Commodity Exports and African Economic Development

Commodity Exports and African Economic Development

Scott R. Pearson
Stanford University

John Cownie
Federal City College

with
James Fry
Sara L. Gordon
Charles Harvey
Valimohamed Jamal
Tony Killick
Ronald K. Meyer
Raymond F. Mikesell
John M. Page, Jr.
J. Dirck Stryker
Teketel Haile-Mariam

Lexington Books
D.C. Heath and Company
Lexington, Massachusetts
Toronto   London

Library of Congress Cataloging in Publication Data

Pearson, Scott R
    Commodity exports and African economic development.

    Includes bibliographical references.
    1. Africa—Commerce—Case studies. 2. Africa—Economic
conditions—1945—Case studies. 3. Commercial products—Africa—Case studies.
I. Cownie, John, joint author. II. Title.
HF3876.5.P4   382'.6'096   73-20275
ISBN 0-669-91959-4

Copyright © 1974 by D. C. Heath and Company

Published simultaneously in Canada.

Printed in the United States of America.

International Standard Book Number: 0-669-91959-4

Library of Congress Catalog Card Number: 73-20275

for our parents

Carlyle and Edith Hope Pearson
John F. and Catherine Bowler Cownie

Contents

List of Tables

Preface

In 1971 a research grant from the Joint Committee on African Studies of the Social Science Research Council and the American Council of Learned Societies launched our investigation of the comparative roles of commodity exports in the economic development of African countries. This book contains the principal results of the study, and we are indebted to the Joint Committee for assisting our research.

Cownie made a reconnaissance trip to several African countries during the summer of 1971. Following that trip we selected a cosmopolitan group of teachers, graduate students, and international civil servants—all of whom had carried out original field research in Africa—and invited them to participate in our study. We provided a methodology which we asked our contributors to use, as appropriate, in their case studies. We owe a strong vote of thanks to our contributing authors for providing balanced, detailed country analyses as well as helpful comments on the methodological and comparative chapters of the book.

Other institutions and individuals have assisted our preparation of this book. Pearson received research grants from the African Language and Area Center, Stanford University, in 1971/72 and from the Center for Research in International Studies, Stanford University, in 1973, and he carried out field work during 1971 and 1972 in Ghana and Ethiopia under the auspices of the U.S. Agency for International Development (A.I.D.). The Food Research Institute, Stanford University, generously made its facilities available to Cownie as a Visiting Scholar in the summer of 1972, and Federal City College allowed him to arrange his commitments so as to concentrate much of his time on research in the summer of 1973. We have benefited from comments received during seminars on parts of this book which Pearson presented to A.I.D., the Department of State, and the World Bank. We are grateful to these institutions for financial assistance and to various individuals in them for intellectual stimulation. Naturally, the conclusions we reach do not necessarily represent the official or unofficial opinions of any U.S. government or international agency, or of the Joint Committee on African Studies.

Several members of the faculty of the Food Research Institute—Walter P. Falcon, Bruce F. Johnston, William O. Jones, Clark W. Reynolds, C. Peter Timmer, and Pan A. Yotopoulos—offered creative discussion and helpful criticism on earlier drafts of this manuscript. Dennis Boland of the Federal City College Economics Department was an occasionally helpful irritant. Thomas G. Rawski provided constructive comments on our methodology. Ronald K. Meyer, the principal author of Chapter 7, contributed enormously to the entire study while serving as Pearson's research assistant. Additional capable research assistance was provided by Betsey A. Kuhn and Gerald C. Nelson. Linda W. Gribbin, occasionally assisted by Anne N. Hoddinott, handled the secretarial chores with efficient aplomb and good humor. Sandra C. Pearson pitched in when the typing load was heavy, edited drafts, and offered continuous encouragement. Elaine Emerson provided vital logistical support to Cownie's 1971 reconnaissance trip. We are deeply indebted to all of these individuals and the many others who by their assistance helped make the completion of this study possible.

Introduction

The nations of Tropical Africa face a strategic dilemma in planning their future economic development.[a] One strategy is to promote growth by means of import-substituting industrialization. In light, however, of the small economic size of most African countries, success in this course of action would depend upon the achievement of regional economic integration. Since few African heads of state have adopted integration as a primary political objective, regional economic cooperation will remain a desirable but elusive goal until political attitudes alter markedly. Under these circumstances import-substituting industrialization must be relegated at least temporarily to a supporting rather than a leading role in African economic development.

The alternative to import substitution is to try to achieve increases in income and employment by concentrating on the production of exports. The success of this strategy will depend in large part upon the developmental effects resulting from expenditure of the incomes, government revenues, and foreign exchange earned in the production and marketing of these export commodities. Over time, successful export-led growth would result in structural shifts—in the economy and in the composition of exports—in favor of manufacturing and against primary production. But development based on the promotion of exports, especially exports of primary commodities, is also beset with difficulties. Uncertain trends and unstable patterns of export earnings are genuine concerns for export-dependent African nations. Although promotion of growth through expansion of exports is neither easy nor always successful, many African countries have achieved success along this path. For most of these economies and for many others in Tropical Africa, exports will play a critical developmental role during the foreseeable future. An informed concern with the economic development of this region therefore requires an understanding of export-oriented growth as it has taken place in individual African countries.

The focus of this book is on the diverse set of relationships between economic development and the growth of commodity exports in Tropical Africa.[b]

---

[a]"Africa" and "African" apply to Tropical Africa, defined here to include the parts of the continent which lie south of the Sahara Desert and north of the Zambesi River. Although important similarities as well as contrasts exist between North or South Africa, on one hand, and Tropical Africa, on the other, we concentrate on comparisons within Tropical Africa.

[b]Although a few African countries have recently begun to export manufactured goods, for a long time to come primary commodities—agricultural crops, timber, and minerals—will continue as in the past to provide nearly all of Africa's export earnings.

Identifying the role of primary exports in African development provides an understanding of the past evolution of African economies and of the prospects for future growth.[c] Yet surprisingly little empirical work exists on the changing historical patterns of income and employment associated with commodity exports in Tropical Africa.[1] In this book, we compare the contributions of selected agricultural, silvicultural, and mineral exports to economic development in eight African countries and seek thereby to enhance understanding of this important developmental process.

The countries and export commodities included in this study are:

Ivory Coast	Timber, Cocoa, and Coffee
Ghana	Cocoa and Timber
Ethiopia	Coffee
Uganda	Cotton
Nigeria	Petroleum
Zaire	Copper
Zambia	Copper
Sierra Leone	Diamonds

The choice of these case studies has been made on the basis of two criteria—suitability for instructive comparisons, and availability of information. Intra-country comparisons between two or more commodities are carried out in the cases of the Ivory Coast and Ghana. Cocoa and timber are compared between these countries, and intercountry comparison is also possible for copper in Zaire and Zambia and for coffee in Ethiopia and the Ivory Coast. The study of diamonds in Sierra Leone involves a comparison of small-scale labor-intensive production by Sierra Leoneans and large-scale production by a government- and foreign-owned firm employing modern technology. The usefulness of our comparative study would clearly be increased if we could include additional African economies and their principal commodity exports, but further comparative analysis is precluded at this time by the scarcity of information on major exports in other African countries.

This book has been prepared with several objectives in mind: (1) to integrate, within a comprehensive analytical framework, previously existing

---

[c]The type of export-led growth with which we are concerned in Tropical Africa is principally of the "vent for surplus" variety. A country with large quantities of land, natural resources, and/or labor available at low opportunity cost can achieve high rates of growth of output and income by allocating these factors to commodity export production. When exports expand to the point where these resources are exhausted, the country can then continue to grow only by improving its technology, by augmenting its supplies of factors of production, or by upgrading their quality. See Hla Myint, "The 'Classical Theory' of International Trade and the Underdeveloped Countries," *The Economic Journal* 68 (June 1958): 317-37, and Richard E. Caves, " 'Vent for Surplus' Models of Trade and Growth," in *Trade, Growth, and the Balance of Payments,* Robert E. Baldwin et al., eds., Rand McNally and Company, 1965, pp. 95-115.

empirical information and new microeconomic data on the export industries themselves; (2) to identify similarities and differences in the experiences of individual exporting countries; (3) to facilitate comparisons among the developmental effects of agricultural, silvicultural, and mineral exports; (4) to evaluate the degree to which governmental policies have enhanced or diminished developmental contributions of exports and to indicate how government policy instruments might be used to improve the levels of future domestic benefits, and (5) to identify the especially critical relationships between individual exports and national economic growth on which future research should be focused.

In designing this book emphasis has been placed on maintaining a common approach among the country studies in order to facilitate comparative analysis. Each study measures to the extent possible the contribution of the export industry or industries under investigation to economic development in the host country. In the first chapter we define an analytical framework focusing on the major issues which arise in measuring interrelationships between exports and development. This framework is then used where appropriate and feasible in the case studies of Chapters 2 through 10. In the final chapter we present an integrated comparative analysis of the nine case studies and draw several implications for governmental policy for primary export activities.

Each case study provides a description of the institutional background of export commodity production, an analysis of the direct and indirect contributions of the export activity to economic development, and a discussion of the implications of the study for past, current, and future governmental policies.

Discussion of the institutional background begins with an historical account of the cultivation or exploitation of the export commodity, stressing investor/host country relationships where appropriate. Further background is generally provided in a summary treatment of the structure of the international market for the export, and in a brief discussion of recent trends in the domestic economy. Past and current governmental policies influencing production and marketing of the export are described in order to set the stage for their later analysis.

A major objective in all empirical analyses of economic development is to achieve a reasonable balance between the application of an analytical framework and the appreciation of those aspects of economic change which either elude quantitative measurement entirely or are omitted from the chosen method of analysis. The analytical framework presented in Chapter 1 is designed to measure changes in domestic income resulting from the production and marketing of export commodities. Important dynamic relationships between exports and development in individual countries are not easily measured, however, and final assessment of these effects rests on intimate, qualitative knowledge of the country and commodity under study. The authors of our case studies have thus supplemented or modified the analytical framework as they deemed appropriate.

The major issues and their implications for policy vary a great deal among countries and commodities. Policy issues emphasized by the authors of the case studies include setting export tax rates for agricultural commodities, deciding levels for producer prices of agricultural exports in countries in which domestic marketing boards exist, establishing contractual terms with foreign concessionaires to divide economic rent associated with mineral exports, setting terms for foreign ownership and governmental participation in the extraction of mineral deposits, and evaluating strategies for membership in international commodity agreements or producer countries' organizations.

Note

1.   Major contributions to the literature of export-oriented development in Tropical Africa include Robert E. Baldwin, *Economic Development and Export Growth: A Study of Northern Rhodesia, 1920-1960* (Berkeley: University of California Press, 1966); R. W. Clower, G. Dalton, M. Harwitz, and A. A. Walters, *Growth without Development—An Economic Survey of Liberia* (Evanston, Ill.: Northwestern University Press, 1966); William A. Hance, *African Economic Development,* rev. ed. (New York: Praeger, 1967); Gerald K. Helleiner, *Peasant Agriculture, Government, and Economic Growth in Nigeria* (Homewood, Ill.: Richard D. Irwin, Inc., 1966); S. Daniel Neumark, *Foreign Trade and Economic Development in Africa* (Stanford, Calif.: Food Research Institute, 1964); and Scott R. Pearson, *Petroleum and the Nigerian Economy* (Stanford, Calif.: Stanford University Press, 1970).

1   A Framework for Analysis

Scott R. Pearson and John Cownie

The analytical framework used in this book allows a comprehensive analysis of the measurable contributions of commodity exports to income.[1] Application of the framework in the case studies and in the conclusion provides a cross-sectional picture in selected countries for one or a few recent years. This picture must be qualified to reflect institutional realities, to incorporate dynamic changes, and to include other effects which are difficult or impossible to measure. Since these considerations are diverse and sometimes specific to one country or commodity, no attempt will be made to discuss them in general in this chapter.

Our analytical framework is designed primarily to measure the contributions of an export activity to income in the local economy. In some instances, however, income distribution or employment generation may be deemed to be more important than gains or losses in income. Hence, in addition to measuring changes in income, it is desirable to try to assess the distribution of export-related income among owners of employed resources and among occupations, the spatial (rural/urban) and regional distribution of employment opportunities, and the regional developmental effects associated with export activities.

Our initial task is to define the contributions to local income by an export activity during a given period of time.[a] Let us consider only a single time period, say one year, and assume that the export activity is represented by a single firm, although the analysis is equally applicable to export production in which hundreds of thousands of small-scale farmers participate. The exporting firm makes a positive direct contribution to local income—to the availability of goods and services—if the value of its output is greater than the value of the inputs, including both primary factors of production and intermediate commodities, which the firm uses in its production process. In addition, the firm may contribute indirectly to local income through the generation of external effects and their impact on other producers or on consumers in the local economy. External effects may, of course, be positive or negative, depending on the nature of their influence.

We define the *net social gain* (NSG) from an exporting activity as the total value of commodities produced minus the value of intermediate commodities

---

[a]We assume throughout this discussion that benefits and costs occurring at different points in time are discounted at an appropriate social discount rate to allow comparability at one point in time. For expositional simplicity, time and the discount rate are not introduced explicitly into the analysis.

and factors used as inputs plus net external effects. Because the case studies focus on the production of exports, a second definition of net social gain is useful. Net social gain can also be calculated as the net value of foreign exchange earned minus the value of domestic resources used in commodity export production plus net external effects. The two definitions of NSG are equivalent, and each will be used where appropriate in our analysis of export activities.

Net social gain is the composite result of three different kinds of economic influences. First, in many export activities, economic rent is associated with a scarce factor of production—for example, natural resources, land, or entrepreneurship.[b] This rent and any monopoly profits the activity might earn compose the residual after costs of other factors of production have been subtracted from the value of the output.[c] In an economy in which the returns to factors of production equal their marginal products and in which monopoly power is absent, the value of intermediate commodities and factors used as inputs would equal the total value of the commodities produced; in this instance the contribution of economic rent to net social gain would be zero. The magnitude of economic rent depends on the extent of the divergence between factor returns based solely on marginal productivity and those based on scarcity values, while the degree of monopoly power is related to the extent to which competition is imperfect in the local economy or internationally. Moreover, the actual contribution of rent to net social gain depends on the nature of ownership of the export activity. When the export firm is wholly owned by domestic interests, all economic rent is an addition to domestic income in the local economy. If foreigners own all or part of an export activity, however, the contribution of rent to local income is decreased to the extent that the foreigners' share of rent (and monopoly profits) is repatriated and thus withdrawn from the domestic economy.

Second, market prices for inputs and outputs in many developing economies often do not properly reflect the scarcity values of factors and commodities. Distortions between private factor incomes and social opportunity costs arise from such institutional and legal considerations as artificial minimum wage levels, maximum interest rate ceilings, and overvalued exchange rates. This divergence between shadow and market prices results in a misallocation of resources and a consequent error in the measured value of output. In order to measure the contribution of an export activity to local income, the authors of case studies in which such distortions seem significant attempt to correct their estimates of net social gain by assigning shadow prices to inputs and outputs in order to reflect more accurately their true scarcity values in the domestic economy.

[b]We measure economic rent at market prices and at the existing exchange rate. As explained below, adjustments to reflect a social valuation of inputs and outputs are carried out in a separate calculation.

[c]Optimal taxation and/or concessions policies would permit the government to extract all economic rent, if the government's principal goal is to maximize its own revenues. In practice, this rent is generally shared between the government and the owner of the firm. By measuring economic rent and monopoly profits in this manner, we incorporate any effects of differential "X-efficiency" deriving from varying degrees of motivation and incentives of managers and employees and from other influences; see H. Liebenstein, "Allocative vs. 'X-Efficiency,' " *American Economic Review 56* (June 1966): 392-415.

Third, export industries contribute indirectly to net social gain and thus to local income through "linkage" effects and through a variety of other indirect economic relationships.[2] Linkage effects occur when export industries increase or decrease the profitability of other industries as a result of intersectoral supply and demand relationships. *Linkage benefits* generally result from economies of scale, productivity gains from the use of underutilized factors, or the creation of positive externalities for other sectors, whereas *linkage costs* stem from the creation of unemployment of local factors or from imparting negative externalities to other sectors. Incremental rents (or monopoly profits) would accrue if gains from economies of scale are reflected in higher profits or greater domestic factor payments rather than in lower product prices.[d] (As with the export industry, the pattern of ownership of linked industries determines their contribution to local income; foreign ownership of linked industries will decrease the domestic contribution of economic rent to the extent that foreigners' shares are repatriated.) Furthermore, gains may arise from a divergence between social and private opportunity costs of factors employed in the linked industry if operations of the export firm allow the linked industry to achieve productivity gains by greater use of previously underutilized factors. Finally, any external benefits and costs resulting from secondary interactions between the linked industry and other domestic industries can be analyzed within the same framework used for primary effects.

Assessment of linkage effects is a key aspect of the country studies. We divide linkage effects into two groups. The first group includes effects associated with the export industry's operations—backward and forward linkages, and technological linkages. Backward linkages involve the use of locally produced intermediate inputs and capital goods by the export industry, while forward linkages arise when outputs of the export industry are used as inputs by other local industries. Technological linkages refer to a variety of external effects imparted by the export industry to other industries in the economy, including the spread of new technologies or methods of organization, and the construction of infrastructure. To the extent that these kinds of linkages occur, the export industry indirectly contributes to economic development through the provision of additional incomes and employment opportunities in the linked industries.

The second group of linkages stems from the expenditure of factor incomes and taxes paid by the export industry. Final demand linkages occur when local purchases are made with incomes obtained from employment in the export industry. A positive final demand linkage effect results when the expenditure of incremental factor incomes generated by the export industry stimulates local manufacturing or agricultural industries. The importance of this effect depends on the extent to which export incomes are saved, spent on local goods and

---

[d]We do not attempt to measure changes in consumer surplus—gains from lower product prices associated with scale economies, or losses from monopoly pricing of products sold domestically—because these effects can generally be assumed to be small for export firms in developing countries.

services, or spent on imports. Fiscal linkage effects are associated with the domestic expenditure of the export industry's payments to government and are especially significant when the government is able to extract large amounts of economic rent from an export activity.[e]

Many other kinds of external effects are often associated with African commodity exports. An export activity's contribution to the supply of scarce factors of production—for example, skilled labor or domestic savings—can be especially important, and most authors of the case studies give special attention to this effect. A wide array of costs and benefits is captured in this residual group of external effects, including, among others, displacement of potential domestic investment by foreign investment and the impact of the export activity on economic stability.[3]

In short, we can evaluate the contributions of an export industry to local income by measuring (1) economic rent, (2) adjustments to reflect the scarcity value of inputs and outputs, and (3) external benefits in the form of linkages and/or other external effects. The first two of these influences indicate the scope for the third—the possible external effects which are at the heart of the dynamic process of economic growth and structural change.

Under some circumstances it is more convenient to use a measure other than net social gain to estimate the social benefits and costs associated with an export activity. The *domestic resource cost* per unit of foreign exchange earned or saved (DRC) measures the opportunity cost of domestic factors required by an activity to generate one unit of free foreign exchange, or value added at world prices.[4] This measure, which is derived from the formula for net social gain, is calculated by dividing the total domestic resource costs involved in the production of the export commodity by the net foreign exchange earnings generated. Because the DRC criterion focuses on foreign exchange, it is valuable for our analysis of commodity exports in Tropical Africa, a region in which foreign exchange availability is often an important constraint to development. Using the DRC criterion, we can analyze the efficiency of the various export activities in generating scarce foreign exchange. The DRC criterion is usually no more difficult to apply than the method of calculating net social gain. In practice the choice of which technique to use will depend upon the focus of the analysis.[5]

It is interesting to observe the implications of an assumption that the domestic resource cost of producing a net unit of foreign exchange is exactly equal to the real worth to the economy of that unit, as reflected in its shadow price. As we would expect intuitively, net social gain to the economy is zero in this case, because we are assuming that the opportunity cost of producing foreign exchange equals the value of foreign exchange produced. Similarly, if DRC is less than the shadow price of foreign exchange, NSG is positive, and if DRC exceeds this shadow price, NSG is negative.

---

[e]The importance of fiscal linkages is difficult to measure because governments almost always derive their revenues from a variety of sources. Unless the export activity is the sole source of government revenue, it is generally not possible to associate specific government expenditures with particular sources of revenue and thus to measure fiscal linkages.

For purposes of comparing different export activities, we define the *net gain coefficient* (NGC) as the ratio of net social gain to total output valued at the shadow price of foreign exchange. The larger the NGC, the greater is the proportional contribution of the activity to national income. The NGC is a product of two effects—the proportion of foreign exchange retained domestically, and a ratio indicating the efficiency of domestic resource use.

Finally, we consider the personal and occupational distribution of income and the generation of employment associated with the export commodity in question. Each of these effects depends upon both the choice of technology employed in the export activity and the relative prices paid to the factors used in the industry. If there is little substitutability among factors in the production process, technology is usually more important than the relative factor prices in determining the distribution of income and levels of employment. If, however, there is a great deal of substitutability among factors in the export activity, the relative factor prices will largely determine income and employment within the industry. In evaluating these effects, it is important to observe the existing patterns of income and employment and to attempt to measure how these patterns are affected directly by operations of the export industry and indirectly by the distribution and expenditure of the rents generated.

Our introduction to the framework for analysis is now complete. This framework is adopted in the individual country studies in greater or lesser degree according to the availability of data and the judgments of the authors of the case studies. In the comparative analysis of the final chapter, we apply the framework as closely as the extent of information permits.

Technical Appendix to Chapter 1

The purpose of this appendix is to define our framework for analysis concisely, using symbolic notation. Readers who are interested more in African development than in economic methodology may wish to skim this appendix or to move directly to the case studies.

In the general case, we have n commodities produced as outputs and/or consumed as intermediate inputs by the firm in question and m primary factors of production used in producing its outputs. Net social gain is then defined as

$$\text{NSG}_j = \sum_{i=1}^{n} a_{ij}p_i - \sum_{s=1}^{m} f_{sj}v_s + E_j \tag{1.1}$$

where $\text{NSG}_j \equiv$ net social gain from the jth export firm,

$a_{ij} \equiv$ quantity of the ith commodity produced by (or used in) the production process of the jth export firm,

$p_i \equiv$ shadow price of the ith commodity,

$f_{sj} \equiv$ quantity of the sth factor used in the production process of the jth export firm,

$v_s \equiv$ shadow price of the sth factor, and

$E_j \equiv$ external benefits (or costs) imparted by the jth export firm to the rest of the domestic economy.

The term containing a_{ij} is positive if the jth export firm *produces* the ith commodity, or negative if the jth firm *uses* the ith commodity as an input. The term containing f_{sj} is subtracted since all factor inputs are costs in the production process. The commodity prices and the factor prices are assumed to reflect scarcity relationships in the economy.

Let us now assume that all the outputs produced by the firm are tradable, either exports that earn foreign exchange or import substitutes that save foreign exchange. The value of all outputs can then be measured in terms of foreign exchange as u_j .

Next we wish to separate the value of each commodity input used in the production process into a foreign exchange component and a domestic factor component. For example, if the export firm uses locally produced fuel oil in its production process, we desire to separate the costs of producing this fuel oil into import costs and domestic factor payments; interest and depreciation payments on imported machinery in the refinery would be import costs, while payments to local labor used in refining would be domestic costs.

If we define the first factor of production as foreign exchange, the direct foreign exchange costs of production are contained in (1.1) as f_{1j} . Indirect foreign exchange costs are found by allocating the costs of commodity inputs as just described. The total, direct plus indirect, value of repatriated earnings of foreign-owned factors of production employed can be defined as r_j and measured in foreign exchange. The direct plus indirect value of imported materials used in production can be defined as $\overline{m}_j$ in terms of foreign exchange. The value of net foreign exchange created by the export industry, i.e., value added at world prices, can then be expressed as $u_j - \overline{m}_j - r_j$. This measure can be converted to local currency by multiplying by the shadow price of foreign exchange, v_1 , expressed as a ratio of local currency to foreign currency.

Direct domestic factor costs of production are defined as

$$\sum_{s=2}^{m} f_{sj} v_s$$

(recall that we have taken f_{1j} as foreign exchange). Indirect domestic factor costs have already been found in the process of allocating all costs of commodity inputs between foreign and domestic sources. Direct plus indirect domestic factor costs can be defined as

$$\sum_{s=2}^{m} \overline{f}_{sj} v_s ,$$

with $\overline{f}_{sj}$ defined below. We can now express a new, but equivalent, definition of the gains from the export firm:

$$\text{NSG}_j = (u_j - \overline{m}_j - r_j) v_1 - \sum_{s=2}^{m} \overline{f}_{sj} v_s + E_j \qquad (1.2)$$

where $u_j \equiv$ value (in foreign exchange) of earnings of the jth export firm,

$\overline{m}_j \equiv$ total (direct plus indirect) value (in foreign exchange) of imported commodities used in the production process of the jth export firm,

$r_j \equiv$ total (direct plus indirect) value (in foreign exchange) of repatriated earnings of foreign-owned factors of production employed by the jth export firm,

$v_1 \equiv$ shadow price of foreign exchange (local currency/foreign currency), and

$\overline{f}_{sj} \equiv$ total (direct plus indirect) quantity of the sth domestic factor used in the production process of the jth export firm.

Equations (1.1) and (1.2) are equivalent. In (1.1) commodities and factors are separated. In (1.2) direct plus indirect foreign factor costs are separated from direct plus indirect domestic factor costs.

Next we reformulate (1.2) to distinguish three components of social gain: economic rent (and monopoly profits), adjustments to reflect the scarcity value of inputs and outputs, and external effects on the domestic economy. The contribution to domestic income via economic rent, measured at market prices and at the existing exchange rate, is:

$$R_j = (u_j - \overline{m}_j - r_j) w_1 - \sum_{s=2}^{m} \overline{f}_{sj} w_s \qquad (1.3)$$

where $R_j \equiv$ net social gain from the jth export firm deriving from economic rent,

$w_1 \equiv$ existing exchange rate (local currency/foreign currency), and

$w_s \equiv$ market price of the sth factor.

Expression (1.4) is a statement of the changes in income which are associated with pricing adjustments that allow a social rather than a private valuation of inputs and outputs:

$$P_j = (u_j - \overline{m}_j - r_j)(v_1 - w_1) + \sum_{s=2}^{m} \overline{f}_{sj}(w_s - v_s) \qquad (1.4)$$

Contributions to net social gain occur to the extent that the market prices of domestic factors of production exceed the shadow prices of these factors, and that the shadow price of foreign exchange is greater than the existing exchange rate (both measured as a ratio of local currency to foreign currency). Inspection reveals that $R_j + P_j$ equals the sum of the first two terms in (1.2). If market factor prices are good approximations of factor scarcity values and if the exchange rate is not overvalued, P_j is zero, and all contributions to income from the first two terms of (1.2) can be attributed to economic rent (and monopoly profits).

External costs and benefits, the third potential source of gain or loss in (1.2), have not so far been expressly identified. Equation (1.5) contains two categories of external effects: linkage effects and all other external effects:

$$E_j = \sum_{k=1}^{q} L_{jk} + \sum_{k=1}^{q} T_{jk} b_k \qquad (1.5)$$

where $L_{jk} \equiv R'_{jk} + P'_{jk} + E'_{jk}$, the prime terms referring to changes in economic rent, adjustments for scarcity values, and secondary external effects on the local economy arising from intersectoral flows between the jth export firm and the kth linked industry,[f]

$T_{jk} \equiv$ other external effects imparted by the jth export firm to the kth linked producer or consumer, and

$b_k \equiv$ social valuation of other external effects on the kth producer or consumer.

Equation (1.5) represents the changes in total domestic net social gain due to intersectoral flows between the export industry and linked industries and the value to the local economy of other external effects generated by the export activity.

Summarizing, the measure of net social gain contains three components, as defined in (1.3), (1.4), and (1.5):

$$NSG_j = R_j + P_j + E_j \qquad (1.6)$$

The domestic resource cost per unit of foreign exchange earned or saved (DRC) is defined in (1.7):

$$DRC_j = \frac{\sum\limits_{s=2}^{m} \bar{f}_{sj} v_s - E_j}{u_j - \bar{m}_j - r_j} \qquad (1.7)$$

[f]A part of the net social gain attributable to backward linkages may be captured in the process of measuring direct plus indirect domestic factor costs.

where $DRC_j \equiv$ domestic resource cost per unit of foreign exchange earned (or
saved) by the jth export firm.

When net gains are zero, the domestic resource cost ratio is equivalent to the
shadow price of foreign exchange. Equation (1.7) can therefore be obtained
directly from (1.2) by setting NSG_j to zero and solving for v_1 .[6]
By comparing (1.2) and (1.7), one can express net social gain in terms of
the DRC ratio:

$$NSG_j = (u_j - \overline{m}_j - r_j)(v_1 - DRC_j) \tag{1.8}$$

When DRC_j is less than v_1, NSG_j is greater than zero, and when DRC_j is greater
than v_1, NSG_j is less than zero. Stated algebraically,

$$NSG_j \gtreqless 0 \quad \text{as} \quad DRC_j \lesseqgtr v_1$$

The net contribution of an export activity to an economy's income is the net
social value of the foreign exchange produced by the activity. This contribution
is represented in (1.8) as the product of the net foreign exchange produced and
the difference between the social value and the social cost of each unit of foreign
exchange.
Finally, the net gain coefficient (NGC), the ratio of net social gain to gross
output evaluated at the shadow price of foreign exchange, is defined as:

$$NGC_j = \frac{NSG_j}{u_j v_1} \tag{1.9}$$

By substituting (1.8) into (1.9), we obtain

$$NGC_j = \left(1 - \frac{\overline{m}_j + r_j}{u_j}\right) \left(1 - \frac{DRC_j}{v_1}\right) \tag{1.10}$$

NGC is the product of two terms: the proportion of foreign exchange retained
in the domestic economy, and a measure of the relative efficiency with which
the export activity uses domestic resources.

Notes

1.   Readers who desire a rigorous statement of our framework for analysis are
      referred to the technical appendix at the end of Chapter 1. The framework
      represents an extension of a methodology developed earlier by one of the
      co-authors; see Scott R. Pearson, *Petroleum and the Nigerian Economy*

(Stanford: Stanford University Press, 1970), pp. 39-54. A related approach is presented by Raymónd F. Mikesell, "The Contributions of Petroleum and Mineral Resources to Economic Development," in Raymond F. Mikesell et. al., eds., *Foreign Investment in the Petroleum and Mineral Industries: Case studies of Investor-Host Country Relations* (Baltimore: The Johns Hopkins Press for Resources for the Future, 1971), pp. 3-28. The methodologies of both of these studies draw particularly on the earlier work of Clark W. Reynolds, "Development Problems of an Export Economy, The Case of Chile and Copper," in Markos Mamalakis and Clark W. Reynolds, eds., *Essays on the Chilean Economy* (Homewood, Ill.:Richard D. Irwin, 1965), pp. 203-357, especially pp. 273-78 and 320-43, and Robért E. Baldwin, *Economic Development and Export Growth: A Study of Northern Rhodesia, 1920-1960* (Berkeley: University of California Press, 1966), especially pp. 58-73.

2.   For a more detailed discussion of linkage effects, see Pearson, *Petroleum and the Nigerian Economy*, pp. 45-50.

3.   See Danial M. Schydlowsky, "Benefit-Cost Analysis of Foreign Investment Proposals, The Viewpoint of the Host Country," Economic Development Report No. 170, Development Advisory Service (Cambridge, Mass.: Harvard University, 1970), pp. 11-14 (mimeographed).

4.   A complete description of the DRC technique is found in Michael Bruno, "Domestic Resource Costs and Effective Protection: Clarification and Synthesis," *Journal of Political Economy* 80 (January/February 1972): 16-33, especially 18-21, and in Bruno's earlier work cited in that article.

5.   This choice is discussed in Scott R. Pearson, "Net Social Profitability, Domestic Resource Costs, and Effective Rate of Protection," Food Research Institute (Stanford University, August 1973, mimeographed).

6.   The relationship between these two concepts was noted in Hollis B. Chenery, "Comparative Advantage and Development Policy," *American Economic Review* 51 (March 1961), p. 46, and demonstrated in Michael Bruno, "The Optimal Selection of Export-promoting and Import-substituting Projects," in *Planning the External Sector: Technique, Problems and Policies* (New York: United Nations, 1967), p. 106.

2

Exports and Growth in the Ivory Coast: Timber, Cocoa, and Coffee

J. Dirck Stryker*

Since the end of the nineteenth century the economic fortunes of the Ivory Coast have depended on a succession of export crops. In 1900 the most important exports of the Ivory Coast, as of most other areas along the West African coast, were palm oil and kernels. While exports of these products remained roughly constant until World War II, at which time they declined as a result of competition in supply from more profitable exports, the impetus for growth came from other sources.[1] For about ten years prior to World War I natural rubber, harvested primarily from wild vines, was the most dynamic export, accounting for 45 percent of the total value of Ivorian exports in 1912. But natural rubber was unable to compete with plantation rubber from Malaysia after that year, and exports virtually ceased by 1914. More important for the future of the Ivory Coast were timber shipments, which grew rapidly and in 1929 accounted for 31 percent of the total value of exports. Following Ghana by thirty years, exports of cocoa from the Ivory Coast expanded quickly during the 1920s to occupy first place, with 37 percent of the total, in 1929. As cocoa's fortunes slowly declined, relatively if not absolutely, during the next four decades, coffee became the leader, increasing continuously to account for 62 percent of all exports by 1954. But then, to come full circle, exports of timber, which had remained static since 1929, began to increase rapidly during the 1950s and 1960s, and had overtaken cocoa in relative importance by 1963.

This chapter is concerned with these last three products: timber, coffee, and cocoa. Together they accounted for 76 percent of the total value of exports in 1970 and for most of the 9 percent average annual rate of growth of real exports over the past twenty-five years. Our interest, however, is not just in the relative importance of these products but also in the insights provided by the ways in which they differ. First, for example, the production of coffee and cocoa takes place almost entirely on small farms cultivated by Africans. The cutting of timber, on the other hand, is accomplished primarily by private companies, owned and managed by Europeans, which use relatively capital-intensive techniques and have many of the characteristics of mining enclaves.[2] Second, the type of capital investment required by coffee and cocoa, on the one hand, and by timber, on the other, also differ. Most of the capital which has gone

*I am grateful for the very helpful comments offered me on an earlier draft of this chapter by Barend deVries, Robert Evenson, and Yoav Kislev.

into the creation of coffee and cocoa plantations has come from the labor of Africans who have cleared the forest, planted their trees, and tended them until after several years they begin to bear fruit, while public sources of investment and foreign exchange have been important for the building of roads and port facilities. Forestry, a more capital-intensive operation, has depended to a much greater extent upon private foreign investment—for the purchase of trucks and other equipment and for the construction of feeder roads leading into the forest from government-maintained roads. Third, the development of coffee and cocoa exports has historically been constrained to a greater degree by demand factors than has timber, whose main constraints have been those of supply.

The objective of this chapter is to investigate the extent to which these and other differences have been associated with factors promoting or inhibiting growth of the export sector and of the rest of the economy. For this purpose coffee and cocoa will be treated together, since they are produced under similar conditions, frequently by the same farmer. In the next section both supply and demand conditions affecting export growth will be discussed within their historical context. Thereafter, an analysis will be made of the impact of that growth on the entire economy. Most of the data for that analysis are taken from the period of the 1960s, for which our quantitative knowledge of the local economy is much greater than for earlier periods. Where possible, however, an assessment of the implications of our results for the years prior to independence will be undertaken.

A History of Timber, Cocoa, and Coffee in the Ivory Coast

Supply Conditions

At the time of colonization by France in the 1890s the Ivory Coast was to the Europeans a largely unexplored and unknown area that had previously been bypassed in favor of more promising centers in Senegal, Ghana, or Nigeria. It was soon realized, however, that the forest area in the southern part of the colony especially was a rich natural resource capable of yielding or producing a variety of products. Yet there were a number of things which stood in the way of the development of this region. Foremost among these was the immediate need to establish effective military and political control over the countryside to prevent violent conflict and to ensure the safe and free passage of traders.[a] Other

---

[a]The local colonial government continued to pursue this goal until 1915 in the western part of the Ivory Coast, where fierce resistance to colonial rule was encountered, thus diverting substantial resources away from development in the east.

bottlenecks included the inadequacy of the transportation network, lack of localized knowledge of and experience in tropical agriculture, and the absence of a reliable supply of labor.

Transportation.   One of the most rapidly growing early exports, timber, though more accessible than in many countries, was nevertheless subject to high costs of transportation. For many years the primary means of transporting logs was to float them down the rivers and across the lagoons to several ports along the coast. At Grand Bassam, the largest port, logs were lifted out of the water by crane and onto rail cars that carried them onto the wharf, extending past the surf to where they were dumped and floated out to ships at anchor in the roadstead. In other areas they had to be rolled for several kilometers across land separating the lagoons from the sea and towed out through the heavy surf. In addition to these costly handling operations, loading depended on sea conditions, and long delays and high losses were frequent.

Beginning in 1903, when the railroad was extended northward from Abidjan, new timber concessions were established along this line.[b] But in 1932, when the railroad was finally linked directly with a newly constructed wharf at Port Bouet, seven miles from Abidjan, the relatively high prices of the 1920s had given way to the depressed condition of the 1930s.

It was not until after the Second World War that the transportation constraint was, for a time, eased.[c] With the opening of the Vridi Canal in 1951 and the construction of a modern deep-water port at Abidjan, costs of transporting timber were lowered to such an extent that many areas of forest previously unexploitable were now within reach. The result was an enormous expansion of production at an average annual rate of growth of 15 percent from 1950 to 1970. Timber camps continued to be concentrated near the railway and various waterways for a time since truck transportation, still relatively expensive, was confined to feeding the railroad and lagoons. During the 1950s, however, public roads were substantially improved. As the areas near the railroad and waterways were depleted, the center of production shifted westward, and trucking directly to Abidjan became increasingly common. By the early 1970s, however, transportation distances were such that several species were not expected to be profitable within a few years. The construction of a new port at San Pedro, in the southwestern part of the country, as part of the 1971-75 Plan, promised to

---

[b]Construction of the railroad passed out of the forest region into the savannah in 1910, having attained a distance of 182 kilometers.

[c]During the interwar period the expansion of transportation facilities was severely constrained by lack of public capital. In France the demand for capital for reconstruction following World War I and, later, the collapse of the capital market due to inflation followed by depression effectively shut off that source. The French West African government was thus dependent on its own resources, which were very meager because of the lack of an adequate tax base. This situation was dramatically reversed in the 1950s when the French began to pour large amounts of financial aid into their empire.

extend timber production for several years, but it was nevertheless clear that the frantic expansion of the previous two decades could not long be continued.

Transportation was a lesser bottleneck in the case of coffee and cocoa, both of which have a relatively high value in relationship to their bulk. In the earlier periods short hauls of relatively small quantities could be accomplished by head porterage, and the lagoons and railway provided avenues for longer hauls. Still, the introduction of the truck and the expansion of the road network during the interwar period opened up many new areas to production.

It was the falling costs of transportation during the post-World War II period, however, which truly revolutionized agriculture in the forest region of the south. This was especially important after 1954, when the high prices received during the first decade following the war were sharply decreased. Even though the prices of many transportation inputs were rising, rates charged for hauling coffee and cocoa declined as a result of increased competition and improved roads. Furthermore, the extension of unimproved feeder roads to most villages, sometimes by the villagers themselves, eliminated the need for head porterage and greatly increased transportation capacity at that stage.

Agricultural Knowledge. More important in limiting the early extension of coffee and cocoa production was the lack of knowledge and management skills necessary to grow these crops profitably. The skills required for timber-cutting were imported with the European or African, usually Ghanaian, entrepreneurs engaged in that business. But the knowledge required for successful cash crop production in the Ivory Coast was more specific to that region and could not be so easily acquired.

The first coffee planted in the Ivory Coast was introduced by Europeans in 1881. Many of the early plantations suffered from a lack of knowledge of local conditions and poor management, and production remained primarily for domestic use for many years. Cocoa was grown only sporadically until 1908, after which it was promoted aggressively among African planters by the colonial government. In the meantime an experiment station had been established at Bingerville, and was conducting research on a variety of tropical fruits, trees, coffee, and cocoa as well as on soil structure and other basic agricultural conditions.[d] By the early 1920s the Ivory Coast was producing cocoa of superior quality which found a ready market in France. Led by African planters and under the impetus of the expansion of road transportation, production of cocoa increased almost sixteen-fold from 1920 to 1929. During the 1930s, however, the rate of expansion of planting decreased because of a decline in world prices

---

[d]This contrasts with cocoa experimentation in Ghana from the first half of the nineteenth century. Ghanaian cocoa planting expanded rapidly from the early 1890s. A similar expansion in the Ivory Coast was delayed until the 1920s. This lag suggests that the length of time required for local testing and experimentation before a crop is profitably grown may be measured in terms of decades. As will be seen, this hypothesis is strengthened by the experience with coffee in the Ivory Coast.

and insect attacks. Production continued to increase fairly rapidly, though, as trees already planted came to maturity.

During the 1920s European planters spread the cultivation of several varieties of coffee throughout much of the southern part of the Ivory Coast. In 1929 an experiment station, concentrating its research on robusta coffee, was established at Man, in the western part of the country. With the collapse of cocoa prices during the Depression most Europeans who had followed the Africans in planting cocoa began to concentrate on coffee, especially the *gros Indénié* variety, which had been developed at the Bingerville experiment station and which was inferior in quality but hardier than the other principal variety, robusta. They were followed shortly by Africans, who, by 1932, had planted more trees than the Europeans. There followed a continuous rise in the exports of Ivorian coffee from 405 tons in 1929 to 17,960 tons in 1939.

The technical problems of these crops were, however, by no means solved. Most of the varieties of coffee in the Ivory Coast, including *gros Indénié*, were severely attacked in 1949-50 by tracheomycosis disease. Vast areas were replanted with *robusta inéac,* a variety which, imported from the Belgian Congo in 1935 by the research center at Bingerville, was resistant to the disease. The replanting program was financed through a coffee fund, which was supported by a portion of the coffee export tax and had been originally established for purposes of stabilization, though by now it was used to aid production. This variety of robusta gave lower yields than previous varieties, however, and could not thrive in some of the dryer areas. The search for more productive robusta varieties continued, and by the late 1960s these efforts were having results. The 1971-75 Plan thus calls for the replanting of most coffee farms with selected varieties under intensive cultivation at the same time that the total area planted to coffee is reduced because of constraints on demand.

Although cocoa experienced less severe technical problems than did coffee, having largely escaped the swollen shoot disease which devastated so much of the cocoa in Ghana, it was not without certain problems. The two principal difficulties after World War II were the age of the cocoa trees, most of which had been planted during the 1920s and were well past their maximum yields, and the losses in production due to capsid insects. During the early 1950s these problems were attacked primarily by the provision of subsidies to farmers for uprooting diseased trees and planting new selected ones and by the spraying of the trees against capsids. The program was financed by a cocoa fund similar to that of coffee. The subsidies were abandoned in 1959, however, because trees were frequently neglected after replanting. The anticapsid program, on the other hand, gained momentum in 1959, and was followed in 1962 by a program for cocoa regeneration. Both of these programs have been quite successful in raising yields. The 1971–75 Plan calls for future planting to be confined to a higher yielding hybrid variety that has been developed recently.

By the time of independence in 1960, it was clear that the Ivory Coast had greatly increased its knowledge of agricultural opportunities and its research infrastructure necessary to add to that knowledge. Experience had been gained in the cultivation of a number of crops over periods of up to fifty or more years. That the production statistics for coffee hardly show the influence of the crippling effects of tracheomycosis attests to the speed with which the agricultural service was able to disseminate a variety immune to the effects of that disease. What was also clear in 1960, though, was the lack of knowledge which existed concerning rural production in general, especially of food crops, and the lack of an effective infrastructure of rural extension services capable of bridging the gap between the results of the experiment stations and the practices of Ivorian farmers.

Labor Supply. The particular mode of production of timber, coffee, and cocoa utilized during the 1950s was the result of the available technology and the relative endowment of factors of production. We will distinguish four of these factors: highly skilled labor or management, modern capital equipment, unskilled labor, and land or natural resources. The first of these inputs, the skills necessary to engage in modern methods of production, was very scarce in the Ivory Coast at the beginning of the colonial epoch but could be imported from Europe, albeit at a cost at least twice that of the same skills in Europe. Modern capital equipment, though equally scarce, could be imported more cheaply than skilled manpower because, unlike human beings, machinery does not eat and drink imported goods or experience a sometimes painful change in climate. The last two factors of production were available in Africa, but, because of the low population density of the Ivory Coast, averaging 12.5 persons per square kilometer in 1965, land was more abundant than labor relative to most of the rest of the world.

The low population density characteristic of the Ivory Coast has had several effects on the supply of labor. On one hand, where very extensive agricultural techniques were employed, manhour requirements necessary to produce a subsistence level of output were likely to be low and very seasonal in nature.[3] This meant that a relatively large number of manhours per person were available during the off-season for other types of work. But since the work required to produce for subsistence needs in the traditional sector was generally slight, Africans were unlikely to enter the full-time labor force during the busy agricultural season unless the wages paid them were relatively high. The result was relatively low-wage labor available on a seasonal basis, but with costs to the employer increased by high turnover rates, and only relatively high-wage labor available year around. In addition, low population densities meant that costs of transportation and communication necessary to assemble a work force of given size were higher than in a more densely populated region.

From the beginning there were frequent complaints of labor shortages on the part of the colonial administration, timber companies, and European planters. Wage rates, which were established in the port areas, where a limited amount of year-around labor was available relatively cheaply, were extended to other areas where the practice of working for wages except for short periods was not well established and where a shortage of labor therefore resulted. Given the unstable nature of the labor force and the belief that Africans were target-income seekers at best, European employers were unwilling to attempt to attract labor by raising wages. Instead they put pressure on the administration to provide them with adequate labor at low wages.

One of the chief instruments of the colonial government's cheap labor policy was the head tax. Since it had to be paid in currency, there was an obligation for Africans to obtain some cash income. Where farmers could not engage in commercial agriculture, this income could only be earned by working for wages. In addition, the government, which obtained a certain amount of involuntary labor for public works projects and military service, frequently recruited at the same time for private European employers as well. There is clear evidence that this recruitment was accomplished only with a strong element of compulsion.[e] In contrast, African planters paying higher wages similar to those paid by cocoa farmers in Ghana seemed to have no difficulty in obtaining labor.

As African cocoa and coffee farming increased during the 1920s and 1930s, providing a viable alternative to wage employment, European employers found it increasingly difficult to obtain local labor. As a result, recruitment shifted to the north and especially to the Mossi country of Upper Volta, where population densities were high and where conditions were unfavorable for commercial crops. The railway in particular was useful in transporting these workers southward to the forest. But the element of compulsion and the poor pay and working conditions offered by Europeans in both Upper Volta and in the Ivory Coast resulted in a massive movement of workers to Ghana, where labor was voluntary and wages and conditions much better.[f]

By the late 1930s African cash crop farming was beginning to draw heavily on the available labor supply. Aside from the higher wages or wage equivalent, workers preferred the greater freedom of hours and methods of work. With the coming of World War II the labor shortage became acute. At the same time that demands increased for bearers because of the gasoline shortage and for Africans to gather rubber to support the war effort, the real value of wages decreased due to the scarcity of imported goods. As a result, labor recruitment was intensified.

Then in 1946 forced labor policies were abandoned by law throughout the

---

[e]Buell, for example, notes that in the mid-1920s about "thirty percent of the fifteen or twenty-thousand laborers employed in the forest industry in the Ivory Coast desert after being recruited." Raymond Leslie Buell, *The Native Problem in Africa,* Vol. 2 (New York: Macmillan, 1928), p. 31.

[f]During the 1930s it has been estimated that about 80,000 workers migrated annually to Ghana from Upper Volta. Estimates of the numbers recruited for work in the Ivory Coast vary, but the number probably did not exceed 10,000 per year during the same period.

French colonial empire. Soon thereafter the demand for workers increased when financing for construction and improvement of roads and the railroad was obtained as part of the first postwar French plan. Employers attempted to lure labor by paying transportation costs to the place of employment and by raising wages, but, even though consumption goods were again appearing on the market, the local labor force was inadequate and high turnover rates resulted in heavy recruitment costs.[g]

It was natural, then, that European employers should turn toward the potential labor pool of Upper Volta, which African planters had been relying upon for several years after the war. Recruitment from this source was organized under the Syndicat Interprofessionel pour l'Acheminement de la Main-d'Oeuvre, which was supported by coffee, cocoa, and banana growers and timber companies and which financed the transportation of workers to and from the forest region of the Ivory Coast. During the 1950s information spread rapidly concerning the opportunities available in the Ivory Coast, and, as it did, the spontaneous flow of migrants toward the south soon exceeded those recruited centrally for European employers.[h] By 1965 it was estimated that out of a population of 4,300,000 there were in the Ivory Coast fully one million Africans who were either themselves born or had at least one parent born outside the country.

The existence of a large pool of labor with few alternative opportunities to earn cash incomes outside the forest region of the Ivory Coast was an important factor in permitting over the past two decades the rapid expansion of the economy with wages being maintained at a relatively high but constant level. There was a substantial real increase in the legal minimum wage during the early 1950s, but this was brought to a halt in 1956 as a result of a decline in coffee and cocoa prices and the relative importance politically of the African planter class. From this date until 1970 there does not appear to have been any increase in real wages in urban areas, and rural wages may actually have declined in real terms, though the price index used here is not very appropriate. It also can be argued that the legal minimum wage is not a good indicator of actual wages paid, especially in the nonmodern sector, but independent evidence indicates actual wages correspond fairly closely, and indeed they may, in some cases, be slightly higher than the legal minimum. A comparison of rural surveys conducted in 1957 and 1963–64 in the southeastern part of the country indicates, moreover, a slight decrease in the real value of rural wages during this period.

It appears, then, that by the mid-1950s information concerning opportunities in the southern part of the Ivory Coast had spread rather effectively to

---

[g]The Chamber of Agriculture around 1950 estimated that 190,000 laborers were required on the Ivory Coast, of which 28,000 were needed by European plantations at harvest time. This can be compared with a total Ivorian population at that time of less than two million.

[h]Between 1952 and 1959 this organization financed the recruitment of 150,000 workers. During the same period at least 500,000 non-Ivorians migrated at least once to the Ivory Coast.

the northern part of that country as well as to Mali and Upper Volta. The result was a massive migration in search of land or wage employment. With economic conditions in these northern areas remaining constant, differences in the subjective opportunity cost of leaving home to go to the rural areas of the south was at least partially offset by the spread of information and growth of the potential labor force. In this way it is entirely conceivable that in the labor surplus areas 550,000 or so migrants out of a population of perhaps 8 to 10 million could be induced to seek work in the south at a roughly constant wage.

At first many of these immigrants were able to obtain land relatively easily, either within a type of sharecropping arrangement or without payment of any kind. As the good land was taken up, however, its value rose and immigrants were forced to settle in less accessible areas. Although the purchase of land was possible by the early 1960s, few migrants had the necessary capital or were able to obtain credit on reasonable terms. At the same time reduced prices for coffee and cocoa put pressure on African smallholders to make their operations more efficient. One result of all this seems to have been a shift from shareholding to the employment of wage laborers on a seasonal basis, perhaps in order to pay each worker the value of his marginal product. A large part of the immigrant labor force was thus left essentially floating and was apt to return to the regions of origin if employment or land was not available.

By the early 1970s, however, there were increasing signs of a shortage of rural labor and of upward pressure on rural wages. In part this may have been the result of rising aspirations on the part of younger Ivorians, who, with a few years of education, were anxious to obtain urban employment. As their number increased, more jobs were created for foreign immigrants in the countryside, and this, together with the overall expansion of demand for labor associated with rapid growth in the agricultural sector, has led to a tighter labor market in rural areas.

From 1956 to about 1969, however, the labor market situation in the rural forest area of the Ivory Coast may be reasonably characterized by a perfectly elastic supply function established at the opportunity cost of labor in the countries supplying workers to the Ivory Coast. The quantity of labor supplied was determined, then, solely by demand factors. Unemployment, to the extent that it existed, was primarily an urban phenomenon and concerned the aspiring white-collar class more than unskilled labor. Underemployment, in which the marginal product of labor differed markedly between sectors, does appear to have been important in the forest area, except perhaps seasonally, due to the high cost of shifting labor between sectors for short periods.

The evolution of the labor situation had important implications for timber, coffee, and cocoa production. For example, in the pre-World War I period, logging was an activity engaged in by both European and African entrepreneurs. Timber camps were located close to waterways or to the railway, and all cutting and hauling of timber to these transportation avenues was by hand. Crews were relatively small, there were no important economies of scale, and capital requirements were minimal. As the most accessible areas were exploited, however, problems of moving timber from the felling areas to waterways or the railroad became more severe. The Europeans solved this problem by laying down track and transporting logs on small flat cars. The greater capital requirements of this method tended to force out African producers, however, and by the 1920s the industry was almost solely in European hands, as it remains today. The shortage of labor and rising costs due to ever-increasing transportation requirements, moreover, resulted in continued pressure for the use of more capital intensive techniques. By the time the industry was poised for its great expansion after World War II, it was almost completely mechanized. One result of the increase in capital intensity of the industry was a tendency for it to become relatively concentrated. In 1968, for example, the six largest out of approximately 150 firms accounted for almost 30 percent of the total value of sales, while the 13 largest accounted for almost 45 percent. Aside from being able to finance the high cost of transport capital, these largest firms also benefited from favorable treatment by government in the issuance of cutting permits and assessment of taxes because they combined logging operations with the running of one or more sawmills or other processing facilities. Most of the smaller timber companies, on the other hand, had no sawmills, but were required after 1962 to sell part of their logs for local processing anyway.

The evolution of coffee and cocoa farming was very different. From the beginning European and African methods of production differed substantially. While European plantations used relatively labor intensive techniques, African farmers used land extensive methods, which, though yields per unit of land were low, nevertheless resulted in a relatively high return to labor. Fundamentally, the African farmer was making greatest use of the most abundant factor of production while his European counterpart made relatively less use of land and more of labor, a scarcer factor. The European could have used more extensive methods, but this would have required his operating over a very wide spacial area in order to earn a return at least as great as his opportunity cost in France. To have done this would have made supervision of his workers very difficult, and good supervisory personnel was the scarcest of all factors of production. The African planter, on the other hand, who was content with a much lower total return, operated on a much smaller scale, and could easily supervise his workers personally. Furthermore, he had access to family labor, which could be used during certain seasons at low opportunity cost—since coffee and cocoa production were at least partially complementary with food production in the timing of their demand for labor.

The nature of the technology was such, furthermore, that it could be easily adopted by African farmers without special technical skills or capital equipment. It is in this important respect that coffee and cocoa farming differed substantially from timber production, for which very capital intensive techniques

could be used to lower costs. In another way, too, the European was at a
disadvantage vis-à-vis the African. In case of crop failure, the European planter,
with his dependence on purchased inputs, was much more vulnerable than the
African farmer, who could easily fall back on his subsistence production.

The crisis came after World War II. During the war the European planters
had been subsidized by the government and provided with forced labor. After
the war these policies were abandoned. Planters were forced to raise wages, and
some attempted to lessen their dependence on labor by introducing tractors
and other equipment. The final blow came, however, in 1949-50, when much of
the coffee in the Ivory Coast was destroyed by disease. Although European
planters had greater access to credit than did the Africans, few tried to re-establish
their plantations, and coffee and cocoa production became almost exclusively
an African enterprise.

By the time of independence in 1960 the basic characteristics of timber,
coffee, and cocoa production were well established. The highly mechanized
timber industry, almost wholly in European hands, was financed privately
from abroad or out of retained earnings. It was heavily dependent, however,
on public investment in basic transportation facilities, which determined the area
over which companies could profitably operate. Coffee and cocoa production, on
the other hand, was undertaken primarily on small African farms using very land
extensive techniques. Financial capital was relatively unimportant for these
enterprises since most farmers continued to grow the bulk of their food needs
and since little modern equipment was required. The capital created on these
farms was obtained instead at the expense of leisure or nonagricultural activities.
Initially, coffee and cocoa farmers were very dependent on government investment in transportation and agricultural research, but, by the 1960s, the constraints on this production came increasingly to depend on market conditions
abroad rather than on supply factors.

Demand Conditions

The market for Ivory Coast exports has had a varied history. Early trade
was characterized by the relative unimportance of France, both as a customer
and as a source of imports. This was in part due to the poor competitive
position of French products in West African markets and in part because the
Ivory Coast by international treaty generally received no tariff preferences
from nor granted any to France.[i] Trade relations with France were gradually
strengthened as a result of licensing during World War I and the commercial
sector becoming more oligopolistic in nature as vertical integration was extended after the war, but the first real pressure for closer ties with France

---

[i]Two exceptions, to be discussed shortly, were coffee and cocoa.

came with the Depression. Tariffs paid by countries exterior to the Franc Zone were increased, quotas were extended, and, for certain products, subsidies were paid to compensate for lower prices and to stimulate production.[j] In 1936 the international treaty exempting the Ivory Coast from preferential duties was abrogated. Finally, at the beginning of World War II exchange controls were imposed and exports outside the Franc Zone were, for the most part, prohibited. Except for several years during the war when French West Africa joined with the Allies, the effect of continuing exchange and price controls in the Franc Zone, as well as in other monetary blocs, was to cause a greater proportion of trade to be contained within the Zone than had been the case prior to the war. After October 1947, for example, exports from the Ivory Coast to France were not subject to control, but exports outside the Zone were subject to licensing and the surrender of foreign exchange on unfavorable terms.

After the devaluation of 1949, export controls were eased and exports of the Ivory Coast to countries other than France began to increase. The next decade or so was characterized by a tariff preference system favoring French exports within the Franc Zone and by benefits for some colonial exports entering France. Export duties on Ivorian coffee and cocoa were in 1950 raised from 6 percent, established in the prewar period, to 15 percent. They were nondiscriminatory in nature. Taxes on the export of timber, also nondiscriminatory, remained at 6 percent and were even reduced to 2 percent during the early 1950s when world prices were depressed for several years. Imports into both the Ivory Coast and France paid a fiscal duty which was nondiscriminatory, whereas imports from non-Franc Zone areas paid a customs duty as well. In addition, Ivorian coffee was effectively protected in the French market by a 20 percent tariff preference vis-à-vis non-Franc Zone countries.

During the mid-1950s stabilization funds backed by the Fonds National de Régularisation des Cours des Produits d'Outre-Mer were formed in the overseas territories. In the Ivory Coast these grew out of separate coffee and cocoa funds established after the war to stabilize prices at controlled levels. These earlier funds had been supplied with part of the export tax assessed on each crop and were used to stimulate production by providing subsidies for planting, research, road construction, agricultural credit, and the use of fertilizers and purchase of equipment. In 1950 the objective of stabilization was eliminated, but as prices dropped after 1954 this problem arose again. The Caisse de Stabilisation des Prix du Café was created in 1955, followed the next year by the establishment of a similar fund for cocoa. The main purpose of these funds was to stabilize the fluctuation of prices received by producers, but a secondary goal was to improve marketing techniques. The Caisse de Stabilisation des Prix du Café, for example, was active in promoting Ivorian coffee on the New York market. It also required coffee to be stocked so as to take advantage of seasonal price fluctuations. In addition to any net receipts of stabilization operations, these funds

---

[j]Throughout this chapter the term *Franc Zone* will be used to denote France and the overseas departments, territories, colonies, and ex-colonies which are bound with her into a customs union, allowing for nonpreferential fiscal duties and the free interconvertibility of currencies.

were also supported by a portion of the export tax of 22.38 CFA francs per kilogram of coffee and cocoa in effect at that time.

In 1959 the drop in the price of robusta coffee, especially on the New York market, resulted in the coffee fund using up its reserves and borrowing from the Fonds National. Prices paid to producers of both coffee and cocoa were reduced, and, in order to pool the reserves of both funds, they were combined in 1962 and later reorganized in 1964 to include the stabilization of cotton prices within a single Caisse de Stabilisation et de Soutien des Prix des Productions Agricoles. Although the promotion of coffee and cocoa production was not an explicit aim of these stabilization funds at the time of falling prices in the late 1950s and early 1960s, the Caisse was explicitly charged in 1966 with financing measures designed to improve productivity and quality in cash crop production and to favor local processing or transformation. Part of this financing was to be direct, but most was to be accomplished by allocations to the general investment budget of the government.

With the formation of the European Economic Community by the Treaty of Rome of 1957 the commercial policy linking the Ivory Coast to its European markets was substantially modified.[4] In general the tariff preferences favoring trade within the Franc Zone were to be dismantled and replaced with external tariffs common to the EEC and its associate members. This would have the effect of granting the French territories in Africa lower preferences but over a larger market. In addition, the various price support schemes for African exports were to be eliminated, and, in compensation, substantial amounts of aid to these countries were to be channeled through the newly created European Development Fund. All this was to be accomplished over a twelve-year timetable, but the Convention of Yaoundé, ratified in 1964, accelerated the process and, at the same time, reduced the ultimate level of common tariff preferences and increased the total amount of aid. To understand the changing trade patterns of the 1960s and 1970s, however, it is necessary to examine each of the three main exports in greater detail.

Timber. Until the twentieth century tropical hardwoods were not well known and were used primarily for aesthetic purposes. In the last seventy years, however, they have increasingly been demanded for a variety of uses to replace dwindling supplies of domestic hardwoods in Europe. In the early years, France was a relatively unimportant customer for Ivorian timber. But the colonial government after World War I did undertake to publicize information concerning the various species and their potential uses. As a result of this publicity and of expanding demand for tropical woods in general, exports increased markedly until 1928, contributing to government revenues obtained from an export tax of 16 francs per ton.

Tropical wood exported from its colonies generally received no tariff protection in France until the Depression. At that time tariffs were raised on timber imports in most industrial countries, but France continued to admit colonial exports duty free. As a result, France, which in 1913 had imported only 25 percent of Ivorian timber exports, by 1933 accounted for almost 70 percent. During World War II timber exports were severely handicapped by the lack of available ships, and it was not until several years after the war that the production and commercial organization was again functioning smoothly. To assist timber companies in expanding production in the postwar period the colonial government reduced export taxes, lowered import tariffs on equipment, granted a subsidy for the use of the railroad, guaranteed loans from commercial banks, and engaged in various other supporting policies in addition to providing an improved transportation infrastructure.

The market for Ivorian timber exports, which during the Depression was concentrated in France, became much more diversified with the easing of controls after World War II, especially in the countries of Western Europe. The French market also expanded as supplies of domestic hardwoods were used up. No tariff preferences were granted the overseas territories on the French market, and, in any event, they would not have been effective since virtually all the French demand for tropical hardwoods was satisfied by the overseas territories. A common external tariff of 5 percent was established for rough timbers by the Rome Treaty but was reduced to zero before being placed in effect. Previous tariffs on tropical timber were low in any case, the highest being that of Italy, 7 percent. In 1964 the United Kingdom also eliminated its preferential duty in return for reciprocal treatment for Commonwealth countries. Thus by the mid-1960s no preferences existed within the major markets for rough logs or sawn timber from the Ivory Coast, though preferences were fairly substantial for processed wood.

Although the tariffs that were removed had already been low, the growth of timber exports to these markets during the 1960s was so rapid that the Ivory Coast today exports twice as much timber as Gabon, its nearest African competitor. The explanation seems to lie less in the effect of tariff reduction than in the result of strong increases in demand. Aside from the effects of rising income during this period, the demand for new sources of supply of hardwoods increased as existing resources in temperate zone countries dwindled. In addition, greater information concerning different species was available as a result of promotional efforts. This is important because there is a wide variety of species, the Ivory Coast exporting about twenty, and the market tends to be fragmented. For this reason and because it is difficult to obtain standardization of quality, expansion of trade depends very much on the establishment of close relations between individual importers and exporters. In the Ivory Coast today, in fact, most timber-cutting companies belong to large integrated foreign companies.

In spite of rising transportation costs, profitability of timber production in the Ivory Coast has, in the past, been maintained, since prices have increased at least as rapidly, at an annual rate of 1.5 to 2.5 percent. This situation will not persist for many more years, however, because the limits of supply are being reached. Given recent world market conditions, it is profitable to export

currently only the most highly valued species, and several of these are already
in short supply in the Ivory Coast. As these are exhausted throughout the world,
consumers will shift to somewhat less highly valued species, of which the
Ivory Coast has abundant supplies, but this shift may take quite some time given
the abundant reserves of Okoumé in Gabon. As a result, although the long-
term prospects for timber exports from the Ivory Coast are quite favorable, over
the shorter term the rate of expansion experienced over the past two decades
is likely to decrease. One possibility for future expansion would involve exporting processed timber, but this will be treated in more detail later.

Cocoa.   Exports of cocoa were nil until about 1910, when they began to
expand rapidly. During the following decade French consumption grew by
over 50 percent, as world prices for cocoa continued their relative decline and
then stabilized during the 1920s. The Ivory Coast in 1911 was granted a tariff
preference of one-half the French import duty of 104 francs per 100 kilograms.
At that time this was equivalent to a preference of about 20 percent of the C.I.F.
value of cocoa imports. During the post-World War I period, however, inflation
reduced the *ad valorem* equivalent of this preference despite an upward revision
accompanying devaluation in 1926. Nevertheless, this tariff preference assisted
the Ivory Coast's capture of 45 percent of the French market by 1929.
By that time, however, virtually all of French imports were being supplied
by French colonies. Since French consumption remained relatively stagnant
during the 1930s, the Ivory Coast had to search elsewhere to market its still
expanding cocoa crops. This occurred just as world prices fell to about 30 percent
of their previous high in 1927, and was an important reason for the shift at that
time from cocoa to coffee planting. Within the Franc Zone, on the other hand,
Ivorian cocoa exports enjoyed a price substantially above that of the world
market but continued until 1936 to pay half the French import duty. During
World War II, prices received by Ivorian planters usually lagged behind cost
increases, and only subsidies to European producers kept them in business. After
the war, exports to France were stimulated by increased demand, in part as a
result of prices being kept artificially low. At the same time unfavorable exchange
rates inhibited exports to other countries until the last of several postwar
devaluations and the relaxation of price and exchange controls in 1949.
This occurred just as world cocoa prices were rising rapidly from an average
of 21.5 cents per pound on the New York market in 1949 to 57.8 cents in 1954.
The reasons for this rise illustrate well the predominant characteristic of the
international cocoa market: instability of prices due to the effect of fluctuations
in weather conditions on the supply of this highly perishable crop and to the
long lag between planting and production. As a result of the decline in prices
over the first two decades of the century, primarily as a result of the growth
of African production, and their continued stagnation until after World War II,
little new planting had taken place since the 1920s. By the early 1950s,
therefore, most existing cocoa trees were well advanced in age and many had

ceased producing altogether. At the same time incomes were rising rapidly with postwar reconstruction, increasing the demand for cocoa. The result was a rapid rise in prices until 1955, when newly planted trees started coming into production and prices broke. Thereafter, there were a series of oscillations due to variations in supply as a result of varying weather conditions as modified by speculative forces.

On the whole, however, prices in the 1960–67 period were considerably below those between 1949 and 1955, especially if we allow for the effects of general inflation. Furthermore, most of the world's most suitable areas for cocoa had already been planted by the mid-1950s, so that increases in production thereafter had to come primarily from increases in yields rather than from new planting, and costs were consequently higher at the time that prices were lower. The Ivory Coast, however, was one of the few countries which still had good land available for planting during the 1950s and even on into the 1960s.

The oscillations in the price of cocoa on world markets, due primarily to short-term variations in supply which are difficult to control, have been the subject of considerable concern. A Cocoa Producers' Alliance has been established among countries producing about 75 percent of the world's cocoa in an attempt to keep excesses of production from forcing prices down in years of favorable harvests, but it has not generally been successful. The primary problem today for the Ivory Coast thus remains short-term price instability, and the major instrument for dealing with that instability as far as the producer is concerned is the stabilization fund. Over the longer term prices are unlikely to be depressed too far because of the negative supply response which would result, but the magnitude and duration of the price slumps that can take place before that response proves effective pose severe problems for these stabilization operations.

Although Ivorian cocoa enjoyed a 25 percent preferential tariff on the French market, in practice this meant nothing, since exports by the overseas territories far exceeded French cocoa imports and French prices correspond closely to prices elsewhere. A common external tariff was established at 5.4 percent in 1964 by the EEC, thus providing some limited protection, and, as expected, there has been a substantial increase of Ivorian exports to Common Market countries other than France. Since almost half of that market is supplied by countries having to pay the 5.4 percent tariff, there may be room for enlargement of the Ivory Coast share at the expense primarily of other African producers. The preference is slight, however, and the gain correspondingly small since all cocoa may be marketed without difficulty at prevailing world prices. Furthermore, the other African producers will also benefit from the preference if they should decide to become associate members of the EEC.

Coffee. In contrast to timber and cocoa, whose principal markets have largely been outside of France, exports of coffee from the Ivory Coast have received important French benefits in the form of direct subsidies and a protected market. Ivorian coffee exports to France benefited in the early years from a rebate of 78 francs on the import tariff of 136 francs per 100 kilograms. Although some coffee was exported as early as 1892, most coffee was grown for many years for local consumption, the profits from coffee exports not being sufficiently great to match those of alternative activities. But with the dramatic decline of cocoa prices in the 1930s, coffee production increased rapidly, almost all of it going to France and Algeria. In 1933 France raised its tariff preference favoring colonial coffee imports to 340.4 francs per 100 kilograms. This was approximately 60 percent of the spot price for Brazilian coffee on the New York market. In 1931 a system of subsidies to colonial coffee producers was established and financed from a surcharge on coffee imports into France. Since most of these imports came from noncolonial areas, the subsidy was essentially paid for by the French consumer. Amounting to 2 francs per kilogram in 1931, almost two-thirds of the F.O.B. price, the subsidy had fallen to 0.3 francs by 1935. The aim and effect of these measures was to stimulate colonial production and enable France to begin to shift imports away from its traditional dependence on Latin America.[k]

With the institution of exchange controls in 1939, severe limitations were placed on coffee imports from outside the Franc Zone at the same time that various forms of subsidy to producers in the Ivory Coast were again increased. Exports of coffee even expanded during the war, though the major market shifted from France to the Allies for several years. After the war, Ivory Coast coffee found a ready market in France, which was faced with a continued shortage of foreign exchange. In 1950 the Franc Zone supplied 73 percent of French imports, and the Ivory Coast accounted for about 40 percent of these colonial exports.

Just prior to World War II about 40 percent of the coffee produced in the Ivory Coast was robusta, the rest being primarily *gros Indénié*. By the mid-1950s, however, after tracheomycosis had eliminated virtually all but the *robusta inéac* variety, which was resistant to this disease, Ivory Coast production was almost solely concentrated on robusta coffee. Robusta had been grown for some time in Uganda and Angola and thus already was part of the world coffee market. Its price was not determined independently, however, but rather was established in relation to that of Brazilian arabica coffee, which dominates the world market and is considered to be of better quality for ground coffee than robusta. The high prices of Brazil in the early 1950s, influenced by the exhaustion of world coffee stocks in 1949, together with the results of Brazilian efforts to hold up prices during the second half of that decade, provided a strong incentive to substitute robustas for more expensive coffee. One result was an expansion of the production of soluble coffee, for which robusta has some distinct advantages, and a narrowing

---

[k]Whereas in the period 1929-33 colonial coffee accounted for only 6 percent of French imports, that figure had risen to 32 percent by 1935.

of the price differential between Brazils and robusta. The most important growth of soluble coffee consumption occurred in the United States, and it was to this market that the Ivory Coast turned increasingly after 1954.

But the expansion of demand for robusta coffee was not limited to the soluble coffee market. In France, especially, as a result of the forced shift from Latin American sources of supply owing to protective tariffs, quotas, and exchange controls, consumers began to develop a taste for robusta. Although the percentage of robusta used in French coffee blends prior to the war had been very low, by 1957 fully 71 percent of blended coffee was made from robusta. The proportion has increased since then, yet soluble coffee represented only 12.5 percent of total French coffee consumption in 1968. Most exchange controls had long since been removed, tariff preferences were relatively low, no quotas were in effect, and the relative price differential between robusta and Latin America coffees on the world market was no higher than before the war. Hence it seems reasonable to conclude that by 1968 French tastes had been markedly altered in favor of robusta coffee. In addition to France, Italy, the Netherlands, and Belgium also consume substantial quantities of robusta in other than soluble coffee form.

After World War II coffee imports from the overseas territories benefited from quotas and a preferential tariff of 20 percent levied by France and 10 percent levied by Algeria on imports from third countries. This tariff applied to virtually all imported arabica coffee, since little of this variety is grown within the Franc Zone. The effect of the tariff and quotas was to establish for a limited quantity of arabica in France a price that was higher than that on the world market. The rest of the demand for coffee in France was satisfied by robustas from within the Zone at a price that might be higher but could not fall lower than the world price for robusta. Until 1954 the combined French and Algerian market was large enough to absorb all Franc Zone robusta coffee at prices above those on the world market, but in that year production increased substantially and lower relative prices on the French market caused Ivory Coast exporters to sell 15 percent of the crop in New York. In order to preserve the higher French price during the next few years a system of licensing known as *jumelage* was used. This system, one form of which had previously been employed for cocoa during the 1930s, required exporters to ship a certain proportion of their coffee to outside markets. World prices continued to fall, however, and the French government agreed in 1959 to maintain a support price for coffee in France and Algeria by fixing quotas on imports from Franc Zone countries.[1] The effect, for several years, was to maintain this price about 60 to 65 percent higher than the world price. Returns to exporters to different markets were equalized, in turn, by the Ivorian stabilization fund.

---

[1] The Ivory Coast quota for the 1959-60 season was 83,000 tons and for 1960-61 it was 93,000 tons. This was almost equal to the quantities previously exported to these two countries.

Associate membership in the European Economic Community has had a number of implications for Ivory Coast coffee. The French price support scheme had to be dismantled, and quotas on foreign exports had to be eliminated. In return, Ivory Coast exports were admitted to the EEC with a 9.6 percent tariff preference beginning in 1964. Since the demand for robusta coffee by this market is currently less than the total supply of the associate members, a means must be found, as in the past, for discriminating between this and other markets in order to make the tariff effective. This could occur through effective cooperation on the part of the various stabilization funds responsible for marketing. To date, however, it does not appear that the external tariff has been effective in raising the EEC price of coffee above world market levels. Of greater importance than the tariff preference, though, has been the amount of aid channeled through the European Development Fund during the past decade, partly to compensate for the loss of French price supports.

Between 1958 and 1962 there were a series of international coffee accords culminating in the International Coffee Agreement of 1962. According to this agreement, the Organisation Africaine et Malgache du Café (OAMCAF) was assigned a quota of coffee which could be exported to participating consumer countries over each of the next five years. OAMCAF in turn assigned the Ivory Coast 5 percent of the total ICO market. The quota was increased to 5.6 percent for the period 1968-73. This agreement has helped to stabilize prices, but it has also created problems of surplus disposal for the Ivory Coast. One alternative was to sell surplus coffee outside the countries signing the agreement, but at a substantially lower price. Another was to try to limit new planting. Production, instead, expanded during the early 1960s, and the Ivory Coast was fortunate in being able to market part of its crop beyond its quota, but within the area of the agreement, because of harvest failure in some countries which were consequently unable to fill their quotas. In 1965, however, the government had to limit new plantings and to attempt to stabilize production. Surpluses continued to accumulate, and during 1967-69, 140,000 tons of coffee were destroyed. It is anticipated that quota exports, which were 172,000 tons in 1971, will be expanded in the future at the rate of about 2.2 percent annually. Further increases in exports must find new markets, in Japan or Eastern Europe perhaps, but at prices much lower than those within the area of the agreement.

The Postwar Record

During the past twenty-five years great changes have taken place in the Ivory Coast economy, many of which have resulted from the rapidly expanding production and export of timber, cocoa, and coffee. As seen in Table 2-1, timber has grown most quickly during these years, followed by cocoa and then by coffee. A quantity index of exports, of which timber, cocoa, and coffee

Table 2–1.
Timber, Cocoa, and Coffee Exports, Quantity Index of Exports, and the Terms of Trade, Selected Years (Ivory Coast)
(quantities in 000s Metric Tons)

Year	Timber Quantity	Timber % Value	Cocoa Quantity	Cocoa % Value	Coffee Quantity	Coffee % Value	Quantity index (1953=100)	Terms of trade (1953=100)
1947	49	4.9	28	19.0	43	55.8	61	28.8
1950	106	4.2	62	34.1	54	48.4	100	86.5
1954	132	3.6	53	32.3	88	62.0	110	136.7
1959	444	11.9	63	43.2	105	47.3	149	105.3
1962	915	19.4	101	22.1	143	39.6	250	81.0
1964	1,526	23.9	124	19.5	204	42.5	339	85.8
1965	1,566	26.9	126	15.9	186	37.8	345	76.2
1967	1,840	27.1	105	17.2	149	31.6	343	89.9
1969	2,695	29.7	119	22.2	178	25.5	435	102.9

Sources: Ivory Coast Territory, Service de la Statistique, Commerce Exterieur de la Côte d'Ivoire et de la Haute Volta de 1931 à 1954 (Abidjan: 1955); Inventaire Economique de la Côte d'Ivoire, 1947-1956 (Abidjan: 1958); Inventaire Economique et Social de la Côte d'Ivoire, 1947-1958 (Abidjan: 1960); Ivory Coast, Direction de la Statistique, Bulletin Mensuel de Statistique (Abidjan: various issues); and estimates from the author's current research on the economy of the Ivory Coast.

comprised about 80 percent of the total value over the entire period, increased
at an average annual rate of 9 percent. During the same period, if we neglect
the immediate postwar years of shortage, the terms of trade, while varying,
did not indicate any clear long-term trend. Thus the purchasing power of exports
has been maintained.

This postwar experience of growth reflects the supply and demand characteristics just discussed. Timber exports, constrained primarily by an insufficient
transportation infrastructure prior to World War II, have expanded rapidly as
this deficiency has been remedied since the war. Cocoa production, after having
been slowed by the low prices of the Depression and wartime difficulties of
marketing, responded rapidly to rising prices during the first ten years of the
postwar period but leveled off after a lag of several years following the 1955 drop
in prices. The production of coffee, which had grown more rapidly than cocoa
during the Depression and war, also increased swiftly in the early postwar years
but began to decline in relative importance by the mid-1960s.

The export growth record only gives part of the picture, however, since it
does not include that part of production which is sold to processing firms for
later export or domestic use. Historically, as seen in Table 2–2, domestic sales
of timber have been much more important as a percentage of total production
then have those of either cocoa or coffee. In recent years, however, domestic
sales of cocoa have increased considerably as a rising proportion of that product
has been processed prior to export. These forward linkages and their effects
will be examined in more detail later.

The impressive record of export growth achieved by the Ivory Coast during
the postwar period has been accompanied by an equally impressive overall
economic performance. Although data with which to examine this experience in
the 1950s are very limited, there do exist reasonably good estimates of the
national accounts for the 1960s. From 1960 to 1970 Gross Domestic Product
in the Ivory Coast rose at an average annual rate in real terms of about 7 percent.
On a per capita basis this amounted to close to a 4 percent annual rate of growth.
At the same time a fundamental restructuring of the economy was taking place
with the proportion of primary production in GDP decreasing from 44 percent
to 28 percent while that of the secondary sector increased from 14 percent to
20 percent. Most of this expansion of industry was concentrated in the production
of energy, construction, and manufacturing of previously imported goods, the
last sector being assisted by substantial private capital inflows. Nevertheless, a
large part of the growth of real investment at an annual rate of about 10 percent
was financed by domestic savings, the savings ratio averaging between 15 and
16 percent of GDP during most of the period. In the foreign trade sector, real
exports increased at about 8 percent annually—sustaining a large and continuously favorable balance of trade—which was used to finance much of the growth
in repatriated profits and remittances sent abroad by foreign workers.

During this period the Ivorian government has worked toward the diversi-

Table 2-2
Production and Domestic Sales of Timber, Cocoa, and Coffee, 1954–67 (Ivory Coast)

	TIMBER				COCOA			COFFEE		
	Production		Domestic sales		Production		Domestic Sales	Production		Domestic Sales
Year	Quantity (000s m³)	Value (million CFAF)	Quantity (000s m³)	Value (million CFAF)	Quantity[a] (000s tons)	Value (million CFAF)	Value (millions CFAF)	Quantity[a] (000s tons)	Value (millions CFAF)	Value (millions CFAF)
1954	292	n.a.	123	n.a.	75	n.a.	—	n.a.	n.a.	n.a.
1955	358	n.a.	149	n.a.	71	n.a.	—	92	n.a.	n.a.
1956	442	n.a.	167	n.a.	73	n.a.	—	114	n.a.	n.a.
1957	407	n.a.	172	n.a.	45	n.a.	—	108	n.a.	n.a.
1958	657	n.a.	190	n.a.	56	n.a.	—	104	n.a.	n.a.
1959	767	n.a.	209	n.a.	62	n.a.	—	153	n.a.	n.a.
1960	1,060	6,504	220	468	85	10,948	—	137	18,221	17
1961	1,260	8,454	260	571	91	8,875	—	172	21,972	23
1962	1,450	9,179	295	744	83	9,190	—	117	16,350	82
1963	1,810	12,293	330	874	99	11,221	—	215	27,805	117
1964	2,270	17,140	410	1,158	133	14,724	40	241	37,111	133
1965	2,605	16,709	700	1,721	115	9,283	772	213	27,439	130
1966	2,600	16,734	778	1,900	163	14,158	1,072	256	31,888	145
1967	3,022	19,963	850	2,125	129	14,859	2,023	157	24,732	190
1968	3,470	23,960	850	2,550	142	22,956	3,460	268	39,212	315

n.a. Not available.

[a]Prior to 1960, data apply to the trading season for which most of production is marketed in the year indicated. From 1960, data are on a calendar year basis. Excess of production over domestic sales differs from exports, given elsewhere, because of changes in stocks and differences in the time of recording.

Sources: Ivory Coast, Service de la Statistique, *Inventaire Economique et Social de la Côte d'Ivoire, 1947-1958* (Abidjan: 1960); Ivory Coast, Direction de la Statistique, *Situation Economique de la Côte d'Ivoire* (Abidjan: various years); Ivory Coast, Direction des Etudes de Développement, *Comptes de la Nation* (Abidjan: various years).

fication of agriculture and the promotion of industrialization concentrated on
import substituting industries and, to a lesser extent, export processing. The
first objective was to be attained by expanding agricultural research and a variety
of programs designed to reach the farmer. Among the more important crops
with which some degree of diversification had been achieved by the early 1970s
were palm products, bananas, pineapples, rice, and cotton. In the manufacturing
sector the major means of attracting foreign capital was the formulation of
a rather liberal investment incentive scheme as well as an absence of restrictions
on repatriation of profits. These policies, together with the expanding Ivorian
market, resulted in a very rapid growth of this sector during the 1960s.

The Direct Contribution to National
Income and Employment

In evaluating the direct contribution of timber, cocoa, and coffee production to national income in the Ivory Coast, an assessment must be made of the
opportunity cost of each factor of production since this contribution should be
measured net of these costs. Where the industry is relatively small, the concept
seems clear, the opportunity cost of an input being equal to the cost of using
that input in its best alternative employment. But where the industry is very
large in relation to the rest of the economy, one must choose between using a
total or marginal concept of opportunity cost. To understand this it is useful to
look separately at timber and at coffee and cocoa.

Although timber in the late 1960s accounted for about one-quarter of the
total value of exports, its impact on factor markets was slight. Skilled labor and
private capital, for example, could be imported from Europe or from other
African countries at fixed prices and helped to earn quickly the foreign exchange
needed to pay for them.[m] Unskilled labor was also available at a relatively constant wage either from within the Ivory Coast or from the countries to the north.
Since the timber industry in the mid-1960s probably employed less than ten
thousand out of a total of over 500,000 workers immigrating from the north,
the effect of that industry on the wage level is likely to have been minimal.

The major constraint on the expansion of timber production during this
period, as we have said, was the availability of public transportation infrastructure. In the early years, when public savings were slight, construction of
these facilities was constrained ultimately by the provision of French public
capital and by the rate at which the government was able to plan and execute
transportation projects. The effect of this investment was to lower transportation

---

[m]One constraint on the use of European personnel which existed in other industries,
pressure for Africanization, was much less important in the timber industry because
Europeans working in timber camps were relatively inconspicuous and because the
demand on the part of Ivorians for this work was not great.

costs to the port and thus raise the economic rental value of land not previously served by public roads. The government, as will be seen later, siphoned off much of this rent with an array of taxes imposed on timber companies, though some of the rent probably went to companies able to gain more favorable geographical positions without paying high taxes.[n] In the strictest sense of the word, of course, the timber reserves opened up to exploitation did have an opportunity cost, that is the return which could have been received by waiting and cutting the timber at a later date when prices might have been higher and the technology more efficient.[o] The choice depended on a comparison of the anticipated rates of return obtained by cutting the timber at various times and the social rate of discount. Because of the uncertain nature of that decision, however, this concept of opportunity cost will be ignored.

It is somewhat more difficult to evaluate conceptually the opportunity cost of factors used in productive activities that dominate the entire economy. Such is the case with the cocoa and coffee sectors, which, if taken together in total, employ factors whose alternative uses would not appear to be nearly as profitable. Even some of the intermediate inputs, such as transportation services, would earn a much lower return in the absence of cocoa and coffee. This presupposes, however, that agricultural research would not have discovered some other equally profitable crop, an assumption which does not seem justifiable given the long history of research in the Ivory Coast.

Rather than attempt to evaluate the opportunity cost of factors in the absence of all cocoa and coffee production, it seems preferable to consider the opportunity cost of these inputs at the margin of their use during the 1960s. Since a very large amount of employed labor originates from outside the country and since rural surveys indicate that agricultural wages during the busy season were above the legal minimum wage, it is reasonable to suppose that the rural wage rate was determined by market forces and that the opportunity cost of labor at the margin was equal to that wage. Family members working fields near their homes may have been willing to work for less, but since it paid to expand production further by employing labor from outside at higher wages, these family workers implicitly earned rents due to their more advantageous position adjacent to areas of production. On the other hand, there is evidence that younger people from the cocoa- and coffee-producing areas were more likely than their northern counterparts to go to school for a few years and then migrate to the cities in search of white-collar jobs. They, in effect, considered their opportunity cost to be higher than the wages paid in agriculture. On balance, the most reasonable alternative is to evaluate the social opportunity cost of labor at the wage rate of rural workers and to assume, for reasons stated earlier, that this wage rate remained constant over the 1960-67 period in which we are interested.

---

[n]It will be shown later, however, that the amount of rent which did not accrue to the government does not appear to have been very great.

[o]Unlike minerals, however, some of the timber held in reserve will rot over time if it is not cut.

The opportunity cost of purchased inputs, both imported and domestic, was also approximately equal to the price paid for those inputs. Private physical capital used in cocoa and coffee production, unlike that employed in the cutting of timber, was not imported from abroad but was made from labor used to clear land and to plant and care for trees until they entered production. The cost of this capital was therefore constant and just equal to the cost of labor used in its creation. The supply of this capital, however, depended upon its rate of return and the ability of farmers to finance the investment. Part of this financing was saved out of agricultural incomes, but when financial capital was not available for hiring workers to extend production, cocoa and coffee farms could be created out of family labor reallocated from leisure or other productive activities. Because of this and the fact that agricultural incomes were growing rapidly, it is reasonable to assume that the supply of capital for planting cocoa and coffee was highly elastic over the relevant range.

Lack of agricultural knowledge, which in the past had been a severe constraint on production, did not limit the expansion of cocoa and coffee during the 1950s and 1960s. The particular varieties planted during these decades had, by this time, established their supremacy—in cocoa very early, in coffee only with the outbreak in 1949 of tracheomycosis. The major constraint seems to have been a combination of public investment in transportation, especially feeder roads, and the vagaries of the international market as influenced by government policies primarily through operations of the stabilization fund. As with timber, the combination of infrastructure, government tax and price policies, the available technology, and the returns to capital and labor, given world prices, determined the rent to land and the division of that rent between the government and the farmer. Again, the opportunity cost of land should be considered in relation to the possibility of postponing this period of rapid growth of what Myint has called the "vent-for-surplus" variety, but the potential gains from postponement appear to be much less important than in the case of timber.[p]

It was possible to estimate quantitatively the returns to the various factors, as well as the payments for inputs of goods and services used in the production of timber, coffee, and cocoa. These estimates were made on the basis of data published in the national accounts and the results of extensive surveys of the

---

[p]Hla Myint, "The 'Classical Theory' of International Trade and the Underdeveloped Countries," *Economic Journal* 68 (June 1958): 317-37. This concept refers to the possibility of achieving high rates of growth of output as land and labor with very low opportunity costs are reallocated to the production of exports as the country is opened to foreign trade. Once these factors are completely absorbed into the export sector, the vent-for-surplus period of growth comes to an end, and further increases in output can be achieved only by increasing the supplies of productive factors, including capital, or by improvements in technology. The Ivory Coast seems to have been very fortunate in the timing of its expansion of coffee production especially, taking advantage of the foreign exchange shortage in France following World War II, which forced France to shift her coffee consumption away from the arabicas of Latin America. The dependence of the Ivory Coast on the French market then pressured France into supporting Franc Zone coffee prices during the late 1950s and early 1960s, and this, in turn, was a major reason for the sizeable assistance granted by the European Development Fund to compensate for the dismantling of these supports within the EEC.

timber industry and of the main cocoa- and coffee-producing regions conducted during the period 1962-66. Details of the estimation procedures are contained in the notes to the tables which follow, but several comments are appropriate here. First, because of wide variations in the value of production of cocoa and coffee due to weather and fluctuating prices, estimates have been calculated for each of the years from 1960 through 1967 even though this required making a number of somewhat arbitrary assumptions. It was presumed, for instance, that the inputs of materials, services, labor, and capital varied as a constant proportion of either the area planted or the quantity produced. This assumption seems reasonable given the relative constancy of the prices of these inputs and the fact that no substantial increases in either yields or labor productivity appear to have taken place over the period. For timber it was assumed that the size of the capital stock varied in proportion to the number of cubic meters produced. Second, in order to treat the timber and the cocoa and coffee sectors on a comparable basis, commercial margins and taxes paid by traders after the purchase of cocoa and coffee from producers were added to intermediate inputs of services and to value added, respectively. Third, all labor input was valued at 200 francs per day, an approximate average of rates obtained from rural surveys for the busy agricultural season.[q] Given an acknowledged margin of error in the estimation of this wage of perhaps 10 percent and the lack of any clear trend in real or nominal rural wages during the period, the wage rate was assumed to remain constant over the entire eight years.

Estimates for the value of intermediate inputs and value added divided into labor costs, payments to government, and a residual are given in Tables 2-3 and 2-4. One of the first things to note is that the shares of intermediate inputs used in the production of timber are nearly twice those found in cocoa and coffee. If transportation services were excluded from the latter sector, moreover, the contrast would be much greater. The low value of these inputs in cocoa and coffee production reflects the relatively simple technology and low yields characteristic of these activities.

Although the absolute value of the returns to labor in cocoa and coffee production is three to four times that in the production of timber, the relative shares of labor in value added, averaging 38 percent for timber, do not differ much. There is, however, substantial year to year variation in this share. Payments to government, on the other hand, differ substantially between these activities, both absolutely and as a share of value added. Rising from 19 percent of value added in 1960, payments by the timber industry averaged 30 percent from 1962 to 1967. The combination of export taxes on cocoa and coffee and

---

[q]Actual rates vary according to conditions of employment, origin of worker, and region of production. The rate of 200 francs includes an implicit valuation of food and lodging and may be compared with the legal minimum wage in 1964 of 178 francs. It is generally recognized that workers on African farms receive higher wages than do unskilled workers in the modern part of the rural sector, who might be expected to receive the legal minimum wage, but that employment is more seasonal. On balance, it seems that 200 francs per day is, if anything, an overestimate, especially if the opportunity cost of family workers is less than that of hired labor.

Table 2-3

Distribution of the Value of Intermediate Inputs and of Value Added in the Timber Industry, 1960-67 (Ivory Coast)

	Expenditures (millions CFAF)							
	1960	1961	1962	1963	1964	1965	1966	1967
Value of intermediate inputs	2,938	3,857	3,675	4,897	6,785	7,792	7,877	8,483
Fuel, electricity	523	603	597	799	1,110	1,253	1,267	1,517
Metals	33	43	37	10	7	12	15	20
Construction materials	7	5	27	36	49	63	65	80
Chemicals	18	15	11	15	21	13	17	28
Vehicles and repair	–	62	64	86	122	1,738	1,756	1,338
Other mechanical and electrical	906	1,231	1,072	1,439	1,996	560	557	658
Tires	152	174	161	215	299	317	320	240
Other industrial products	4	4	17	23	33	50	72	56
Construction	10	17	31	42	58	84	115	45
Transportation	1,246	1,652	1,560	2,100	2,907	3,380	3,410	4,110
Rent	13	17	40	54	75	60	64	50
Other services	26	34	58	78	108	262	219	341
Value-added	3,566	4,597	5,504	7,396	10,355	8,917	8,857	11,480
Labor costs	1,454	1,896	1,533	2,257	2,857	3,481	3,039	3,663
Payments to government[a]	699	983	1,573	2,090	3,041	3,038	2,876	3,424
Residual (profits, etc.)	1,413	1,718	2,398	3,049	4,457	2,398	2,942	4,393
Value of production	6,504	8,454	9,179	12,293	17,140	16,709	16,734	19,963

	Factor shares of the value of production							
	1960	1961	1962	1963	1964	1965	1966	1967
Value of intermediate inputs	45.2	45.6	40.0	39.8	39.6	46.6	47.0	42.5
Fuel electricity	8.1	7.1	6.5	6.5	6.5	7.5	7.6	7.6
Metals	0.5	0.5	0.4	–	–	–	–	–
Construction materials	0.1	–	0.4	0.3	0.3	0.4	0.4	0.4
Chemicals	0.2	0.2	0.1	0.1	0.1	–	–	0.2
Vehicles and repair	–	0.8	0.7	0.6	0.7	10.4	10.5	6.7
Other mechanical and electrical	14.0	14.5	11.7	11.8	11.6	3.3	3.3	3.3
Tires	2.3	2.1	1.7	1.8	1.7	1.9	1.9	1.2
Other industrial products	–	–	0.1	0.1	0.2	0.4	0.4	0.3
Construction	0.2	0.2	0.3	0.3	0.3	0.5	0.7	0.2
Transportation	19.2	19.5	17.0	17.2	17.0	20.2	20.4	20.6
Rent	0.2	0.2	0.5	0.4	0.4	0.4	0.4	0.3
Other services	0.4	0.5	0.6	0.5	0.6	1.6	1.4	1.7

Table 2–3 (cont.)

	1960	1961	1962	1963	1964	1965	1966	1967
			Factor shares of the value of production					
Value-Added	54.8	54.4	60.0	60.2	60.4	53.4	53.0	57.5
Wages and salaries	22.4	22.4	16.7	18.4	16.7	20.8	18.1	18.3
Payments to government	10.7	11.6	17.1	17.0	17.7	18.2	17.4	17.2
Residual (profits etc.)	21.7	20.4	26.2	24.8	26.0	14.4	17.5	22.0
Value of production	100	100	100	100	100	100	100	100

[a]Includes estimates for the payment of direct taxes as well as indirect taxes taken from the national accounts.

Sources: Ivory Coast, Direction des Etudes de Développement, *Comptes de la Nation* (Abidjan: various years); Ivory Coast, Ministère de l'Agriculture, *Economie Forestière de la Côte d'Ivoire* (Paris: Société d'Etudes pour le Développement Economique et Social, 1967).

Table 2–4

Distribution of the Value of Intermediate Inputs and of Value Added in Cocoa and Coffee Production, 1960-67 (Ivory Coast)

	1960	1961	1962	1963	1964	1965	1966	1967
			Expenditures (millions CFAF)					
Value of intermediate inputs[a]	6,098	7,014	5,791	6,794	9,750	8,927	10,968	6,111
Fuels	20	26	18	32	36	32	38	24
Fertilizer	25	27	29	31	32	32	33	34
Pesticides, insecticides	45	47	49	52	54	56	57	58
Mechanical equipment, tools	64	66	70	73	77	79	81	82
Bags	84	100	76	119	134	124	159	109
Construction	11	11	11	11	12	13	13	13
Decortication	562	706	480	882	990	875	1,053	644
Transport and commerce	5,287	6,031	5,058	5,594	8,415	7,716	9,534	5,147
Value-added	23,071	23,833	19,749	32,232	42,085	27,795	35,078	33,480
Labor costs[b]	8,882	9,921	8,342	11,556	12,857	12,150	13,983	10,726
Payments to government[c]	2,731	2,688	5,976	10,134	12,509	3,202	6,492	11,745
Residual (profits, etc.)	11,458	11,224	5,431	10,542	16,719	12,443	14,603	11,009
Value of production	29,169	30,847	25,540	39,026	51,835	36,722	46,046	39,591

Table 2-4 (cont.)

	1960	1961	1962	1963	1964	1965	1966	1967
	Factor shares of the value of production							
Value of intermediate inputs	20.9	22.7	22.7	17.4	18.8	24.3	23.8	15.4
Fuels	0.1	0.1	0.1	0.1	0.1	0.1	0.1	0.1
Fertilizer	0.1	0.1	0.1	0.1	0.1	0.1	0.1	0.1
Pesticides, insect-icides	0.1	0.1	0.2	0.1	0.1	0.2	0.1	0.1
Mechanical equip-ment, tools	0.2	0.2	0.3	0.2	0.1	0.2	0.2	0.2
Bags	0.3	0.3	0.3	0.3	0.3	0.3	0.3	0.3
Construction	–	–	–	–	–	–	–	–
Decortication	1.9	2.3	1.9	2.3	1.9	2.4	2.3	1.6
Transport and commerce	18.2	19.6	19.8	14.3	16.2	21.0	20.7	13.0
Value-added	79.1	77.3	77.3	82.6	81.2	75.7	76.2	84.6
Labor costs	30.4	32.2	32.7	29.6	24.8	33.1	30.4	27.1
Payments to gov-ernment	9.4	8.7	23.3	26.0	24.1	8.7	14.1	29.6
Residual (profits etc.)	39.3	36.4	21.3	27.0	32.3	33.9	31.7	27.9
Value of production	100	100	100	100	100	100	100	100

[a]Estimates of the value of material and service inputs were obtained for each year by multiplying the ratio of this value to either tons of cocoa and coffee produced or hectares in production, as estimated by regional surveys for 1962-64, times the quantities produced or area in production each year. To this was added the cost of transportation and commercial transactions after deduction for taxes paid and the net balance of stabilization operations.

[b]Two hundred francs per day multiplied by the estimated number of man-days used in production, assuming 17 days for cocoa and 28 days for coffee per hectare for tree maintenance and 50 days for cocoa and 150 days for coffee per ton for harvest operations. These requirements are based on information gathered in a survey of the southeast area of the country conducted in 1963-64.

[c]Includes export tax estimates and the net flow of stabilization operations.

Sources: Ivory Coast, Direction des Etudes de Développement, *Comptes de la Nation* (Abidjan: various years); Ivory Coast, Ministère du Plan, *Région du Sud-Est: Etude socio-économique* (Paris: Société d'Etudes pour le Développement Economique et Social, 1967, *Region de Daloa-Gagnoa: Etude socio-économique* (Paris: Bossard Uniter, 1967); *Etude Générale de la Région de Man* (Paris: Bureau pour le Développement de la Production Agricole, n.d.), *Etude Régionale de Bouaké, 1962-1964* (Abidjan: 1966); annual data on the number of hectares of cocoa and coffee in production obtained from the planning ministry of the Ivory Coast.

operations of the stabilization fund resulted in wide variation in payments to government from this source because of fluctuations in weather, international prices, tax rates, and prices paid to the producer, but the average share of value added was 22 percent, substantially less than that of timber.

The remaining portion of value added is broken down in Table 2-5 into an allowance for amortization, the net return to capital, and a residual rent. It has been estimated that the sales value of producing cocoa and coffee farms in the southeastern part of the Ivory Coast was roughly 50,000 francs per hectare for cocoa and 30,000 francs for coffee in 1963-64. These values were each approximately three and one-half times the net return to land and capital per hectare of cocoa and coffee trees after deducting the estimated return to labor and amortization of capital from agricultural income. This was equivalent to capitalizing the returns to land and capital at about 29 percent per annum. Since the capital market for borrowing was very imperfect, however, this rate was probably somewhat higher than the true opportunity cost of capital in an investment of equivalent risk. Consequently, the return to capital invested in cocoa and coffee trees has been calculated at an assumed rate of interest of 20 percent. Although this rate is slightly arbitrary, the results are not much affected by a change of a few percentage points in either direction.

This 20 percent rate of return may be compared with the ratio of net profit to capital stock in the timber industry, which averaged just under 9.5 percent annually for the eight years. Although some of this profit may have been a form of rent to companies with more favorably located concessions, the average return is so low that we will assume all of it was a return to capital. One reason for the low estimated rate of return may be the relatively short service life, averaging 6.7 years, of capital equipment invested in the industry. This together with favorable market conditions implies that risks were considerably lower in this industry than in the coffee and cocoa sectors, where investments had payoffs over periods of more than fifteen years and returns were subject to fluctuations of prices and weather conditions. Finally, profits in the Ivory Coast timber industry may also have been low because local firms are usually vertically integrated with companies in Europe which may be more interested in maintaining assured sources of supply of this very heterogeneous product than in reaping large profits at the primary level.

Of greatest interest, perhaps, are the substantial rents to land devoted to cocoa and coffee production after deduction for the returns to all other factor services. In the southeast, where practically all rural families grow at least some cocoa or coffee, the average return to labor per hectare in 1964 was 14,300 francs per year. For cocoa land in the entire nation over the eight-year period, the average annual residual return was 7,160 francs, somewhat lower than that for the Southeast region. If we consider only family labor valued at 8,100 francs per hectare in the Southeast in 1964, the return to land in cocoa was very close to that of labor. Returns to land planted in coffee were lower, and this is

Table 2-5

Capital and Factor Returns in the Production of Timber, Cocoa, and Coffee, 1960-67 (Ivory Coast) (millions CFAF)

	1960	1961	1962	1963	1964	1965	1966	1967
Timber								
Capital[a]	5,668	6,737	7,753	9,678	12,138	13,929	13,902	16,159
Amortization[a]	850	1,010	1,163	1,452	1,820	2,089	2,085	2,424
Net profit[b]	220	320	987	1,312	2,525	−417	146	1,557
Ratio of net profit to Capital	3.9	4.7	12.7	13.6	20.8	−	10.5	9.6
Cocoa and coffee								
Agricultural income[c]	20,061	21,144	13,773	22,098	29,574	24,592	28,586	21,736
Cocoa	7,535	6,472	5,268	6,506	9,070	6,909	10,461	8,851
Coffee	12,526	14,672	8,505	15,592	20,504	17,683	18,125	12,885
Labor costs[d]	8,882	9,921	8,342	11,556	12,857	12,150	13,983	10,726
Cocoa	1,787	1,933	1,931	2,145	2,317	2,363	2,870	2,549
Coffee	7,095	7,988	6,411	9,411	10,540	9,787	11,113	8,177
Capital[e]	27,127	27,093	28,336	29,338	31,571	32,388	32,840	33,287
Cocoa	9,900	10,800	11,624	12,240	12,528	12,852	13,140	13,320
Coffee	17,227	16,293	16,712	17,098	19,043	19,536	19,700	19,967
Amortization[f]	1,643	1,590	1,695	1,751	1,895	1,944	1,970	1,997
Cocoa	495	504	581	612	626	642	657	666
Coffee	1,148	1,086	1,114	1,139	1,269	1,302	1,313	1,331
Return to capital at 20%	5,425	5,419	5,667	5,868	6,315	6,477	6,568	6,657
Cocoa	1,980	2,160	2,325	2,448	2,506	2,570	2,628	2,664
Coffee	3,445	3,259	3,342	3,420	3,809	3,907	3,940	3,993
Residual rent[g]	4,111	4,214	−1,931	2,923	8,507	4,021	6,065	2,356
Cocoa	3,273	1,875	431	1,301	3,621	1,334	4,306	2,972
Coffee	838	2,339	−2,362	1,622	4,886	2,687	1,759	−616
Residual rent per hectare (CFAF)								
Cocoa	11,901	6,249	1,334	3,826	10,405	3,736	11,797	8,032
Coffee	1,566	4,622	−4,551	3,054	8,261	4,428	2,875	−993

[a]Based on benchmark estimates obtained from a survey conducted in 1960 and on the assumption of a constant ratio of capital to the volume of timber produced in subsequent years.

[b]Obtained as a residual after deducting estimates for amortization, direct taxes, and payments for financial services.

[c]Equal to production valued in terms of prices paid to the farmer minus the value of intermediate inputs purchased by the farmer.

Table 2-5 (cont.)

---

[d]See Table 2-4.

[e]Estimated from the imputed value at 200 francs per day of labor used in clearing, planting, and maintaining cocoa and coffee trees until they enter production. It was assumed that only one-half of actual clearing costs are attributable to cocoa and coffee, the remaining half going to food production, which frequently is combined with the planting of cash crops the first year. Labor requirements were estimated as 180 days per hectare for cocoa and 161 days per hectare for coffee from the southeast rural survey cited in Table 2-4.

[f]Straight-line depreciation over 20 years for cocoa and 15 years for coffee, the approximate periods of yield.

[g]Obtained by deducting labor costs, amortization, and the return to capital from agricultural income.

Sources: See sources of Tables 2-3 and 2-4.

consistent with the general impression, confirmed by land use estimates, that farmers were tending to switch to cocoa during this period.[r] It must be remembered, moreover, that the rents to land shown in Table 2-5 do not include payments to government but only that portion retained by the farmer.

Not only was the development of these exports of interest to African farmers, it was also a net gain to the whole economy. If it is assumed, in accordance with our previous discussion, that the social opportunity cost of all factors except land was equal to prevailing factor prices, this net gain was equal to the sum of payments to government and the residual rent received by cocoa and coffee farmers. The ratio of the net gain from timber production to the total value of this production climbed from .107 in 1960 to .171 in 1962 and remained roughly constant thereafter. For cocoa and coffee, however, this net gain coefficient was much higher, averaging .359 during the entire period with no clearly discernible trend.

An alternative way of considering the net gain is to examine its importance relative to the total amount of accumulated public investment in the Ivory Coast. Since much of this investment had as its effect the opening up of new areas to export trade, the returns to government and to land may be viewed as a return on this public capital, the major constraining factor on development. At the beginning of 1960 it has been estimated that the value of this capital in terms of that year's prices was 83.7 billion CFA francs. Assuming that the 1960-66 investment program was spread out equally over the next seven years, the value of the capital stock may be estimated for each year. The total net gain to the economy from timber, cocoa, and coffee production during this time averaged about 12 to 13 percent of the value of this accumulated investment. If only that part of

---

[r]During the period 1960-67 the estimated number of hectares producing cocoa increased more than twice as rapidly as the number producing coffee. This is especially noteworthy because coffee can be grown in many areas in which cocoa cannot. It should be noted, however, that these estimates are subject to a relatively high degree of error.

investment which contributed directly to export expansion, such as capital expenditures on transportation and agriculture, is included in the capital stock, that percentage is much higher—perhaps 30 to 40 percent. Thus it is clear that the economic gains which directly resulted from this investment were very important.[8]

The employment and income resulting from these export activities, shown in Tables 2–6 and 2–7, differ markedly. Total employment in the timber industry in 1963 has been estimated as 16,636 persons, of which approximately 45 percent were Ivorians. In the cocoa- and coffee-producing regions, on the other hand, there were about one million persons working in agriculture, spending on the average approximately 40 percent of their time devoted to agriculture in the production of these cash crops. Of these almost 90 percent were Ivorians.

Other important facts are revealed by looking at incomes. In terms of absolute size, coffee and cocoa generated substantially larger incomes than did timber. Timber production, on the other hand, a relatively capital and skill intensive activity, employed fewer workers but paid each of them on average substantially more than did cocoa and coffee farming. The largest share of income, moreover, went to the European owners and managers of these firms. Total salaries received by Europeans were more than two-thirds as great as the wage bill paid to Ivorians and equaled 27 percent of total labor costs. Non-Ivorian Africans, though employed proportionately more in the lower skill grades than Ivorians, nevertheless received almost as much in total wages because of their greater numbers. In addition to a larger total income, Ivorians producing cocoa and coffee received by far the largest share of income from their labor, capital investment, and ownership of land. For cocoa and coffee, in fact, non-Ivorian workers received only slightly more than one-quarter of the total wage bill and 13 percent of total income. Because of lower skill levels and the seasonality of employment, however, each worker on average received substantially less than did workers in the timber industry.

The regional variation in cocoa and coffee production is also striking. The Southeast area of the country has had the longest history associated with these cash crops and is the most commercialized. In that region 25 percent of the total labor force, including family workers of whom many devote only part of their time to agriculture, is hired from outside. In the Daloa-Gagnoa area, located in the center-west of the country where production has grown most rapidly in recent years, 19.5 percent of the labor force works for wages. Man and Bouaké, in the western and central parts of the country, are more marginal areas of production and are less dependent on hired labor. Also indicative of the

---

[8]This calculation ignores amortization and current maintenance and operating expenses paid out of general tax sources. In addition, some past operating expenditures, such as those on agricultural research, should probably be considered as investment. For these reasons and because some general public investment undoubtedly contributed indirectly to the expansion of exports, it is not unreasonable to presume that the return to government investment was not far from the 20 percent rate of return used in the preceding calculations as the opportunity cost of capital.

Table 2-6
Distribution of Employment and Income from Timber Production by Origin of Recipient, 1963 (Ivory Coast)

	Region			
	Ivorian	Non-Ivorian African	Non-African	Total
Employment[a]	7,541	8,604	491	16,636
Yearly income (millions CFAF)	848	792	1,925	3,565
Wages and salaries[b]	848	792	613	2,253
Net profit[c]	–	–	1,312	1,312
Average wage (CFAF/yr)[d]	112,451	92,050	1,248,472	135,420
Share of income (%)	24	22	54	100
Wages and salaries	24	22	17	63
Net profit	–	–	37	37

[a]Estimated by averaging data for 1961 and 1966 (see reference note 9) and adjusting for undercoverage as reported in the timber-industry survey cited in Table 2-3.

[b]Estimated on the basis of average-wage rates by skill group, given in the timber-industry survey, and adjusted to the total wages and salaries shown in the national accounts for 1963.

[c]See Table 2-5. Since almost all timber companies are owned by Europeans, it was assumed that all of net profits went to this group.

[d]Obtained by dividing estimated wages and salaries by the number of employees in each category.

Sources: See Table 2-3 sources.

Table 2-7
Agricultural Employment, Proportion of Agricultural Time in and Distribution of Income from Coffee and Cocoa Production by Region, 1962-64[a] (Ivory Coast)

	Region				
	Southeast	Daloa-Gagnoa	Man	Bouaké	Total
Employment (000s persons)					
Heads of Farm	99	84	72	71	326
Family workers	163	143	110	181	597
Local hired workers	2	1	0	0	3
Nonlocal hired workers	90	54	6	12	162
Ivorian	22	21	1	2	46
Non-Ivorian	68	33	5	10	116
Total	354	282	188	264	1,088
Proportion of agricultural time in coffee and cocoa (%)					
Heads of farm and family workers	50	46	19	12	32
Hired workers	84	81	80	74	82

Table 2-7 (cont.)

	Region				
	Southeast	Daloa-Gagnoa	Man	Bouaké	Total
Yearly income (millions CFAF)	13,394	6,436	1,888	1,339	23,057
Heads of farm and family workers	10,735	5,307	1,752	1,062	18,856
Return to labor[b]	3,462	1,821	877	617	6,777
Rents, return to capital, etc,	7,273	3,486	875	445	12,079
Hired workers[c]	2,659	1,129	136	277	4,201
Ivorians	694	439	22	46	1,201
Non-Ivorians	1,965	690	114	231	3,000
Average income per recipient (CFAF/yr)					
Heads of farm and family workers	41,000	23,400	9,600	4,200	20,429
Return to labor	13,200	8,000	4,800	2,400	7,342
Rents, return to capital, etc.	27,800	15,400	4,800	1,800	13,087
Hired workers	28,902	20,500	22,700	23,100	25,510
Rents, return to capital, etc., per hectare (CFAF/ ha)	16,945	18,444	13,177	5,933	15,901
Share of income (%)	100.0	100.0	100.0	100.0	100.0
Heads of farm and family workers	80.1	82.4	92.7	79.3	81.7
Return to labor	25.8	28.2	46.4	46.0	29.3
Rents, return to capital, etc.	54.3	54.2	46.3	53.3	52.4
Hired workers	19.9	17.6	7.3	20.7	18.3
Ivorians	5.1	6.9	1.3	3.5	5.3
Non-Ivorians	14.8	10.7	6.0	17.2	13.0

[a]Data for the Man and Bouaké regions were obtained for 1962-63; all other data apply to the season 1963-64. Output in each region was valued in 1963-64 producer prices.

[b]Obtained by estimating the total return to labor, using the method described in the notes to Table 2-4, and subtracting the return to hired workers estimated on the basis of the observed number of days they worked in cocoa and coffee. This is a slight overestimate of labor time spent by hired workers in current production, since it is impossible to separate out the number of days devoted to the maintenance of trees not yet in production. Clearing and planting time, however, are not included.

[c]The distribution of the wage bill paid to Ivorian and non-Ivorian hired workers is based on the relative numbers employed in each region.

Sources: Ivory Coast, Ministère du Plan, *Côte d'Ivoire 1965: Population; Etudes Régionales 1962-1965-Synthèse* (Abidjan: 1967); regional surveys cited in Table 2-4.

greater concentration of cocoa and coffee in the Southeast and Daloa-Gagnoa regions is the higher proportion of agricultural time devoted to these crops, especially among heads of farm and family workers, who are not hired primarily for this work.

As expected, average incomes from cocoa and coffee decrease as one moves from the Southeast toward the newer and more marginal regions of production. This is as true of the returns to family labor as it is of the returns to capital and land. The average income of hired workers in Daloa-Gagnoa, however, is lower than in any other region, probably because hired labor is used for clearing and planting, activities which have been more important in this region in recent years than elsewhere but for which wages are not included in the table. In the Southeast the income of hired workers is higher than elsewhere since these laborers are more likely to work all year round or at least for an entire agricultural season.

Also interesting is the value of residual rent and return to capital per hectare of land in production. In the Southeast, where trees in some areas are past their prime and declining in yields, returns are somewhat lower than in Daloa-Gagnoa, where cocoa and coffee have been planted more recently. Clearly indicated, too, is the marginal nature of the other two regions, especially of Bouaké, where, after deduction for labor costs, returns per hectare are less than one-third those of Daloa-Gagnoa. It is important to note, however, that while Bouaké is a marginal region in terms of land use, especially outside of the southern part, coffee growers are nearly as well developed commercially as the farmers in the Southeast and in Daloa-Gagnoa, as evidenced by the high share in total income of wages going to hired labor.

Linkage Effects

Linkage effects, defined as economic benefits and costs associated with the impact of export expansion on other sectors of the economy, may result from interrelationships in production, consumption, savings, and investment. In a strict sense they should be valued net of opportunity cost, that is the net gain which arises from the exploitation of scale economies, externalities, the use of underemployed resources, or, from the national point of view, the attraction of capital and other scarce resources from abroad. In a broader sense, however, the objectives of economic development may be multiple, and linkage effects should be defined to include progress toward achievement of all goals. Even if there is no gain of income after considering social opportunity cost, linkage effects that increase equality of income distribution, for example, may be desirable.

It is also important to define the concept of net gain over a relatively long period of time. One of the arguments associated with the desirability of industrialization is that long-term prospects are not good for the continued growth of traditional exports at a rate sufficiently rapid to stimulate sizeable increases in per capita income. In the Ivory Coast, for example, we have seen that prospects for a rapid growth of cocoa and coffee exports are limited by demand conditions, whereas supply constraints affecting timber production are likely to become increasingly important in the next few years. The current profitability of these long-established exports, however, makes it difficult, and not necessarily desirable, to undertake any immediate, large-scale reallocation of resources.

Yet there are a number of reasons why the current restructuring of the economy in the directions of agricultural diversification and industrialization is important. For one thing, although there appears to be no underemployed rural labor during the busy season, there is a good deal at other times of the year. The difference between the average income of unskilled workers in the timber industry, which employs labor throughout most of the year, and that in cocoa and coffee production is strong evidence of this. Severe difficulties, moreover, lie in the way of gainfully employing rural labor outside of agriculture during the slack season because of the reduction of efficiency and high turnover costs involved. Only through the development of a diversified range of activities, therefore, will it be possible to provide year-round employment for the bulk of the population and develop a modern, stable work force.

Another good reason for current efforts to promote industrialization is that the Ivory Coast is a small country with a limited market, which, if it is going to have a substantial industrial sector, must find export markets for its manufacturers. To be competitive in world markets these goods will have to be produced by a labor force sufficiently skilled to manufacture high quality products at relatively low cost. The development of those industrial skills in a population now largely engaged in agriculture is a major task that will require some time.

The growth of industry in recent years has been extremely rapid, stimulated in part by liberal government investment incentives and a moderate degree of tariff protection. So too has been the expansion of agricultural products other than cocoa and coffee. Our concern here is to outline some of the ways in which this fast pace of industrialization and diversification, as well as the growth of the tertiary sector, has been encouraged by the expansion of the three main exports.

Production Linkages

The timber and cocoa and coffee sectors may generate linkages, either backward or forward, which increase capacity utilization or induce new investment in other sectors. Backward linkages, generated by the demand for intermediate inputs of goods and services, appear to be relatively weak for timber. Although the share of estimated local purchases of these inputs rose from 49 percent in 1960 to 80 percent in 1967, most of this was for the transportation of logs to the port. This is an activity which is conducted primarily by the timber companies themselves and can be considered as being within the same enclave, though it does provide employment for a number of Africans. Aside from transportation, the most important stimulus to backward-linked production comes from the demand for fuel oil for heavy equipment and trucks, which, since 1966, has been refined locally. Capital expenditures are less likely to affect the local economy since equipment tends to be highly specialized and could not be efficiently produced within the Ivory Coast at this time. Out of estimated capital expenditures of from 1.9 billion francs in 1960 to 4.8 billion francs in 1967, approximately 85 percent represented purchases from abroad.

Backward linkages in cocoa and coffee are even less important as a percentage of the total value of production, as can be seen from a comparison of Tables 2–3 and 2–4, but their impact on the local economy, especially in the transportation and commercial sectors, is probably greater. These sectors tend to be much more diffused, to involve a much larger number of Africans, and to generate returns to both capital and labor which are more likely to go to Africans, though not necessarily to Ivorians, than is the case with timber. Of some importance, too, is the decortication of coffee, much of which is performed by larger planters who have invested in the necessary machinery. Of lesser importance is the stimulus given to the local manufacture of jute bags, pesticides, and insecticides. Investment in the planting of cocoa and coffee trees, because it is such a labor-intensive activity, also contributes to African incomes, though the expansion of this investment was not as rapid during the 1960s as it was a decade earlier. Nevertheless, it is clear that the failure of most farmers to use substantial amounts of purchased inputs has limited the backward linkage effects of these two crops.

Forward linkages, on the other hand, are much more important, especially for timber. In 1954, as seen in Table 2–2, sales of timber to local sawmills and other processing installations accounted for 42 percent of total production, whereas processing of cocoa and coffee, aside from preliminary activities carried out in the village such as sorting and drying, was limited to conditioning prior to export. By 1968, the proportion of local to total sales of timber had fallen to 24 percent, but local processing of cocoa and coffee, extended principally to the manufacture of soluble coffee and the intermediate products, cocoa butter and cake, accounted for 1 and 15 percent, respectively, of the total values of production of coffee and cocoa and was expanding rapidly. During the first years of production, as seen in Table 2–8, virtually all of the cocoa butter and cake and about 80 percent of the soluble coffee was exported.

Despite the relatively large quantity of timber processed domestically, the Ivory Coast does not appear to have a strong comparative advantage in exporting processed wood. Historically, the timber supplied to local sawmills has been of inferior quality or damaged in transit so as to be unacceptable for export, but since 1962 the government has required timber companies to process locally a part of their production which would otherwise be exported as logs. In 1966 the tax laws were changed so as to provide a further incentive for local processing. The growth of the domestic market has not been as great as that of local production, moreover, so that about 60 percent of locally processed timber has been exported in recent years, as compared to about 40 percent from 1960 to 1964. A study of the timber industry undertaken in the mid-1960s revealed, however, that exporting unprocessed logs was considerably more profitable and contributed more government revenue and foreign exchange per unit of capital

Table 2-8
Value of Production and of Exports of Processed Timber, Cocoa, and Coffee, 1960-67[a] (Ivory Coast) (millions CFAF)

	1960	1961	1962	1963	1964	1965	1966	1967	1968
Lumber, plywood, veneer									
Production	1,397	1,733	2,185	2,672	3,682	5,740	5,686	5,909	6,566
Export	680	810	950	1,030	1,990	3,492	3,357	3,599	4,106
Cocoa, butter and cake									
Production	—	—	—	—	59	1,193	1,657	2,614	4,369
Export	—	—	—	—	59	1,153	1,555	2,693	3,996
Soluble coffee									
Production	—	—	188	235	305	450	591	611	953
Export	—	—	132	190	242	384	472	486	746
Roasted coffee									
Production	42	60	100	170	170	110	92	82	96
Export	22	30	55	90	90	35	40	32	47

[a]Production and export figures differ from year to year because of variations in inventories as well as domestic sales.
Sources: Ivory Coast, Direction des Etudes de Développement, Les Comptes de la Nation (Abidjan: various years).

investment than did primary processing prior to export.[5] The latter activity, in fact, was undertaken by timber companies primarily in order to satisfy the government's requirement. With the change in tax legislation in 1966, the private profitability of exporting unprocessed logs decreased, but this did nothing to increase the social profitability of exporting processed timber products. Nevertheless, there may be a social gain from processing associated with the acquisition of skills and the use of species that are not exportable in raw form but that can be used domestically or exported to a limited extent as timber or plywood.[t]

The extent to which backward and forward linkages result in gains to the economy net of social opportunity cost is difficult to evaluate quantitatively, but these gains do not appear to be very great. First, as we have seen, the linkages themselves are not strong, especially the backward linkages excluding the transportation sector. Forward linkages are more important in relation to the value of production, but value added, in the production of cocoa butter and cake especially, is not great and timber processing is achieved at the cost of some loss of efficiency in the allocation of capital. Second, where important linkages do exist, there are few economies of scale to be exploited in most of the linked sectors since the optimum scale of each establishment is, in most cases, well short of the incremental demand or supply created. There are exceptions, of course, such as petroleum and the production of jute bags, but they are not numerous. Third, there do not appear to be any important externalities except those associated with the acquisition of skills and the advantages gained by agglomeration. From a distributional point of view, however, one of the important characteristics of the timber-processing industry may be its dispersed character, providing some manufacturing employment in rural areas. Finally, these linked sectors use few, if any, otherwise underemployed productive factors. Cocoa and coffee transportation, which because of its flexibility is able to employ people seasonally, experiences its greatest demand for labor at approximately the same time that workers are needed in agriculture. Management, capital, skilled labor, and even unskilled labor are imported from abroad at fixed factor prices in most of the other industries, while the one factor which is still underutilized, land, is not an important input.

---

[t]Because virgin tropical forests are made up of mixed species rather than homogeneous stands of timber, some privately unprofitable trees must usually be cut down or damaged in order to gain access to the most valued species. Since the market for timber land is very undeveloped, and since timber companies retain concessions for relatively short periods of time, the only cost to the companies of cutting down unprofitable trees is that involved in the felling process itself. From a social point of view, however, the opportunity cost of cutting down currently unprofitable trees includes the discounted present value of those trees if they were preserved until rising prices eventually made their exploitation profitable. By requiring firms to process a certain proportion of cut timber and sell to the local market at a loss, the government is causing them to absorb part of this opportunity cost to the current benefit of the Ivorian consumer. This is not the most efficient solution, however, since this cost to the timber companies is imposed on the felling of profitable species as well.

Final Demand Linkages

In evaluating the linkages associated with the demand for goods and services resulting from the incomes generated in the export sector, we are disadvantaged by the difficulty of obtaining reliable estimates of the distribution of incomes among savings, consumption of imported goods, and consumption of domestically produced goods. Budget studies in rural areas have been conducted, but this allocation of income is extremely difficult to estimate accurately. We can use estimates from the national accounts instead, but they apply to the entire country. Because of the pervasiveness of cocoa and coffee cultivation, however, the national accounts estimates may be of some use along with various qualitative observations.

First of all, it is clear that the impact on final demand of incomes generated in cocoa and coffee has been enormous. In 1960 agricultural income earned in the production of cocoa and coffee was 23 percent of disposable personal income. Although this proportion had dropped to 18 percent by 1966, cocoa and coffee income still rose by 40 percent during these six years. Even given leakages out of the income stream due to taxes, savings, transfers abroad, and expenditures on imported goods, the impact of this sector on total consumer demand must have been very important.

In contrast to production linkages for which net gains appear rather low, moreover, the gains associated with the expansion of demand are quite substantial. In the first place, the total magnitude of the effect is more important because incomes generated in cocoa and coffee production are three or four times the value of intermediate inputs plus value added in processing. Second, economies of scale, which were relatively unimportant in production-linked local industries such as transportation, are much more extensive in the import-substitution, consumer goods industries. The sustained industrial expansion of the last decade has, in fact, been possible only because of the simultaneous increase in size of the domestic market. Investments have frequently been made well ahead of the expansion of demand because capacity utilization rates have increased rapidly. It is worthwhile noting, too, that for purposes of market expansion it makes little difference whether incomes are paid to Ivorians or to other Africans, except in so far as the latter transferred part of their earnings out of the country. Third, the externalities associated with the agglomeration of industry, urbanization, and the creation of a pool of skilled labor are likely to have been important in the past, though they may be giving way now to problems associated with congestion and too rapid a rate of rural-urban migration. Fourth, there is the quesiton of whether any underutilized factors have been brought into production or whether most factors have been imported from abroad or reallocated from other sectors. Much of the expansion of the labor force in industry, for example, has been achieved by non-Ivorians. Nevertheless, it is possibly true that many of these immigrants will continue to live in the Ivory

Coast for years, and one should not distinguish too sharply between African nationalities in assessing the benefits of expanded employment opportunities. Furthermore, the expansion of industry has increased the number of white-collar jobs, to which many Ivorians feel they are more suited by virtue of their education, and this has been a net social gain. In addition, incomes from cocoa and coffee have expanded demand for the output of the small-scale manufacturing and services sector, which presumably is more flexible in providing employment on a seasonal basis. Finally, to the extent that labor has been reallocated from seasonal employment in agriculture to year-round employment in industry or the services, there has been a net increase in factor utilization.

It should be remembered, however, that a large part of industry is subsidized by the investment incentive program, by low interest rates, and by mildly protective tariffs. Although the investment incentives are supposed to be temporary, it is recognized that some firms are never likely to be able to operate without them. Since all these measures represent a cost to the consumer and to other sectors, any net gain is reduced accordingly.

Most of these effects exist for the final demand generated by the timber industry as well, but the impact is much smaller. Salaries earned by Europeans, for example, are more likely to be transferred abroad or to be used to purchase imported goods than is the income earned by Africans. The higher proportion of non-Ivorians in the timber industry also implies that a greater proportion of African wages will be transferred outside the Ivory Coast. Finally, most of the profits earned by European companies are either transferred abroad or used to purchase imported equipment, whereas the profits of African farmers are more likely to be spent at home.

It seems clear that there are substantial savings by cocoa and coffee planters, but they are difficult to measure because of a certain amount of secrecy and the tendency to hoard savings as cash rather than to place them in banks or postal savings accounts. There are also wide fluctuations with changes in yearly income. Nevertheless, there is substantial evidence that farmers, in addition to expanding the area of cultivation, have also been able to finance the construction or purchase of schools, home improvements, agricultural implements and small machinery, vehicles, and, in some cases, urban houses. Some of these investments, such as purchases of taxis, of houses (in some cases), and of land, have been for business purposes. In recent years savings have also been used to finance diversification into other agricultural products such as oil palm.

There is little information concerning the rate of savings. The regional study of the southeast in 1964 estimated the savings rate as 15 percent of family income, but failed to include a number of investment expenditure items as part of savings. The national accounts estimates of all personal savings are about 8 to 10 percent of disposable personal income, but it is recognized that this is a residual item containing all the errors of other estimates. In any case, it seems clear that, in addition to forced saving from government taxation, there is a substantial amount of voluntary saving.

Technological Linkages

There have been a number of external economies associated with the production of timber, cocoa, and coffee. One of the most important has been the construction of feeder roads by timber companies and African farmers for the evacuation of their products. These roads have later served as transportation routes for a variety of purposes. In sparsely populated areas of the country, immigrating Africans have often established their villages near the roads previously built for the transportation of felled timber. Among the gains resulting from this improved transportation network, aside from the direct effect of a reduction in the cost of transport, are increased competition among commercial traders at the local level and greater access to agricultural extension services, health facilities, and schools.

In addition to roads, transportation vehicles and commercial networks established primarily for the export trade are available during the off-season for other tasks. Historically, the network supplying imported goods throughout the year frequently coincided with that set up for exports. Although these networks tend to be more distinct today, there is still substantial overlap, with some equipment and personnel employed in both sectors. At the same time that these two directions of trade have reinforced each other, however, their lines of communication have been such as to inhibit purely internal exchange.

In the same way that the development of linked industries has helped to build up a pool of skilled labor, so have timber, cocoa, and coffee contributed directly to the acquisition of skills available for other uses. Truck driving, road building, and tree clearing are some of the skills employed in the timber industry which have application elsewhere. The African farmer, as he becomes increasingly commercial by planting new land and hiring labor, develops entrepreneurial abilities that can be applied to a variety of enterprises, nonagricultural as well as agricultural.

Pecuniary and especially technological economies and diseconomies are likely to be quite important in the Ivory Coast at its present stage of development because of the long durability of infrastructure, because of the importance of locational specificity in a sparsely populated country whose transportation infrastructure is still far from completely developed, because of the uncertainty which is so prevalent, and because markets are often poorly, if at all, organized. The existence of important pecuniary effects operating through the market may call for government planning and other efforts to reduce uncertainty, but they do not necessarily require government intervention.[6] Technological externalities outside the market, on the other hand, may be in conflict with various government objectives, and cannot usually be corrected without some form of policy action. Thus it is important to try to distinguish between these effects and to estimate the impact of technological externalities on social objectives such as growth and equity. The expansion of timber, coffee, and cocoa in the Ivory

Coast has, on balance, favored growth by providing skills and transportation infrastructure, but the lack of developed markets for human capital and land indicate that government intervention is needed to gain full advantage from these investments.

Fiscal Linkages

Some of the most important effects of the expansion of timber, cocoa, and coffee production have taken place via the fiscal system. As can be seen in Table 2-9, all of these exports have contributed in an important way to government revenues. The receipts from cocoa and coffee have been especially important in years in which stabilization operations favored the government. Although these funds were received primarily for stabilization purposes during the first part of the period, in recent years an increasing proportion has been allocated for development. Of greater importance as a consistent source of revenue from coffee and cocoa, however, has been the export tax, which provided more than twice the resources contributed by the timber industry until the new tax laws regarding that industry became effective in 1967, raising the effective rate of taxation from about 15 percent of the F.O.B. value of exports to about 18 percent. Nevertheless, the greatest expansion of revenue has been that derived from timber, the result both of the expansion of production and of a steady increase, since the early 1950s, in the rate of taxation.

In addition to the direct contribution of timber, cocoa, and coffee, averaging 18 percent of total government revenue from 1960 to 1967, the impact of these crops on the rest of the economy has strengthened the general tax base. More important at this stage, the foreign exchange earnings of these exports have permitted imports to grow rapidly, and it is import duties which are the most important single source of taxation, averaging nearly half of the total. As a result, total revenues more than doubled during this period and enabled the government to operate with a substantial surplus, used, in turn, to finance capital expenditures. Out of about 93 billion francs in public investment, including that of public corporations, between 1960 and 1966, the Ivorian public sector was able to finance about 73 percent, the rest coming from foreign aid. Of this total, 18 percent went to general administration, 11 percent to education and health, 12 percent to agricultural development, and 46 percent to economic infrastructure such as transportation and electricity generation. From 1967 to 1970, on the other hand, public investment accelerated rapidly, and the Ivorian government was able to finance only 55 percent—8 percent going to administration, 9 percent to education and health, 26 percent to agriculture, and 45 percent to economic infrastructure.

One question that has caused considerable debate is the desirability of an export tax or of a stabilization fund acting as a fiscal agent.[7] It is generally

Table 2-9

Payments to Government from the Production of Timber and Cocoa and Coffee, Total Government Revenues, and Government Surplus on Current Account, 1960-67 (Ivory Coast) (millions CFAF)

	1960	1961	1962	1963	1964	1965	1966	1967
Payments to government	3,430	3,671	7,549	12,224	15,550	6,240	9,368	15,169
Timber	699	983	1,573	2,090	3,041	3,038	2,876	3,424
Indirect taxes	432	650	1,027	1,379	1,920	2,562	2,384	2,476
Direct taxes[a]	267	333	546	711	1,121	476	492	948
Cocoa and coffee	2,731	2,688	5,976	10,134	12,509	3,202	6,492	11,745
Export tax[b]	5,885	6,386	5,451	6,307	7,354	6,985	7,122	6,543
Stabilization operations	-3,154	-3,698	+525	+3,827	+5,155	-3,783	-630	+5,202
Total government revenue	28,000	35,000	39,000	46,000	56,000	57,000	60,000	67,000
Government surplus on current account	5,000	7,000	13,000	16,000	22,000	14,000	17,000	17,000
Payments to government of timber, cocoa and coffee as a percentage of total government revenue (%)	12	10	19	27	28	11	16	23

[a]Estimated as a proportion of total production and of net profits using coefficients calculated for 1963.
[b]Estimated by multiplying the equivalent specific tax rate times the quantity of exports.

Sources: See Tables 2-1 and 2-3. Total government revenue and government surplus on current account are taken from a reclassification of the national accounts undertaken by the author in order to put them in a form recommended until recently by the United Nations.

held that this tax is easily administered, and may increase savings if the government is inclined to save and invest more than producers, but that it destroys incentives and does not have the most desirable distribution effects. For the Ivory Coast until the late 1960s the export tax may have been particularly appropriate and preferable in some ways even to a land tax, which, though frequently suggested as being ideal from a theoretical point of view, is much more difficult to administer. Because of the very elastic supplies of all factors of production except land, the export tax has fallen primarily on land and probably, to a much lesser extent, on local capital. It differs from a land tax, however, in that it is not the value of land that is assessed but the value of the produce which that land yields.[u] Better land pays more taxes per hectare than poorer land, but, since other costs per hectare do not vary proportionately with output, the residual rent net of taxes must be higher on better than on poorer land. This was seen empirically earlier in comparing these residuals for different regions of the Ivory Coast.

One effect of the export tax, then, is to keep marginal areas out of production. This is held to be desirable by the Ivorian government because of uncertain marketing prospects for cocoa and coffee and the durability of capital invested in these trees. Instead, areas which would otherwise be planted to cocoa and coffee can be devoted to other crops, such as cotton, rice, or oil palm. This, in fact, has been the case in the 1960s under the joint influence of lower prices and sustained government taxation. One possible disadvantage, however, is the effect that the tax has on agricultural techniques, since it serves to discourage production on the intensive as well as on the extensive margin. If, as some people believe, agricultural modernization is more likely to be achieved under conditions of intensive cultivation, the tax may have an adverse developmental impact.

From a distributional point of view, the export tax is not as desirable as a land tax, though it may be more attractive than some other forms of taxation. In particular, a properly administered land tax could siphon off all the rent to land, leaving the return to labor and capital, which would be more evenly distributed geographically. On the other hand, an export tax does have the advantage of requiring richer farmers to pay more taxes than do farmers cultivating less profitable land. Consequently, though the tax is largely proportional rather than progressive among cocoa and coffee planters, it is progressive relative to taxes on other sources of income in the rural area as a whole. To the extent that savings and capital investment depend on the tax rate, however, it may be desirable to avoid too progressive a tax system.

Contributions of Factors of Production

Until the end of World War II, growth in the Ivory Coast was constrained by two interrelated factors. First, the difficulty of obtaining foreign capital

[u]The value of land may be related to geography as well as to climate and soil conditions. Since cocoa and coffee are everywhere paid the same price, this is not an important consideration for these crops, though it is very important for timber.

and the limited domestic resources of the colony severely inhibited the development of transportation infrastructure and prevented the three principal exports from growing at more than a relatively moderate pace. Agricultural research might also have been accelerated if more capital had been available, but, given the moderate level of capital investment required, the results of this activity were probably related more to time and to skills of those involved than to the amount of financial resources available. At any rate, by the mid-1930s most of the research and experimentation had been done, thereby setting the stage for later expansion of these exports. Second, the constraints on the supply of capital, together with the existence of an important group of European planters and managers anxious to obtain cheap labor, led the colonial government to institute policies designed to force Africans to work either without compensation or at low wage rates. As a result of attempts at evasion and of the failure to communicate to large number of Africans the potential advantages to be gained by working in the Ivory Coast, the supply of unskilled labor during the prewar period was inadequate to sustain the magnitude of growth which occurred after the war.

Following World War II both of these constraints were dramatically eased. By the late 1950s the large amount of public investment as well as spreading knowledge of profitable private opportunities resulted in supplies of unskilled labor and private foreign capital in the form of direct investment, supplies which can be considered as an approximation, as perfectly elastic with respect to price. Foreign exchange needed to pay for these factors of production either came with the imported capital or was obtained from export earnings. Although tariffs helped to lessen the demand for some imported consumer goods, there were few direct controls on trade, especially after exchange controls were lifted in 1958.[v] Repatriation of profits was without restriction except insofar as firms were required from 1962 to contribute modestly to the repayment of the public debt unless they reinvested a certain proportion of their profits within the country. Given the rapid expansion of exports and foreign aid, as well as access of European-owned firms to overseas sources of private capital, foreign exchange does not appear to have been a constraint on growth during this period.

The chief constraints appear, instead, to have been the rate of inflow of public capital and the absorptive capacity of the Ivory Coast to undertake investment projects. The latter was substantially lessened by the ability to purchase the services of skilled manpower from external sources. Although the cost of this manpower was relatively high, the profitability of investment in this potentially rich country, which had been for so long frustrated by limits on the supply of public capital, was such that skills were readily imported. By the mid-1960s it was estimated that there were approximately thirty thousand Europeans living in the Ivory Coast. Despite this, however, the organizational difficulties

---

[v] These were controls placed by the Franc Zone on exchange transactions in other currencies, there being no controls on currency exchange within the Zone. During the late 1960s and early 1970s exchange restrictions were reimposed and lifted several times, but this was solely because of the international monetary crisis of that period and resulting efforts to protect the French franc.

involved in sustaining a very high rate of investment were such that absorptive capacity must at times have been the chief constraint on growth. Furthermore, the demands for Africanization since independence have applied increasing pressure to lessen dependence on imported skilled labor.

To assess quantitatively the relative importance of investment resources, foreign exchange and absorptive capacity as constraints on development, it is useful to examine some of the variables suggested by Chenery and Strout as being important indicators.[8] During this period from 1946 to 1960 the real value of public investment in the Ivory Coast grew at an average annual rate of 10 percent.[w] We have no figures on private investment during this period, but it is unlikely that it grew more rapidly, except perhaps for the planting of cocoa and coffee trees. Public investment continued at about the same pace during the first eight years of the next decade, but accelerated sharply in 1969 and 1970. Private investment, on the other hand, expanded more rapidly at about 19 percent per year for the first five years, leveled off during 1966 and 1967, and then renewed its previous pace during the rest of the decade. On the average, total gross investment increased annually at about 15 percent during 1960-65 and about 12 percent during the entire first eight years of the 1960s. For a period of over twenty years this is a high rate of sustained investment growth, and occasionally the absorptive capacity constraint must have been effective, especially during the first half of the 1960s.

When this constraint was not binding, growth was dependent on the rate of inflow of public foreign capital and on the ability of the country to generate its own public and private savings. Once invested, these helped to create the profitable opportunities which induced the inflow of private foreign capital. In 1947 about 75 percent of public investment capital came from foreign sources. By 1960 this figure had fallen to 28 percent. Forty-five percent of the capital for the public investment program of 1967-70 came from foreign sources, but, unlike the 1950s, most of this was in the form of loans rather than grants. The marginal savings rate, defined as the ratio of the increment of gross domestic savings exclusive of net capital inflows to the increment of Gross Domestic Product, was equal to .17 from 1960 to 1967. Since this is slightly less than the ratio of total investment to GDP, the indication is that the Ivory Coast, still substantially dependent on foreign capital inflows to finance a large part of its rapidly expanding investments, is likely to remain so for some time.

Foreign exchange, on the other hand, is not at present a binding constraint. The marginal import ratio of .30 from 1960 to 1967 was about the same as the average ratio of imports to GDP during the entire period. About one-half of these imports, moreover, were consumer goods, many of a luxury variety. Since consumer goods have not declined substantially as a proportion of total imports and since the import ratio is high and roughly constant, the foreign exchange

---

[w]All growth rates, the marginal savings rate, and the marginal import ratio were obtained from linear trends fitted to time series.

required to purchase capital and intermediate goods for the growing industrial sector must have come from the expansion of exports and from inflows of capital. Exports, in fact, increased even more rapidly than GDP at the same time that there were, on balance, substantial capital inflows, all of which financed not only imports but substantial remittances and repatriation of profits. If capital inflows were to be reduced, this would have an immediate effect on investment, but foreign exchange shortages could be avoided for a short time by policies aimed at reducing the demand for imported consumer goods or restricting the repatriation of profits and wages. In the long run, it is expected that the demand for imports of capital and intermediate goods will increase and that foreign exchange earnings must grow rapidly enough to pay for these as well as for the repatriation of profits and wages and a moderate growth of consumer goods imports. At present, however, the outlook for continued rapid expansion of traditional exports is not promising and whether new agricultural products and manufactured goods can successfully take up the slack remains to be seen. Furthermore, the Ivory Coast is handicapped in one way by its membership in the West African Monetary Union, which prevents its use of a policy instrument that may become increasingly needed: the exchange rate. Consequently, it is important to see the net effect on foreign exchange earnings, as well as on the supply of skills and capital, of the past expansion of timber, cocoa, and coffee.

Skills

Because of the high cost of importing human skills from abroad and because of the desire of Ivorians for an increase in the pace of Africanization, it is important to examine the contribution that the export sector has made to the acquisition of skills. We have already made references to skills acquired in linked industries and to those associated with technological externalities. Here we are concerned only with the magnitude of the skills of Africans acquired in the timber, cocoa, and coffee sectors, but available, perhaps, for use elsewhere.

Estimates of the number of employees in the timber industry by skill level and by origin are available for the period 1961-66.[9] A relatively large number of workers (more than one-third of the total in 1966) are at least semiskilled. As a rough measure of the value of those skills, these workers earn on the average perhaps twice as much as unskilled workers. Even the latter earn about 60,000 francs per year, substantially more than agricultural workers who averaged about 25,000 francs per year in the early 1960s. Although this partly reflects the greater seasonality of labor in agriculture, as was explained earlier, it also results from a greater acquisition of skills even on the part of "unskilled" labor.[x]

[x]The difference in the value of skills is not nearly as great as the difference in annual incomes, however, since workers in the timber industry have substantially less leisure time than those working in agriculture.

A second important feature of timber-industry employment is the increasing importance of non-Ivorian Africans, especially in the more skilled positions. Although in 1961 these workers were concentrated predominantly in the unskilled category, by 1966 substantial numbers had moved into higher categories, being even more numerous than Ivorians in semiskilled work. The number of European foremen also increased markedly, whereas the number of Africans filling this position dropped. This might be the result of the increased demand for talented Africans created by the expansion of industry, but there is no direct evidence.

The composition of the labor force in cocoa and coffee production was previously given in Table 2–7. Although the numbers involved in this sector are much greater than those working in the timber industry, the average annual return to labor, and probably the skills as well, are considerably less. The market also appears to value much more highly the skills and supervisory talents associated with timber production than it does the entrepreneurial capabilities of the average cocoa and coffee planter, especially when it is acknowledged that much of the residual income accruing to heads of farms from these agricultural activities is a return to capital and to land use. Nevertheless, the acquisition of skills in cocoa and coffee production cannot be ignored because of the large numbers involved and because, in contrast to timber, of the predominance of Ivorians as heads of farm and family workers especially.

In addition to those employed at any single time, a large number of Africans have acquired skills in these activities and have later left to pursue other employment. Furthermore, for every three hired workers currently employed in cocoa and coffee production it is estimated that there is one person not currently employed but who is likely to return at some time in the future. The seasonal nature of agriculture, moreover, implies that skills applicable to other activities may be utilized during the off season. If it is assumed that all workers and heads of farm in the cocoa- and coffee-growing areas have available 250 working days per year, then, out of a total of 272 million man-days available for work, perhaps 200 million man-days may be devoted to activities other than the production of cocoa and coffee. Although there is no way of measuring the value of the net addition to the supply of skills, the relatively high turnover rates of labor and the relatively short busy season in agriculture imply that the potential is great to the extent to which these skills can be used outside of the export sector.

Investment Resources

The investment resources generated or imported by the export sector are shown in Table 2–10. For the sake of completeness it was assumed that 15 percent of agricultural income from cocoa and coffee production, after

Table 2-10
Investment Resources Generated or Imported by Timber, Cocoa, and Coffee Producers, 1960-67 (Ivory Coast)
(millions CFAF)

	1960	1961	1962	1963	1964	1965	1966	1967
Timber								
Resources supplied	2,618	3,009	4,661	6,002	6,652	5,100	7,218	8,243
Capital inflow[a]	1,919	2,026	3,088	3,912	3,611	2,062	4,342	4,819
Payments to government[b]	699	983	1,573	2,090	3,041	3,038	2,876	3,424
Resources used								
Gross Investment[a]	1,919	2,026	3,088	3,912	3,611	2,062	4,342	4,819
Net contribution	699	983	1,573	2,090	3,041	3,038	2,876	3,424
Cocoa and Coffee								
Resources supplied	5,230	5,290	7,563	12,785	16,207	6,193	9,977	14,390
Gross savings[c]	2,499	2,602	1,587	2,651	3,698	2,991	3,485	2,645
Payments to government[b]	2,731	2,688	5,976	10,134	12,509	3,202	6,492	11,745
Resources used								
Gross investment[a]	1,609	2,833	2,697	3,984	2,712	2,396	2,417	n.a.
Net contribution	3,621	2,457	4,866	8,801	13,495	3,797	7,560	n.a.

[a]Estimated from the difference between the value of the capital stock in successive years plus amortization.
[b]See Table 2-9.
[c]Estimated as 15% of total agricultural incomes from cocoa and coffee after deduction for wages paid to hired workers. It was assumed that these represented the same proportion of total labor cost in each year as in 1962-64.
Sources: Tables 2-5 and 2-9.

deduction for estimated wages paid to hired workers, was saved, but it is recognized that this proportion is little more than a guess. For the timber industry, the only net savings are those going to government, since all profits are assumed to be repatriated abroad due to the predominantly European ownership of the industry. At the same time, however, capital investment, even if it actually took the form of a reinvestment of earnings, is treated as a capital inflow from abroad which is used entirely by the timber industry. The generation of investment resources in the form of savings by cocoa and coffee planters, on the other hand, does not necessarily equal investment, and, in fact, is frequently greater than that investment, leaving a sizeable quantity of resources available for investment in other sectors.

The importance of the particular form of investment resources generated in the export sector must be emphasized. While the Ivory Coast has had ready access to private foreign capital for direct investment, its supply of public investment resources has not been unlimited, but instead has been the chief constraint on growth over the past twenty years. Nor have African farmers had unlimited access to capital via the banking system or other lending institutions. The high cost of obtaining information concerning prospective borrowers in rural areas and the resulting uncertainty concerning their prospects for repayment have effectively shut off this source of funds for long-term investment purposes. Thus the generation of savings by the export sector has been of considerable importance in helping to overcome these two potential bottlenecks to development.

Foreign Exchange

The net contribution of foreign exchange resulting from the production and export of timber, cocoa, and coffee was derived from estimates of various items for the period 1960-67.[10] Virtually all of the exchange earned from export sales of cocoa and coffee went to local factors of production. While the balance-of-payments impact of timber sales was less important, it increased much more rapidly than did that of cocoa and coffee. Furthermore, it also increased as a percentage of export sales, rising from 62 percent in 1960 to 72 percent in 1967. This was due partly to increased purchases of locally produced materials, such as fuel oil, and partly to the increased rate of government taxation. The inflow of capital into this industry has also consistently been greater than the outflow of profits, reflecting the high rate of growth of timber production.

In summary, the balance-of-payments impact of these traditional exports has been the major reason for the lack of a binding foreign exchange constraint during the past twenty years. In order to furnish the foreign exchange necessary for continued rapid growth the Ivory Coast must find new export activities which can be expanded rapidly and which will not require too high a rate of growth of imported inputs. Since many manufactured products are produced today using fairly capital intensive techniques and requiring a high proportion

of imported intermediate goods, it may be difficult to generate a rapid growth
of net foreign exchange earnings from exports of these products. New agricultural exports, on the other hand, require fewer imports in their production, and,
if they can be expanded rapidly, should contribute more to the balance of
payments.

Conclusion

The expansion of timber, cocoa, and coffee exports has been viewed here
as an example of "vent-for-surplus" growth. The productive factor most abundant
in supply with very low opportunity cost in the early years was land. But in
order for land to be used in production for export, there had to be developed
a knowledge of agricultural possibilities and a transportation infrastructure.
Local labor, available from leisure time or other productive activities, was
sufficient to initiate cultivation but not to sustain the expansion that ensued
during the post-World War II period. For that, a labor market developed, relying
upon migrant workers from the north. Private capital and human skills were also
imported, especially from Europe, to ease other potential constraints.

On the demand side the Ivory Coast benefited in one way from delayed development. Whereas in Ghana much of the best cocoa land had already been planted
by the end of the 1920s, in the Ivory Coast at that time this process had just
begun. When the Depression arrived and cocoa prices plummeted, planters
in the Ivory Coast shifted easily to coffee, enjoying the benefit of a protected
market in France. During and after the war the expansion of this market was
rapid, too, due to the necessity, because of exchange resitrictions, for France
to rely on colonial coffee. The constraints long imposed on the development of
the timber industry, preventing the Ivory Coast from exploiting this resource
at a time when world market conditions were not well developed, have also
resulted in greater diversification today.

The period of rapid expansion of these traditional exports is, however,
nearing an end. Much of the best cocoa and coffee land has already been planted,
and the stock of currently marketable timber species is such that some of these
will be approaching exhaustion within a decade if their exploitation is not slowed.
Cocoa is subject to highly unstable world prices and coffee exports, subject to
an international agreement, are limited to an annual growth rate in traditional
markets of about 2.2 percent. Though more rapid expansion of the coffee
market is expected in Eastern Europe and Japan, the prices offered in these
markets are very low.

The contributions that these exports have made to Ivorian development
have been considerable. The net gain directly obtained in the form of payments
to government and the residual rent to cocoa and coffee farmers has been high,
averaging 25 percent of the total value of production, which, in turn, accounted
for almost one quarter of GDP. Cocoa and coffee have accounted for the largest

share of this net gain, but timber production has increased its share rapidly from 6.5 to 15.9 percent. Cocoa and coffee have, in addition, not only generated more employment and more income than has timber, but these have gone in much greater proportions to Ivorians. On the other hand, important regional inequities have also resulted. Whereas per capita income in the southern part of the country averaged 49,000 francs in 1965, three-quarters of it in monetary form, income per head in the north was 18,600 francs, of which only 5,400 francs were received as cash, the rest being imputed subsistence production. The ultimate solution to this problem of regional disparity is seen partly as migration towards the richer areas of the south and partly via the introduction of new commercial crops, such as rice and cotton, in the north.

Aside from direct contributions, the production of these exports has generated linkage effects throughout the rest of the economy. Although backward and forward linkages in production do not appear to be very important, those resulting from increases in final demand have been enormous, especially for cocoa and coffee. Most of the expansion of the Ivorian economy has, in fact, depended upon them. Technological linkages have probably also been important, especially the construction of feeder roads and the acquisition of skills, but the value of these is impossible to measure quantitatively. The combination of direct and indirect payments to government resulting from production in the export sector, furthermore, has enabled the Ivory Coast government to finance a large part of its own investment program. This has been heavily weighted in favor of economic infrastructure in the past, but is being increasingly directed toward agricultural development.

The contribution of the export sector to the total supply of productive factors has also been important. African workers in the timber industry have acquired skills of greater depth, but those learned in the cocoa and coffee sector have been diffused much more broadly, and, to the extent that they are transferable, may be employed during the slack season. Investment resources generated or imported have been slightly more important for cocoa and coffee than for timber. Timber, however, has channeled an average of 31 percent of value added toward the important public investment sector, a percentage which has been growing rapidly, whereas this proportion of value added in the production of cocoa and coffee has oscillated widely around an average of 22 percent with no clearly discernable long-term trend. Cocoa and coffee, on the other hand, have contributed to scarce rural savings used for a variety of investments while the profits from timber have generally been either repatriated abroad or reinvested within the industry. Production of cocoa and coffee has also contributed more to foreign exchange earnings, both absolutely and as a proportion of export sales, though the net contribution of timber has grown more rapidly.

As this phase of rapid growth of these traditional exports is coming to an end, the Ivory Coast government has adopted a program of agricultural diversification and industrialization designed to restructure the economy and expand its export base. Although the growth of exports is expected to slow somewhat, it is not expected to fall in real terms below 6.8 percent before 1980. To take up the slack resulting from the slower growth of unprocessed coffee, cocoa and timber, exports of cocoa butter, soluble coffee, canned pineapple and pineapple juice, canned fish, vegetable oils, raw cotton, paper pulp, textiles, and iron ore are expected to increase rapidly. Since these products are based on locally produced raw materials, they require few imported inputs and thus avoid one of the difficulties, noted earlier, associated with the export of manufactured products.

Most of the domestic raw materials going into these industries will be the result of the diversification program which is taking advantage of the Ivory Coast's favorable natural endowment and rich heritage of agricultural research.[y] Past experience indicates strongly the importance of this broad base of local research in developing new agricultural products. Where this experience may not be of much help, however, is in showing how new techniques can be spread from experiment station to farmer. In the past, expansion has occurred over empty land using the most extensive techniques. Today much of that land has a relatively high opportunity cost in terms of the cocoa or coffee which may be grown. Future expansion will therefore have to come increasingly from shifts to more highly valued crops and from increased yields. This will require among farmers, researchers, and suppliers of agricultural inputs a continuous flow of information which has not existed in the past. To develop its extension services, the government has for several years been active in a variety of pilot programs designed to introduce new crops or improve techniques. Success has varied, but the real test is only now coming as these programs are expanded to encompass most Ivorian farmers, thus placing a greater strain on their administration. Twenty-five years of rapid export growth have contributed the resources required to place the Ivory Coast economy firmly on this more difficult path of sustained development. Whether, in fact, the path will be attained depends now only upon the wisdom and skill of the Ivorian leaders.

Notes

1. Descriptive portions of this chapter for which sources are not indicated are taken from a larger body of research on the Ivory Coast economy currently being undertaken by the author.

2. See Robert E. Baldwin, *Economic Development and Export Growth; A Study of Northern Rhodesia, 1920-1960* (Berkeley, Calif.: University of California Press, 1966), pp. 58-73, for a discussion of these characteristics.

---

[y]Evenson and Kislev have collected data on scientific man-years which indicate that the Ivory Coast in 1967 spent more scientific man-years in agricultural research than any other country in sub-Saharan Africa except Nigeria, Rhodesia, South Africa, and possibly Kenya. On a per capita basis, research in the Ivory Coast clearly exceeded all countries except South Africa. See Robert E. Evenson and Yoav Kislev, "Investment in Agricultural Research and Extension: A Survey of International Data," Center Discussion Paper No. 124, Economic Growth Center (New Haven: Yale University, August 1971).

3. Ester Boserup, *The Conditions of Agricultural Growth: the Economics of Agrarian Change under Population Pressure* (Chicago: Aldine, 1965).

4. Much of the description and analysis concerning the implication of the Ivory Coast's associate membership in the EEC is taken from Roger Lawrence, "Primary Products, Preferences, and Economic Welfare: The EEC and Africa," in Peter B. Kenen and Roger Lawrence, eds., *The Open Economy* (New York: Columbia University Press, 1969).

5. Ivory Coast, Ministère de l'Agriculture, *Economie Forestière de la Cote d'Ivoire* (Paris: Société d'Etudes pour le Développement Economique et Social, 1967), p. 253.

6. Tiber Scitovsky, "Two Concepts of External Economies," *Journal of Political Economy* 62 (April 1954): 143-51.

7. Gerald K. Helleiner, *Peasant Agriculture, Government, and Economic Growth in Nigeria* (Homewood, Ill.: Irwin, 1966), pp. 178-84.

8. Hollis B. Chenery and Alan M. Strout, "Foreign Assistance and Economic Development," *American Economic Review* 56 (September 1966): 679-733.

9. Ivory Coast, Office de la Main d'Oeuvre, *Statistiques* (Abidjan; various years); Ivory Coast, Ministère de l'Agriculture, *Economie Forestiere de la Côte d'Ivoire* (Paris: Société d'Etudes pour le Développement Economique et Social, 1967).

10. Ivory Coast, Direction des Etudes de Développement, *Les Comptes de la Nation* (Abidjan, various years).

3

The Role of Cocoa in Ghanaian Development

Sara L. Gordon

Institutional Background

Cultivation of Cocoa

Cocoa farming in Ghana commenced during the 1880s. Output of the cocoa industry expanded rapidly, allowing Ghana to become the world's leading cocoa supplier by 1911. Although cocoa is grown on large plantations in South America, in West Africa cocoa is produced by small-scale farmers. From its inception, Ghana's cocoa industry was developed by African entrepreneurs, with minimal participation of the colonial government and foreign capital. All the initiative, factors of production, and techniques were provided by local entrepreneurs.

The early history of Ghana's cocoa-farming industry has been chronicled by Polly Hill.[1] Hill has shown that Akwapim farmers, a migratory people with a history of production and trade in palm products and rubber, initiated the industry. In the 1890s these migratory farmers bought land upon which to grow cocoa in Akwapim and Akim Abuakwa. These land transactions gave rise to a market for land for use in cocoa production; by 1906 the going price for cocoa land was about £1 per acre.[2] With development of the cocoa industry, land to be used in cocoa growing acquired a value and became a factor of production which could be bought and sold.

Most of the capital used by the Akwapim people to develop the industry came from their earlier production and trade in palm products, which had become important during the first half of the nineteenth century following the abolition of the slave trade. After 1885, when the price of palm products fell, capital was transferred into cocoa, where profits were relatively higher. During the early stages of cocoa production the farmer and his family provided the necessary labor services. The farmer used hired labor only when the farm was sufficiently established to pay for labor out of the cocoa earnings. Growth of the industry was facilitated by the *abusa* system, under which a laborer was paid a share of the proceeds.

The industry developed rapidly. From Akwapim and Akim Abuakwa, cocoa farming spread to other parts of the Eastern region, to Ashanti, the Western region, and the Volta region.[3] During the first four decades of this century, the world supply of cocoa grew steadily. A large part of this growth occurred in Ghana, where output rose continuously until World War II. From 80 pounds in 1891 cocoa output rose to 1,000 tons in 1901 and to 39,700 tons in 1911, when cocoa contributed 46 percent of the value of Ghana's exports.

Between 1916 and 1920, Ghana exported an average of 106,000 tons of cocoa, and between 1936 and 1940 it exported an average of 263,000 tons. But then output levels fell and remained low for almost two decades. During the 1940s output levels were extremely low. In 1949 production began to recover somewhat. In the early 1960s output levels soared again, and during the first quinquennium Ghana exported an average of 450,000 tons.

The British colonial government and foreign capital contributed little to the development of the cocoa industry. The government was more concerned with promoting external trade between the colony and the United Kingdom, providing infrastructure and basic services in the colony, and maintaining a good climate for foreign investment than in promoting indigenous enterprise.[4] For example, to provide transport facilities for foreign-owned gold mines in Western Ghana, the government constructed 188 miles of rail line between 1898 and 1903. Though this investment of capital in the gold mines and the railroads did contribute to growth of gold exports, by the second decade of this century cocoa exports provided the central stimulus for Ghana's economic growth.

The government had done little to develop transportation facilities for the cocoa-producing areas. By 1911, only 36 miles of railroad had been built into cocoa areas, and roads in areas somewhat distant from Accra were not suitable for motor vehicles.[5] Nevertheless, cocoa absorbed a large part of Ghana's resources and contributed significantly to the value of exports and national output. Out of a population of 1.5 million in the Gold Coast Colony and Ashanti, about 185,000 were employed in producing cocoa, and a large number of others were involved in transporting cocoa to the ports or rail lines. In many instances groups of cocoa farmers themselves built roads and even bridges into cocoa-producing areas to facilitate the transport of cocoa. During the second and third decades of this century, in belated recognition of the cocoa farmers' achievements, the colonial government finally constructed railways and roads into cocoa-producing areas. It also built a deep water port at Takoradi.

In the early days of cocoa growing, farmers made their own arrangements to bring cocoa to the large European export firms situated at the ports. Later a marketing system evolved which employed thousands of African middlemen in the purchase, assembly, and transport of the crop. Generally the middlemen used capital supplied by the European firms. This system continued under the West African Produce Control Board (1942-47) and the Ghana Cocoa Marketing Board (GCMB) until 1961 when the United Ghana Cocoa Farmers' Cooperative Council took over the function of buying cocoa.

The Organization of the International Market for Cocoa[6]

Five countries—Ghana, Nigeria, Ivory Coast, Cameroon, and Brazil—produce close to 80 percent of the world's output. The United States, Western Europe, and Japan consume the bulk of this output.

The marketing of cocoa in the main producing countries is affected by the activities of public and semipublic organizations. In Ghana and Nigeria, as well as in Sierra Leone and Jamaica, cocoa is collected and marketed by statutory marketing boards which purchase the entire output at fixed prices, act as sole exporters, and collect export taxes and other levies on the produce. In countries affiliated with the Franc Zone, the Caisses de Stabilisation fix the price to be paid to the producer at the beginning of the crop year. The marketing and export operations are undertaken by private firms, with the Caisses acting essentially as price-stabilizing agents for both traders and producers. In Brazil, a government agency sets the producer price as well as the minimum price for export markets to isolate the farmer from price fluctuations.

Private firms undertake the international marketing of cocoa and its distribution within the main consuming countries. These firms are either dealers who carry stocks to meet the needs of manufacturers or manufacturers who purchase cocoa directly in the producing country. The fact that most of each year's cocoa crop becomes available during the late fall and early winter when the main crops in West Africa and Brazil are harvested, means that the manufacturers and dealers in consuming countries must purchase supplies in advance of production needs. Much of the trading in cocoa takes place in the markets for futures. Though some large manufacturers purchase directly in the producing country, price quotations (on a C.I.F. basis) in the main markets for futures are considered accurate indicators of the price level for most of the cocoa bought and sold. Prices are determined mainly in the futures markets of New York and London, but the markets in Hamburg, Amsterdam and Paris also exercise some influence on price.

Wide variations in world supply coupled with a relatively inelastic world demand cause the price of cocoa to be more unstable than that of almost any other commodity exported by the developing countries. The purpose of the International Cocoa Agreement, which became effective on June 30, 1973, is to stabilize international cocoa prices. To accomplish this objective, the agreement would leave market price formation and transactions in cocoa trade largely in the hands of existing institutions while influencing the market supply of cocoa through the operation of export quotas combined with a buffer stock scheme.

Out of forty-four producing countries, the nine (Ghana, Nigeria, Ivory Coast, Brazil, Cameroon, Dominican Republic, Equatorial Guinea, Togo, and Mexico) which account for 95 percent of world production would have to observe supply management commitments in accordance with the agreement. No quotas would be applied to countries producing less than 90,000 tons of ordinary cocoa a year or to countries producing fine flavor cocoa. After deducting exports from these countries from the anticipated level of world demand, the remaining amount of world demand would be allocated to the nine countries which are subject to quotas. These quotas have been made proportionate to the highest annual production in these countries during the preceding eight years. Market developments during the year may necessitate a change in the annual export quota. For instance, when prices fall below 20 cents per pound, quotas would be adjusted in a downward direction; quotas would be suspended above 29 cents per pound. Presently, the intervention range within which the Cocoa Council will attempt to stabilize prices falls within the range of 23-32 U.S. cents per pound.

Because of the wide variations that occur in world supply, the operation of a buffer stock could help to stabilize the world cocoa price. In principle, to mitigate against a continued decline in price, purchases are made into a buffer stock when prices fall below a given level and when prices rise above a certain amount, sales from the buffer stock occur. The arrangements provide for the establishment of a buffer stock having a maximum capacity of 250,000 tons. Purchases will be made from producing countries subject to quotas up to cumulative maximum entitlements of the individual members that are proportionate to their basic quotas. Buffer stock purchases can be made only from those countries subject to quotas. When prices fall to a level where quotas are reduced below 100 percent of quota, countries may sell to the buffer stock. After the country has sold a quantity of cocoa equal to its individual entitlement, all additional sales to the buffer stock would realize only such a price as could be realized by the disposal of the cocoa beans for nontraditional uses. When prices rise to a level of 6 cents above the minimum price, quotas are suspended, and at levels of 8 cents above the minimum price, sales from the buffer stock shall commence. Sales shall continue until the indicator price falls to the maximum price or until all cocoa in the buffer stock has been exhausted.[7]

The Direct Contribution of Cocoa to Ghanaian National Income and Employment

Historical Data

Historical data on total cocoa output, export and producer proceeds, and world and producer prices for selected years from 1900 to 1970 are shown in Table 3-1. Output expanded almost continuously during the period preceding World War II, but unstable world prices caused large year-to-year fluctuations in the value of Ghana's cocoa exports. Until the 1930s the average annual value of this output rose. For example, the average annual value of cocoa exports grew from £2.3 million between 1911 and 1915 to £5.4 million between 1916 and 1920, £6.5 million between 1921 and 1925 and £7.5 million between 1926 and 1930. Even though growth in the quantity of cocoa continued during the 1930s, a large reduction in world prices caused the value of cocoa exports to fall to an average of £5.0 million between 1931 and 1935. The average value recovered to £6.4 million between 1936 through 1940, but then fell to £4.2 million between 1941 and 1945 as a result of swollen shoot disease, which contributed to a large reduction in output, and controlled wartime prices.

Table 3-1
Cocoa Statistics (Ghana)

Crop year ending Sept. 30	World price (£ F.O.B./ton)	Ghana producer price (£/ton)	Ghana total output (000s tons)	Ghana total cocoa export proceeds (£Millions)	Ghana total producer proceeds (£Millions)
1900	50.9	--	.5	.03	--
1905	36.7	--	5.1	.19	--
1910	38.3	39.5	22.6	.87	.89
1915	47.2	46.5	55.9	3.6	2.2
1920	80.6	75.5	144.5	10.0	10.0
1925	37.7	33.0	210.9	8.2	7.0
1930	36.6	32.0	231.9	7.0	7.0
1935	19.4	14.0	276.0	5.2	3.9
1940	20.1	15.9	241.7	4.5	2.9
1945	30.8	22.4	228.7	7.1	5.1
1946	40.2	27.1	209.4	9.5	5.7
1947	92.3	51.3	192.1	16.6	9.9
1948	196.8	74.7	207.6	42.2	15.4
1949	129.1	121.3	278.4	34.0	33.8
1950	204.0	84.0	247.8	54.6	20.8
1951	262.8	130.7	262.2	60.7	34.3
1952	247.8	149.3	210.7	55.4	31.5
1953	237.3	130.5	247.0	58.3	32.2
1954	395.0	134.4	210.4	85.6	28.3
1955	318.4	135.0	220.1	65.6	29.6
1956	217.8	148.5	228.8	52.0	34.4
1957	195.5	149.2	263.7	50.9	39.4
1958	315.7	134.2	206.6	62.5	27.5
1959	274.9	131.9	255.5	69.9	33.8
1960	219.4	112.0	317.1	67.4	35.5
1961	170.9	112.0	432.2	70.8	48.4
1962	159.0	100.8	408.6	70.7	40.9
1963	158.4	100.8	421.3	67.0	42.2
1964	168.0	100.8	421.0	68.1	42.3
1965	226.0	100.8	571.3	68.1	52.0
1966	193.3	74.7	410.0	56.8	30.6
1967	238.0	84.0	376.0	51.8	31.6
1968	319.5	99.0	415.0	93.4	41.4
1969	415.5	106.6	334.0	78.1	35.6
1970	305.5	121.9	409.0	119.3	49.9

Sources: 1900-62—M. J. Bateman, *Cocoa in the Ghanaian Economy* (Unpublished Ph.D. dissertation, Cambridge, Mass.: Massachusetts Institute of Technology, 1965), pp. 206, 208, 211-12. Permission to publish these results here is gratefully acknowledged.
1963-70–*Cocoa Market Report* (London: Gill and Duffus, Ltd.); D. Scott, *Economic Policy in Ghana* (Unpublished Ph. D. dissertation, Cambridge, Mass.: Harvard University, 1967), pp. 189, 190; *Economic Survey* (Accra, Ghana: Central Bureau of Statistics, various issues); *1964 Statistical Yearbook* (Accra, Ghana: Central Bureau of Statistics); *External Trade Statistics of Ghana* (Accra, Ghana: Central Bureau of Statistics, various issues).

Between 1946 and 1959 increases in world prices produced large increments in the value of exports. But the unstable nature of these prices combined with fluctuations in output caused wide fluctuations in value. Between crop years 1946-47 and 1953-54, total cocoa proceeds rose from £16.6 million to £85.6 million. But with the fall in world prices during 1955-56 and 1956-57 proceeds averaged only £51.1 million for these two years. The recovery of world prices in 1957-58 brought total proceeds up to £68.8 million. Beginning with the 1959-60 crop year, world prices were greatly reduced as a result of world overproduction relative to demand. Large increases in Ghana's production of cocoa caused the value of total proceeds to average about £70 million between 1960-61 and 1964-65. Prices remained low until 1965-66, but with a decline in world production prices increased, remaining at fairly high levels until 1970-71. Though Ghana's output of cocoa was somewhat lower than during the first half of the 1960s, the value of exports was considerably higher during the late 1960s, because of increased world prices.

Net Social Gain

Before estimating the net social gain resulting from the production of cocoa in Ghana, it is necessary to evaluate the social opportunity costs of the factors of production used in cocoa. In evaluating the opportunity costs of the factors of production used in cocoa, it is assumed that the industry competes with other industries for casual and unskilled labor. Because of the existence of considerable unemployment and underemployment in Ghana, it is assumed that an unlimited supply of labor is available at a given wage rate, that the marginal product of labor employed in cocoa is equal to the given wage rate, and that the social opportunity cost of labor is equal to the given rate. Because it has been shown that the wage rate in cocoa is equivalent to the minimum wage for unskilled labor,[8] the value of the minimum urban wage for unskilled labor will be used for the purpose of calculating the value of labor services used in cocoa. Since the capital stock used to produce cocoa is made by labor services required to clear land, plant trees, and care for the trees, the cost of labor used in its creation may be considered the opportunity cost of this capital. The value of the capital stock employed in cocoa during 1960 was estimated at £360 million.[9] This value was obtained by estimating the present value of a stream of earnings from acreage under cocoa over a twenty-year period. Output in the early 1960s was about the same as during the late 1960s. But, as a consequence of greatly reduced world and producer prices during that decade, there was then little new planting of cocoa, and by the late 1960s, the age structure of the capital stock was much older than in 1960. To reflect the increasing age structure of the capital stock, the value of cocoa capital was reduced to £270 million. In 1969 the interest rate charged by commercial banks in Ghana varied between 6.5 percent and 10 percent: thus it was arbitrariliy assumed that the rate of return to capital in cocoa could not be lower than 7 percent. Using straight line depreciation, the capital stock under cocoa was amortized over a twenty-year period. Intermediate inputs include transport and marketing services as well as the few inputs such as insecticides and sprayers used in the production of cocoa. The opportunity cost of these inputs can be assumed to be equal to the price.

Estimates of the returns to the various factors of production, as well as the payments for inputs of goods and services used in the production of cocoa, are presented in Table 3-2. Because of wide variations in the volume of output, estimates have been calculated for each of the three years 1967-68 through 1969-70. It is assumed that labor inputs and the value of intermediate goods and services vary in relation to the volume of output. To obtain aggregate labor costs, the number of days required to produce a ton of output was first multiplied by the number of tons produced. Payment to the government includes the export duty as well as a local duty imposed on cocoa. The remaining portion of value added is broken down into the net return to capital, an allowance for amortization, and the residual which is considered to be rent.

The results of the calculations in Table 3-2 indicate that the development of the cocoa industry has produced substantial benefits for the economy as a whole. Since it is assumed that the social opportunity cost for all factors (except land) was equal to the prevailing factor price, the net gain is equal to payments to the government plus the residual for rent received by cocoa farmers. The net gain coefficient averaged .249 for the three-year period.

The Distribution of Income and Employment

In addition to contributing substantially to the national income of Ghana, development of the cocoa industry had profound effects upon the distribution of income and employment. According to the 1960 census, of 2,561,000 persons in the labor force, one-fifth—including some 300,000 cocoa farmers— were engaged in cocoa. Because the number of farmers was large, ownership of cocoa capital was dispersed widely throughout the economy. But this capital was not dispersed equally among cocoa farmers. Hill has demonstrated that there were wide variations in the size of farms and in the number of farms owned by one individual and that variation in total acreage owned per farmer was even greater than the variation in farm size.[10] This unequal distribution was also reflected in the ownership of other types of capital. Wealthier cocoa farmers not only invested in land and new cocoa farms, but they also invested in other productive assets such as trucks and houses to rent.

Table 3–2

Distribution of the Value of Cocoa Production between Value Added and Intermediate Inputs (Ghana) (millions £ sterling)

	1967-68	1968-69	1969-70
Value of production[a]	93.4	78.1	119.3
Value of intermediate inputs[b]	20.0	17.0	20.0
Value-added	73.4	61.1	99.3
Labor costs[c]	(21.1)	(17.0)	(20.8)
Payment to government[d]	(31.7)	(32.6)	(50.9)
Return to capital	(18.9)	(18.9)	(18.9)
Depreciation	(13.5)	(13.5)	(13.5)
Residual	(−11.8)	(−20.9)	(−4.8)
Net gain[e]	19.9	11.7	46.1
Net gain coefficient[f]	.213	.149	.386

[a]The value of cocoa beans plus cocoa products exported.

[b]Includes an allowance for the costs involved in transporting and marketing the produce plus some estimate for the value of intermediate inputs.

[c]Obtained by multiplying the 162.2 man days required to produce a ton of cocoa by the average rural wage rate (assumed equivalent to the daily minimum wage rate) of £0.306 (N₵ 0.75). The labor cost per ton was then multiplied by the number of tons produced to obtain labor costs.

[d]Includes receipts from the export duty plus local duty.

[e]The sum of payments to government plus the residual.

[f]The net gain divided by the value of production.

Sources: Ghana, Central Bureau of Statistics, *External Trade Statistics for Ghana* (various issues), *Quarterly Digest of Statistics* (various issues), *Statistical Yearbook* (1967-68; B. E. Rourke and S. K. Sakyi-Gyinae, "Agricultural and Urban Wage Rates in Ghana," *The Economic Bulletin of Ghana,* vol. 2, no. 1 (1972), pp. 3-13.

Social Opportunity Costs of the Alternatives Foregone

In the preceding discussion that evaluated the direct contribution of cocoa
to the Ghanaian economy it was possible to assume that the social opportunity
costs of productive factors were equal to their market prices. Because one-
fifth of Ghana's labor force, more than one-fourth of the capital stock and much
of the best land in the forest belt are devoted to cocoa production, it is possible
to assume that given the structure of the economy, alternative economic activities
might not be as profitable as cocoa. However, at the time when the industry was
developing, alternative activities might have prospered had not cocoa been more
profitable. Within a historical context, it becomes feasible to evaluate the social
opportunity costs as the alternatives foregone by the development of the cocoa
industry.

It has been argued elsewhere that labor services provided for cocoa had
previously been consumed in the form of leisure.[11] It is more plausible to assume
that the profitable opportunities offered by cocoa were capable of drawing
labor services away from other activities in which they had been previously engaged. Writing in 1968, William O. Jones supports this explanation, and suggests
that "labor can be attracted away from the production of less highly valued
goods when it is presented with an opportunity to produce things more highly
prized or to earn money to buy such goods. . . . The labor required to earn these
rewards may come from anywhere in the system, but it seems safe to infer that
it is drawn from activities that resulted in something less prized than the new
product; it could have come from craft manufactures, personal or household
services, production of food or any of the political, administrative, social, educational, or religious services."[12] Within this context, it is reasonable to assume
that a substantial amount of domestic labor services used to produce cocoa
could have come from activities in which they had been previously engaged,
such as the production of other export crops and craft manufactures. Kola nuts,
copra, palm kernals, palm oil, rubber, and coffee were traditional export crops
of the forest area. By the 1930s, most factors of production had been shifted
into the production of cocoa; the export of kola nuts, palm oil, palm kernels, and
rubber had become negligible. Craft manufactures could have been another source
of labor services. When it became cheaper in terms of labor services rendered to
grow cocoa and use the proceeds to purchase imported manufactures rather than
to produce (or purchase) local manufactures, labor services were shifted into
production of the export crop.

In addition to contributing to the decline of traditional exports, the growth
of the cocoa industry may also have influenced the decline of the gold-mining
industry. Though gold dust had been exported since the earliest days of Ghana's
trade, gold mining began in earnest only in the beginning of the twentieth

century after completion of the Sekondi-Tarkwa railway. During the first few years of this century investment was dominated by railroad construction and mining development. This investment was followed by a large rise in gold exports, which between 1905 and 1918 contributed an average of one-third of total exports. The mines created a large demand for labor, and by 1911, 19,000 workers—only one-third of whom were Europeans and migrant laborers— were employed in the mines.[13] But by the second decade of this century increasing quantities of labor were used both for cocoa farming and for carrying cocoa to the railroad centers and to the ports. Elsewhere it has been argued that economic opportunities created by cocoa drew labor away from the mines as the price of labor was bid upwards.[14] Because labor services were drawn out of other economic activities such as the production of traditional export crops, the social opportunity costs of using these services in alternative economic activities were substantially greater than zero at the time when the cocoa industry was developing.

Investment Linkages

The cocoa industry has direct input-output relations with the chemical industry, which is backward linked, and with the cocoa-processing industry, which is forward linked. The chemical industry produces the insecticide, Gammalin 20, which was introduced during the 1950s to control capsid disease. Part of Ghana's cocoa is processed into cocoa butter and cocoa paste before being shipped abroad for processing into chocolate products in the importing country. In addition, since the cocoa industry is best defined to include internal marketing as well as production, cocoa may be considered as being backward linked with the road transport industry and the cocoa bag industry.

The Cocoa-Processing Industry. The main advantages to be gained by processing a raw material in the producing country are the savings in transport cost if the raw material loses a considerable amount of weight in the manufacturing process or in processing if a large amount of required fuel is locally available.[15] Cocoa processing commenced in 1947 and under the *Seven-Year Development Plan* (1963-70), the government increased processing capacity. During the processing the liquid is first separated from the bean and is then separated into cocoa butter and cocoa paste. In the newest of Ghana's factories about 70 percent of the weight of the bean is recovered in the form of liquid. Given the cocoa butter to cocoa beans price ratio prevailing on world markets during the period 1961-66, foreign exchange earnings would have been slightly higher had raw beans been exported instead.[16] For instance, in 1964 with total cocoa exports of £68 million, export earning losses due to processing part of the crop equaled more than £1.5 million. In addition, being capital-intensive, processing involved a high foreign exchange cost because of the need to import capital equipment and building materials from abroad. Although processing resulted in foreign exchange losses, other gains may have helped to counteract this disadvantage. In 1966 the industry employed more than one-thousand persons and contributed £255,000 in domestic factor earnings. In the long run, the industry could help augment Ghana's scarce supply of skilled labor and management.

Cocoa Bags. During the early 1960s the government established Ghana Fiber Bags Manufacturing Corporation, which by 1963 was producing 4 million bags per year. Although the import of cocoa bags fell, imports of jute required to produce the bags increased. An evaluation of the performance of the factory in 1968 showed that the cocoa bag industry created several positive benefits.[17] Balance of payments effects were derived by subtracting the foreign exchange costs of production from the C.I.F. costs of an equivalent amount of imports; and from this remainder was subtracted an allowance for the effects that an increase in income of the domestic factors of production would have upon imports. Net foreign exchange savings equaled almost £0.5 million for 4.7 million cocoa bags produced. The plant produced other benefits. By deriving an explicit exchange rate of 77 percent of the official rate (the ratio of domestic cost to direct foreign exchange savings) for the project, it was shown that the project was able to use Ghanaian resources efficiently. Also, because the firm's machine shop and foundry had excess capacity which was used to sell repair services and spare parts for other plants in the Kumasi area, it produced external economies. The plant, which in 1968 employed more than one thousand also contributed towards the employment of labor and upgrading of Ghanaian labor skills. Conclusions concerning the plant's effects upon savings were also favorable. In 1968 the firm was generating savings; a large part of the inflow from profits and depreciation was being used for new investment.

Chemicals. In 1960, the subsidized value for insecticides purchased from the manufacturing sector equaled £0.7 million. The insecticide used in the prevention of capsid disease was prepared from imported concentrates and was sold to farmers at a subsidy. Use of imported concentrates greatly reduced value added and limited foreign exchange savings. Though the production of insect-icides in Ghana is backward-linked with cocoa, the net gains to the economy were small.

Linkages with Road and Rail Transport. The most significant investment linkage occurred in the development of transportation. Since the second decade of this century growth in the value of cocoa exports has continued to influence transport developments. Before World War II the large growth in cocoa produc-tion induced investment in rail and road transport. Though output between 1940 and 1960 was lower than the peak yields of the 1930s, the large growth in the value of cocoa resulting from higher world prices was still instrumental in inducing investment in transport.

Growth in cocoa influenced the government to invest in roads and railroads. Whereas at the turn of the present century gold mining provided the main impetus for development of the railroads, by 1911 the colonial government had begun the construction of railroad lines into cocoa-growing areas. These thou-sands of miles of newly-built roads helped reduce transport costs and made the attracted investment in the road transport industry profitable.

The road transport industry became important during the 1920s and re-mains one of Ghana's most important industries. During the interwar period as well as in the post-World War II period, the purchase and operation of trucks provided an outlet for savings earned in cocoa.[18] By increasing the demand for trucks to convey cocoa to the buying centers and to the ports, the cocoa industry was directly able to induce investment of the economy's savings in the road transport industry.[19] Even though the railway was the principal carrier of cocoa and bulk commodities destined to the ports after World War II, road trans-port remained an important carrier of cocoa and local foodstuffs because the rail system penetrated only a small area in Ghana and because road transport proved to be cheaper than rail. After the war, there was much investment in the road transport industry, and expansion of this industry was one of the fac-tors contributing to Ghana's economic growth during the 1950s.

A number of benefits resulted from the linkage between cocoa and road transport, an industry employing a substantial amount of Ghana's resources. In 1960, of the 60,000 persons employed in transport, almost two-thirds worked on trucks and a further 11,500 repaired motor vehicles. In addition to being a large user of labor services, the road transport industry represents a large invest-ment in fixed capital, and it was estimated that in 1960, 2.6 percent of Ghana's capital stock consisted of vehicles.[20] Road transport itself has induced investment in filling stations, tire-retreading shops, truck body building shops, motor vehicle repair shops, and blacksmithing firms.

Technological Linkages

The Introduction of New Techniques. The technological characteristics of the production function in the export industry are strong determinants of the extent to which that industry can diffuse new techniques and skills to other sectors of the economy. When the export industry teaches industrial skills and techniques to local labor, growth of this industry can spread new techniques throughout the economy.[21] As noted earlier, cocoa employs one-fifth of Ghana's labor force. If techniques used in cocoa production required the teaching of industrial and managerial skills, the export industry could have helped to change the quality of the labor force and diffuse new skills and techniques throughout the economy. Cocoa did involve a large segment of the population of the forest belt in cash crop production, but the techniques involved were not new since kola nuts had been produced on farms and traded internally or exported long before cocoa was introduced. Not being dependent upon technological change, development of the cocoa industry did not change the quality of the labor force and, thereby, contribute to the diffusion of skills and techniques. Techniques required for cocoa production—clearing the bush and planting cocoa as well as harvesting and processing the bean—do not require complex skills.

Technological improvements were introduced after World War II. To eliminate swollen shoot disease, many trees were cut out and young trees planted. And during the mid-1950s the government introduced on a wide scale spraying against capsid disease. These improvements, in particular capsid control, did contribute substantially to productivity increases in the early 1960s. Because, however, there is little evidence ascertaining that these technological improvements encouraged use of disease control to raise productivity in other sectors of the agricultural economy, it cannot be concluded that they produced technological linkages.

Promotion of Mass Education. Although the cocoa industry did not produce a trained labor force, cocoa farmers frequently spent large amounts of earnings from cocoa to educate their children. Hence development of the industry indirectly affected the educational level of a wide segment of the population.

Diffusion of the cocoa industry is historically related to the development of eduation within Ghana's different regions. Until the 1920s, education had been confined to Southern Ghana, where for many decades trade and commerce had been important and the cash economy had undergone its greatest expansion. Cocoa production originated in the Eastern region of Southern Ghana, and it was not until the second decade of this century that much cocoa was produced in

Ashanti. Because growth of the cash economy in Ashanti occasioned social change and a breakdown in the traditional structure, the society became more receptive towards education, and by the late 1920s the pace of the expansion in education in Ashanti had rapidly accelerated.[22]

A survey conducted during the early sixties has shown a positive relationship between number of students receiving advanced secondary schooling and number of students coming from cocoa-farming backgrounds. In a country where only one-third of the farming community is made up of cocoa farmers, two-thirds of all students from farming backgrounds (16 percent of all sixth-form students) had parents who were cocoa farmers.[23]

Cocoa did contribute to the spread of mass education, but the strongly academic nature of this education prevented the population from attaining technical and industrial skills as well as the entrepreneurial and managerial skills required by a country undertaking economic development. Since this spread of mass education was not instrumental in producing the trained labor that could have facilitated development of other industries by helping to reduce their costs of production, technological linkages from the production of cocoa were limited.

Construction of Infrastructure. Technological linkages may arise if the expanding industry constructs infrastructure which helps other sectors of the economy reduce their unit costs. In Ghana, the transport of cocoa to market required the development of an intricate transportation network penetrating remote areas, and for at least half a century native authorities and private groups of cocoa farmers constructed roads and even bridges into cocoa-producing areas, thereby contributing to the development of this network.[24] Once built, such infrastructure can be used as an input in other economic activities such as the development of other export crops and transportation of domestic foodstuffs to market. Even though large-scale development of additional export crops has not occurred, after World War II production of some traditional crops was renewed. However, privately constructed roads have facilitated the movement of domestic food supplies to markets within Ghana, and foodstuffs are carried long distances before arriving at their final destination. Because economic development requires that a supply of basic wage goods be readily forthcoming, by facilitating distribution of locally produced foodstuffs, construction of infrastructure could have contributed towards economic growth in Ghana.

Final Demand Linkages

Import data and the household surveys conducted during the 1950s and early 1960s indicate a large market size for a number of mass-produced goods. But even though market size was large, the development of industries to supply these demands was slow.

By the late 1920s, which was a period of prosperity in Ghana's cocoa industry, growth in cocoa had made a significant impact on the size of the market for a number of importables. Though population and per capita income were much lower than during the 1950s, movements in the importation of sixteen basic consumer goods reveal that during the late 1920s the quantities of canned meat and iron sheets imported almost equaled their 1955-57 levels, and imports of wheat and flour, beer, tobacco, cotton fabrics, sewing machines, watches and clocks, lamp oil, and soap were also high.[25]

During the 1950s, another prosperous period for Ghana's cocoa farmers, Ghana's Office of the Government Statistician conducted several household surveys. Two surveys were conducted in cocoa-producing areas during the mid-1950s, one in the Oda-Swedru-Asamankese area, in Ghana's Eastern region, and the other in Ashanti.[26] The expenditure patterns for these two areas, which together produced one-half of Ghana's cocoa, show that cocoa farmers consumed a fairly wide range of goods and services. The largest proportion of household expenditures went for food (62 percent in Oda-Swedru and 55 percent in Ashanti), of which only about two-fifths was consumed in kind. The fact that in Ashanti, where total monthly household expenditures were larger than in Oda-Swedru—315 shillings as opposed to 255 in Oda Swedru—the proportion spent on food was lower is suggestive of an Engel effect (whereby as income levels rise, the proportion of total expenditure for food falls). The two next most important expenditure categories were clothing and the drink and tobacco group, which in Oda-Swedru accounted for 17.4 percent and 7.4 percent, respectively, and in Ashanti for 18.6 percent and 9 percent.

The 1961-62 National Household Survey, which showed a large final demand for a wide range of goods and services, confirmed the results of the earlier surveys. Although a substantial proportion of expenditures upon food, drink and tobacco, clothing, health and hygiene, and durables went for importables, a large part went for domestic goods. In addition to imported cloth, cocoa farmers also purchased a substantial amount of locally produced cloth. Purchases of domestically produced goods such as beer and palm wine, furniture, cooking utensils, and floor covering were also important.

Because household surveys indicate that during the mid-1950s cocoa farmers had a high average propensity to save—one-fourth in Oda-Swedru and one-third in Ashanti—upon examining final demand it is also important to consider investment of savings from cocoa farming. Traditionally, cocoa farmers have used savings to educate their children, buy trucks and land, build houses, and establish new cocoa farms,[27] and during the 1950s this process continued. However, because the import component in trucks and houses was high, final demand linkages from cocoa were greatly reduced.[a]

---

[a]The purchase of trucks and house construction did generate some final demand linkages. With trucks, generally an imported chassis is fitted with a cheap, locally made, wooden body produced with local labor and materials. And, in addition to using imported materials, in particular cement and corrugated iron roofs, house construction also uses local labor and materials.

During the 1950s, a period of rapid economic growth, much of the increase in demand was supplied by imports, and between 1950 and 1961 an average of 20 percent of consumer spending went for imports.[28] Imported food, which averaged over 16 percent of total imports between 1950 and 1965, rose from 10 percent of purchased food in 1950 to 13 percent in 1961. Per capita expenditure elasticities of demand for imported food during these years were high, ranging from 0.98 to 1.52 in urban areas and 1.07 to 1.32 in rural areas.[29] Importation of food rose because the domestic economy was not capable of supplying most of the more exotic or "western" type foods which were demanded. Large amounts of rice, wheaten products, sugar, milk products, meat and fish products were imported. Though Ghana produced fish and rice and some meat, little, if any, of the other products were produced in Ghana.

Import substitution was successful in the production of beverages and tobacco, and between 1946 and 1965, beverages and tobacco fell from about 6.0 percent to about 0.9 percent of total imports. Though local production of beer commenced in 1933, it was only during the 1950s that import substitution of beverages became important. High import duties combined with other restrictions imposed during the early 1960s furthered this process, and production of beer, distilled spirits, and soft drinks increased. Given the large role of the beverage industries, it would have been possible for them to have had investment linkages with a number of input supplying industries. But it was not until the mid-1960s that attempts were made to produce sugar, an important input in beer and soft drinks. Import substitution in the production of tobacco products and unmanufactured tobacco has also been successful. Commercial production of tobacco commenced in 1953. However, by the mid-1960s two-thirds of domestic manufacturers' requirements of unmanufactured tobacco were still being imported.

Textiles and clothing made up the second most important expenditure grouping in the household surveys. By the mid-1960s, local production, though rising, was still minimal, and it was not until the late 1960s that import substitution in the production of clothing and textiles became more important. Because of the necessity of importing considerable quantities of inputs for these industries, value added was low. In addition to food, beverages and tobacco, and clothing and textiles, several other consumer goods imports were significant. Trade statistics for the period following World War II indicate that Ghana imported large quantities of soap, pharmaceuticals, and footwear. By the early 1960s some import substitution had taken place in the production of soap and pharmaceuticals, and as a consequence the relative importance of these imports declined. It was not until the late 1960s that domestic production of footwear became significant.

One industry in which import substitution has been successful is furniture. The production of furniture in small-scale establishments dates back to before World War II.[30] Given the presence of hardwoods required for furniture production, Ghana has a significant advantage in transport costs.

It may be concluded that even though development of the cocoa industry had been successful in significantly raising the purchasing power of a large segment of the population, final demand linkages resulting from growth of the industry were somewhat limited in scope. Only the production of furniture and beer had commenced before World War II. And even after the war, the large growth in purchasing power resulting from the upsurge in cocoa proceeds was not instrumental in generating strong final demand linkages. Beginning in the early 1950s, as the standard of living rose, imported food became a more important component in consumer expenditures. Import substitution in beverages and tobacco had become significant by the mid-1960s. Although domestic production of clothing and textiles was substantial by the end of the decade, the necessity of importing large quantities of inputs for these industries reduced their overall impact upon the economy.

Fiscal Linkages

Fiscal linkages are the external effects which arise from the expenditure of funds that the government receives from the cocoa industry. The allocation of these funds is made by decision makers in the public sector, and the linkage effects created by their expenditure are analogous to the linkages created by the cocoa industry. In view of the difficulties encountered in attempting to identify separately the effects of government expenditure of revenues received from cocoa, no attempt is made here to discuss the scope and importance of fiscal linkages. Such an analysis requires a detailed examination of the role of government in Ghanaian development. This kind of analysis has been carried out elsewhere for the period 1947-64.[31]

Contributions of Factors of Production

To determine the cocoa industry's contribution of scarce factors, it is first necessary to specify the factors which were in scarce supply and thus placed constraints upon the process of development. During the 1950s, cocoa prices were generally high and the economy was growing at the rate of about 5.5 percent a year. The cocoa industry made a major contribution to Ghana's foreign exchange reserves, which remained high throughout the decade and reached a peak of over £200 million in 1955. Cocoa was also the major contributor to public savings, which, though declining during the late 1950s also remained high during that decade. It is apparent, however, that development of the cocoa industry did not contribute the type of trained manpower required by a developing economy, and that a deficiency of such manpower constrained development by limiting the economy's absorptive capacity.

Implications for Policy

This study of the direct and indirect impacts resulting from growth in the value of cocoa has explained why cocoa was unable to produce diversification around the export base and, hence, could not propel sustained economic growth. The direct impact of cocoa exports continued to comprise a large share of gross national product, and the industry contributed significantly to Ghana's supplies of investment resources and foreign exchange. But important linkage effects from growth in the value of cocoa were few. Since the 1920s, the road transport industry which is backward-linked with cocoa, has made important contributions to Ghana's economic growth. Development of the cocoa bag industry may also be considered one of the stronger investment linkages, but the impact of the cocoa-processing industry is questionable. External economies created by the investment of private resources and public sector revenue derived from cocoa in physical infrastructure produced significant net gains for the economy. Although the investment of earnings in education, through both the public sector and the private sector, improved the educational level of Ghana's population, the type of education provided in the past could not satisfy the economy's requirements for trained manpower.

The impact of the cocoa industry was limited by both the technological characteristics of its production function and the institutional framework imposed upon the economy. The technological characteristics of the production function influence the extent to which the growing industry is capable of propelling economic growth. Growth in final demand can be significant when inputs used by the export industry fit local factor availability because a substantial part of the industry's earnings remain to add to final demand for goods and services. On the supply side, when the export industry induces investment linkages and/or changes the quality of the labor force, important repercussions may result.[32] Because cocoa was able to develop using the services of local factors of production—land and unskilled labor—the industry contributed greatly towards raising demands for goods and services.

But on the supply side repercussions with other sectors of the economy were limited. Because the production process for cocoa was not dependent upon the use of manufactured inputs, investment linkages were few. An export industry can favorably affect growth in other sectors of the economy if it teaches skills that can easily be adapted to manufacturing. But because the cocoa industry developed by using simple productive techniques, it was incapable of producing a supply of trained labor which would subsequently be used to reduce production costs in other industries.

The institutional framework within which the economy was forced to operate can also constrain the development process. In Ghana, marketing arrangements for cocoa, inappropriate development planning, and colonial financial and monetary institutions could have hindered the transmission of economic growth.[b]

The Ghana Cocoa Marketing Board was established in 1947 to take over the functions performed by the West African Produce Control Board, which the United Kingdom had established in 1942 to control the export and sale of agricultural export produce in the West African colonies. According to a government White Paper,[33] the West African cocoa marketing boards were to be established to stabilize cocoa producer prices and incomes through the operation of buffer funds. Cocoa statistics for Ghana for the crop years 1947-48 through 1960-61 show that not only were interseasonal producer prices destabilized but aggregate producer earnings from cocoa were even more unstable than were export earnings from cocoa. Although the Ghana Cocoa Marketing Board did not effectively stabilize producer prices and incomes, by separating the world price from the producer price, the public sector mobilized large amounts of savings, most of which were used for development expenditures on social overhead capital.

Between 1947-48 and 1963-64, cocoa proceeds totaled over £1,000 million, of which approximately one-half was paid out to producers and about one-third accrued to the public sector in the form of GCMB surpluses and public revenue from export and local duties. Until the mid-1950s, most of these funds were accumulated in Great Britain in the form of overseas sterling assets, and by 1955-56 overseas assets derived from cocoa totaled £145 million. Ghana, along with other members of the Colonial Empire and some independent members of the Sterling Bloc, built up large overseas reserves by exporting capital on current account. At a time after the war when many countries were depleting their sterling balances, Ghana not only maintained its sterling balance, but also made substantial contributions to Britain's scarce supply of dollars. Because most of Ghana's reserves were invested in long-term securities, large losses resulted from the fall in bond prices when these securities were redeemed during the late 1950s and early 1960s.

Public sector savings from cocoa earnings permitted Ghana to undertake a large amount of development spending. In addition, the GCMB spent some of its surpluses to rehabilitate the cocoa industry which was suffering from swollen shoot and capsid diseases. Rehabilitation, coupled with the new plantings encouraged by high producer prices during the 1950s, led to a large growth in output during the following decade. But during the mid- and late 1960s, world prices fell, and the GCMB reduced producer prices and stopped promoting disease control in order to discourage increases in output (which could have continued to depress world prices). As an outcome of the low level of real producer prices paid during many years since 1963-64, the structure of the capital stock in cocoa is now much older than in the early 1960s.

Several policy implications follow from the above discussion of the GCMB's

---

[b]Ghana achieved independence in 1957, at which time many of the colonial institutional arrangements were still deeply ingrained in the economic structure.

activities. Though the policies pursued by the board did help mobilize large amounts of public savings, these policies did not succeed in stabilizing producer incomes. The high producer prices of the 1950s encouraged greater output during the following decade, but the board's conservative policies during the 1960s have limited the economy's potential to maintain future output levels. Given the instability inherent in the world cocoa market, implementation of the International Cocoa Agreement may help to stabilize producer incomes and the world supply of cocoa by providing more reasonable expectations about future price levels. Moreover, the policy of transferring economic rents from the agricultural sector has undoubtedly retarded the accumulation of private capital. It is plausible that by reducing the earnings of cocoa farmers, the high tax on cocoa hindered the accumulation of private capital which might have been transferred into other productive activities such as manufacturing or the diversification of exports.

Banking was controlled by expatriate banks whose main function was to service the needs of foreign traders who required self-liquidating loans. Since surplus funds were exported to London, Ghana was deprived of investment funds and a capital market could not develop.

The philosophy which emphasized maintaining the financial self-sufficiency of the colonies and the type of development planning which emanated from this philosophy also restrained Ghana's development. The First and Second Development Plans emphasized social overhead capital as opposed to directly productive activities and encompassed a number of different projects unrelated to economy-wide goals and targets. Until the mid-1950s, Ghana's overseas reserves continued to increase. To justify not using these reserves to undertake an imaginative economy-wide development program stressing industrialization and diversification, the administration contended that these reserves would generate the confidence required to attract large inflows of foreign capital.

Cocoa remains Ghana's leading sector and principal earner of foreign exchange. Given the variable export duty and high prices currently prevailing on world markets, the export crop does make a substantial contribution to public sector resources. But continuous problems have beset the cocoa industry. As an outcome of the low level of real producer prices paid since 1963-64 few new plantings have taken place, and the age structure of the capital stock under cocoa is much older than during the 1960s. Also, output levels have fallen below the peak levels of the early 1960s, and the industry continues to be plagued by capsid and swollen shoot diseases. Policy measures aimed at preventing deterioration of the industry continue to be necessary. These include price incentives to encourage new plantings and proper horticultural techniques, a continuation of the government's program aimed at controlling swollen shoot disease, and further encouragement of capsid control.

There remains ample scope for the cocoa industry to exert a strong positive impact upon the Ghanaian economy. Ghana now has a better physical infrastructure and a better educated population than most developing countries.

Cocoa linkages can be greatly strengthened if development policy provides required manpower skills, expands the Ghanaian manufacturing sector, and broadens the base of agricultural development.

Notes

1. Polly Hill, *Migrant Cocoa Farmers of Southern Ghana* (Cambridge: Cambridge University Press, 1963).
2. Ibid., chaps. 2 and 3.
3. Polly Hill, *The Gold Coast Cocoa Farmer* (London: Oxford University Press, 1956).
4. Steven Hymer, "The Political Economy of the Gold Coast and Ghana," in *The Government and Economic Development,* ed. Gustav Ranis (New Haven: Yale University Press, 1971).
5. Robert Szereszewski, *Structural Changes in the Economy of Ghana, 1891-1911* (London: Wiedenfeld and Nicholson, 1965).
6. This section is based largely on information contained in the following: Food and Agriculture Organization, *The International Organization of Commodity Trade—Case Study on Cocoa,* January 1966, TD/B/AC. 2/3. United Nations, UNCTAD, *Marketing and Distribution Systems for Primary Commodities, Cocoa,* June 1971, TD/B/C. 1/116/add .1.
7. See United Nations, UNCTAD, United Nations Cocoa Conference, *Preparations of an International Agreement Embodying International Measures Considered Desirable,* TD/Cocoa, 3/8, October 1972.
8. B. E. Rourke and S. K. Sakyi-Gyinae, "Agricultural and Urban Wage Rates in Ghana," *The Economic Bulletin of Ghana,* vol. 2, no. 1 (1972), pp. 3-13.
9. Robert Szereszewski, "Capital," in *A Study of Contemporary Ghana, Vol. 1: The Economy of Ghana,* Walter Birmingham, I. Neustadt, and E. N. Omaboe, eds., (Evanston, Ill.: Northwestern University Press, 1966).
10. Hill, *The Gold Coast Cocoa Farmer,* chap. 8.
11. Robert Szereszewski, *Structural Changes in the Economy of Ghana,* pp. 75-85.
12. William O. Jones, "Labor and Leisure in Traditional African Societies," *Social Science Research Council Items,* vol. 22, no. 1 (March 1968), pp. 1-6.
13. Robert Szereszewski, *Structural Changes in the Economy of Ghana,* p. 62.
14. Allan McPhee, *The Economic Revolution in West Africa* (London: George Routledge and Sons, 1926), p. 54.
15. William Arthur Lewis, *Report on Industrialization and the Gold Coast* (Accra: Government Printing Office, 1953), p. 1.
16. Sara L. Gordon, *Aspects of Economic Development in Ghana* (unpublished PH. D. dissertation, Stanford, Calif.: Stanford University, 1971), pp. 142-155.
17. Unpublished government study.
18. Hill, *Migrant Cocoa Farmers,* p. 190; F. R. Bray, "Cocoa Development in Ahafo, West Ashanti" (mimeographed, Achimoto, 1959), p. 37.
19. Polly Hill, "The Indigenous Economies," *Economic Development and Cultural Change,* vol. 13, no. 1 (October 1966), p. 16. During the interwar years

cocoa farmers in Western Nigeria also purchased vehicles to convey cocoa from the farms or villages. Sara Berry, "Cocoa and Economic Development in the Nigerian Economy," in *Growth and Development of the Nigerian Economy,* eds. Carl Eicher and Carl Liedholm (East Lansing: Michigan State University Press, 1970).

20.   Szereszewski "Capital."

21.   Robert Baldwin, *Economic Development and Export Growth: A Study of Northern Rhodesia, 1920-1960* (Berkeley: University of California Press, 1966), pp. 58-73.

22.   G. E. Hurd, "Education," in *A Study of Contemporary Ghana, Vol 2: Some Aspects of Social Structure in Ghana,* Walter Birmingham, I. Neustadt, and E. N. Omaboe, eds., (Evanston, Ill.: Northwestern University Press, 1967), p. 220. P. T. Foster, *Education and Social Change in Ghana* (London: Routledge & Kegan Paul, 1965) pp. 126-128.

23.   Hurd, op. cit., pp. 326-38.

24.   Kwamina B. Dickson, *A Historical Geography of Ghana* (Cambridge: University Press, 1969), p. 22. Peter Gould, *Transportation in Ghana,* Northwestern University Studies in Geography, No. 5 (Evanston, Ill.: Northwestern University Press, 1969) pp. 43-44, 66, and 144-47. Fredrick Gordon Guggisberg, *The Gold Coast, A Review of the Events of 1920-26* (Accra: Government Printer, 1927), pp. 80-81. Hill, *Migrant Cocoa Farmers,* pp. 243-47. H. P. White, "Environment and Land Use in the Eastern Savanna of the Gold Coast," West African Institute of Social and Economic Research, Annual Conference Proceedings, 1956 (Ibaden University College, 1956), pp. 74-78.

25.   W. O. Jones and C. Merat in "Consumption of Exotic Consumer Goods as an Indicator of Economic Achievement in Ten Countries of Tropical Africa," *Food Research Institute Studies,* Vol. 3, no. 1 (February 1962), pp. 35-60, have contrasted import statistics for consumer imports to calculate indices for relative level of living. And the Stanford University Food Research Institute has calculated movements for consumer imports between 1927 and 1962.

26.   Ghana, Office of the Government Statistician, *Survey of Population and Budgets of Cocoa-Producing Families in the Oda-Swedru-Asamankese Area,* Statistical and Economic Papers, No. 6 (Accra: Office of the Government Statistician, 1958) and *Survey of Cocoa Producing Families in Ashanti, 1956-1957,* Statistical and Economic Papers, No. 7 (Accra: Office of the Government Statistician, 1960). Subsequently, Ashanti was divided into two separate regions—Ashanti and Brong-Ahafo.

27.   Hill, *The Gold Coast Cocoa Farmer,* chap. 9.

28.   Edinburgh University, Department of Political Economy, *Ghana: Projected Level of Demand, Supply, and Imports of Agricultural Products in 1965, 1970, and 1975,* Economic Research Service, Foreign Agricultural Service, U.S. Department of Agriculture, p. 19.

29.   Ibid, p. 49.

30.   Lewis, *Industrialization and the Gold Coast,* p. 2.

31.   Gordon, op. cit., pp. 289-363.

32. Baldwin, *Economic Development and Export Growth,* pp. 58-73.
33. Great Britain, *Parliamentary Papers* (House of Commons and Command), 1945-46, Vol. 20 (Reports, Vol. 6), Cmnd. 6950, November 1946, *Statement on Future Marketing of West African Cocoa.*

4 The Timber Industry and Ghanaian Development

John M. Page, Jr.*

A Brief History of Timber Exploitation in Ghana

Timber has been exported from Ghana since Elizabethan times, when ekki, a hard, heavy wood used in European ship building, was sold to coastal traders. It was not until the colonial period, however, that large-scale exploitation of Ghana's forests was undertaken.[1]

Recorded log exports commenced in 1888 and consisted of mahogany cut from forests in the Western province. Lack of transportation facilities limited resource exploitation to the coastal regions and to the few forests bordering on navigable rivers. Producers, utilizing the limited fluminary system, floated logs downstream to the surf-port at Axim, which was to become one of the major mahogany logging ports in the world by the turn of the century.[2] High transport costs and the uncertainty of surf-port operations resulted in very limited resource use within exploitable forests. Loggers generally cut only the highest valued mahogany trees and expended considerable effort in the search for figured trees, which commanded high prices on the export market.

The opening of the railroad line from the port at Sekondi to the Tarkwa gold fields in 1901 greatly expanded the area of forest accessible to exploitation, and the extension of the line to Kumasi two years later opened additional areas of forest in Ashanti. Timber concessionaires clustered along the railroad lines. Felled logs were hauled by hand from the forest to railway sidings and shipped as backhaul goods by rail to the port at Sekondi. Rail transport brought about a substantial decline in operating costs. Producers faced high and relatively stable export prices. The combination of events led to spectacular increases in logging output. By the outbreak of World War I log exports had increased in annual

*The field work on which the following study is based was financed by the U.S. Agency for International Development Mission to Ghana. Some of the arguments contained herein may be found in S. R. Pearson and J. M. Page, "Development Effects of Ghana's Forest Products Industry," report submitted to the USAID Mission to Ghana, December 1972. The views expressed are held by the author and do not represent the position of the USAID or any other government agency.

91

volume to 3 million cubic feet, of which 95 percent was mahogany.

The war interrupted the export trade, and Ghanaian production fell sharply to only 620,000 cubic feet in 1917. Recovery in the postwar period was relatively swift, and by 1922 exports had reached 2.5 million cubic feet of logs. The opening of the Accra-Kumasi railway line in 1923 made forests in the Eastern region exploitable for the first time. There was some shift of production from the Western province as loggers extended the search for mahogany into the eastern forests. The Western region continued to provide the bulk of log exports, however, and total log output did not increase.

The opening of the deep water harbor at Takoradi in 1928 reduced the high handling costs and losses associated with surf-port operations. Logs were railed directly to Takoradi harbor, floated in the log pond, and lightered aboard freighters. The decline in handling costs might have generated further increases in output, but the general economic depression of 1929-39 caused international prices to decline sharply between 1929 and 1933. By 1933 log exports had fallen to less than one-tenth of their level in the mid-1920s. The industry began to recover immediately prior to World War II. Log exports increased during the war years and reached 2.7 million cubic feet by 1945.

During the period before 1945 most of the loggers operating in Ghana's forests were small-scale local entrepreneurs, who also engaged in farming and cocoa trading.[3] Production methods were highly labor intensive and required little investment in fixed capital. Entry into and exit from the industry were relatively easy. Concession and felling agreements were undertaken with the local "stool," and the colonial government exercised little control over the pattern or intensity of resource utilization.[a] Marketing and shipment of exports were concentrated in the hands of European log buyers operating in the principal logging ports.

Processing activities began in 1903 with the construction of a sawmill to provide timbers to the Tarkwa gold mine. Non-mining demand for sawn timber was met by Ghanaian pit sawyers, who handcut trees for use in local construction. By 1946 the number of sawmills had grown to seven, several of which were producing sawn timber for export sale.[4] In contrast to logging production, investment in sawmilling was of European origin. Sawmillers acquired extensive concession areas over which they exercised felling rights for both export and saw-log production.

Major foreign investments in logging and wood-processing activities were undertaken in the period after 1945. A concessions act regularized procedures for alienating common-hold lands to private producers. The security of tenure provided by new concession agreements coupled with construction of additional transport infrastructure and rising postwar export prices increased the attractiveness of large-scale investment by foreign, principally British, companies.

---

[a]Most timber lands in Ghana are communally owned by the tribe resident in the area and administered by the local chief or "stool." Recently the government has begun to administer unreserved forests on behalf of the local owners.

Foreign investors established large- and medium-scale, vertically integrated companies producing logs and processed timber for export. The new firms introduced productive techniques that were radically different from those employed by smaller-scale Ghanaian firms. Log haulage was mechanized, feeder roads were constructed into the forest, and road transport was used between felling sites and the rail head. The new techniques increased the capital intensity of logging production and raised fixed costs per unit of output and per unit of forest area harvested. At the same time, however, these innovations served to reduce marginal costs and permitted substantial increases in the speed and volume of logging operations. Thus firms in the foreign subsector of the industry tended to exploit the forest more intensively than Ghanaian logging contractors. Species of timber with relatively low commercial values were extracted, and logs which were of less than export quality were processed into sawn timber or sold on the local market.

Many of the innovations introduced by the foreign firms spread to Ghanaian producers. Government programs of feeder-road construction made road transport viable for firms that did not build their own roads into forest areas. Wheeled tractors and bush lorries replaced gangs of men as the principal methods of log haulage for small-scale firms. In general the lower level of technical expertise and capital intensity of Ghanaian firms prevented them from achieving the levels of efficiency in resource exploitation exhibited by the foreign companies. Higher marginal production costs often forced Ghanaian loggers to leave the lower-valued trees which foreign companies harvested. Nevertheless, the additions to transportation infrastructure coupled with the innovations adopted by both local and expatriate firms led to increases in yields per unit of forest area harvested and substantial increases in log output.

The expanded output of logs increased the attractiveness of investment in local wood-processing activities. By 1957 thirty-one sawmills were in production and two plywood-veneer mills were in operation. Processing activities tended to cluster in Kumasi and Takoradi, where local markets in sawgrade logs were well established and where sawmillers had access to adequate transport facilities. Firms supplying services to the processing industry grew up in these cities and further increased the locational advantage of the two sites.

Investment in sawmilling was undertaken by foreign investors and expatriates resident in Ghana. The relatively high initial capital costs and level of technical ability required by sawmilling operations tended to preclude Ghanaian investment in timber processing during the late colonial period. Non-British resident expatriates were barred by law from holding forest concessions. These investors either entered into felling agreements with Ghanaian logging contractors or purchased logs on the local market. Sawmilling technologies were designed for processing the low-grade log inputs available. Wastage was high, and producers compensated by milling logs at high speed to increase the volume of throughput. The bulk of sawn-timber production was exported; local construction demand continued to be met by the output of Ghanaian pit sawyers.

Colonial government policy did not greatly affect the development of the industry. Forestry practices were regulated within the reserved forest areas, but the unreserved forests were not subject to strict control. Although revenues were collected in the form of export taxes and royalties, the government did not attempt to use fiscal measures to control the composition or level of output. Foreign investment, which was encouraged by colonial policy, was uncontrolled with the exception of the restrictions on concession holdings of non-British expatriates.

Foreign and domestic private investment in the forestry sector continued into the post-independence period, although the pace of new investment began to slacken somewhat by the end of the decade following independence. The most marked trend during the 1960s was the increase in timber-processing facilities. The number of sawmills grew from forty-three in 1962 to sixty-one in 1970, and plywood-manufacturing plants increased in number from two to five during the same period. Ghanaian investors became increasingly involved in the industry, as investments in both logging firms and vertically integrated sawmills were undertaken by Ghanaian entrepreneurs. By 1970 Ghanaians controlled twenty-four sawmills, two plymills, and more than one hundred small logging operations.

Five large firms currently dominate the timber industry with respect to the area of forest held under concessions and the share of industry output. Three of the five enterprises are subsidiaries of foreign-owned multinational corporations. One is jointly owned by Ghanaian and expatriate investors, and the fifth is wholly Ghanaian owned. All of the major firms employ expatriate management and technical staffs. The major firms alone marketed approximately 40 percent of the value of logs, 47 percent of lumber, and 82 percent of plywood and veneer exported from Ghana in 1970.

Medium- and small-scale firms are owned chiefly by Ghanaian nationals or expatriates resident permanently in Ghana. Approximately half of the firms in these groups hold forest concessions. The remainder enter into felling agreements with timber contractors or purchase logs on the local market. Medium-scale firms produce over 80 percent of their output for export sale, while the small-scale firms concentrate on supplying local demand.

Independence marked the beginning of more active government intervention in the timber industry. Policies were implemented to increase Ghanaian ownership of timber firms. Measures were taken to increase utilization of the resource, and efforts were made to expand local processing activities and to reduce the relative level of log exports.

Successive governments have used concessions policies, frequently combined with subsidy measures, to encourage Ghanaianization of the timber industry. In the late 1960s the government granted forest concessions and soft loans for the purchase of capital equipment to large numbers of Ghanaian logging contractors, a policy which resulted in the proliferation of many small Ghanaian firms working the forest at less than minimum efficient scale. Default rates on the government loans were high, and the bulk of small Ghanaian contractors have become increasingly dependent on loans of funds or equipment from sawmillers and timber merchants.

Ghanaianization efforts have recently been directed at gaining control over the large multinational timber corporations operating in Ghana. In late 1972 the government assumed control of a majority equity in the principal international companies. Although management and technical control of the firms will be retained by the foreign parent, the government will undertake overall direction of the company policy within Ghana. The effects of this policy are uncertain at present. It is impossible to establish a priori whether equity ownership of the foreign companies will yield greater social benefits than the application of well-designed tax and royalty policies.

Subsidy measures intended to lower producer costs were instituted as part of an effort to increase the harvest of species with low commercial values. The government offered full rebates on the cost of shipping low-valued logs by the state railways during the 1969-71 period. Despite the government's action, output of these logs failed to increase significantly due to weak international demand for the relatively unknown timber and to the inability of the railroad to expand capacity sufficiently to haul both traditional export species and lesser valued logs. Producers, confronted with a transportation bottleneck, continued to ship the relatively more profitable export species by rail despite the rebate scheme, and failed to harvest low-valued species.

Recent policy actions have centered on attempts to expand timber-processing activities in Ghana and to reduce the relative importance of log exports. Policy actions to increase domestic processing of exportable logs have included applying an *ad valorem* tax to log exports and granting an export bonus to plywood exports. To augment these measures the government has also attempted to institute a partial ban on the export of logs.

Government efforts to encourage utilization of export logs within Ghana are limited by the technology of present sawmilling capacity in Ghana. Ghanaian sawmills were designed to process low-quality logs at a high volume of throughput. Conversion of log volume to sawn timber volume is low compared with mills in Western Europe and the United States, and no market exists for waste products. Thus despite the apparent transport cost advantage of local processing, Ghanaian sawmillers are unable to saw profitably the highest-priced export logs with the existing technology. Processing facilities employing techniques of a more recent vintage would raise the capital intensity of sawn-timber production significantly. Government policy options thus include allowing the export of high-quality logs, subsidization of private producers, milling export logs with existing plant and equipment, or promotion of public or private investment in new processing facilities.

Surprisingly, the government has failed to use tax or royalty policies as instruments to achieve its goals of increased forest utilization and reduction in the relative level of log exports. Royalties are charged at a specific rate per tree harvested which does not alter with fluctuations in commercial value. No device in Ghanaian leasing policy allows the government to extract the incremental rents accruing to producers with favorably located concessions. Hence the royalties policies that the government has pursued appear to have been inefficient both as policy instruments and as revenue-raising devices.

The Market for Ghanaian Hardwood Exports

Historically Ghana has conducted the majority of its export trade with Western Europe. Geographical proximity and the traditional links between Ghanaian exporters and agents and buyers in the United Kingdom largely explain the evolution of a trading pattern in which Western Europe including the United Kingdom has purchased more than 80 percent of Ghana's annual exports of logs and sawn timber since World War II. Exports from Ghana compete on the Western European market with those of such other West African countries as Ivory Coast, Gabon, Congo (Brazzaville), Cameroon, and Nigeria.

Although Ghana is a major producer of tropical timbers, it does not occupy a dominant position as a supplier in any geographical market. The largest single market for Ghanaian log exports is the U.K., where Ghana had an average market share of 13.5 percent between 1966 and 1970. Ghanaian log exports ranked third among African producers and eighth among world producers of tropical hardwoods in 1968, supplying approximately 2 percent of world demand. Yet Ghana occupies a more important world position as an exporter of lumber. In 1969 it ranked fourth among world exporters of tropical sawn timber—supplying approximately 11 percent of world demand. Ghana's share of geographical sawn-timber markets ranged from approximately 6 percent of the United States market to 25 percent of the market in the United Kingdom in 1968.[5] These data tend to support the hypothesis that Ghana faces a nearly perfectly elastic demand for its timber exports on both world and regional markets. It is therefore doubtful that government policies to expand or restrict the output of tropical timber will significantly affect the price that Ghana receives for its exports of major species.

Demand-side constraints operate to limit the export of lesser-known or "secondary" species of timber, however. Hardwood importers show strong preferences for the major timbers entering international trade. This is due to buyer conservatism and to the unknown working properties of the secondary species. Attempts to expand output through the sale of lesser-known species therefore present some difficulty. Stocks of accepted timbers in other West African and Asian producing countries are sufficiently large to supply world demand in the short to medium term. Thus attempts to expand exports through the diversification of species exported will involve major promotional efforts and incur high selling costs. Although Ghana can apparently increase its exports of

major timbers without difficulty, significant increases in the exports of secondary species appear unlikely in the short to medium term.

Marketing of timber exports takes two forms in Ghana. The multinational
corporations supply timber through sales affiliates in the United Kingdom and
Continental Europe, and thus introduce the possibility of international transfer-
pricing by the companies. Such transfer prices are particularly difficult to detect
in the timber industry because of quality differences in the various grades of
logs and lumber. Small- and medium-scale firms sell either directly to export
merchants in Ghana or to foreign purchasers through agents in Europe or Britain.
The agents serve as financial intermediaries and provide marketing services for
which they charge on a commission basis.

The Ghana Timber Marketing Board was established shortly after independence to serve as a vetting authority to control the quality and oversee the invoicing
of log and lumber exports. It collects revenues in the form of export taxes—
Marketing Board Levies—on the export of primary species of logs, and has used
these revenues to provide financial and technical assistance to small-scale loggers
and sawmillers.

Marketing Board intervention in the export market for forest products
has varied substantially over time. For a brief period in the early 1960s the
board undertook all export sales of Ghanaian timbers, setting producer prices
and serving as overseas agent for direct sales to importing firms in Europe and
North America. Under the National Liberation Council and the subsequent
civilian government, the board's functions were confined to vetting of individual
export contracts for underinvoicing. Recently the board has begun to engage in
more active market intervention. Minimum prices for timber sales have been
established and enforced. Active promotion of secondary species has been undertaken, and the board has recently established a public corporation to market
export sales of small Ghanaian logging contractors.

Extent of the Resource

Ghana possesses approximately 31,000 square miles of forest. Of this area,
6,940 square miles are held in forest reserves and the remainder consists of
unreserved forests. Unreserved areas are intended for initial timber exploitation
followed by agricultural settlement, whereas the reserves are to be held in
perpetual forest production.

During the last two decades Ghana has come to rely increasingly on the
forest reserves for timber production. The share of timber production originating
in reserved forests increased from 11 percent in 1959 to 41 percent in 1969.[6]
The most recent inventory estimates predict complete exhaustion of unreserved
forest areas in eight to fifteen years, after which all timber production will
originate in reserved areas.[7]

The forest inventory in the reserves will not, however, support the present levels of log output under existing harvesting policies. Estimates based on current yield programs indicate that the maximum potential output of timber from reserved forests is 78 percent of 1970 output.[8]

Confronted with a limited resource the government can either accept a lower level of log production or alter yield policies. Current forestry practice emphasizes a sustained annual yield policy that gives the maximum perpetual output of logs from a given area of forest. Recent work by economists has demonstrated that such sustained yield policies may be suboptimal in the presence of a social rate of discount.[9] Although determination of optimum yield policies based on both economic and environmental considerations are beyond the scope of the current paper, this issue will have to be faced in the near future by planners in Ghana.

Industry Output 1950-70

The volume and value of export and local sales of logs during the 1950-70 period are summarized in Table 4-1. The data indicate that although the industry has grown substantially during the two decades, the period of most rapid expansion was from 1950-60. Increases in output and exports did not continue at the same pace into the decade of the 1960s. Export volumes moved cyclically with peaks in 1960, 1964, and 1969. The average annual rate of growth over the entire period was 2.3 percent. Exports increased at the rate of 13.5 percent per annum from 1950 to 1960. The volume of exports declined sharply between 1960 and 1961 and remained constant between 1961 and 1970.

Total output of timber exhibited a pattern similar to that of log exports. Local sales of logs increased from approximately 9 million cubic feet in 1950 to a peak of 37 million cubic feet in 1962 and declined thereafter. Local sales moved steadily to occupy a larger share of total output. Averages for five-year periods indicate that during the periods 1950-54 and 1966-70 the logs sold on the local market represented 33.8 percent and 61.0 percent, respectively, of the volume of total log production.

The increase in output and exports is consistent with the growth of investment and the pattern of resource depletion in the industry. Major investments were undertaken in the late colonial and early independence period, when unreserved forests were made accessible by expansion of the transport network and government policies were favorable to foreign investors. In the 1960s the more accessible forests were being rapidly depleted. Increasing reliance was placed on forest reserves with their restricted forestry practices and lower yields, and government policy had turned against both foreign investment and export logging.

In the past no direct trade-off existed between production of logs for

Table 4-1
Volume and Value of Log Production 1950-70 (Ghana)
(Volume, cu ft million; value, ¢ million)

	Export logs		Local consumption		Total production	
	Volume	Value	Volume	Value	Volume	Value
1950	10.39	3.52	9.24	n.a.	19.63	n.a.
1951	9.13	6.36	12.69	n.a.	21.82	n.a.
1952	7.53	6.48	15.80	n.a.	23.33	n.a.
1953	10.39	6.48	16.33	n.a.	27.38	n.a.
1954	12.62	7.28	19.32	n.a.	31.94	n.a.
1955	16.90	8.88	23.33	n.a.	40.23	n.a.
1956	19.61	10.20	24.65	n.a.	44.26	n.a.
1957	24.55	10.80	24.43	n.a.	48.98	n.a.
1958	27.03	12.44	25.65	n.a.	52.68	n.a.
1959	35.60	15.94	26.40	n.a.	62.00	n.a.
1960	35.90	19.64	28.85	n.a.	64.75	n.a.
1961	21.48	18.10	31.35	14.11	52.83	32.21
1962	20.34	11.58	37.50	16.88	57.84	28.46
1963	23.65	14.44	33.39	15.03	57.04	29.47
1964	24.26	16.16	36.86	16.58	61.12	32.74
1965	19.72	13.26	36.49	16.42	56.21	29.68
1966	16.82	10.88	32.24	14.50	49.06	25.38
1967	17.86	12.83	29.55	13.30	47.41	26.13
1968	20.10	16.26	28.95	13.03	49.05	29.29
1969	24.60	24.12	31.72	14.27	56.32	38.39
1970	16.14	20.29	27.21	12.25	43.35	32.54

Sources: Economic Survey 1960, 1965, 1969, Central Bureau of Statistics; author's estimates.

local consumption and for export. Logs sold on the local market were traditionally of a quality inferior to the minimum grade entering international trade and therefore were nontradable joint products of export logging production. The issue of a trade-off arises when local purchases of export quality logs are made. At present no sawmills in Ghana find it privately profitable to process export quality logs. The potential for the development of processing activities utilizing export-grade logs and the possibilities of future trade-offs are discussed in the concluding section.

The Direct Contribution to National
Income and Employment

Estimates of input and factor shares in the gross output of Ghana's logging industry are given in Table 4-2. The data are taken from a sample survey of firms in the industry conducted for the fiscal year 1970-71, and the estimates refer to logging operations conducted both by vertically integrated firms and firms not vertically integrated.

Table 4-2
Shares in Logging Output and Net Gain from Logging, 1970-71 (Ghana)

	Input and factor shares		Net gain coefficient
Imported intermediates		.0755	Value of output	1.0000
Locally purchased intermediates		.0772	Less foreign input costs	-.3633
Fuels		.0700	Less foreign factor costs	
Payments to foreign contractors		.0435		
Payments to local contractors		.1096	Labor[a]	-.0053
Road and rail transport		.0814	Capital[a]	-.0901
Electricity and water		.0153		
Financial services		.0180	Less local input costs	-.1292
All intermediates	.4925		Less local factor costs	
Wages and salaries	.1343		Skilled labor	-.0605
Expatriate		.0133	Unskilled labor[b]	-.0302
Ghanaian			Capital[c]	-.0338
Skilled		.0605		
Unskilled		.0605	Less rents repatriated by foreign investors	-.0704
Payments to government	.0970		Net gain	.2172
Direct taxes and royalties		.0794		
Export taxes		.0176	Components of net gain coefficient	
Residual (profits, depreciation, rents retained by private sector, etc.)	.2762		Excess payments to unskilled labor	.0302
			Payments to government	.0970
Total output	1.0000		Rents to local investors	.0900

[a]Based on an annuity computed for machinery with a life of 10 years at 15 percent and buildings with a life of 20 years at 15 percent. Import costs of capital as well as repatriated normal profits are included.
[b]Based on an estimated overvaluation of 50 percent in the social cost of unskilled labor.
[c]Returns to local investor based on the annuities computed as specified in note a.
Source: Author's survey of timber firms.

Several important assumptions and limitations of the estimating procedure warrant discussion. The sample year appears to have been relatively representative of industry operations in the period from 1960 to 1970. Although output in 1970 was below levels for the previous decade, production increased in the second half of the year and continued to increase into the first half of 1971. Hence, output and capacity utilization for the accounting year were similar to the levels experienced in the 1960s. Firms surveyed during the accounting year may have enjoyed greater than normal access to imported intermediate inputs owing to the operation of the Open General Licensing System. Therefore, the sample estimates may tend to overstate the consumption of imported intermediates in comparison with recent levels.

The completed sample of firms engaged in logging was biased toward large-scale, vertically integrated, foreign firms, and underrepresented small-scale logging contractors. To correct for this bias, production coefficients for each subsector of the industry were calculated separately. The aggregate Leontief production function in Table 4-2 consists of an average of the individual subsectoral production functions, weighted by each subsector's share in the volume of log output in the sample year. Due to a lack of basic accounting data, however, the smallest, most labor intensive, and least technically efficient firms were those which failed to enter the sample. Thus the weighted entry for small-scale logging probably overstates the actual capital intensity and technical efficiency of the subsector. The production function thus remains somewhat biased in favor of the more capital intensive and efficient firms in the industry.

In order to derive factor shares in total logging output it was necessary to price the output of logs produced by vertically integrated companies and provided to their own milling operations.[b] The price was taken as equal to the average local market price for identical species purchased by similar processing activities. Such an estimation procedure ignores the possibility of quality differences in the logs used by firms which are vertically integrated and those which are not. In the absence of evidence of quality differences, it was felt that the procedure gave a consistent estimate of the value of total logging output.

Input costs represent 49 percent of the value of output. Value added accounts for the other 51 percent of gross output and consists of wages and salaries, payments to government, amortization of capital, profits, and economic rent. Wages and salaries account for 13 percent of the value of output. Payments to government represent an additional 10 percent of production costs, and the residual consisting of amortization of capital, profit, and privately held rents represents 28 percent.

---

[b]An alternative procedure would have been to attempt to divide logging costs between those for export logs and those for sawmill-grade logs. Such a procedure would have allotted logging costs of sawmill logs to the sawmilling operations, but it would also have served to obscure the role of rents in providing net gains in logging.

The Computation of Net Gain

The computation of net gain from the logging industry involves estimating shadow prices of the factors employed in logging production. The forestry sector (including processing activities) is sufficiently small in relation to both total employment and output of the Ghanaian economy that its effect on the market (and accounting) prices of factor inputs is probably negligible. Hence the definition of factor-accounting prices appears clear; it is the opportunity cost to the economy of the factor employed in its best alternative use. The opportunity cost measure gives an indication of the loss in output resulting from the shift of a marginal unit of the factor input from elsewhere in the economy into the logging industry. To the extent that market failures or institutional factors cause social and private valuations of factor inputs to diverge, the accounting price will differ from the market price and the net gain coefficient will be altered. The following section consists of a brief discussion of the sources of divergence between social and private factor costs in the Ghanaian economy and of some estimates of the accounting prices of factor inputs into the logging industry. The factor-accounting prices which will be discussed are those of foreign exchange, skilled and unskilled labor, foreign and domestic capital, and land.[10]

Estimating the shadow price of foreign exchange is a complex task. Although the Ghanaian economy clearly suffers from a critical shortage of foreign exchange and from overvaluation of the exchange rate, little empirical research has been undertaken to determine the possible value of a shadow price of foreign exchange.[11] Rather than make an arbitrary valuation, however, the shadow price was taken as equal to the official exchange rate. Net gain is thereby understated if net foreign exchange earned is positive and overstated if it is negative.

The shadow price of skilled labor and management was taken as equal to its market wage. Skilled labor is in limited supply in Ghana, and it is therefore likely that the wages and salaries paid by the logging industry reflect the value of skilled labor's marginal product elsewhere in the economy.

Casual and unskilled labor are not in limited supply. Available evidence suggests that considerable unemployment and underemployment of unskilled labor exists. Estimates of the level of unemployment reveal that an average of 11.1 percent of the labor force was unemployed during the 1966-69 period.[12] In addition, substantial underemployment of casual labor may exist in the agricultural sector during much of the year.

Logging firms are rural enterprises that draw their unskilled labor either directly or indirectly from the agricultural labor force. Thus an indication of the social opportunity cost of unskilled labor employed by the industry is the marginal product of unskilled labor in agricultural production. One estimate of the marginal product of agricultural labor is the daily wage rate paid to hired laborers for peak season agricultural work. It may be expected that farmers will pay hired labor up to the value of its marginal product during such peak periods.

The limited empirical data available indicate that the average daily wage of unskilled labor in logging production exceeds the peak period agricultural wage by approximately 40-70 percent.[13] Several factors serve to explain the divergence in wage rates. First, industrial minimum wage rates apply to logging-production workers. The legal minimum sets a floor under payments to unskilled labor by the industry, a floor that is higher than the opportunity cost of such labor. Second, large- and medium-scale firms are subject to union pressure in setting wages, and the average level of wages in the industry is increased by union-negotiated minima for large and medium firms. Finally, the timber firms are forced to offer some wage premium to attract migrant labor into uninhabited forest areas. This final factor is an economic cost of the industry's operation, and will reduce to some extent the divergence between market and social prices implied by the first two factors. Because the relative magnitude of the various factors is unknown, a point at the low range of the scale was chosen and the wage rate in logging was assumed to exceed opportunity cost by 50 percent.

Private investment opportunities in Ghana generate high rates of return. One estimate of the rate of return on marginal investments yielded a nominal rate of return of 15 percent. Bank lending rates range between 11.5 and 14.5 percent, and the government uses a rate of return of 15 percent in evaluating public investment projects.[14] On the basis of this evidence, a rate of return of 15 percent was chosen as the opportunity cost of capital supplied by Ghanaian and resident-expatriate investors.

The shadow price of foreign investments is more difficult to establish. If foreign investors in the timber industry would not have invested elsewhere in the Ghanaian economy, the opportunity cost of their investments is zero. However, the investment generates a stream of repatriated profits which reduce net gains from the foreign operations. If the net gain is computed over the life of the investment, the factors may be considered separately. In attempting to estimate a net gain coefficient for a single year, however, an alternative approach is needed. It is reasonable to assume that the expected present value of the repatriated profits from the foreign investment (discounted at the investor's test rate[c] of return) is at least equal to the cost of the invested capital. Thus an annuity based on the test rate of discount will give an estimate of the cost of foreign capital when profits are repatriated. Little information exists on alternative investment opportunities or attitudes toward risk of foreign firms in Ghana's forest products industry. Fifteen percent was taken as the anticipated rate of return on foreign investments; yet, it represents nothing more than a guess based on the author's conversations with management personnel in the industry.

Because forestry ties up extensive tracts of land in reserved areas, it may

---

[c]The test rate of discount is defined as the rate of return at which the present value of a marginal investment project contemplated by a foreign firm is equal to zero.

generate social costs if the land has alternative economic value. Evidence suggests that some areas of forest reserve have high potential for cocoa farming. The shadow rent of such land is equal to the net gain at accounting prices of a unit of forest in cocoa production. Unfortunately the available data do not permit computation of the shadow rent or provide an indication of the extent of the cocoa land available in reserved forests. Nevertheless, the reader should be aware that net gains will be reduced where forest lands show positive social rents.

An estimate of the net gain coefficient is given in Table 4-2. Division between foreign costs and domestic costs was based on the experience of firms that could provide detailed information on the composition of inputs and on interviews with firms supplying inputs to the industry.

An important assumption was made concerning the valuation in terms of foreign exchange of logs sold on the local market. Locally purchased logs serve as inputs into processing industries that produce for export or input substitution. It was assumed that the market price of locally purchased logs accurately reflected the value of their marginal product, and thus the cedi values of locally purchased logs were converted to foreign exchange values without adjustment. This assumption would be incorrect to the extent that processed timber producers exercise some monopsonistic power in the local market, but monopsony does not appear to be a prominent feature of Ghana's processing industry. Companies not vertically integrated compete actively for log inputs, and market prices probably equal social costs.

Finally, an assumption was made in the computation of net gain that foreign-owned companies would repatriate all of their profits arising from economic rent. In fact much of this profit has been reinvested in further processing activities. It is assumed, however, that the present value of the repatriated profits from the additional investment will equal the value of unremitted profits. Hence all profits were treated as remitted abroad.

The estimated net gain coefficient for logging production is approximately 21 percent of the value of output. It is composed of extra incomes accruing to local capitalists, payments to government, and that component of wages to unskilled labor which exceeds opportunity cost. The net gain from extra capitalists, income, which is 9 percent of gross output, is substantially less than the rents accruing to capitalists of 16 percent of gross output because of the assumed repatriation by foreign-owned companies.

The relative magnitudes of the gain from extra capitalist's income and from payments to government call into question the effectiveness of government royalty and tax policy. It appears that government policies did not efficiently transfer economic rents from the private to the public sector. Additionally, more appropriately designed fiscal policies could have transferred rents from foreign-owned firms to the government and increased the net gain coefficient through the reduction in repatriated profits.

The net gain coefficient computed in Table 4-2 ignores linkages and externalities discussed below; nevertheless, it is apparent that net gains from the industry have been substantial, and that the potential exists for increasing net gains through the revision of fiscal and leasing policies.

Forward Linkages

Timber-processing activities have come to play an increasingly important role in the forest-products industry of Ghana. The availability of saw-grade logs at low cost relative to the price of sawn timber provided the initial stimulus for investors to install sawmilling capacity. Government policies have since encouraged further investment in sawmilling and plywood manufacturing as part of a program to increase local processing of primary exports.

Lumber exports grew substantially during the 1950s, but remained virtually constant in the 1960s. In 1969 exports equaled 7.73 million cubic feet, valued at ¢14.96 million. Sales of sawn timber on the local market increased slightly during the 1960s, and in 1969 equaled 5.17 million cubic feet, valued at ¢ 6.94 million. Ghana is unusual among West African timber producers in that a major portion of sawn timber is exported. Wood is not a popular construction material for mass housing or large-scale construction in Ghana. Thus, although efforts have been made to increase local utilization of wood products, domestic demand for processed timber has not grown significantly.

Two types of forward-linked firms exist in Ghana's forestry sector. Many primary producing companies have established processing activities vertically integrated with logging operations. These producers utilize low-grade logs in their sawmills and plywood-manufacturing plants and export the processed output. All the major foreign-owned companies are vertically integrated, and an increasing number of small- and medium-scale Ghanaian-owned firms are establishing processing plants. At present vertically integrated companies produce 84 percent of processed timber output. Firms not vertically integrated are owned by expatriates resident in Ghana. These firms also produce timber for export, but they purchase log inputs on the local market.

The trend toward vertical integration may be explained in large measure by two factors. First, government concessions policy favors firms with processing activities. Hence some form of processing plant is seen as a prerequisite for obtaining extensive concession areas. Control over a concession allows the firms to engage in the highly profitable export logging business as well as in timber processing. Thus firms are often willing to engage in processing activities of marginal profitability in order to undertake export logging. Additionally, vertical integration permits greater use of installed capacity by assuring a supply of log inputs. Firms not vertically integrated have periodically had difficulty in obtaining consistent supplies of sawmill logs.

Benefits from forward-linked activities arise when timber processers employ factors of production which have an opportunity cost below their market price, when excess profits are retained locally either as extra income accruing to capitalists or as payments to government, or when second-round linkage effects or externalities are generated.[d]

The computation of net gain is complicated by the presence of vertically integrated firms. Such firms do not normally price log inputs into their milling operations, nor do they divide logging costs between those for export logs and those for sawmill-grade logs. There are two possible approaches to evaluating the net gain from the processing activities of vertically integrated firms. The first is to price log inputs in the manner discussed in the preceding section and compute the net gain of the processing activity alone. In this way rents accruing to the resource are not reflected in the net gain to the processing activity. An alternative approach is to compute the total net gain from all operations of a vertically integrated firm. This approach is preferable where doubt exists concerning the applicability of market prices to log inputs of vertically integrated firms. The approach does not allow separate analysis of net gains in each type of activity, but it does permit more accurate comparisons between net gain coefficients for firms of different ownership.

Both approaches were employed in the following analysis. First aggregate net gain coefficients were computed for sawmilling and plywood manufacturing by pricing the log inputs of vertically integrated firms. Second, firms were divided by ownership into Ghanaian, foreign, expatriate and jointly owned groups, and net gain coefficients for the combined activities of each ownership group were computed.

Table 4–3 contains Leontief production functions and estimated net gain coefficients for sawmilling and plywood manufacturing. Factor-accounting prices were assumed to be the same as those given in the preceding section. Foreign-owned firms were assumed to repatriate all excess profits. The net gain coefficients for both sawmilling and plywood manufacturing are low in relation to the net gain from logging. Net gain from sawmilling is estimated at 4.9 percent of the value of gross output. The net gain coefficient for plywood manufacturing is 5.6 percent.

Net gain in each case is composed of excess payments to unskilled labor, payments to government, and extra income accruing to capitalists. Sawmilling was the more labor intensive of the activities and had the greater proportional excess payments to unskilled labor. Although plywood manufacturing had a greater residual element of extra incomes accruing to capitalists, the high proportion of foreign ownership in the subsector reduced net gain substantially.

Positive net gains for sawmilling and plymilling indicate that the logging

---

[d]The terms *excess profits* or *extra incomes accruing to capitalists* are used interchangeably to refer to capitalists' income in excess of the normal rate of return based on the opportunity cost of capital. Such profits may arise from privately held rents to the resource, monopoly or monopsony profits, or the managerial or technical efficiency of the firm.

Table 4-3
Shares in Sawmilling and Plywood Output and Net Gains from Processing Activities, 1970-71 (Ghana)

Input and factor shares

	Sawmilling	Plywood manufacture
Log inputs	.3224	.3081
Imported intermediate inputs	.0832	.1299
Domestic intermediate inputs	.0526	.0337
Fuels	.0334	.0070
Payments to foreign contractors	.0309	.0400
Payments to local contractors	.0654	.0367
Road and rail transport	.0620	.0150
Electricity and water	.0115	.0382
Financial services	.0271	.0102
Total intermediates	(.6985)	(.6188)
Wages and salaries		
Expatriate	.0266	.0503
Ghanaian		
Skilled labor	.0800	.0553
Unskilled labor	.0700	.0500
Payments to government	.0088	.0162
Residual (amortization, profits, etc.)	.1161	.2092
Total output	1.0000	1.0000

Net gain coefficients

	Sawmilling	Plywood manufacture
Value of output	1.0000	1.0000
Less foreign input costs	.3004	.3132
Less foreign factor costs		
Labor	.0266	.0503
Capital	.0792	.0923
Less local input costs	.3981	.3056
Less local factor costs		
Skilled labor	.0800	.0553
Unskilled labor	.0350	.0250
Capital	.0267	.0674
Less excess profits repatriated by foreign-owned firms	.0053	.0344
Net gain coefficient	.0487	.0555
Components of net gain		
Payments to government	.0088	.0162
Excess payments to unskilled labor	.0350	.0250
Extra capitalists' incomes retained	.0049	.0143

Source: Author's survey of timber-processing firms, 1970-71.

industry served to generate further benefits through forward-linked processing activities. The relatively low net gain coefficients tend to cast doubt on the assumption that increases in the local processing of exports with present techniques will result in substantial gains to the Ghanaian economy, but important distinctions must be made. Low levels of technical efficiency, high wastage, and the tendency to view sawmilling as a cost of export logging operations explain much of the low net gain from sawmilling. Plywood-manufacturing firms, on the other hand, are of recent vintage and exhibit less wastage than sawmills. Two of the plywood-manufacturing firms, however, were in the initial phase of operations and therefore experienced abnormally high production costs. These "infant industry" effects reduced the net gain coefficient for the sample year.

Net gain coefficients for total operations of vertically integrated firms are presented in Table 4–4. Firms were divided into three ownership groups, foreign, Ghanaian, and joint, and into three size categories. Net gain coefficients for the aggregate operations of each group containing more than one firm were computed under each of two assumptions: (1) that all profits and rents of foreign firms are retained in Ghana and (2) that all profits and rents of foreign firms are remitted abroad.

The analysis reveals that all but one of the ownership groups of vertically integrated firms yielded positive net gain coefficients. No single category clearly dominates all others. Under assumption (1), large, foreign-owned firms have the highest net gain coefficient. Allowance for profits remitted abroad, however, reduces the net gain by 45 percent and places large foreign firms in the mid-range of the sample. The coefficient for large Ghanaian and jointly owned firms probably understates the actual net gain from this group owing to the fact that one firm in the sample had an extremely bad year with production falling proportionately more than costs.

Medium-scale Ghanaian firms exhibit the highest net gain coefficient under assumption (2) and also compare favorably with foreign and jointly owned firms under assumption (1).

Small Ghanaian firms were the only ownership category to exhibit negative net gains. The source of the negative coefficient is a large negative entry for residual rents indicating that value added at world prices was less than domestic factor costs.[e] This may be due to the relatively recent inception of most small Ghanaian firms. Such firms tend to have high learning costs and utilize less of their installed capacity than do other firms in the industry. Small foreign-owned firms also exhibited negative residual rents, but of a much lower magnitude. Net gains from this subgroup were positive because payments to government and excess payments to unskilled labor outweighed negative residual rents.

In sum, vertically integrated operations of large and medium scale have

---

[e]This would be equivalent to a domestic resource cost of foreign exchange greater than the test exchange rate if the Bruno measure were employed.

Table 4-4
Net Gain Coefficients for Total Operations of Vertically Integrated Companies, 1970-71 (Ghana)

	Large foreign firms		Large Ghanaian and jointly owned firms		Medium foreign and jointly owned firms		Medium Ghanaian firms	Small foreign firms		Small Ghanaian firms
	(i)	(ii)	(i)	(ii)	(i)	(ii)		(i)	(ii)	
Payments to government	.0532	.0532	.0546	.0546	.0356	.0356	.0240	.0165	.0165	.0403
Excess payments to unskilled labor	.0393	.0393	.0612	.0612	.0311	.0311	.0401	.0545	.0545	.0584
Residual rents retained locally	.0742	--	-.0312	-.0312	.0833	.0416	.0826	-.0285	-.0285	-.2156
Net gain coefficient	.1667	.0925	.0846	.0846	.1500	.1083	.1467	.0425	.0425	-.1169

(i)　All profits and rents assumed to be retained in Ghana by foreign companies.
(ii)　All profits and rents assumed to be repatriated by foreign companies.
Source: Author's survey of timber-producing firms, 1970–71.

apparently generated substantial net gains. The bulk of the net gain arises from primary production, as indicated by the prominence of residual rents. Processing activities provide some additional net gains, but exhibit net gain coefficients below those for logging or for combined operations.

Backward Linkages

Backward linkage effects arise when the operations of a producing activity give rise to new investments by supplying firms, or permit existing firms to utilize excess capacity or underemployed factors of production or to achieve economies of scale. The interindustry flows between the forestry sector (including both processing and logging firms) and the rest of the Ghanaian economy are of limited magnitude. Products of local origin used in timber production include fuels, tires and tubes, protective clothing, and paper products. Timber-industry demand for these items in relation to total output is low, and available evidence does not suggest that the forestry sector has been responsible for assisting the supplying industries to achieve scale economies or to increase capacity utilization.

Services provided to the forestry sector consist principally of road and rail transport and repairs to equipment. During the period of early operations of the railroad, the logging industry permitted increased capacity utilization by providing back-haul goods. Currently, however, increased capacity utilization is limited by inefficiency in the railway, and the industry cannot generate further linkage benefits in this sector.

Road transport contractors may have achieved increases in capacity utilization by hauling logs and lumber during periods of slack demand for other transport services. Quantification of the benefit accruing from this linkage is impossible, but it cannot have been of great importance since contracted road haulage is only occasionally employed by most firms in the industry.

Local servicing and machinery-repair firms are important suppliers of inputs to the forest-products industry. Such firms, however, have as their major inputs imported spare parts and skilled labor. Thus no linkage gains arise from use of unemployed factors of production. Scale effects in the repair-services industry are of extremely limited importance and appear to have been exhausted. Capacity is fully utilized and limited by the lack of spare parts. It is doubtful, therefore, that a significant linkage gain results from the demand for services.

Thus backward linkages resulting from the operations of logging and timber-processing firms are of negligible importance to the Ghanaian economy. The level of technical expertise and the high standards of quality control necessary to machine parts and tools for woodworking limit the ability of the Ghanaian economy to provide inputs into the forest-products industry. The limited amount of locally produced inputs purchased at present does not appear to generate substantial linkage gains.

Externalities

The forestry sector constructs extensive networks of feeder roads and trains small quantities of skilled labor which are of potential importance to other sectors of the Ghanaian economy. These activities represent external gains to other sectors if those sectors are able to appropriate benefits from roads and skilled workers without cost. In a country with well-developed markets for human capital and land, producers of such external benefits might be compensated. In Ghana, however, market imperfections prevent firms in the timber industry from recovering expenditures on labor training and road construction which benefit other industries.

The construction of feeder roads appears to be potentially the more important of the two external benefits. Firms in the timber industry constructed more than 850 miles of roads of varying quality during 1970-71. In areas of unreserved forest these roads are later used by immigrant farmers to transport produce. Estimating the pecuniary value of the benefit to farmers and consumers derived from lower transport costs would involve determining the frequency of travel over the logging roads by goods vehicles, computing transport costs for the route, and comparing these costs with transport costs for alternative routes. Required data do not exist. Discussions with government and industry officials indicate that feeder-road construction has been of particular importance in the Western region in areas of concessions worked by the major foreign and Ghanaian firms. If this is indeed the case, the external benefits from road construction will increase the net gain coefficient for logging by large firms.

The construction of feeder roads in reserved forest areas does not generate any gains to other sectors, because other forms of economic activity are prohibited within forest reserves. Hence the importance of feeder-road construction to net gains from the industry will diminish as production shifts from unreserved to reserved forests.

Both logging and processing firms provide limited on-the-job training for skilled and semiskilled laborers. This training will benefit other sectors of the economy if the skills taught are transferable and if workers move into other industries.

Skills such as heavy-equipment repair, surveying, carpentry, and technical trades are transferable. Only one firm in the industry, however, has organized programs to provide training in such skills. Other firms tend to use on-the-job training to upgrade the basic skills acquired by laborers outside the forest-products industry. Thus it appears that skilled labor training by timber firms does not offer a substantial gain to other sectors of the Ghanaian economy.

Employment and Income Distribution

Recently policy makers in Ghana have placed increasing weight on the objectives of expanding employment opportunities for Ghanaians and increasing the share of national income accruing to lower- and middle-income groups. The following section briefly considers the available evidence on the structure of employment and income distribution within Ghana's forest-products industry.

In 1969 employment in the forestry sector totaled 23,558, which represented less than 2 percent of the nonagricultural labor force. Workers were divided evenly between the logging-production industry, which employed 11,666, and the processing industries, which employed the remaining 11,892. The five major firms in the industry employed 30 percent of the forestry sector's Ghanaian labor force and 62 percent of the industry's expatriate personnel.

The scope for employment creation within the forest-products industry is defined by the existing factor intensities, the scope for labor-capital substitution, and the relationship between increases in output and employment. Factor intensities, as measured by the full-capacity capital-output ratio, differ widely among the various stages of timber- and wood-processing production[f]. The most capital intensive activity is plywood manufacturing, whose capital-labor ratio of 3.10 exceeds the capital-labor ratios for logging and sawmilling by 46 percent and 103 percent, respectively. Sawmilling is the least capital intensive of the three stages of production. Capital intensity in sawmilling, however, tends to vary with the size of firm and with the choice of technique. New technology sawmills exhibit considerably higher capital-labor ratios than the average Ghanaian plants. The two sawmills currently employing more advanced techniques of production in Ghana have capital-labor ratios that exceed the national average for sawmills by 40 percent.

Logging is relatively capital intensive due to the need for heavy investment in haulage and transport equipment. Capital intensity of production does not appear to vary significantly with the size of firm, although some very small enterprises may continue to use hand-felling techniques, which would raise the labor intensity of production within those firms.

The scope for expanding employment within the logging sector is limited by the extent of the resource, which under existing yield policies will prevent employment creation through further increases in output. Hence increases in employment will have to come through substitution of labor for capital. No estimates of the elasticity of substitution in logging production exist. The nature of the production process, however, appears to indicate that the only real scope for substitution of labor for capital would be in a return to hand-felling techniques. The net employment effect of such a shift is difficult to predict, but there does not appear to be grounds for great optimism concerning the elasticity of substitution.

Within the processing sector, scope for increasing employment by expanding output continues to exist. Although evaluation of the potential employment effect of expanding a processing activity is best accomplished by computing the

---

[f]The concept is defined as the ratio of the depreciated value of the capital stock in thousands of cedis to the full-capacity labor force.

incremental labor-output ratio for each activity, data limitations compel the use of a more crude measure. Average labor-output ratios were computed for saw-milling, plywood manufacturing, and several other manufacturing activities for the years 1967 through 1969. It was found on the basis of the labor-output ratio that sawmilling and plywood manufacturing both rank favorably in comparison with the manufacturing sector as a whole and with alternative manufacturing in-dustries in terms of their potential employment effect. As expected from the data on factor intensities, sawmilling appears to have the greater potential em-ployment effect. Nevertheless, the labor-output ratio for plywood manufac-turing is more than double the average for all manufacturing, and thus also presents an attractive opportunity for employment expansion.

The influence of various components of the industry on the distribution of incomes can be assessed, with the aid of data contained in the preceding discus-sion of net gains. Factor payments were divided between payments to capital and payments to five occupational groups—expatriate managers, Ghanaian managers, Ghanaian supervisors, and Ghanaian skilled and unskilled laborers.

Capital costs—amortization and normal profits—are quite uniform as a per-centage of gross output across groups of firms. Residual rents accruing to cap-italists are highest among foreign- and Ghanaian-owned medium-scale firms. Logging generates the greatest proportion of extra capitalists' income, which is consistant with the high levels of rents to the resource accruing to concession holders. The greatest proportion of extra capitalists' incomes retained within the local economy accrues to medium-scale Ghanaian-owned firms.

The distribution of wages and salaries varies considerably among various categories of firms. Multinational firms pay the highest proportion of wages to expatriate managers. Large-scale Ghanaian and jointly held firms have the highest Ghanaian wages and salaries component in gross output and the highest compo-nent of payments to unskilled labor. Large firms have the highest component of payments to skilled labor, followed by small-scale firms. Medium-scale firms have the smallest component of wages and salaries in gross output and the smallest coefficient of payments to unskilled labor. Across all size categories foreign- and expatriate-owned firms have a smaller coefficient of payments to unskilled labor than do Ghanaian firms. Thus foreign ownership appears to favor expatriate- and skilled-labor income groups relatively more than does domestic ownership.

Among the various stages of production plywood manufacturing most favors expatriate and management personnel. Sawmilling has both the highest skilled labor and unskilled labor coefficients, while log production ranks between the two processing activities in terms of its payments to skilled and unskilled labor.

Policy Issues and Conclusions

The analysis in the foregoing sections speaks directly to two sets of policy issues. The first concerns the extent to which components of the forest-products industry contribute to the growth of income and employment in Ghana and whether the levels of activity of each component can be altered to achieve more efficient attainment of social goals. The second involves the question of whether increasing the level of public or private Ghanaian ownership of the industry might advance or impede development objectives.

The study was limited in scope to three broad economic objectives—the growth of income, expansion of employment, and improved distribution of income. Major emphasis was placed on the objective of growth of income largely because of the feeling that it is inappropriate to base policy decisions for an important export industry employing less than 1 percent of the labor force on employment or distributional considerations.

Decisions concerning the desirable structure of the timber industry hinge on the degree to which various components of the industry contribute to the economic objectives held by the government. The analysis reveals that each component of the forest-products industry contributes positively to the growth of income. Logging makes the greatest contribution via rents to the resource which are retained within the local economy. Sawmilling is more marginal as a contributor to the growth of income, but it has the most favorable properties from an employment and income distributional viewpoint. New technology sawmills, however, tend to show higher net gains in income at the expense of employment creation and improved distribution of income. Future investment in plywood manufacturing should yield positive net gains in income. It is the least efficient of the three components of the industry, however, at increasing employment or altering the distribution of income.

The expansion of the industry is constrained principally by the extent of the resource. Therefore if the government wishes to expand export logging sales, for example, it must be prepared to accept a higher rate of exploitation of the forest or contraction of processing activities. Conversely, increasing the output of processing activities will entail either increasing the rates of exploitation or utilizing some export-quality logs in local production. The data indicate that increased processing of high-quality logs is perhaps best accomplished by expansion of plywood manufacturing and new technology sawmilling. Programs to encourage the use of export-grade logs in sawmills of existing technology do not appear to offer substantial net gains to income, although they may be desirable in fulfilling an employment objective.

It is important to note that the forest-products sector has few significant links with the rest of the Ghanaian economy. Linkage effects for both the logging and processing stages of the industry are of limited magnitude, and net gains arise wholly from payments to government, capitalists' incomes and excess payments to unskilled labor. Because it is quite likely that the government may place a higher valuation on government revenues than on extra income accruing to capitalists, an important area for further study is the nature of optimal leasing arrangements for the resource. The available evidence indicates that present leasing policies are efficient neither at extracting the economic rent accruing to the resource nor at achieving other possible policy objectives of the government. Hence maximization of future net gains from the timber resource will depend in large measure on the implementation of more efficient leasing and royalties policies.

The issue of Ghanaian ownership has been emphatically brought to the fore by the recent partial nationalization of the major multinational timber companies.[g] The present analysis offers no conclusive evidence that changes from foreign to private Ghanaian ownership will improve the net gains from timber extraction and processing. Large Ghanaian and jointly owned firms performed less well than large- and medium-scale foreign-owned firms, even when full allowance was made for profits remitted. On the other hand, medium-scale Ghanaian firms showed the highest net gains per unit of output.

Answers to the question of whether to undertake public or private Ghanaian investments in logging or timber processing will require careful cost-benefit analysis of the investments in question. Additionally, the government should consider the desirability of appropriate tax and royalties policies as an alternative to public investment in foreign-owned companies.

Notes

1. A. Foggie and B. Piasecki, "Timber Fuel and Minor Forest Produce," in *Agriculture and Land Use in Ghana*, J. B. Wills, ed. (London: Oxford University Press, 1962).
2. W. E. M. Logan, "Timber Exploitation in the Gold Coast," *Empire Forestry Review* 26 (1947): 30-53.
3. Ibid.
4. Ibid.
5. For data on tropical hardwood production, see FAO *Yearbook of Forest Products Statistics*, 1969. For data on Ghana's shares of various geographical timber markets, see D. K. Agbetsiafa, "Analysis of The Institutional Market for Ghanaian Tropical Hardwood" (mimeographed, University of Ghana, 1972).
6. Republic of Ghana, *Economic Survey*, 1961, 1965, 1969.
7. Canadian International Development Agency, *Ghana Forest Products Transport Study*, prepared by Swan-Wooster Engineering Company, Vancouver, B. C., 1972.
8. Ibid.
9. See, for example, C. G. Plourde, "A Simple Model of Replenishable Natural Resource Exploitation," *American Economic Review* 60 (1970): 518-22.

---

[g]The nationalization was imposed by the Extractive Industries Decree of 1973 and applied to the largest three foreign-owned companies. Terms of the settlement are as yet unclear.

10. Readers familiar with the recent literature on project evaluation in developing countries will recognize the brevity and incompleteness of the treatment of accounting prices in this paper. A more detailed analysis would have involved estimation of commodity accounting prices, and more detailed efforts to estimate the shadow prices of unskilled labor and foreign exchange. For an example of the techniques involved in estimating accounting prices, see I. M. D. Little and J. A. Mirrlees, *Manual for Industrial Project Analysis in Developing Countries* (Paris: OECD Development Centre, 1968).
11. Michael Roemer and J. J. Stern, formerly of the Harvard Advisory Group in Ghana, have estimated that the shadow price of foreign exchange may lie between ¢ 1.50 and 1.70 per dollar.
12. T. Merrit Brown, "Economic Statistics of Ghana," part 1, *Economic Bulletin of Ghana*, 1972.
13. B. E. Rourke and S. K. Sakyi-Gyinae, "Agricultural and Urban Wage Rates in Ghana," *Economic Bulletin of Ghana*, vol. 2, no. 1, Second Series. (1972), pp. 1-13.
14. Nathan Consortium for Sector Studies, *Economic Assumptions and Coordination* (Accra, Ghana: Ministry of Finance and Economic Planning, May 1970).

5

The Impact of Coffee on the Economy of Ethiopia

Teketel Haile-Mariam

Coffee accounts for more than 50 percent of Ethiopia's export earnings. This study analyzes the influences of coffee exports on Ethiopian income, stressing both direct income effects and linkages. In addition, policy guidelines are recommended for government participation in the production and marketing of coffee and for government plans for diversification.

Trends in the Economy of Ethiopia

Ethiopia, located in the northeastern part of Africa, occupies an area of about 122 million hectares inhabited by some 24 million people. The main physiographical features of the country are the rugged mountains and plateaus dissected by a rift valley that runs from north to south through the heart of the country. Coffee is grown in the temperate and cool highland regions.

Agriculture accounts for more than 50 percent of the total GDP and employs more than 87 percent of the total population. Many farmers are tenants. Productivity in traditional agricultural subsectors is low. Farming practices employed by most of the Ethiopian farmers are traditional, with the oxen, wooden plough, and the hoe providing the principal capital inputs. The effective demand for nonfarm inputs like fertilizers, pesticides, herbicides, and fungicides by the majority of farmers is quite small, with the exception of a very few large-scale commercial farmers who employ mechanized farming practices.

The manufacturing sector constitutes the "modern" industrial sector of the economy. It is composed basically of import-substituting industries, some of which receive high tariff protection. The most important manufacturing industries include food, beverages, tobacco, textiles, leather and shoes, wood and wood products, chemicals, and nonmetallic mineral products.

Exports accounted for 8 percent of total GDP and 13 percent of monetary GDP in 1969. The value of exports increased at an average annual rate of 5.3 percent from 1960 through 1969, compared to an approximate GDP rate of growth of 4 percent per annum during the same period. Agricultural products compose the predominant exports, with coffee accounting for about 60 percent of the total. Other major export commodities include hides and skins, oilseeds and kernels, pulses, and fruits and vegetables. The composition of exports tends to be rigid with small changes in the relative importance of the major export commodities.[1]

The Production of Coffee in Ethiopia

The total supply of coffee can be estimated at 134,000 tons for 1970.[a] Fifty-eight percent of this total is exported, while the remainder is consumed domestically. Coffee is produced on more than 80,000 hectares by over 100,000 small holder farmers, in seven provinces of the country. These provinces are Harerge in the southeast, Sidamo and Gemu Gofa in the south, Kefa and Illubabor in the southwest, Welega in the west, and Arusie in the central part of the country. The area under coffee represents only one-tenth of 1 percent of the total agricultural lands in the country, or seven-tenths of 1 percent of the total cultivated land.

Coffee is believed to have originated in Ethiopia. It is often alleged that a large proportion of Ethiopian coffee is harvested from coffee trees that grow wild. For instance, the National Coffee Board of Ethiopia reports that forest coffee accounts for 60 to 65 percent of total coffee production in the country.[2] Although coffee trees originally grew under natural forest habitat unattended by man, indications are that almost all productive coffee trees are now cultivated. In Kefa, Ilubabor, and Welega, the growth of coffee takes one of three forms: coffee trees growing in a wild environment intermingled with trees that are not yet producing; coffee farms established by clearing fields on which wild trees grew by rearranging the old trees, and by planting additional new seedlings on these cleared fields; or coffee farms established entirely by cultivating virgin lands and by planting young coffee seedlings. In the four other producing provinces, the coffee trees are virtually all planted. Therefore, the popular view that most Ethiopian coffee comes from wild trees that grow under natural forests is largely inaccurate.[3]

Farm Ownership

Land ownership in Ethiopia can, in general, be classified into four types—private, communal, government, and church. There are various forms of private land ownership, but basically they originate from personal purchases and/or grants from the state to nobles, soldiers, members of the royal family, and various officials in different parts of the country. Lands allocated by the government to

---

[a]My estimate of total supply is lower than the official estimate of 200,000 tons see Teketel Haile-Mariam, *The Production, Marketing, and Economic Impact of Coffee in Ethiopia* (unpublished Ph.D. dissertation, Stanford, Calif.: Stanford University, 1973), pp. 35-41.

the Coptic Church, on which men serving the Church make a living, are classified as Church lands. In addition to direct government land grants to the Church, private owners are allowed to transfer their holdings to the Church, and the Church reserves the right to collect land, tithe, and education taxes that otherwise would have gone to the government from persons settled on the land.

In most areas the number of tenant holdings exceeds that of resident owners, although there are variations in the ratio of tenant holdings to resident owners among different subprovinces; up to three-fourths of farm income accrues to the landlord.[b]

The distribution between landlords and tenants of the increments of production resulting from making permanent improvements on farms and the extent to which farmers are compensated for making innovative improvements play important roles in determining the nonagricultural inputs purchased and the extent to which technologies are adopted to improve the quality of coffee. The decision to make new plantings of coffee trees depends, first, on the decision of the landlord to allow such improvements and, second, on the expectations of the tenant about the opportunity he has of staying on the farm to reap the fruits of the long-term investments. Although there are some contracts of tenancy to ensure security of tenure for the tenants, they are usually oral, a characteristic that reduces their operational value. The landlords and the tenants are not equal partners and do not have equal bargaining power when designing policies that deal with security of tenure, because the landowning class has much greater political power in Ethiopia.

Factors of Production

Labor and land are the most important factors used in the production of coffee. Purchased inputs, including imports, are only a small proportion of all inputs used in production. Family labor accounts for most of the labor input used; other sources of labor are communal labor and migratory labor from non-coffee-producing regions.

The cultivation of coffee has not substituted for either the production of food crops or the production of other export commodities. In view of the availability of unused land in the country—only 15 percent of the total agricultural land is cultivated—and of the unsuitability of jungle and mountainous

---

[b]A report (Kebede Koomsa, "Problems of Agricultural Tenancy in Ethiopia") presented in 1970 at a seminar on agrarian reforms, sponsored by the Ministry of Land Reform and Administration of Ethiopia, states (p. 54): ". . . the tenants in Shewa province made payments of one-quarter to two thirds of the crop . . . in Arusie tenants paid one-quarter to two-thirds of the crop, in Welega, the sharecroppers pay less than half to over 50 percent of the crop. It should be further noted that in all the cases cited, all variable inputs, such as oxen power and the like, are provided by the tenants. . . . Landlords contribute only land as a factor of production."

coffee-growing fields for other crops, land areas occupied by coffee trees have low social opportunity cost. Although there are competing demands for labor, it would seem that the country has the potential to increase both agricultural output (including food crops) and the production of other export commodities without being seriously constrained by a labor shortage.

Government Control of Marketing

The economic and political importance of coffee in the national economy has led to the formation of the National Coffee Board of Ethiopia, whose primary short-run objective is to maximize export earnings and export duty from coffee. The policy of the Board has consistently emphasized control of the movement of coffee among markets together with attempts to control the movement of some factors of production within the coffee industry. The Board attempts to control the coffee industry through licensing schemes, including licenses to coffee exporters and other market participants.

The National Coffee Board attempts to impose a compulsive control on sales to external markets as long as there is a demand for them, regardless of what the domestic retail prices might be. All coffee produced in the country, whether for export or for domestic consumption, is required by law to be inspected by the Board. Coffee may be sold to the domestic market only if it is graded as of nonexportable quality or if quota markets have been filled up and no further external markets are available.

Two additional government bodies have a direct impact on the coffee trade. The Customs Department collects export duties, and the National Bank of Ethiopia attempts to control export prices of coffee through its export license scheme. The National Bank of Ethiopia does not interfere directly with the export of coffee. Yet, to safeguard its foreign exchange earnings, it attempts to make sure that the prices received by any coffee exporter do not fall "much" below the international prices. The Bank tries to prevent artificially low price quotations by an exporter who sells to his own agent in another country in order to avoid taxes by the Ethiopian government. The Board facilitates tax revenue flows through its intermediation between the International Coffee Organization and the exporters and through its licensing schemes, which direct the flow of coffee to a focal point and make it easy to tax.

Coffee Exports and Quotas

Ethiopia is a member of the International Coffee Organization (ICO). Ethiopia's quota, which represents 2.5 percent of the total coffee exports to

Table 5-1
Coffee Quotas and Exports (Ethiopia)
(thousand tons)

Year	Authorized Quota	Actual Exports		
		Quota Countries	Nonquota Countries	Total
1961-62	–	–	–	59.4
1962-63	–	–	–	64.5
1963-64	n.a.	n.a.	n.a.	75.6
1964-65	65.9	76.3[a]	3.3	79.5
1965-66	71.0	60.1	10.8	71.0
1966-67	72.3	70.8	10.9	81.7
1967-68	73.8	73.7	4.6	78.3
1968-69	76.6	71.5	8.1	79.7
1969-70	82.8	78.3	2.1	80.4

[a]"Export Certificates of Origin" were not established. The certificates are instruments designed to avoid export of coffee by any producer-member beyond the authorized quota through a third country.
Source: Ministry of Finance files (Ethiopia).

ICO countries, has recently been about 83,000 tons. Quota exports represented 97 percent of total exports in 1969-70, a representative year evidenced in Table 5-1. During most years between 1964 and 1970 Ethiopia was not seriously constrained by the ICO quota system since exports to quota countries were below the authorized quota.

Direct Impact of Coffee Exports on National Income

The distribution of income from export sales and gross value added by coffee to GDP are presented in Table 5-2 for the years 1964-69. The gross value added to GDP from coffee exports is equal to F.O.B. proceeds from exports minus the sum of payments for purchased inputs used on the farm, values of inputs and services used in the domestic marketing of coffee, and returns to exporters and other merchant middlemen.

The production of coffee for export contributes to national income only if its social marginal product is greater than its social marginal cost. The crucial part in the analysis of net contribution to national income is the evaluation of the social marginal cost of producing a net unit of foreign exchange. The measure we use to estimate the social marginal cost of a net unit of foreign exchange obtained from coffee exports and to evaluate the efficiency with which domestic resources are used in the production of foreign exchange is the domestic resource cost per net unit of foreign exchange (DRC).

Table 5-2

Coffee Exports, 1964-69 (Ethiopia)

(E$ million)

Distribution of proceeds	% Share[a]	1964	1965	1966	1967	1968	1969
Transport	2.7	4.3	5.1	4.2	3.8	4.1	4.7
Taxes and duty	8.3	13.2	15.6	12.9	11.6	12.7	14.4
Cleaning	1.0	1.6	1.9	1.6	1.4	1.5	1.7
Packaging	1.1	1.7	2.1	1.7	1.5	1.7	1.9
Commission	0.3	0.5	0.6	0.5	0.4	0.4	0.5
Labor	0.6	0.9	1.1	0.9	0.8	0.9	1.0
Insurance	0.2	0.3	0.4	0.3	0.3	0.3	0.3
Net margins to:							
Exporters	11.7	18.6	22.0	18.3	16.3	17.8	20.3
Other middlemen	2.5	4.0	4.7	3.9	3.5	3.8	4.4
Residual[b]	71.6	113.6	134.6	111.8	99.9	109.3	124.5
Total	100.0	158.7	188.1	156.1	139.5	152.6	173.7

		1964	1965	1966	1967	1968	1969
Proceeds from exports		158.7	188.1	156.1	139.5	152.6	173.7
Marketing sector:							
Taxes and duty		13.2	15.6	12.9	11.6	12.7	14.4
Marketing services and inputs		5.0	6.1	5.0	4.4	4.8	5.4
Exporters' and other merchant middlemen		22.6	26.7	22.2	19.8	21.6	24.7
Farm purchased inputs[c]		1.7	2.1	1.7	1.5	1.7	1.9
Gross value-added to GDP[d]		116.2	137.6	114.3	102.2	111.8	127.3
Value-added as a percentage of total GDP		4.4	5.0	4.0	3.3	3.1	3.3

[a]Estimated distribution of income for the series of years is based on an assumption that the share of F.O.B. price of each recipient remains unchanged for all years.

[b]Refers to gross farm income.

[c]This is estimated by taking the F.O.B. price share of farm tools and implements—which amounts to roughly 1.1 percent—and multiplying this percentage by the value of coffee exports for the respective year.

[d]This is the same as value added to GNP, since net foreign factor payments are negligible.

Sources: Data are from: 1962, Central Statistical Office, *Summary Report on Ethiopia's External Trade, 1953-1963*, p. 28; 1963-65, National Bank of Ethiopia, *Quarterly Bulletin*, no. 20 (December 1968), p. 30; 1965-66, Central Statistical Office, *Statistical Abstract-1967 to 1968*, pp. 103-7; and 1967-69, Central Statistical Office, *Statistical Abstract-1970*, pp. 98-102.

Our DRC ratio estimate amounts to 1.18 for 1970. This ratio does not exceed the official exchange rate obtaining when our data were collected.[c] Even if we consider what may be an overvalued exchange rate established after devaluation of the United States dollar—which apparently reduces the social marginal product of foreign exchange and net contributions of coffee to national income—the DRC ratio for coffee is still considerably lower than the official exchange rate. This means that the transformation of domestic resources into foreign exchange through activities involving the production of coffee for export provides for net additions to national income. The net contribution to national income per unit of foreign exchange obtained from coffee exports amounts to E$1.32. This is obtained by subtracting the esti-mated DRC ratio from the official exchange rate between the Ethiopian dollar and the U.S. dollar. The net gain coefficient amounts to 0.53. This means that 53 percent of Ethiopia's total earnings from coffee exports is net contri-bution to national income.

Contributions of Coffee Exports to Savings

The transfer of savings from the coffee industry to noncoffee sectors of the economy provides further growth of national income if increases in output would otherwise be constrained by a lack of domestic investment resources. A complete assessment of the coffee sector's contributions to domestic saving would involve knowledge of the propensities to save of all income recipients who are involved in the processes of producing and marketing the coffee. In this study, however, we estimate only direct government revenue from coffee exports because the information we have does not provide us with an adequate basis for estimating other classes of saving that may be contributed by the coffee sector.[d]

A comparison of the tax revenue from coffee exports with public saving gives an indication of the probable contributions of coffee to government saving. In estimating government saving, however, a comparison of total government revenue and total government current expenditure gives a mis-leading picture of domestic public saving if total government revenue includes external assistance or loans. In our estimation of apparent domestic public saving, we have excluded external components of total government revenue

[c]The exchange rate between the Ethiopian dollar and the U.S. dollar prior to January 1, 1972, was E$2.50 = U.S.$1.00. Ethiopia's refusal to devalue the currency after the first devaluation of the U.S. dollar resulted in a new official exchange rate of E$2.07 = U.S.$1.00.

[d]Private savings take place with village-level savings institutions, "under the mattress," and with commercial banks. Although we cannot tell what portion of deposits with all commercial banks come from the coffee sector, evidence indicates that business activities of commercial banks located in the different coffee provinces follow the pattern of coffee production and marketing.

and current expenditures. Thus apparent domestic public saving equals domestic public revenue minus domestically financed current expenditures. Although there were wide fluctuations from year to year, apparent domestic public savings for the period 1965-66 thru 1969-70 averaged E$20.0 million annually; tax revenue from coffee exports averaged E$19.3 million annually for the same period.

Linkages

Linkages are intersectoral relationships between the coffee industry and other sectors of the national economy. The most important linkage effects to be considered here are backward linkages, resulting when the coffee industry purchases inputs and services from other sectors; forward linkages, resulting if the coffee industry's output is used as an input in other domestic sectors; and final demand linkages, arising when expenditures of coffee incomes generate demand for locally produced consumer goods. The strength of benefits or costs from linkages is affected by the definition of the industry that is used, the structure of the regional or national economy, the coffee production function and composition of marketing inputs used, and the income distribution of the proceeds from coffee sales.

If the coffee industry is defined to include activities on the farm only, more linkages would be "created" because all other sectors serving or being served by the narrowly defined industry would benefit through increased employment of factors or better utilization of presently employed resources. On the other hand, if the coffee industry is defined to include both production and marketing, we then narrow down the apparent linkages by including sectors that would have served or are being served by the coffee industry. In this study, the coffee industry is defined to include production up to the farm gate. All activities involved in the process of marketing are considered to be outside of the industry.

The structure of the domestic economy affects the magnitude of backward linkage effects. If the inputs are not produced in the domestic economy, there are no linkages. Instead, the derived demand for the inputs becomes a leakage out of the economy. Production and marketing functions influence income accruals to suppliers of inputs; and the income distribution of proceeds from coffee sales affects the direction and strength of final demand linkages.

Each round of expenditure of receipts from coffee sales has its own linkage effects, and with each round of linkage analysis, measurement errors expand. Most of the present analysis focuses on first-round effects. But even here we have less than adequate data to look at all induced employment of factors or the extent to which the efficiency of use of the presently employed resources has been increased. Therefore, appraisal of some of the first-round linkage and leakage effects must be qualitative.

Backward Linkages

The strength and direction of benefits to the domestic economy resulting from the expenditures by the coffee industry in the purchase of inputs can be indicated by using the ratio of expenditures on domestically produced inputs to the total value of coffee produced. Small-holder coffee farmers incur only about 6 percent of their total production costs through the purchase of various farm tools and implements. This amount is equivalent to roughly 1 percent of export proceeds. Most of the inputs used by farmers are supplied domestically. Labor, which is primarily supplied by the farm family, is the main recipient of most of the income from coffee production that accrues to non-land factors of production. Hence, the benefits to the domestic economy resulting from the purchases of inputs by the coffee industry are quite small, and the foreign exchange cost to the domestic economy resulting from the industry's demand for imported inputs is even less.[e]

Forward Linkages

Forward linkages include purchases of transport services, packaging supplies used for transporting coffee, and other marketing services. Demand by the coffee marketing sector for transportation may provide economic stimulation for firms that supply railway, truck, airline, and mule transport services. In 1969, total payments to the railway company from exports were roughly E$2.4 million. Airline and truck transport received roughly E$2.3 million, most of which accrued to truck services. Payments to mule transport cannot be determined. Accruals to the transport services are distributed among labor, depreciation on machines, spare parts, fuel, electricity, and profits; some of these provide gains from linkages while others result in leakages.

The bag manufacturing industry operates at less than full capacity.[4] Hence, the demand for packaging supplies by the coffee-marketing sector perhaps allows some economies of scale and most probably increased employment of local labor and materials. The demand by the coffee export marketing sector amounted to roughly 23 percent of total production of textile bags in 1969. If we add probable purchases of bags to transport coffee from the provinces to Addis Ababa, the percentage share of textile bags used by the coffee-marketing sector would be considerably more than 23 percent. The share of total twine production used by the coffee sector is at least 15 percent.

---

[e]A marginal increase in domestic demand will result in a net welfare gain if the stimulated local industry employs (otherwise) underutilized factors or benefits from economies of scale. Given the limited importance of backward linkages in this study, no attempt has been made to consider the extent of gains from these intersectoral relationships.

Purchases of coffee bags and twine for export in 1969 amounted to a minimum of E$1.9 million. A substantial amount accrued to Ethiopian employees of the bag-manufacturing industry and to suppliers of locally purchased inputs such as *enset (Enset edulis)* and *dum*. Data collected from the bag-manufacturing industry reveal that in 1969 total Ethiopian employment in the industry was 1,182, or roughly 5 percent of total employment within the textile-manufacturing sector in that year.

Some market participants save and invest money outside the coffee industry. Most exporters engage in import-export businesses involving many commodities; some have large hotels and motels. Similarly, other domestic merchants trade in eggs, poultry, salt, edible oil, soap, kerosene, and food grains; others are engaged in activities such as ownership of hotels, motels, and bars, real estate speculation, and money lending. Thus, the savings from the coffee sector are being used for investment in other sectors. Such a flow of funds among industries stimulates economic interaction.

Final Demand Linkages

Expenditure patterns of income recipients in the coffee industry provide an indication of the extent to which demand for local goods and services stimulates domestic economic activities. In 1969, coffee exports raised gross farm incomes by over E$100 million; this amount could be nearly doubled if it were possible to account for domestic sales of coffee. This income was distributed over more than 100,000 farmers. For many farmers, annual gross income can be estimated at over E$500 per household. If allowance is made for production costs and rent (if the farmer is a tenant), net income would decline accordingly.

As determined by availability of data, our analysis of final demand linkages is based on estimates of rural expenditures of households in the different coffee regions. Expenditure studies of households in the coffee areas can give a first approximation of the extent of final demand linkages. Rural consumption surveys conducted by the Ethiopian Central Statistical Office are used here to indicate expenditures of households.[5] Analysis of the expenditure patterns focuses on cash expenditures, current consumption, current expenditures on enterprises, capital formation, and deposits with village savings institutions. Reported per capita figures were converted to household units by multiplying these figures by estimated average size of the rural household in each province. Rankings of broad groups of expenditure items in order of their relative magnitude in the different provinces are given in Table 5-3.

The results show, first, that expenditures on food and on clothing and footwear hold significant importance in all provinces, with expenditures on food alone accounting for more than 48 percent of consumption expenditures

Table 5–3
Rankings of Broad Groups of Expenditure Items in Order of Relative Magnitude in the Coffee Provinces (Ethiopia)

Expenditure Group	Harerge	Arusie	Welega	Ilubabor	Kefa	Gemu Gofa	Sidamo
Final demand linkages[a]							
Food	1 (48)	2 (49)	1 (52)	1 (63)	1 (52)	1 (37)	1 (50)
Clothing and footwear	2 (26)	3 (28)	2 (18)	4 (11)	3 (18)	2 (35)	3 (27)
Drinks and tobacco	6 (10)	5 (11)	4 (13)	3 (21)	5 (9)	7 (5)	5 (11)
Services	5 (13)	7 (8)	6 (11)	7 (2)	4 (16)	5 (15)	7 (7)
Household durables	7 (3)	8 (4)	7 (6)	6 (3)	7 (5)	6 (8)	6 (5)
Other linkages							
Expenditures on enterprises	3	4	5	5	6	4	2
Other investments	4	1	3	2	2	3	4
Savings	8	6	8	8	8	8	8

[a]The figures in parentheses indicate the percentage of total consumption expenditures accruing to each consumption expenditure group.
Source: Teketel Haile-Mariam. *The Production, Marketing, and Economic Impact of Coffee in Ethiopia* (unpublished Ph.D. dissertation, Stanford, Calif.: Stanford University, 1973), pp. 174-76.

in all provinces except Gemu Gofa. The kinds of foods that the rural households purchase are more likely to be those that are produced domestically and sold in the local markets rather than imported canned foods. Canned foods (such as fish, meat, cheese, butter, evaporated milk) are luxury items for the farmers and are, therefore, mainly consumed by the high-income group and by the foreign community dwelling in the country. Second, the nonfood items on which the consumers spend their money are more likely to be produced domestically than imported. Most nonfood items are produced by village craftsmen and by domestic import-substituting firms.

Variations in absolute expenditures on each item in the different provinces can be attributed to differences in tastes, cultural values, religious backgrounds of the consumers, and in income positions of households chosen for the interviews. Differences in cash expenditures can also reflect the degree of specialization in production by the particular household interviewed. The less cash the household spends on a certain consumption item, the more may be the probability that the household supplies its own needs, assuming all other things remain unchanged.

It is interesting to examine whether differences exist in the consumption expenditure patterns of small-holder peasants, landlords, and merchant middlemen. Expenditure patterns of landlords who are residents of the coffee areas seem to be similar to those of other local farmers, though at higher levels and with small variations in the mixture of goods and services. Polygamy is practiced in almost all coffee-growing areas. The richer one is, the more wives he can have and hence the more children he may father. As a result, receipts from coffee sales tend to be spread thinly over the members of the household. Also, the income position of the rich landlord does not stay the same over time inasmuch as he has to distribute part of his property every time one of his sons marries.

Another group of landlords is made up of outsiders, usually government officials. The expenditure patterns of members of this group vary depending on how far up in the hierarchy one is. The further up, the more that may be spent on imports. Merchant middlemen (many of whom live in the provinces) have patterns of consumption similar to those of other rural people, although with relatively higher demands for income-elastic luxury foods and with different modes of consumption of the more common types of foods.

The static expenditure pattern reveals that most of the commodities on which the largest proportion of total expenditure goes are food items that can be purchased from local markets. Inasmuch as base rural income is low, incremental income would not change significantly in the short run the mixture of goods and services on which people spend their money. Let us demonstrate this, using expenditures on food as an example, since food is the most common item on which the rural households spend their money. With a slight increase in the income of the household, the volume and the degree of complexity of the meals might be increased a bit. The difference in consumption might take the form of the frequency of eating per day, the volume eaten per meal, and the nature of the supplementary foods. At least in the short run, the mixture of commodities and services for which incremental incomes have stimulated production for the market would not change significantly.

The evidence indicates that local producers of goods and services stand to gain from the consumption expenditures of households. Income receipts from coffee are also linked with the demand for goods and services in other provinces. Some migrant laborers bring money to their relatives at the end of the coffee season, money which is then used to purchase goods and services in these localities. Equally important is the extent to which the evolution of specialized agencies to supply the needs of consumers is accelerated by growth in income and by increased complexity of the associated demand for goods and services. The level of per capita income required to induce evolution of specialized agencies to supply complex consumer needs may not be realized in the very near future. But the existence of specialized infant village industries that supply some of the needs of the consumers and the existence of a market-oriented society provide a basis from which increasingly specialized groups would evolve with each rise in economic well-being of the society.

Summary

Analysis of coffee production reveals that values of purchased farm inputs account for a minor proportion of the value of total output. Levels of purchased marketing inputs are more significant. Domestic factors and agencies receive more than 85 percent of coffee income. This income is distributed among a large number of small-holder farmers, merchants, and other market participants. Farmers and others earning incomes from coffee create a broadly based effective demand for domestically produced goods and services, and hence strong final demand linkages. Forward linkages are not as strong, but are important. Backward linkages are quite weak.

Implications for Policy

In this section, we consider government participation in the production and marketing of coffee, and the extent to which the diversification of the economy away from coffee may or may not require the diversion of land areas now occupied by coffee trees to other uses. In suggesting policies, however, it is helpful to remember that attempts to remove specific distortions in the production and marketing of coffee may only increase the cost of policy making and reduce the impacts of new policies unless other complementary problem areas are dealt with at the same time. It is even doubtful whether an attempt should be made to design policies that are specific to the coffee industry without at the same time considering their repercussions on other sectors of the economy.

Government Participation in Production and Marketing

An important contribution of the National Coffee Board is its control of the quality of the coffee exported—although very little attention is given to the quality of coffee consumed domestically—and its introduction of grading and standardization systems into the coffee trade. Grading and standardization enhance pricing of the commodity. They ease the language of communication between the consumers and the producers by transmitting the specific quality of coffee that the consumers prefer to buy at specific prices back to the producers.

The primary functions of the Board from the government's viewpoint seem to be to increase efficiency in collecting government revenue and to promote foreign exchange earnings from coffee exports. Although the Board specifically attempts to control all coffee produced in the country in the name of "inspection and grading," the main reason for this seems to be the facilitation of tax collection. Together, the activities of the National Coffee Board, the National Bank, and the Customs Department referee the transfer of revenue from coffee exports to the government.

The primary activities of the National Coffee Board do not seem to be consistent with the coordination of the interests of all parties in the coffee trade, including farmers, merchants, and domestic consumers. Such coordination would require that market participants be allowed to sell coffee to buyers who are willing to pay the most—either domestic consumers or consumers in the international market—and that there be a smooth interaction between consumers and producers. Restriction by the Board of the free movement of the participants reinforces obstacles from natural barriers to entry into any market.

Despite the desirability of minimizing controls of the marketing process, there is a tendency for increased control. The National Coffee Board now requires wholesalers (market intermediaries who purchase coffee in major provincial terminal markets and sell it to exporters in Addis Ababa or Dire Dawa—the largest domestic terminal markets) to surrender all coffee to an auctioneer who, employed by the Board, then sells the coffee to the exporters through auction and returns the proceeds to the wholesalers. Such a system is believed to minimize the "exploitation" of wholesalers by exporters. Although we have no evidence of such exploitation, the setting up of the auction system may increase the intensity of competitive trading among wholesalers and

exporters. The usefulness of such a system to the whole coffee economy, however, depends on how much it increases the income of other market participants,
and the increase in the speed and accuracy with which it allows prices to carry
necessary market information back to the farm; probably, the full benefits of
such an auction system do not reach the farm.

Government facilitation of the production and marketing of coffee would
benefit society more if it emphasized the construction of road systems in the
coffee areas, which, in general, also have the best agricultural potential. Road
construction is a long-run investment whose benefits to the national economy
can be measured not only through its expected beneficial effects on the coffee
sector alone, but also in the use of the roads by all the agricultural economies
of the regions and in their use by the suppliers of nonagricultural commodities
to these regions.

An expansion of road construction by itself does not guarantee increased
production for market, however. The role of more efficient communication
systems in accelerating economic interactions and growth will increase with
each round of reforms that is undertaken, including expanded credit facilities
to market participants, and a change in the relationship between landlords
and tenants. One of the most important questions of rural development in
Ethiopia revolves around land, the political and cultural institutions that are
interwoven with the ownership of land and that, in turn, influence the relationship between landlord and tenant. Prolonged delay in establishing policies
on the question of land reform may only add to hopes and fears, with the
potential of a violent explosion. The resource costs of some policy changes
designed to accelerate growth and development of the agricultural sector
probably are low. Basic changes in the institutions that affect the relationships
between the tenant and the landlord can have high initial payoffs in terms of
accelerating growth and development of the economy, and such policy changes
probably have low initial resource costs, since they basically require changes
in the laws and regulations governing the existing landlord-tenant relationships and the enforcement of these new laws and regulations.

Government Plans for Diversification

Diversification may imply either or both of the following: reducing the
share of coffee in the national income of the country by increasing the share of
other sectors; or increasing the share of other export commodities in the total
exports of the country. According to official estimates of national income, the
value of coffee produced was about 8 percent of the total GDP in 1969. Hence,
the share of coffee production in the overall economic activities of the nation
is quite small, and on this account alone the economy is not highly dependent
on coffee. Furthermore, the quantity of the factors of production used by the

coffee industry is insignificant compared to the total resources of the nation. Even if it were desired to expand the production of food crops in the coffee areas, coffee would not provide serious competition for most of the important factors. The social opportunity cost of land used by coffee is low, and increasing the production of food crops would not require reduction in the amount of land used by coffee.

Since the share of coffee in the national income is already quite small, diversification basically means diversifying exports rather than reducing the share of coffee in the gross domestic product. How best can the export base of the nation be diversified? Let us first see how the Ethiopian government uses the "diversification fund" of the ICO to diversify the economy away from coffee.

The International Coffee Organization requires payment to its diversification fund by the coffee-producing member countries of E\$1.50 for every bag (each 60 kilograms) of coffee over 100,000 bags that each producing member country exports to quota countries. Any project that would diversify the economy away from coffee would qualify for support if the particular product directly or indirectly lessened the dependence of the economy on coffee and curtailed the flow of production factors toward coffee.[6] Alternative projects chosen on the basis of these criteria include national range development, an agricultural credit program, forestry and sawmill projects, development of rural handicrafts, and development of small regional agricultural package programs in both the coffee and noncoffee provinces of Ethiopia.

The choice open to the government in its use of the diversification fund is either to undertake projects itself or to use public funds to encourage private entrepreneurs to undertake desired development projects. Whichever alternative the Ethiopian government chooses, it would be poor policy to attempt to curtail factor movements towards the coffee industry. An optimum allocation of scarce resources (and hence an optimum development program) requires that factors of production move to those activities that have the highest return. Furthermore, since the resources used by the coffee industry are quite small compared to the total resources of the country, and since coffee does not compete significantly for factors of production with other export commodities, the goal of diversification will not be achieved by attempting to curtail the flow of factors of production to the coffee industry. In fact, no attempt should be made to lower the supply of coffee since the country does not have surplus production problems. Indeed, as long as the domestic market for coffee grows, agricultural policies designed to increase production of coffee for sale to this market would increase contributions of the industry to national income.

At least in the short run, the development projects chosen (with the possible exception of the national range development program) seem to have weak prospects for diversifying the export base. In the short run, the country probably has a better prospect of diversifying exports if resources from the diversification fund are used to expand the production for market of pulses and oilseeds. In the long run, an accelerated diversification of the export base and the development of the economy might be achieved better by a genuine campaign to increase marketed production of the other major export commodities through the increased construction of roads and through the design of other agricultural policies (including land reform) that will increase production above the consumption needs of farmers. The accelerated transformation of the economy would probably be served better by the facilitation of increased local and regional economic interaction than by any attempt to divert the use of scarce resources from one industrial sector to another.

Notes

1. For a detailed breakdown, see Ministry of Commerce and Industry, *Economic Progress of Ethiopia* (Addis Ababa, 1955), p. 90 (1945-52), and three reports put out by the Central Statistical Office: *Summary Report on Ethiopia's External Trade: 1953-1963* (Addis Ababa, 1963), pp. 13-16 (1953-62); *Statistical Abstract—1967 and 1968* (Addis Ababa, July 1969), pp. 103-7 (1963-66); and *Statistical Abstract—1970* (Addis Ababa, September 1971), pp. 98-102 (1967-69).
2. National Coffee Board of Ethiopia, *Coffee Processing Project* (Addis Ababa, June 1970), p. 2.
3. For more detail on the historical setting of coffee production in Ethiopia, see Teketel Haile-Mariam, op. cit., pp. 27-35.
4. Ministry of Commerce and Industry, *Excess Capacity in Manufacturing Industry in Ethiopia* (Addis Ababa, June 1970).
5. Central Statistical Office, "Draft Report on Rural Household and Consumption Survey: December 1966-June 1968" (unpublished report, Addis Ababa, January 1971).
6. Institute of Agricultural Research, *Report on Coffee Diversification* (Addis Ababa, September 1969), p. 28.

References

Awash Valley Authority of Ethiopia. *A Survey of the Bag Manufacturing Industry*. Addis Ababa, May 1967.

Bruno, M. "Domestic Resource Costs and Effective Protection: Clarification and Synthesis." *Journal of Political Economy* 80 (January-February 1972): 17-33.

Central Statistical Office. "Draft Report on Rural Household and Consumption Survey: December 1966-June 1968." Unpublished report, Addis Ababa, January 1971.

_____. *Report on the 1965 Survey of Cost of Production of Coffee*. Addis Ababa, 1966.

_____. *Report on a Survey of Welega Province, and 7 Other Volumes.* Addis Ababa, July 1970.

_____. *Statistical Abstract–1967 and 1968.* Addis Ababa, July 1969.

_____. *Statistical Abstract–1970.* Addis Ababa, September 1971.

_____. *Summary Report on Ethiopia's External Trade: 1953-1963.* Addis Ababa, 1963.

Dub Liben. *Main Features of the National Accounts Estimates of Ethiopia.* Addis Ababa, February 1970.

Hirschman, A. O. *The Strategy of Economic Development.* New Haven: Yale University Press, 1958.

Imperial Highway Authority. *Ethiopia: General Road Study.* Addis Ababa, November 1969.

Institute of Agricultural Research. *Report on Coffee Diversification.* Addis Ababa, September 1969.

Koomsa, Kebede. "Problems of Agricultural Tenancy in Ethiopia." *Seminar Proceedings on Agrarian Reform.* Addis Ababa, Ministry of Land Reform and Administration, 1970.

Krueger, A. O. "Some Economic Costs of Exchange Control: The Turkish Case." *Journal of Political Economy* 70 (October 1966): 466-80.

Ministry of Commerce and Industry. *Economic Progress of Ethiopia.* Addis Ababa, 1955.

_____. *Excess Capacity in Manufacturing Industry in Ethiopia.* Addis Ababa, June 1970.

National Bank of Ethiopia. *Quarterly Bulletin,* No. 18, Addis Ababa, June 1968.

_____. Quarterly Bulletin, No. 27. Addis Ababa, June 1971.

National Coffee Board of Ethiopia. *Coffee Processing Project.* Addis Ababa, June 1970.

_____. *The Story of the National Coffee Board of Ethiopia, 1957-1968.* Addis Ababa, July 1969.

_____. *Rules for Export of Coffee.* Addis Ababa, 1970.

Teketel, Haile-Mariam. *The Production, Marketing, and Economic Impact of Coffee in Ethiopia* (unpublished Ph.D. dissertation, Stanford, Calif.: Stanford University, 1973).

6

The Role of Cotton in Uganda's Economic Development

Valimohamed Jamal*

Uganda's economic development has been based largely on exports of two crops, cotton and coffee. Both of these crops were introduced into Uganda in the early years of the British Protectorate—cotton in 1904 and coffee a few years later. Until 1940, cotton completely dominated the Uganda economy. Its exports in most years provided 80 percent of export earnings, while coffee exports, though always second in importance, provided no more than 10 percent of the total. Cotton was grown in most areas of Uganda by a majority of the farmers, and hence it affected an overwhelming majority of the people. Coffee, on the other hand, was confined to European estates. With the emergence of peasant-grown robusta in Buganda in the 1940s, the scene changed. Coffee acreages expanded, and because of steep price increases in the early 1950s, coffee gained in importance and by the late 1950s surpassed cotton as Uganda's main export.

Even though cotton export earnings have recently been only about 40 percent of coffee earnings, cotton's importance in the Uganda economy is greater than shown by its export position for two reasons. First, cotton has given rise to significant linkages with local industries, which themselves are an important part of Uganda's manufacturing sector. Second, for farmers in the eastern and northern regions cotton remains the main and, in some instances, the only cash-earning activity, and in these regions cotton remains as dominant as ever. In spite of the recent development of the coffee industry, cotton is grown by many more farmers than is coffee and affects the lives of a greater share of Uganda's population.

The objective of this paper is to consider the role of cotton in Uganda's development. Several historical questions are also discussed: the major episodes in the expansion of cotton; the development of infrastructure that aided this expansion; the impact of cotton on the rural and urban sectors of the economy; and the historical importance of cotton incomes. Moreover, we consider recent impacts of cotton on development in Uganda: the modern organization of the cotton industry; the principal characteristics of the economy; and quantification of cotton's direct and indirect impacts.

*This paper is based on my dissertation, "The Role of Cotton and Coffee in Uganda's Economic Development." I should like to acknowledge funds for research provided by the Ford Foundation in connection with a wider study of rural development and structural transformation by Professors B. F. Johnston, W. J. Chancellor, and Peter Kilby.

Cotton in the Economy of Uganda, 1904-47

Expansion of Cotton Acreage

Cotton was introduced into an almost nonmonetized economy. The nineteenth century Arab trade had been conducted with chiefs who organized the collection of ivory and received most of the imported goods for their own personal use. The ten years of Indian trade preceding cotton cultivation, which came with the establishment of the British Protectorate, had affected a wider population. The Indians had begun to settle in the country and to trade directly with the farmers, exchanging cloth, hoes, beads, and so forth for local produce. The rupee had been introduced as the currency of the country and familiarity with money and what money could buy was increasing. The mass of the people, however, remained outside the exchange economy. In an attempt to draw the people into productive work to make the country economically viable, the government imposed a hut tax at a rate of Rs.3 (or Sh 4/-) per hut.[a] In the early years the government allowed the tax to be paid in kind, and the people responded with produce and livestock, which the government found difficult to dispose of.

With the completion of the Uganda Railway at the end of 1901, the possibilities of trade increased and many local products began to be exported. At about this time the government and the Uganda Company imported four tons of cotton seed. The seed was given to Baganda chiefs for distribution to farmers. The government was in effect making it possible for the people to pay the hut tax by exporting a commodity that was then in strong demand in England. Most people found cotton-growing a more acceptable means of earning money for the tax than having to subject themselves to employment in the public works department or on European estates.[b]

From Buganda the cotton frontier quickly moved outward to Busoga, where the climate and social factors were similar, and from there into Teso and rather less spectacularly into Lango in the northern region. The foundation of the industry was laid between the years 1913 and 1925. Acreages in these twelve years expanded elevenfold at an annual rate of growth of 22 percent (see Table 6-1). After 1925, the rate of growth slowed considerably. However, the industry was expanding from a wider base and the figures of acreage

---

[a]One effect of the hut tax was that it led to overcrowding because the Africans were reluctant to build new huts that might become subject to the hut tax. Partly for this reason and partly to widen the tax base, the form of taxation was changed in 1909-1910 to a poll tax levied on all adult African males at the rate of Rs. 3. Non-Africans paid no direct tax until 1919.

[b]Given the prices then being paid to farmers and average yields, a farmer would have to cultivate 0.2 acres to earn enough cash to pay the poll tax. This represents about 100 manhours of labor time. Wages were $1\frac{1}{3}$-2 pence per day, at which rate 40-60 days of labor would be required to pay the tax. These calculations apply to 1914. Data from *Blue Book*, 1914.

expansion were impressive; acreage expanded by 1.2 million acres between 1925 and 1938. Between 1938 and 1948 cotton acreages contracted sharply, mostly due to falling acreage in Buganda, where coffee was then becoming an important cash crop. Within a few years, however, cotton acreages had again reached their late 1930s levels and continued to expand thereafter as expansion in the Eastern and Northern regions counteracted the fall in Buganda. In recent years cotton acreages have stabilized around the 2 million mark.

The acreage distribution figures show that by 1913, the leading region in export cultivation was the Eastern region, i.e., the Busoga, Teso, and Bukedi districts. In 1913, the Easterners planted three-quarters of the cotton acreage in Uganda, and the Baganda accounted for just under a quarter. In this period the Eastern region had about 40 percent of Uganda's population and Buganda about 25 percent. Hence, per capita (or per family) acreages in the Eastern region were higher than the national average. Some rough estimates show that in 1914, acreage per family in the Eastern region was 0.38 against 0.18 in Buganda.[c] Thereafter, due to a faster rate of growth in Buganda, the Eastern region's share fell. By the early 1930s Buganda had caught up with average acreages in the Eastern region and by the late 1930s surpassed them, but Buganda's leading position in the cotton industry proved to be short-lived. In the 1940s Buganda cotton acreages declined sharply as a result of competition from coffee, and, after some recovery in 1948 and 1950, declined further in the 1950s and 1960s. In recent years Buganda has contained only 8 percent of Uganda's cotton acreage compared with 60 percent in the Eastern region and 25 percent in the Northern region.

Development of Infrastructure

Cotton cultivation in all areas—especially in the Eastern region—spread much faster than either the transport network or ginning capacity. The effect was to make the availability of labor a severe constraint in cotton cultivation because a great amount of labor was required to head-transport seed cotton. Lint makes up only one-third of the weight of seed cotton, and cotton seed could not be exported in this period because of high international transport costs. Farmers were in effect having to head-carry three pounds of seed cotton to sell one pound of lint. The problem was gradually solved as both the ginning industry and the transport network expanded. The ginning industry was developed first, and continual improvements were made in the transport system.

In the early years the ginning industry lagged behind cotton production, and even the capacity that existed was badly distributed. As a result, between 1907 and 1915 much cotton had to be exported unginned, especially from

---

[c]These figures imply that in 1914, Buganda farmers were growing just enough cotton to pay the poll tax. See footnote b.

the remote areas of the Eastern region. In 1910, only 60 percent of the crop could be ginned. Thereafter, ginning capacity expanded somewhat faster than cotton production, so that in 1913, 84 percent of the crop was ginned. After 1918 all the cotton crop was exported ginned. By that time the maldistribution of ginneries had also been corrected, as a result of the willingness of Indian ginners to push into the interior.[d]

Expansion of the road network had also lagged behind cotton acreages, especially in the Eastern region. In 1913, there were only 30 miles of all-weather roads in the Eastern region, while Buganda had over 300 miles of such roads. The Eastern region had to rely on railway and lake transport (on Lake Kioga), and long journeys had to be made transporting seed cotton to the steamer or to the train, or between steamer and train. Ox-carts helped to ease the burden somewhat, having been introduced into the Eastern region by Indian merchants around 1910.[e] The great boom in road building came in the 1920s. In 1919, a cotton export tax had been imposed which greatly widened the tax base and made available increased revenue, some of which was used for the development of the cotton industry.[f] The road network was greatly improved and extended in the 1920s. In 1920, there were 600 miles of all-weather roads and 800 miles of dry-weather roads for light cars. By 1934, in contrast, there were 1,024 miles of first-class roads and 880 miles of second- and third-class roads.

Trends in Output, Earnings, and Prices

Table 6-1 presents data on output and value of cotton exports. Cotton dominated Uganda's exports until the early 1950s; thereafter, coffee—both because of expanding quantity and increasing prices—bypassed cotton as Uganda's principal export. Before this change, cotton in most years accounted for 60-75 percent of the value of export earnings.

Broad trends in prices may be discerned in Table 6-1. In the 1920s and 1930s prices generally declined. The steepest price increase occurred between

---

[d]For the first decade in which cotton was grown in Uganda, the ginning industry had been the preserve of the Europeans. Indians then began to enter the industry to fulfill capacity needs, especially in the interior. By the mid-1920s there was excess capacity in the ginning industry, and in 1931 only 130 out of 194 ginneries were being worked.

[e]In 1914, a daily average of twelve ox carts used the Jinja-Iganga road, and nine used the Iganga-Mbale road. In comparison, there were 496 Africans with head-loads on Jinja-Iganga road and 561 on Iganga-Mbale road. Uganda, *Annual Report of the Public Works Department* (Entebbe: Government Printer, 1914).

[f]When the cotton export tax was imposed, its avowed objective was to provide funds for the cotton industry. In the first year, out of a total export tax of £47,227, £25,759 was earmarked for road construction, £5,778 for two cotton research stations, and £1,500 for cotton stores. *(Blue Book, 1921.)* In subsequent years, the revenue from the cotton export tax was credited to general revenue.

Table 6-1
Cotton Acreage and Exports, Uganda, 1905-70, Selected Years

	Acreage (000)	Quantity (000 bales)[a]	Value (000£)	F.O.B. price (Sh/100 lb)
1905		(56)	(235)	21
1913	50	26	254	49
1917	134	28	538	96
1920	162	47	1,210	166
1925	556	196	4,686	107
1933	1,071	295	2,682	45
1937	1,485	333	4,269	63
1940	1,268	300	3,760	62
1946	1,146	227	5,620	124
1948	1,037	170	7,458	214
1949	1,555	391	17,343	222
1950	1,629	339	16,698	240
1951	1,535	346	28,742	415
1952	1,514	380	29,954	396
1953	1,472	320	16,802	251
1956	1,586	364	19,285	256
1965	2,138	438	16,762	191
1969	2,084	291	12,548	216
1970	2,176	430	17,549	204

[a]A bale contains 400 lbs of lint. £=20 Uganda shillings here and throughout the chapter.
Sources: Data for early years from Uganda Protectorate, *Blue Book* (Entebbe: Government Printer). Other sources: Uganda, *Annual Report of the Department of Agriculture* (Entebbe: Government Printer); Colonial Office, *Report on Uganda* (London: HMSO); Kenya Colony and Uganda Protectorate, *Annual Trade Report of Kenya and Uganda* (Nairobi: Government Printer); Uganda, *Statistical Abstract* (Entebbe: Government Printer).

1938 and 1948 and helped to counteract the fall in output in those years. Movements in export prices and earnings assume greater meaning when they are compared with price movements of imports. Using the C.I.F. price of cotton cloth as a proxy for prices of all imports,[g] we find that when export prices

[g]This is a simplifying assumption we make in the absence of official price series. Based on visual inspection there is close correspondence between prices of imported cloth and prices of other imported goods. This and the fact that cotton cloth formed a large proportion of total imports and of Africans' budgets makes cloth prices a suitable proxy for our purposes. The discussion in the text is based on the following indices:

	1914	1927	1937	1947
Lint F.O.B. price	100	156	91	274
Cotton cloth C.I.F. price	100	234	86	586
Lint output	100	378	888	523

Sources: *Annual Trade Report, Blue Book, Annual Report of the Department of Agriculture,* relevant years.

rose, import prices rose even more; when export prices fell, import prices fell to an even greater extent. As a result the apparently unfavorable years between 1925 and 1938 were, in fact, very favorable. Between these years F.O.B. prices declined by 42 percent, but C.I.F. price of cloth declined by 63 percent. The period around 1937 was also the peak period for cotton production so that in terms of real income the late 1930s were prosperous years for Uganda. In contrast, between 1937 and 1947 F.O.B. price rose threefold, while import prices increased almost sevenfold; at the same time cotton acreage and output fell catastrophically, and the late 1940s were extremely unfavorable years for Uganda.

Historical Development of the Ugandan Economy

Economic development in Uganda, while based on export crops grown by small-holder farmers, was similar to that of a plantation economy. Division of labor followed racial lines: Africans provided the labor, willingly or unwillingly, and Asians and Europeans provided the capital, skills, and entrepreneurship. The disparities in incomes were as acute as in any plantation economy with the same differences in consumption patterns.

The pattern of development in Uganda can be characterized as the grafting of a modern economy on a traditional economy. In the modern economy— comprising commerce, industry, and government—imported factors of production combined with local labor to produce largely new goods and services. In the traditional economy, the traditional factors of production combined with imported hoes to produce the same array of food crops and crafts and, with some reallocation of labor time, cotton. The successful adoption of cotton was facilitated because the crop fitted well with the traditional forms of agriculture.

The impact of development on traditional crafts was varied. Of the prominent crafts extant in the economy, bark-cloth making and iron smelting declined due to competition from imports; pottery, and basket and mat making, on the other hand, experienced a positive impact as a result of new demand from the modern sector.

By and large, there was no disruption of the traditional economy—either agricultural or nonagricultural. This should be regarded as a positive factor. However, the traditional economy was left to develop very much on its own and the positive impact on it was slight or non-existent. The demands for new skills were satisfied by Indian *fundis* (artisans); exports and imports were handled by the Indian *duka-wallahs* (traders); accounts in the ginnery and *duka* were kept by Indian bookkeepers. Having come with an advantage in skills required by a modern economy, the Indians monopolized these skills.[h]

---

[h]It happened that the Ugandan economy developed on a racially based division of labor, but it may be conjectured that similar urban-modern-rural-traditional disparities would have come about regardless of who controlled the modern sector.

Development in Towns

The most significant development in the Ugandan economy occurred in the towns and most prominently, until 1950, in Kampala. Although the prosperity of Uganda clearly depended on numerous cotton growers spread over a wide area, its wealth was concentrated in a few hands in the main towns. Through them crops were exported and imports channeled to the mass of cotton growers. And when final demand industries began to be established, they catered to the needs of the expatriate communities.

In 1903, there were nine industrial establishments in the country (four ginneries, one cotton-baling press, two soft drink plants, one *jaggery* (crude sugar) mill, and one dairy)—all in Buganda and six in Kampala alone.[1] In 1911, there were twenty-four establishments and the list is indicative of the direction in which the country was progressing.[i] Within the next two years several traditional Indian artisan industries were established including carpenters, smiths (gold, silver, and iron), and shoemakers. Along with ginneries, several small-scale industries—watermills and handmills to make flour, oil presses, and tanneries—spread into the rural areas to process local produce.

Some of these industries—ginneries, coffee hulleries, and to some extent the jaggery mills—were export-oriented. Other plants catered to local demand which, by and large, at this time came from the expatriate communities. In the 1920s two significant import-substituting industries were established: the sugar plantation factories of Mehta and Madhvani, and the cigarette- and tobacco-manufacturing plant of the British American Tobacco Company. These large-scale factories were perhaps the first industries which specifically catered to the African market.[j]

By 1945, the manufacturing sector had become as important as agriculture as an employer of wage labor. There were then 546 establishments in the manufacturing sector, including 194 ginneries; 60 saw mills and furniture factories; 63 processing plants for coffee, sugar, rubber, and tea; 37 auto repair shops; 37 flour and oil mills; 11 soft drink plants; and 5 soap factories.

Importance of Cotton Incomes in Early Development[2]

How important were cotton incomes in generating growth in the Uganda economy? For the period before 1950, the lack of national income estimates

---

[i]Industries in 1911 included:

6 Ginneries	2 Soft drink plants	4 Sawmills	1 Government printery
1 Baling press	1 Dairy	2 Coffee pulpers	1 Lemon distillery
2 Jaggery mills	1 Oil press	2 Brickworks	1 Motor workshop

[j]On average, each of the million or so African families consumed about 10 pounds of sugar and 1 pound of tobacco per annum. In aggregate this provided sufficient demand for the establishment of these industries.

precludes a definitive answer, but available data clearly show the preponderant place of cotton in Uganda in the early period. In generating foreign exchange, money income for Africans, and tax revenues, cotton played an important role. In 1937, incomes of cotton farmers were five times as great as wages of African employees; cotton exports provided 82 percent of foreign exchange; and revenues from cotton incomes provided 33 percent of central government revenues. In all these respects cotton's predominance continued until the early 1950s. Cotton incomes remained of great importance in stimulating distribution and local manufacturing industries especially, since the bulk of cotton incomes accrued to farmers whose expenditures were confined to necessities that could be locally manufactured. Over 40 percent of the expenditure of a typical cotton farmer was on cotton textiles, whose local manufacture was established in 1957. Next in importance were tobacco and sugar, both of which were supplied from local industries beginning in the early 1930s.[k]

One aspect of the colonial economy which adversely affected establishment of local industries was great inequality in the distribution of income; moreover, the inequality was further aggravated by regressive taxation. Cotton industry statistics illustrate these points. In 1937, total cotton exports (lint and seed) amounted to £4,661,000. Deducting the cost of marketing and ginning, around £3,661,000 was available for local distribution. The government received £133,000 in export duty, 800,000 farmers received £2,913,000, and 143 ginners received £600,000. Out of their incomes farmers paid an estimated £495,000 poll tax and £266,000 in local taxes—a rate of taxation of 26 percent. In contrast, the total income tax collected from *all* non-Africans (i.e., ginners, nonginner Asians, and Europeans) was £30,000, which as a proportion of ginning profits works out to just 5 percent.

The total taxes collected from cotton incomes (export tax and poll tax) contributed 40 percent of government revenues in 1927 and 33 percent in 1937, and Africans paid other taxes as well.[l] But while providing the bulk of government revenues, Africans received much less than their share of benefits from government expenditure. For example, in 1937, the number of persons per government hospital bed was: European, 62; Asian, 336; African, 2,769. In 1927, the government spent 3.7 percent of total revenue on African education which amounted to Sh 4/27 cts per African child attending school; by contrast, expenditure per Indian child amounted to Sh 82/30 cts; European children attended school in Kenya and Britain with some financial assistance from the government.

Two points emerge clearly. Until the late 1940s cotton incomes were the major part of the Ugandan monetary economy; to Africans cotton provided

---

[k]Indications of patterns of consumption in the foregoing paragraph are based on typical budgets of cotton farmers compiled by the author. See also footnote j.

[l]Customs and excise taxes contributed a further 34 percent in 1937—60 percent of it coming from Africans.

the most important, and in a majority of cases, the only means of earning cash. And within the Ugandan cotton industry as in the economy at large, great disparities in incomes existed; these were further aggravated by the system of taxation.

Diversification of the Ugandan economy led to a gradual reduction in the importance of cotton. The decline of cotton's role accelerated after 1955 with the rise of the coffee industry.

The Recent Role of Cotton in the Ugandan Economy

The Economy of Uganda

Uganda is a poor country by any standards. In 1969, Gross Domestic Product per capita amounted to £39. Nearly one-third of this was the value of subsistence consumption, so that monetary per capita income was £27. There are wide disparities on racial and occupational lines. The average African wage was £154, and the average Asian wage, £803. Cotton and coffee farmers, on the other hand, were at the lower end of the income distribution scale; cotton farmers on average earned around £15, and coffee farmers, £35.[m]

Growth in the economy has been steady if unspectacular. At current prices, the rate of growth of monetary GDP between 1963 and 1969 was 8.5 percent per annum. In real terms, growth amounted to 5.4 percent per annum, and to 1.6 percent per capita per annum. For the average person, this has meant a growth in real income of £2 during the period.

The relatively poor performance of the economy can in some degree be attributed to poor performance of cotton and coffee export earnings. Between 1963 and 1969 monetary GDP in current terms increased by around 75 percent; in the same years the value of cotton exports fell by 12 percent, while the value of coffee exports increased by 42 percent. Cotton and coffee together now form no more than 20 percent of monetary GDP; nevertheless, since many local industries and businesses are dependent on cotton and coffee incomes, the two exports still have a much wider overall impact on the Uganda economy.

Sectoral breakdown of GDP is typical of most LDCs. Agriculture dominates the economy with 32 percent of monetary GDP, followed by miscellaneous services (27 percent) and commerce (18 percent). The manufacturing sector is still comparatively small (11 percent). In keeping with the poor

---

[m]These again are average figures, and wide disparities exist among cotton and coffee farmers. It may be noted that figures are not on a strictly comparable basis. We are comparing monetary incomes, which, for wage-earners, was their only income, whereas the farmers also had subsistence income, which would boost their real income. The farmers' income figures are per holder or per family, whereas the wage figures are per wage-earner.

performance of the economy, sectoral shares have changed little between 1963 and 1969.

In Table 6-2 we give some indications of the place of cotton in the economy, and for comparison we also provide figures for coffee. It is estimated that the number of owners of cotton-growing farms equals 44 percent of the number of adult Ugandan males and that there is an average of 1.75 adult males per farm; cotton therefore employs nearly 80 percent of Uganda's adult males. Cotton is much more dispersed geographically than coffee, which is confined to Buganda (robusta) and Bugisu (arabica). In all areas where cotton is grown, except Buganda, cotton is the main, and in some instances the only, cash-earning activity available to the farmers; it thus affects the fortunes of a great majority of the people.

Cotton exports in recent years have been about 40 percent of coffee exports, and have provided in recent years just over 20 percent of foreign exchange. They form about a fifth of the value of monetary agriculture and 6 percent of monetary GDP.

Organization of the Cotton Industry[3]

The cotton industry comprises the growers, the ginners, and the marketing board. The growers are the most important part of the industry and receive the largest part of cotton incomes.

Most growers operate rather small farms—less than five acres, of which a quarter to a third may be devoted to cotton or coffee and the rest to several food crops of which millets dominate in the North and plantain in the South. Apart from these two food crops, which are regionally specialized, there are normally six to eight other food crops which are grown on most farms in all areas. These include the root crops—cassava and sweet potatoes—and a variety of pulses and oil seeds.

On a typical cotton farm 1½ acres of cotton are grown, usually interplanted with food crops. In the Eastern and Northern regions, which are the two most important cotton areas, rather larger acreages of cotton are grown. In most areas the bulk of the cotton crop is planted in June and July. In Teso, because of the use of the ox-plough, farmers manage to plant their cotton earlier. The Department of Agriculture recommends that cotton be planted by mid-June, since late planting results in a loss in yields. Farmers often do not meet this deadline because at this time they are also engaged in planting their food crops.

Few inputs are used in agriculture. The commonest tool is the hoe which is used in preparing land, planting, and weeding. The ox-plough has long been used by the Iteso, enabling them to cultivate significantly larger acreages than the average Ugandan farmer. But even in Teso, few other ox-drawn implements

Table 6–2
Place of Cotton and Coffee in the Ugandan Economy, Recent Years

	Year	Cotton	Coffee (robusta and arabica)
Acreage ('000)	1969	2,111	703
Total cultivated area (%)	1969	16	5.6
Holders ('000)	1969	875	675
Holders/Males 20-64 years (%)	1969	44	34
Total exports ('000£)	1967-69 (Average)	14,164	35,285
All exports (%)	1967-69	21.3	54.7
Monetary agriculture (%)	1967-69	13.1	49.2
Monetary GDP (%)	1967-69	6.0	15.5
Total GDP (%)	1967-69	4.2	10.8

Sources: From Uganda, *Statistical Abstract, 1971,* (Entebbe: Government Printer, n.d.), except number of cotton and coffee holders which were projected from figures given in Uganda, Ministry of Agriculture and Co-operatives, *Report on Uganda Census of Agriculture vols 1-4* (Entebbe: Government Printer, 1965). The *Census* estimated that there were 738,000 cotton growers and 496,000 robusta growers in 1963-64. These figures were projected at roughly 3 percent per annum. An estimated 90,000 arabica growers have been included in the total for coffee growers. Export figures and the related proportions are averages for 1967, 1968, and 1969.

have been adopted. Chemical inputs—pesticides and fertilizers—are very seldom used. Paid labor is also rarely employed except at peak times to weed the cotton and coffee plots. This labor is mostly paid for in kind in the non-Buganda regions.

Cotton is harvested in November and December. It is then sold to local cooperatives for bulking and transport to the ginneries. The ginneries operate for five months following the harvest. During this time they employ over seven thousand workers who are laid off at the end of the ginning season. Most jobs at a ginnery are unskilled, and the seasonality of the industry perpetuates its low skill syndrome.

The ginneries are now all owned by cooperatives. With the cooperative take-over, ginnery numbers fell from 130 in 1965-66 to 53 in 1970-71. This decline came about partly because there was excess capacity in the industry, especially in Buganda; the cooperatives phased out some ginneries to bring capacity into line with regional seed cotton output. Some ginneries, however, were simply legislated out of existence in order to avoid paying compensation. As a result there is now a shortage of ginning capacity, and there are plans in the third five-year plan period to build up the ginning industry.

Ginneries act as agents of the Lint Marketing Board (LMB). The LMB pays ginners for lint and seed according to a cost-plus formula with some allowance for quality of the lint produced. Lint and seed are sold at auctions in Kampala to licensed exporters, of whom there are normally fifteen. Some lint may be exported directly by the Lint Marketing Board, as in the case of exports to China and Eastern bloc countries. Seed not retained for re-planting is sold to oil mills.

Present-day Impacts

Direct Impact.   In Table 6-3 the gross output of the cotton industry for 1969 is divided into value added and intermediate inputs. The year 1969 was fairly typical of the recent period in terms of quantity (about 425,000 bales) and F.O.B. price (Sh 200/- per 100 lb lint, F.O.B. Mombasa), and hence these results are quite representative.

Several significant characteristics of the cotton industry reflect the fact that the industry is dominated by small-scale peasant growers. First, inter-mediate inputs form only 16 percent of the gross output of the industry. As a result, the backward linkages are small in relation to the incomes generated by cotton, though they may be sufficient to provide a market for local supply industries. Second, the industry is a meager user of imported inputs; nearly 90 percent of export income is net foreign exchange. Third, wages—growers' payments, ginnery, and LMB workers' wages—dominate the cost structure with 64 percent of gross output. Of these, payments to growers are the most im-portant, constituting 58 percent of gross output. (See also Table 6-4.) Finally, the government receives a sizeable part of cotton incomes in taxes, mostly from the cotton export tax.

To give some perspective to the figures we have derived, we provide some comparisons with other components of GDP. Value added by cotton amounted to £16m, contributing 6.1 percent to monetary GDP. Payments to cotton growers amounted to £12m, an average of £15 per grower; in comparison African wage-earners received £44.5m, an average of £154 per worker.

Value added consists of the income that accrues to factors of production in the export industry. However, not all of this income can be regarded as net addition to the economy. If labor and capital could have earned as much in alternative uses as in the cotton industry, there is no net gain to the economy. This requires that we consider the opportunity costs of factors of production, and in the following paragraphs we present arguments that enable us to get some notion of these opportunity costs. We also present alternative calculations of the domestic resource cost (DRC) ratio. We first assume that the social opportunity cost (SOC) of each factor is equal to its market price (MP); we then make a second calculation in which some SOCs are varied to test the sensitivity of our results.

Payments to labor, primarily to cotton farmers, make up 64 percent of the costs of the cotton industry and therefore assumptions that we make about the

Table 6-3
Local and Foreign Payments in the Cotton Industry, Uganda, 1969
(items as percentage of gross output of cotton)

| | | Percentage breakdown of costs between local and foreign components | | | |
| | | First round | | Second round | |
	(1) *Total*	*(2)* *Local*	*(3)* *Foreign*	*(4)* *Local*	*(5)* *Foreign*
Intermediate inputs					
Electricity, water	0.4	0.4	–	0.3	0.1
Packing materials	2.2	0.5	1.8	0.3	1.9
Tools	4.3	2.0	2.3	1.2	3.1
Services	5.1	4.7	0.4	3.9	1.2
Other inputs	3.7	2.0	1.7	0.8	2.9
Total	15.7	9.5	6.2	6.5	9.1
(£, thousands)	2,966	1,793	1,174	1,236	1,731
Value-added					
Wages	63.9	63.9	–	63.9	–
Interest	1.7	1.7	–	1.7	–
Depreciation	1.8	0.5	1.3	0.5	1.3
Profit	5.5	5.5	–	5.5	–
Government Tax	11.5	11.5	–	11.5	–
Total	84.3	83.0	1.3	83.0	1.3
(£, thousands)	15,976	15,740	237	15,740	237
Total, inputs and value-added (= gross output)	100	92.6	7.4	89.6	10.4
(£, thousands)	18,943	17,532	1,411	16,975	1,968

Sources: Based on Uganda, Statistics Division, Ministry of Finance, Planning and Economic Development, *Survey of Industrial Production, 1969* (Entebbe: Government Printer, 1972); Lint Marketing Board *Annual Report 1969* (Kampala: n.d.); East African Community, East African Customs and Excise, *Annual Trade Report of Tanganyika, Uganda and Kenya, 1969* (Mombasa: East African Customs and Excise Department, 1970); and, estimates derived from author's own survey of cotton farmers and cotton-related industries. Steps involved in derivation were as follows:

1. Leontief production functions (i.e., cost columns, similar to column (1)) were first derived for growers, ginners and Lint Marketing Board. Growers' column was based on aggregation from own survey and *Trade Reports*. Ginners' column was based on *Survey of Industrial Production* and *LMB Reports*. LMB column on *LMB Reports*.

2. The three columns were consolidated into a single column representing the production function of the cotton industry. The breakdown was similar to column (1) except that inputs initially were valued *as purchased,* i.e., distribution costs had not been subtracted.

3. Distribution costs were subtracted to obtain local inputs at ex-factory prices, and imports at C.I.F. In most cases a markup of 20 percent on ex-factory and C.I.F. prices was assumed. Distribution costs after being netted out from inputs were included with other services—repairs, LMB international fees (the first-round foreign component of services). This gives us column (1).

4. Inputs were broken down into local and foreign components. The *Survey of Industrial Production* does not give inputs according to source. Knowing the industrial structure

in Uganda, however, it was comparatively easy to identify local inputs—electricity and water, of course, baling hoops, hoes, etc. The results were confirmed with past ginnery owners. This gives us columns (2) and (3).

5. Local inputs were further broken down into *their* local and foreign components. This was done using cost structures of supply industries. This gives us columns (4) and (5) where column (5) contains direct and indirect foreign inputs.

opportunity cost of growers' labor have a sizeable impact on net gain calculations We contend that there is little or no divergence between the SOC and the very low MP for cotton farmers of £15 per family per annum (compared to a minimum yearly wage in the modern sector of £90). In our alternative calculation we set SOC = 0.8MP. There is greater room for question as to whether ginnery and LMB workers have SOCs equal to the wages they command. In our alternative calculation we set SOC = 0.5MP for these workers.

There is an element of rent in ginning profits insofar as ginners are paid a premium for quality which is unrelated to cost. Ginners on average may receive 5 to 7 cents per pound as a premium. Calculating at 6 cents per pound, we may regard £510,000 as rent. (The £2.2m received by government in the form of export taxes may also be regarded as economic rent, and these rents together constitute net gain when all SOCs equal corresponding MPs. See Table 6-4.) Remaining profits of £534,000 constitute a factor payment for the services of the ginners, who are assumed in both calculations to have a SOC equal to MP. Depreciation and interest costs are also assumed to accurately reflect SOCs, and foreign costs are simply subtracted from gross foreign exchange earnings.

For local intermediate inputs, we set SOC = 0.7MP in our alternative calculation to correct for any overvaluation in their wage components.

Table 6-4 presents the two sets of calculations. Assuming no divergences between SOCs and MPs, a positive net gain of £2.7m arises from economic rent, as noted above. Net gain from cotton would be £5.8m if all of the lower SOCs assumed in our alternative case were in fact true reflections of factor costs. The true net gain from cotton almost certainly falls between these alternative estimates.

The efficiency of the export industry as a foreign exchange earner may be calculated using the DRC, domestic resource cost per unit of foreign exchange earned. In calculating the DRC, we shall assume that all of the cotton-industry output is either exported or substituted for imports on a one-to-one basis. The DRC for the cotton industry is less than the exchange rate in each set of calculations, implying that the cotton industry is an efficient earner of foreign exchange. The relative efficiency of the industry in earning foreign exchange may be judged by expressing DRC as a percentage of the exchange rate. To earn a dollar by growing cotton requires 16 to 34 percent fewer resources than shown by the exchange rate.

Table 6-4

Domestic Resource Costs and DRC Calculations for Cotton Industry, Uganda, 1969

	Domestic Resource Costs (£000)		
		Assumptions about SOC	
	No divergences between SOC and MP	SOC equal to a stated proportion (in parentheses) of MP	
Growers' receipts	11,018	(0.8)	8,814
Ginnery wages	488	(0.5)	244
LMB wages	598	(0.5)	299
Profit	534	(1.0)	534
Local inputs	1,236	(0.7)	865
Interest and depreciation	420	(1.0)	420
Total domestic costs	14,294		11,176
Net foreign exchange	16,975		16,975
Net gain	2,681		5,799
DRC Calculations—Exchange Rate (Sh per $) = 7.14			
Net foreign exchange (000$)	47,549		47,549
Domestic costs (000 Sh)	285,880		223,520
DRC (Sh per $)	6.01		4.70
DRC ÷ exchange rate (%)	84.2		65.8

Source: From data of Table 6-3.

Cotton and Linked Industries.   Industries related to cotton have long been an important part of Uganda's industrial scene. As noted above, some of the first factories in Uganda were ginneries. After World War II, many oil mills were established to crush cotton seed. In recent years a cotton textile industry has been established in Uganda serving the whole East African market. In this section we analyze the contribution of these cotton-related industries to development.

The cotton industry purchases an important part of agricultural tools, baling hoops, and tins and drums. These backward-linked industries could not survive without the market provided by the cotton industry. Since the cotton industry is dominated by growers, however, backward linkages are limited. Only 8 percent of the output of the growers is represented by intermediate inputs. Of these the main item is hoes, which are now locally produced. For the entire industry (growers, ginners, and marketing board) intermediate inputs are somewhat more important, comprising 17 percent of gross output.

Several important inputs—agricultural tools, baling hoops, and gunny bags—comprising 5 percent of the output of the cotton industry are now locally produced.

As for forward linkages, the oil mill industry is clearly an offshoot of the cotton industry; its purchases of cotton seed amount to 60 percent of its output. For textiles, inputs of lint represent 26 percent of total output. The importance of cotton products to these industries shows up even more in a ratio expressing purchases from the cotton industry as a percent of intermediate inputs. For textiles this ratio is 52 percent and for oil mills, 72 percent.

There are some additional interindustry flows between cotton and other industries which may be mentioned. The baling hoop industry is an offshoot of the steel-rolling mill at Jinja, which itself supplies a small proportion of the steel flats used by the hoe industry. A small part of the oil-industry output consists of soap stock used in the manufacture of soap. A small part of the by-product of the oil industry, cake, is used in the manufacture of animal feeds. The textile industry produces yarn, which is used in knitting mills, and some of its waste is used in the manufacture of blankets.

In Table 6-5 we present the most important indicators of the impact of cotton and related industries. These industries are a fairly important part of the industrial sector. Around 25 percent of industrial gross output, employment and wages, and just over 20 percent of value added are concentrated in these industries. The textile industry by itself is a sizeable part of the industrial scene with 12.5 percent of value added and 13.9 percent of employment.

Expenditure Linkages. As we have seen previously (Table 6-3) 83 percent of the gross output from cotton is paid to factors of production within Uganda—58 percent of this total going to growers. The consumption pattern of cotton growers thus has an important bearing on the stimulation of other economic activities.

A survey of fifty cotton farmers was carried out by the author in the eastern region of Uganda to ascertain expenditure patterns. Farmers spent only about 10 percent of their income on imports, a large part of their income being spent on necessities locally produced. Eleven percent of their income was spent on farm inputs; one-third were modern industry inputs, the rest being supplied from within the traditional sector. The highest proportion of income—29 percent—was spent on food, notably meat, sugar, oil, and bread. Traditional foods like millet, sorghum, beans, and roots did not figure to any great extent in food purchases except at pre-harvest shortage periods, because most farmers grew most of their requirements of these foods. The survey results were aggregated according to the origin of goods and showed that 36 percent of income was spent within the rural areas on such items as meat, baskets, services, and social ceremonies; 30 percent on locally manufactured industrial goods; 10 percent on imported goods; 12 percent went to pay taxes; and 8 percent to pay for health services and education.

Table 6–5
The Place of Cotton and Linked Industries in Uganda's Manufacturing Sector, 1969

	Economic indicators of cotton and linked industries					
	Ginning	Cotton textiles	Cotton seed oil milling	Agricultural tools	Total	All manufacturing
Gross output (000£)	15,394	6,743	4,350	465	26,952	108,107
Value-added (000£)	1,409	3,056	326	186	4,977	24,414
Salaries and wages (000£)	474	1,694	200	41	2,409	9,432
Employment	5,089	6,343	1,218	118	12,768	45,778
Shares of cotton and linked industries in total manufacturing (items as percentage of all manufacturing)						
Gross output	14.2	6.2	4.0	0.4	24.9	100
Value-added	5.8	12.5	1.3	0.8	20.3	100
Salaries and wages	5.0	18.0	2.1	0.4	25.5	100
Employment	11.1	13.9	2.7	0.3	27.9	100

Sources: Derived from Uganda, Statistics Division, Ministry of Finance, Planning and Economic Development, *Survey of Industrial Production, 1969* (Entebbe: Government Printer, 1972). Estimates had to be made of certain magnitudes for two reasons. (1) Industries in which there are less than three firms are aggregated with other industries to avoid divulging confidential information. In our case, cotton textile industry was reported along with blankets and rayon textile industries; agriculture tools industry was reported with other metal industries. (2) Oil mills crush groundnuts besides cotton seed, and also undertake flour milling, etc. To overcome these problems, estimates were derived as follows:

1. *Cotton textiles.* Gross output and employment obtained from appendix tables of *Survey of Industrial Production.* Value-added and wages were then estimated assuming that share of cotton textiles in value-added and wages in the composite industry (cotton textiles + blankets + rayon textiles) was the same (90 percent) as its share of gross output.

2. *Agriculture Tools.* From appendix tables of the *Survey* relating to industry 3811.

3. *Oil milling.* The survey statistics include grain milling since many oil mills also operate grain mills. Estimates were made of economic indicators relating to grain milling only and subtracted. Secondly, adjustments were made to relate figures to cotton seed oil only. To give an indication of adjustments required, noncotton oil and grain milling output comprised under 15 percent of gross output of oil industry. The other economic indicators were correspondingly scaled down by the same proportion.

An important question for the development of local industry is the percentage of the local consumer goods output absorbed by cotton incomes. We have estimated that 30 percent of cotton incomes—about £3.6m in 1969—went to purchase local industrial goods. Compared to this the total market for locally manufactured consumer goods was £40m, and hence cotton incomes provided 9 percent of this market. Cotton incomes accounted for approximately 5 percent of consumer imports and 7 percent of total consumer goods. These proportions can be compared with the 4.6 percent share of growers' cotton incomes in monetary GDP.[n]

An important question is the extent to which expenditures out of export incomes provide a stimulus for rural development, and thus bring about a more equitable distribution of income and provide a wider base for further development. As noted above, farmers spend around 36 percent of their income on rural goods and services—baskets and pots, meat, furniture, tailoring services, and bicycle repair being some of the main items. Most of these goods and services are supplied by nonspecialists. Division of labor remains very rudimentary. There is as yet little division of labor between agriculturists and non-agriculturists; and there is no division of labor between export-oriented agriculturists and food agriculturists. The result is that the process of income generation is short-circuited beyond the second round. Farmers purchase meat, but cattle owners do not need to purchase food, and most of their incomes are expended on nonrural goods. Cotton incomes leak out of rural areas by the second or third round of expenditures. This process occurring over a number of years has resulted in great geographical disparities. Most economic activities are concentrated in two urban areas—Kampala and its suburbs, and Jinja-Kakira. They account for 68 percent of gross industrial output, 56 percent of the total African wage bill, 37 percent of licensed traders, and 34 percent of total sales. All the sectors which comprise monetary GDP—government, transport, electricity, manufacturing industry—are concentrated in these two areas.

There is no doubt that economic dualism has increased in recent years. Industries continue to locate at Kampala or Jinja. The impact of the Ugandanization policy was to further increase this dualism, for as Indian *dukawallahs* and *fundis* were confined to larger towns, they left a vacuum in the rural areas.

Summary and Conclusion

Uganda's economic history has run through two phases. In the first phase, lasting until the late 1940s, cotton reigned supreme, providing the largest share

---

[n]It should be emphasized that our estimates relate to cotton incomes only. Cotton farmers also receive other incomes, and the quantity of consumer goods absorbed by cotton farmers is correspondingly increased.

of export earnings and money incomes. In the second phase, covering the last quarter century, cotton began to be relegated to a less important position, first by coffee and then by wages in the modern sector. At present cotton ranks third after wage employment and coffee as a generator of income for Africans. Directly, cotton accounts for 6 percent of monetary GDP, and indirectly through linked industries it contributes perhaps an additional 6 percent.[o] In the third five-year plan, 1972-76, cotton output is targeted to expand from approximately 0.4 million to at least 0.6 million bales annually. Coffee production, on the other hand, will not be increased and may even be cut down due to market limitations. Hence, the role of cotton in the Ugandan economy is assured and may in fact be enhanced in the future.

Notes

1. These data and what follow are from *Blue Book* of the relevant years. *Blue Book* information includes name of industry, name of owner and location.

2. The statistical data in the following sections are based on Colonial Office, *Report on Uganda* (London: HMSO, relevant years); Harris, Sir Douglas, *Development in Uganda, 1947 to 1955-56* (Wisbech, England: Balding and Mansell Limited, n.d.); Lord Hailey, *Native Administration in the British African Territories Part I, East Africa: Uganda, Kenya, Tanganyika* (London: HMSO, 1950); and Uganda Protectorate, *Report of the Cotton Commission, 1938* (Entebbe: Government Printer, 1939).

3. The discussion relating to farmers is based on Uganda Government, Ministry of Agriculture and Co-operatives, *Report on Uganda Census of Agriculture, vols. 1-4* (Entebbe: Government Printer, 1965). The census was carried out in 1963-64, but the data are considered applicable to the present period.

References

Colonial Office. *Report on Uganda.* London: HMSO.

East African Community, East African Customs and Excise. *Annual Trade Report of Tanganyika, Uganda and Kenya.* Mombasa: East African Customs and Excise Department.

---

[o]Forward- and backward-linked industries were 14 percent of manufacturing GDP, which itself was 14 percent of monetary GDP; hence, contribution of linked industries was 2 percent. Of the consumer goods market, 25 percent was attributed directly to cotton incomes, and consumer goods industries form about one-half of local industries, i.e., 7 percent of monetary GDP; hence, the contribution due to cotton expenditures was approximately 2 percent. The contribution of the service sector (in distributing inputs and consumer goods to the cotton industry and growers) can be estimated from the data of Table 6–3 and from the expenditure survey at £5m, again approximately 2 percent of monetary GDP.

Hailey, Lord. *Native Administration in the British African Territories Part I, East Africa: Uganda, Kenya, Tanganyika.* London: HMSO, 1950.

Harris, Sir Douglas. *Development in Uganda, 1947 to 1955-56.* Wisbech, England: Balding and Mansell Limited, n.d.

Lint Marketing Board. *Annual Report.* Kampala: n.d.

Uganda Government. *Statistical Abstract.* Entebbe: Government Printer.

_____ . Ministry of Agriculture and Co-operatives. *Report on Uganda Census of Agriculture vols 1-4.* Entebbe: Government Printer, 1965.

_____ . Statistics Division, Ministry of Finance, Planning and Economic Development. *Survey of Industrial Production.* Entebbe: Government Printer.

_____ . *Uganda's Plan III, Third Five-Year Development Plan, 1971/72-1976/77.* Entebbe: Government Printer.

_____ . *Blue Book.* Entebbe: Government Printer.

_____ . *Annual Report of the Department of Agriculture.* Entebbe: Government Printer.

_____ . Ministry of Commerce, Industry and Tourism. *Manufacturing Industry of Uganda in Figures, 1969 and 1970.* Kampala: 1971 (unpublished).

_____ . *Annual Report of the Public Works Department.* Entebbe: Government Printer.

Uganda Protectorate. *Report of the Cotton Commission, 1938.* Entebbe: Government Printer, 1939.

7

Contributions of Petroleum to Nigerian Economic Development

Ronald K. Meyer and Scott R. Pearson*

In the short span of 15 years, the production of crude petroleum has risen from insignificance and has emerged as the leading activity in Nigerian economic development. Following a rapid expansion of output during the mid-1960s, the accelerating importance of oil in Nigeria was interrupted during the two and one-half years of the Nigerian civil war, but was renewed with vigor after the conflict ended in January 1970. The focus of this study is on the postwar role of oil and gas in the economy of Nigeria, partly because the developments of the 1960s have been analyzed elsewhere,[1] and partly because of the highly significant events that have taken place in the past three years. During this brief period, the output of petroleum has expanded to a level nearly three times its prewar peak, Nigeria has joined the Organization of Petroleum Exporting Countries (OPEC), the Nigerian government has followed the lead of the other OPEC countries and has successfully negotiated a doubling of the effective tax rate on oil exports, the Nigerian National Oil Corporation (NNOC) has been established and has taken equity participation in many petroleum companies operating in Nigeria, and important advances have been made in planning for the exploitation of Nigeria's large discoveries of natural gas. In the following discussion, we place these changes in historical perspective and show how they have influenced the contributions of petroleum to Nigerian economic development.

Trends in Nigerian Economic Development

Even before the discovery of petroleum in 1956, Nigeria had long benefited from rapidly growing exports. Between 1900 and 1929 the volume of exports—mainly palm produce, ground nuts, cocoa, rubber, and cotton—grew at an average annual rate of 5.5 percent.[2] Although relative economic stagnation set in during the Depression, after 1945 Nigerian economic growth again continued upward. The Gross Domestic Product (GDP) at factor cost in constant 1962 prices grew at annual rates of 4.1 percent between 1950 and 1957 and 5.7 percent between 1958 and 1966.[3] During the years of the Nigerian civil war, economic growth stagnated, both because of a forced cessation of production in the war-torn areas and because a large portion of government revenues was devoted to military

*The authors are grateful to Alan Logan for providing valuable information for this study.

expenditures. Following the resolution of the conflict, economic growth resumed rapidly, but the basis of this expansion was very different from that of prewar economic development. Although GDP at constant prices increased by nearly 10 percent in 1970-71 and 12 percent in 1971-72, almost all traditional exports suffered a decline in both volume and value.[4] Nigeria continues to enjoy the advantages of having varied and substantial natural resources and export products in addition to oil and gas, but economic growth has become increasingly dependent upon the production of petroleum.

Pattern of Ownership in the Nigerian Petroleum Industry

The search for petroleum in Nigeria began in 1908 when a German company, Nigerian Bitumen Corporation, drilled fourteen wells before ending operations with the outbreak of World War I. In 1937 a consortium of Royal Dutch/Shell and British Petroleum was formed to search for oil in Nigeria. Between 1938 and 1941 this consortium, later to become the Shell-BP Petroleum Development Company of Nigeria, carried out preliminary geological reconnaissance. After a five-year interruption caused by World War II, Shell-BP undertook a series of geophysical surveys between 1946 and 1951, and drilled its first wildcat well, a dry hole, in 1951. During the next four years, the company concentrated its efforts in the areas around the Niger delta, but made no discoveries. After shifting focus to the delta itself, Shell-BP made its first commercial strike in 1956 at Oloibiri. With this discovery Nigeria entered the international oil scene.

Even before Shell-BP started exporting oil from Port Harcourt in 1958, other companies were showing interest in Nigeria. Mobil carried out reconnaissance work in northwestern Nigeria in the 1950s and then shifted to the western coastal area between 1958 and 1961. Following Shell-BP's release of a portion of its original acreage, Tenneco, Gulf, Agip, Safrap, and later Phillips obtained onshore oil prospecting licenses. Additional onshore oil exploration licenses were later granted to Esso, Safrap, and Great Basins.[a]

In 1960, Nigeria divided its offshore continental shelf into twelve blocks of about 1,000 square miles each. Ten of these blocks were leased in 1961, one in 1964, one in 1967. Texas Overseas Petroleum made Nigeria's initial offshore discovery in 1963.

The Nigerian government issued in November 1969 new petroleum legislation which provides for government participation up to an agreed percentage in each prospecting license and mining lease if this participation is

---

[a]Oil exploration licenses (OELs) are valid for periods of one to two years and confer non-exclusive rights to make geological and geophysical studies, but not to drill for oil. Oil prospecting licenses (OPL's) are valid for four years with a one-year renewal option, involve an obligation on the part of the company to meet certain minimum drilling requirements, and grant exclusive rights for exploration and retention of oil discovered. Upon expiration, no more than one-half of an OPL can be converted into oil mining leases (OMLs) with the other half of the acreage reverting to the government.

considered to be in the public interest. In May 1971, the Nigerian government formed the Nigerian National Oil Corporation (NNOC) to engage in all phases of the petroleum industry's activities, from exploration to transporting and marketing.[5] NNOC may enter into contracts or partnerships in order to carry out its operations. All provisions relating to commercial petroleum licenses or leases also apply to the NNOC, except that there is no limit on the duration of its licenses and leases.

From the moment of its creation, NNOC had oil production of its own as a result of an agreement between the Nigerian government and Safrap, a French company. Safrap's initial requests to resume operations after the Nigerian civil war were refused, probably because of French support of the Biafran regime. Nevertheless, Safrap was allowed to produce again in May 1971, following NNOC's acquisition of a 35 percent interest in the company. This share is scheduled to increase to 50 percent if production reaches 400,000 barrels per day (b/d). In accord with an earlier agreement giving the Nigerian government a future option to take equity participation, NNOC also acquired a $33\frac{1}{3}$ percent share in the company owned jointly by Italy's state-owned AGIP and by Phillips. NNOC pays for both of these newly acquired equity holdings with its accruing revenues from crude oil production, thereby reimbursing Safrap and AGIP/Phillips for its shares of past and ongoing expenses.

In 1971 NNOC secured a 51 percent equity share in Occidental Petroleum's new offshore concession in Nigeria. If Occidental begins commercial production, NNOC will pay 51 percent of all applicable expenses and investments from the time of the agreement's signature. In return, Occidental has agreed to pay an initial bonus of £N2 million, plus further payments based on future production rates. Occidental will also market the government's share of production on a commission basis.[6] In addition to its majority share with Occidental, NNOC has concluded similar ownership agreements with Japan Petroleum, Henry Stephens and Sons, and Deminex/Niger Petroleum. NNOC's association with Henry Stephens and Sons is the Nigerian government's first joint venture with a private company that is 100 percent Nigerian-owned.

More importantly, in June 1973 Nigeria acquired a 35 percent interest in the operations of Shell-BP. Under the agreement, Nigeria's equity share will increase to 51 percent by 1982. Both NNOC and Shell-BP will direct the management of future investment and operations, and Nigeria will pay for its share on the basis of Shell-BP's updated book value in four semiannual installments.

Still to be established are association agreements with Gulf and Mobil, each of which has offered the government a 20 percent participation, and with Texaco/Chevron, Mobil/Tenneco/Sun DX, and Pan Ocean/Delta Oil. To date Gulf's and Mobil's offers have been turned down by government negotiators, who seek at least the 35 percent share received in other participation agreements.[7]

Table 7-1 contains a summary of the equity shares and affiliations of the companies operating in Nigeria at the beginning of 1973. No new oil concessions

Table 7-1
Petroleum Companies Operating in Nigeria, July 1973

Company	Equity share (%)	Affiliation
Nigerian Agip Oil	33.3	subsidiary of the Italian State Company, ENI
Phillips Oil (Nigeria)	33.3	subsidiary of Phillips Petroleum Company of United States
NNOC	33.3	Nigerian National Oil Company
Deminex	44	subsidiary of German oil consortium
NNOC	51	*
Niger Petroleum Company	5	Nigerian independent
Gulf Oil (Nigeria)	100	subsidiary of Gulf Oil Company of United States
Japan Petroleum (Nigeria)	49	Japanese consortium
NNOC	51	*
Japan Petroleum (Nigeria)	40	*
NNOC	51	*
Niger Oil Resources	9	Nigerian independent
Mobil Producing Nigeria	100	subsidiary of Mobil Oil Corporation of United States
Mobil Producing Nigeria	50	*
Tenneco Oil (Nigeria)	37.5	subsidiary of Tenneco Incorporated of United States
Sun DX Nigeria	12.5	subsidiary of Sun Oil Company of United States

Company	%	Description
Occidental Petroleum (Nigeria)	49	subsidiary of Occidental Petroleum Company of United States
NNOC	51	*
Pan Ocean Oil (Nigeria)	n.a.	subsidiary of Pan Ocean of United States
Delta Oil	n.a.	Nigerian independent
Safrap (Nigeria)	65	subsidiary of French Elf Erap group
NNOC	35	*
Shell (Nigeria)	32.5	subsidiary of Royal Dutch Shell of United Kingdom and Netherlands
British Petroleum (Nigeria)	32.5	British Petroleum Oil Company of United Kingdom
NNOC	35	*
Henry Stephens and Sons	49	Nigerian independent
NNOC	51	*
Texaco Overseas Petroleum (Nigeria)	50	subsidiary of Texaco of United States
Chevron Oil (Nigeria)	50	subsidiary of Standard Oil of California of United States

* listed elsewhere on table

n.a. not available

Source: *Annual Review of 1972–Nigeria*, March 1973

will be granted to any individual or company since all future concessions as well as any surrendered concessions will be vested in NNOC. However, NNOC is free to employ oil companies as contractors or minority partners in its own areas.

Financial Arrangements Facing the Nigerian Petroleum Industry

The basic fiscal terms for the petroleum companies were first established in the Petroleum Profits Tax Ordinance of 1959. (Although exact financial arrangements are specific to each individual company, several major financial provisions apply uniformly to all companies.) Under this law, a producing company applied its realized price (an internal company transfer price) to the volume of crude oil produced and exported in order to calculate royalties and profits taxes. In the calculation of taxes on profits, operating expenses and usable capital allowances were subtracted from gross proceeds to arrive at chargeable profits. Fifty percent of this amount was paid to the government. Royalties, rentals, and other minor taxes could be used to offset the profits tax and thus were included in the total payment. In short, a company's total tax obligation to the government could never be greater than one-half of its chargeable profits.

In 1966 the Nigerian government modified the capital allowance legislation affecting the oil industry by cutting nearly in half the rate at which the companies were allowed to depreciate their capitalized investment. As a result, capital allowances were decreased, and chargeable profits and hence the share of profits accruing to the Nigerian government were increased.

A more important alteration of the financial arrangements took place in 1967. Although Nigeria was not yet a member of the Organization of Petroleum Exporting Countries (OPEC), in Decree 1 of 1967 the Federal Military Government introduced what were essentially OPEC terms.[b] The new decree required, first, that the companies agree to establish a posted price—a tax reference price on which petroleum profits taxes and royalties would be calculated—and, second, that royalties be treated as expenses rather than as tax offsets. Under the provisions of 1959, companies could use all royalties as an offset against petroleum profits taxes, but under the new provision, 50 percent of the value of royalties accrued to the government as additional taxes on profits. Following the

---

[b]Differences between the Nigerian terms and the OPEC terms existed because the Nigerian government had not yet negotiated the phasing out of the "percentage allowance" discount and the "gravity allowance" discount.

introduction of these changes, in November 1967 Shell-BP announced a posted price of U.S.$2.17 per barrel (of API 34° crude).[c] The required deductions of harbor dues, a gravity allowance, a percentage allowance, and a marketing allowance effectively reduced the base posting to a tax reference price of $1.95 per barrel.[d]

In September 1970, the Nigerian government negotiated an increase of $0.25 per barrel in the posted price, so that this price increased from $2.17 to $2.42 and the effective tax reference price increased to $2.18. Following the OPEC settlement in Spring 1971, the companies operating in Nigeria agreed to a substantial increase in the posted price to $2.78 per barrel. In addition to the changed posting, the government negotiated an increase in the rate of taxation of chargeable profits from 50 to 55 percent, a reduction in the rate of generation of capital allowances of approximately 30 percent, the elimination of deductions for harbor dues and the other allowances mentioned above, and the addition of a complex set of premia and escalations to the base posting.[e] The net result of this change was an increase in the tax reference price to $3.21. Finally, in 1972, a third increase in the base posted price to $3.02, negotiated to compensate for the devaluation of the U.S. dollar, resulted in a new tax reference price of $3.42 per barrel of API 34° crude.

The series of changes in the posted price had an important impact both upon the petroleum industry and upon the Nigerian government. As a result of the increase in the effective rate of taxation, the Nigerian government was able to secure a significantly larger portion of the economic rent associated with petroleum production. Following the 1970 and 1971 changes, the amount of economic rent accruing to government from onshore production increased from $.86 to $1.70 per barrel (of 34° API crude). After the February 1972 change, the per barrel payments to government rose further to $1.90.[8]

---

[c]A most-favored-company clause exists in each company's covenant with the government, stating that no one company will receive better treatment than any other. In effect, when one company sets a posted price, the other companies must eventually establish the same price. Consequently, all other companies later posted the same price as Shell-BP. Technically, the parent companies, Shell and BP, actually posted the price of $2.17 for crude in the API range 34-34.9° (less harbor dues). There was a $0.02 variation for each whole degree of gravity; for example, the posted price for 27.0-27.9° API crude was $2.03.

[d]The deductions were $0.06 per barrel for harbor dues, $0.137 for percentage allowance, $0.02 for the gravity differential, and $0.005 for the marketing allowance.

[e]The new provision includes the following additions to the posted price (to raise the tax reference price): a Suez allowance of $0.12, a temporary freight premium of $0.09, a $0.10 low sulfur premium that will increase by $0.02 a year, and three annual inflation escalations of $0.05 plus 2.5 percent beginning in January 1973. *Petroleum Press Service,* May 1971, p. 163.

**Production and Cost Structure of the
Nigerian Petroleum Industry**

To set the stage for an analysis of the impact of petroleum production on the Nigerian economy, it is useful to summarize the principal factors influencing oil company operations, to review the history of petroleum production and export growth, and to examine the cost structure of the petroleum industry.

Factors Affecting Company Operations

Several factors influence oil company operations in Nigeria. The government's role in oil production and the financial arrangements under which the oil companies operate have already been discussed above. In addition to these policy influences, the development of petroleum in Nigeria is favorably affected by Nigeria's location and by the quality of the crude produced. Nigerian petroleum production is advantageously located with respect to both costs and security of international shipping routes. Oil companies operating in Nigeria have good competitive access not only to the markets of Western Europe, but also to those of North and South America. Furthermore, Nigeria enjoys a competitive advantage because of the low sulfur content of its crude oil, an especially important consideration as the concern with air pollution in consuming countries increases. Nigerian crude is also attractive because of its relatively high fuel yield and its excellent blending properties.

Production and Exports

As late as 1953, L. Dudley Stamp, the noted British geographer, wrote:[9] "Apart from the fields along the shores of the Gulf of Suez in Egypt and a small yield from three tiny fields in Alteria and four in Morocco, Africa has no oil. The conditions favoring the accumulation of oil in quantity, in folds among sedimentary rocks on the margins of great sedimentary basins, do not exist in Africa." Fortunately for Nigeria (and the other African oil-producing countries), Stamp proved to be a poor prophet. As of March 1973, Nigeria was the ninth largest producer and sixth largest exporter of oil in the world.[10]

Table 7-2 illustrates the rapid growth of output and exports following the commencement of oil production by Shell-BP in 1958. Until the outbreak of the Nigerian civil war in mid-1967, at which time petroleum production was severely curtailed, there had been a continual upward trend in oil production. After the conflict ended in January 1970, the oil industry lost no time in resuming production. Much of the immediate postwar jump in crude oil output resulted from the delayed development of prewar discoveries. Consequently, since the beginning of 1972, production has been growing at a slower rate.

From 1958 through 1964 all production was by Shell-BP. Beginning with Gulf in 1965 and Safrap in 1966, the number of producing companies has

Table 7-2
Petroleum Production and Exports, Nigeria, 1958-1972

| Year | Volume (000 b/d) | | Value (million £N)[b] | |
	Production[a]	Exports	Production	Exports
1958	5	5	0.9	0.9
1959	11	11	2.6	2.6
1960	17	17	4.2	4.2
1961	46	46	11.3	11.3
1962	68	68	17.2	17.2
1963	76	76	20.1	20.1
1964	120	120	32.0	32.0
1965	270	266	69.1	68.1
1966	415	383	99.7	92.0
1967	317	300	76.6	72.4
1968	142	142	36.6	36.6
1969	540	540	139.4	139.4
1970	1084	1064	280.4	276.3
1971	1531	1490	523.9	486.2
1972	1817	1772	710.1	692.6

[a]For the years 1958-64 all production is Shell-BP; 1965: Shell-BP 243, Gulf 27; 1966: Shell-BP 352, Gulf 51, Safrap 12; 1967: Shell-BP 243, Gulf 55, Safrap 19; 1968: Shell-BP 44, Gulf 98; 1969: Shell-BP 352, Gulf 188; 1970: Shell-BP 807, Gulf 217, Mobil 51, Agip/Phillips 5, Texaco/Chevron 4; 1971: Shell-BP 1108, Gulf 277, Safrap 25, Mobil 72, Agip/Phillips 39, Texaco/Chevron 10; 1972: Shell-BP 1208, Gulf 325, Safrap 55, Mobil 167, Agip/Phillips 52, Texaco/Chevron 10.
[b]Production and exports are valued at authors' estimated realization prices.
Sources: Data for 1958-68 from S.R. Pearson, *Petroleum and the Nigerian Economy*, p. 56. Data for 1969-72 from *Monthly Petroleum Report* (Lagos: Ministry of Mines and Power).

gradually increased. Gulf was able to continue to produce and export through-out the Nigerian Civil War, since its production was completely offshore in the Midwestern State. Shell-BP and Safrap, however, were forced to discontinue operations in July 1967. Shell-BP began producing again at a reduced scale in October 1968, but, as explained earlier, Safrap was prohibited from resuming operations until it associated with NNOC in May 1971.

Shell-BP is the most important producer of crude oil in Nigeria, with 66 percent of total output in 1972, followed by Gulf (18 percent), Mobil (9 percent), Safrap/NNOC (3 percent), Agip/Phillips/NNOC (3 percent), and Texaco/Chevron (1 percent). However, Shell-BP's relative importance has decreased somewhat since 1971, when it produced nearly three-fourths of total output. Of the other petroleum companies granted concessions in Nigeria, only Occidental/NNOC and Japan Petroleum/NNOC had announced petroleum discoveries by early 1973. In 1972, crude petroleum accounted for more than four-fifths of Nigeria's total exports and was shipped to practically all areas of the world. The United States continues as Nigeria's largest single market for petroleum, purchasing almost one-fourth of total exports in 1972. The United Kingdom, France, and the Netherlands follow the United States, together taking one-half of Nigerian petroleum exports. Japan is likely to become an increasingly important market for Nigerian petroleum in the near future, in part because of the association of the Japanese consortium with NNOC. Shipments to Japan began in 1971 and amounted to approximately 4 percent of total exports in 1972.

Barring any major changes in the technology of energy production or in governmental policy concerning energy use in the industrialized countries, it appears that Nigeria need have little concern about continuing high external demand for petroleum. A recent study predicts that between 1971 and 2000 total world energy demand and the demand for petroleum will increase at average annual rates of 4.3 percent and 4.7 percent, respectively.[11]

Cost Structure

In spite of the relative youth of the petroleum industry in Nigeria and the disruptions it faced during the civil war, it is possible to identify the dominant characteristics of the industry's cost structure. Cost data for the period 1963-71 are presented in Table 7-3. The proportions of the total value of output devoted to local purchases and to local wages and salaries have fallen over the last several years. In 1963 these two items comprised more than 45 percent of gross output; by 1967 their share had fallen to 30 percent and by 1971 to only 11 percent. Similarly, the share of imports of goods and services markedly decreased, falling from 50 to 16 percent of gross output over the nine-year period. Nevertheless, in 1971 the share of imports was almost 50 percent greater than the combined shares of local purchases and wages and salaries.

In contrast, payments to government have continually increased over this same period. The government receives the following kinds of payments directly from the petroleum companies: petroleum and natural gas royalties, profits taxes, rentals for oil exploration and mining leases, premia paid for the acquisition of concessions, and miscellaneous fees (such as oil pipeline fees). Profits taxes and royalties are the most important sources of government revenue from petroleum. As a result of the several alterations in financial provisions governing the petroleum companies and the exhaustion of accumulated depreciation allowances, the share of direct payments to government (including harbor dues and port charges) in the value of gross output rose from 27 percent in 1963 to almost 60 percent in 1971. This increase, coupled with the large expansion in petroleum output, resulted in payments to the Nigerian government in 1971 at a level more than fifty times that of 1963.

As production has increased, the residual accruing to foreign investment— interest, return of capital, profits, and economic rent—has turned positive and become an increasingly larger absolute and proportionate share of total expenditures. In 1970 the residual share comprised almost 11 percent of the total value of output and in 1971, 14 percent.

By combining these cost trends with other available information, we can summarize the nature of the production process of the Nigerian petroleum industry. The production of petroleum in Nigeria is carried out with technologically advanced methods that allow little room for input substitution and require relatively large amounts of capital equipment, skilled labor, and sophisticated imports. It is conducive to the generation of enormous economic rents, part of which accrue to the government and part to the producing companies. As production has increased over time, these rents have also increased, forming a continually growing portion of gross output. Because of its requirements for skilled labor and imported inputs, the production of Nigerian petroleum engenders only moderate levels of domestic wages and salaries and uses only relatively small amounts of local materials.

The Direct Contribution to Income at Market Prices

Table 7-4 presents figures for net social gain (NSG), net gain coefficients (NGC), and domestic resource costs (DRC) for the years 1963, 1965, 1969, 1970, and 1971 under the assumption that the opportunity costs of all factors are equal to their market prices. Comparison of these five years shows the changes in the contribution of the petroleum industry to Nigerian income in response to changes in the policies affecting the petroleum companies' operations. Although the NSG results indicate a growing absolute contribution to income over time, they do not provide a measure of the proportion of total output contributing to increased national income.

We therefore focus on NGC and DRC. NGC expresses the contribution to national income per unit of earnings of the petroleum industry, while DRC measures the domestic costs incurred by the petroleum industry in earning a net unit of foreign exchange. From 1963 to 1965, prior to any major changes in governmental policies, NSG comprised approximately one-fourth of gross output, that is, NGC was about .25. In 1971, NSG increased to almost 60 percent of gross output, reflecting the introduction of the financial changes and the expansion of production, discussed earlier.

The DRC results indicate that the petroleum industry was highly efficient during each of the selected years. Moreover, with the passage of time it has required increasingly smaller amounts of domestic resources per dollar of foreign exchange generated.[f] In 1963, £N .212 was required to generate $1

---

[f] An export industry is efficient if its DRC is less than the country's shadow price of foreign exchange. Each of the selected years' DRC is considerably less than Nigeria's exchange rate of .357 £N/$.

Table 7-3
Cost Structure of the Petroleum Industry in Nigeria, 1963-1971

	Industry Expenditures (millions £N)								
	1963	1964	1965	1966	1967	1968	1969	1970	1971
Gross output[a]	20.7	32.8	69.1	100.6	80.6	36.9	139.4	280.4	523.9
Local purchases of goods and services	7.2	10.3	18.5	27.9	21.9	11.2	22.8	36.1	51.1
Local wages and salaries	2.0	2.3	2.7	2.7	2.5	1.8	2.8	4.4	6.0
Payments to government[b]	5.0	12.3	13.3	18.7	27.0	15.8	60.5	126.8	306.3
Harbor dues and port charges	0.6	1.0	2.0	2.7	2.4	0.4	3.3	7.9	4.3
Imports of goods and services	10.6	24.0	35.7	58.0	51.2	48.4	60.8	74.7	83.1
Residual (interest, return of capital, profits, economic rent)	-4.7	-17.0	-3.3	-9.5	-24.5	-40.7	-10.8	30.5	73.1

Factor Shares Based on Total Expenditures

	1963	1964	1965	1966	1967	1968	1969	1970	1971
Gross output[a]	1.000	1.000	.999	.999	1.000	1.000	.999	1.000	1.000
Local purchases of goods and services	.346	.315	.268	.277	.277	.304	.163	.129	.098
Local wages and salaries	.097	.070	.039	.027	.031	.051	.020	.016	.011
Payments to government[b]	.242	.375	.193	.186	.335	.428	.434	.452	.584
Harbor dues and port charges	.030	.030	.029	.026	.030	.011	.023	.028	.008
Imports of goods and services	.513	.731	.517	.636	.636	1.312	.436	.266	.159
Residual (interest, return of capital, profits, economic rent)	-.228	-.520	-.047	-.094	-.304	-1.103	-.077	.109	.140

[a] 1963-68 figures include local sales of natural gas.

[b] 1963-68 figures are actual payments to government for each calendar year; 1969-71 figures are authors' estimates based on generation of payments to government per barrel of output, rather than on accruals.

[c] Residual is calculated as total proceeds less imports of goods and services less gross total expenditures in Nigerian currency.

Sources: Data for 1963-68 from S. R. Pearson, *Petroleum and the Nigerian Economy*, p. 61. Data for 1969-71 from unpublished sources and authors' estimates.

Table 7-4
Net Social Gain, Net Gain Coefficients, and Domestic Resource Cost Ratios, at Market Prices, for Selected Years (Nigeria)

	1963	1965	1969	1970	1971
Net social gain (millions £N)	5.6	42.8	63.8	134.7	310.6
Net gain coefficient	.271	.221	.458	.480	.593
Domestic resource cost ratio[a]	.212	.195	.093	.075	.050
Efficiency factor[b]	.406	.453	.739	.791	.861
Foreign-exchange factor[b]	.668	.495	.381	.608	.689

[a]Foreign component of local goods and services for the selected years is estimated from Pearson's 1965-68 data on the share of indirect imports in local goods and services. See S. R. Pearson, *Petroleum and the Nigerian Economy*, p. 81.
[b]See footnote g for a definition of this term.
Source: Table 7-3.

of foreign exchange, but in 1971 this figure had fallen to only £N .050, resulting in a savings of £N .162 per unit of foreign exchange generated.

It is of considerable interest to examine further the changing pattern of the petroleum industry's contribution to Nigerian income. In the last two rows of Table 7-4 we separate NGC into two factors: the proportion of foreign exchange retained in the economy, and the relative efficiency with which the petroleum industry uses domestic resources. NGC is, of course, the product of these two factors.[g]

As illustrated by the DRC analysis, the relative efficiency with which the petroleum industry uses domestic resources has increased over time. Hence the efficiency factor has more than doubled between 1963 and 1971. However, the proportion of foreign exchange retained domestically decreased from almost 67 percent in 1963 to 38 percent in 1969 but rebounded to 69 percent in 1971. The earlier decrease can be explained by re-examining Table 7-3. Although the proportion of foreign exchange flowing out of the economy as direct or indirect imports of goods and services remained at approximately 60 percent of the total output from 1963 to 1969, over this same period net income paid abroad became less negative. Consequently, the share of the total value of gross output flowing out of the economy increased from 33 to 62 percent.

With the rapid recovery of production in 1970, the picture again changed. Imports fell to 27 percent of gross output, and the total share of gross output remitted abroad decreased to 39 percent. The last major financial change, enacted in April 1971, has led to a further decrease in the outflow of foreign exchange to 31 percent of gross output. Hence the positive effect of the increasing efficiency of domestic resource use has been partially offset by expenditures on imports and foreign remittances. The share of these leakages of foreign exchange in gross output, however, has recently been decreasing. If both of these trends continue, the production and export of petroleum will have an increasing positive direct impact on Nigerian income.

The Direct Contribution to Income at Shadow Prices

The actual contribution of petroleum depends on the opportunity costs of the factors used in production. Because precise and reliable data on factor opportunity costs are nearly impossible to obtain, we vary our assumptions about opportunity costs in order to test the sensitivity of the results to these assumptions.

Prior to 1971, foreign exchange seems to have been a serious constraint on Nigerian development. From the end of 1959 to the end of 1970, Nigerian

---

[g]See Chap. 1 and the technical appendix for a complete discussion of these measures. In terms of the notation employed there, the efficiency factor is $(1 - DRC_j/v_1)$, and the foreign exchange factor is $[1 - (\bar{m}_j + r_j)/u_j]$.

reserves of foreign exchange dropped almost 80 percent. Although much of this decline took place during the civil war, the supply of foreign exchange was already severely constrained before the outbreak of the conflict. In 1968 Nigeria was forced to adopt an import rationing system in order to control the outflow of foreign exchange. Following the end of the war in early 1970, foreign exchange reserves began to rebound, largely as a result of petroleum exports.[h] In early 1973, because foreign exchange earnings were sufficiently high, Nigeria considerably liberalized its policies on payments for imports and remittance of dividends.[i] Hence, foreign exchange availability no longer appears to be a constraint to growth. We assume for simplicity, however, that there was no divergence between the market rate of exchange and the shadow price of foreign exchange during the entire period under discussion.

With respect to skilled and unskilled labor, it is useful to make alternative assumptions concerning factor opportunity costs. Skilled labor has been in short supply throughout the recent development of the Nigerian economy. Consequently, it is probable that this factor would receive nearly its equivalent payment in alternative employment. Conversely, it is likely that the market wage of unskilled labor is overvalued. The first progress report on the 1970-74 Development Plan indicated that 7.8 percent of the labor force was unemployed in 1970.[12] In addition, the vast majority of the employed labor force is engaged in low-productivity occupations. In order to reflect the relative abundance of unskilled labor, we make two calculations, one in which the opportunity cost of unskilled labor is assumed equal to its market wage and one in which wages and salaries are taken as 50 percent of the actual total.

If we assume that only 50 percent of wages and salaries reflect true opportunity costs, the estimated annual net direct contributions (in million £N), net gain coefficients, and domestic resource costs, respectively, become: 1963: 6.6, .319, .186; 1965: 16.6, .241, .181; 1969: 65.2, .468, .087; 1970: 136.9, .488, .066; and 1971: 313.6, .599, .044. When these figures are compared with those of Table 7-4, it is clear that the results of the previous section remain almost unchanged. This outcome reflects the relatively small amounts of local labor required in petroleum production.

Linkage Effects

Among the indirect influences associated with the petroleum industry in Nigeria are linkage effects, including backward and forward linkages, technological linkages, final demand linkages, and fiscal linkages.

---

[h]In 1971 and 1972 petroleum was responsible for almost 60 percent of Nigeria's increasing supply of foreign exchange. *Marches Tropicaux et Mediterraneens,* 28 January, 1972, p. 273, and *Barclay's International Review,* January 1972, p. 9.

[i]The 1973 liberalization abolished the 180-day deferred payments procedure for imports and allowed foreign companies to remit arrears on dividends for 1971 in full and up to 25 percent of dividends due in 1972. "New Deal for Nigeria's Farmers," *West Africa,* 13 April, 1973, p. 458.

Backward Linkages

Although no definitive statements can be made without a detailed firm-by-firm analysis, it is possible to reach some general conclusions concerning the importance of backward linkages of the petroleum industry with the Nigerian economy. Information contained in Table 7-3 allows us to establish an upper limit to the magnitude of potential gains that might have been achieved from exploiting economies of scale or using underemployed factors. Between 1963 and 1971, from 10 to 35 percent of total petroleum industry expenditures were paid to suppliers and contractors operating in Nigeria. Of these expenditures a large part involved local services rather than local goods, and approximately one-seventh leaked out of the Nigerian economy as indirect imports. Hence there appears to be small scope for gain through the exploitation of scale economies.

Nor does it appear that there are significant benefits from the employment of previously underutilized resources. Many of the firms supplying the petroleum industry are foreign-owned and managed, large relative to other firms, and were established prior to the growth of oil production. Hence, the payments to these suppliers mainly constitute additions to foreign incomes rather than to the employment of underutilized domestic resources. In general, backward linkages have not had substantial effects on Nigerian development. There is scope for greater Nigerian participation in the supplying and servicing industries, but because of the sophisticated nature of petroleum technology, this scope appears to be quite limited for the near future.[j]

Forward Linkages

Any discussion of forward linkages must be largely speculative. Several forward-linked industries have been proposed, but very few have actually been established. The forward linkages discussed in this section include the processing of petroleum and the production and export of natural gas which is associated with crude oil production. Both crude oil and natural gas can be used as raw materials in processing industries, and natural gas, of course, is itself an excellent source of energy.[k]

The Nigerian Petroleum Refining Company (NPRC)—a joint venture among the Nigerian government (50 percent), British Petroleum (25 percent), and Royal Dutch/Shell (25 percent)—was established in 1965. In May 1972, the Nigerian government boosted its participation to 60 percent with the shares of Shell and British Petroleum each decreasing by 5 percent. NPRC operates Nigeria's only refinery at Alesa-Eleme near Port Harcourt. The refinery began operating in 1965 and continued until the outbreak of the civil war in July

---

[j]A backward-linked industry about which there has been much discussion is the proposed iron and steel industry which could be a supplier of pipe to the petroleum industry. Although no final decision has been made, £N10 million has reportedly been set aside to initiate the project, and a study has been undertaken to decide on siting. *Barclay's International Review,* November 1972, p. 19.

[k]For convenience we treat the utilization and processing of natural gas as a forward linkage with crude oil production. Actually, natural gas is a joint product with crude oil, and local processing of natural gas should be treated as a forward linkage of the gas industry itself.

1967. Following reconstruction to repair damage, the refinery resumed operations in May 1970.

The NPRC refinery currently has a processing capacity of 60,000 b/d.
In 1970 it produced over 7 million barrels of major finished products. Exports
of petroleum products totaled 1.7 million barrels, 70 percent of which consisted of shipments of fuel oil to the United States, the Bahamas, Curacao and
Holland, with the remainder going mostly to neighboring African countries.[13]
The refinery fulfills the local demand for most petroleum products consumed
in Nigeria. Petroleum products not produced by the refinery include bitumen,
asphalt, lubricating oil, and aviation gasoline. In addition to its supplying of
refined products to the Nigerian economy, the net foreign exchange benefits
of the refinery are substantial, as is its contribution to Nigerian income.

There are plans to construct a second refinery in an effort to provide
locally for expanded future demand for refined products. The new refinery
is expected to have a crude capacity of approximately 60,000 b/d and to be
sited at Warri in the Midwestern state.[14]

The Nigerian petroleum industry made its first deliveries of natural gas
as a source of energy in January 1963. These sales were made to the Electricity
Corporation of Nigeria and the Trans-Amadi Industrial Estate, both located in
Port Harcourt. From 1963 until the outbreak of the civil war—and again after
its resolution—sales of natural gas as fuel to Nigerian utilities and industries
increased rapidly, reaching 12 million cubic feet/day (cf/d) by the end of 1970.
In 1972, Nigeria produced an average of over 1.6 billion cf/d of natural gas
in association with crude oil production, an increase of 32.4 percent over
natural gas production in 1971. Almost all of this gas was flared (i.e., burned
during oil production) except for 0.7 percent consumed by the oil industry
itself and 0.9 percent sold to industrial consumers. Hence, the quantity of
natural gas actually utilized is exceedingly small compared to the volume of
gas produced and to the size of potential exports.

In an effort to use the natural gas currently flared at the oil fields, the government plans to construct the country's first liquefied natural gas (LNG) facility,
which is scheduled to begin production in 1977. Shell-BP, Gulf, and the Agip/
Phillips group have all drawn up plans for the project. Through NNOC the
government intends to hold a 55 percent interest in the plant, the construction
of which would allow both the domestic use and export of a resource with an
opportunity cost near zero.

Plans are also underway to extract liquefied petroleum gas (LPG) from
the associated deposits of natural gas. The government has signed an agreement
giving the Guadalupe Gas Products Corporation of Texas a 40 percent share in
the plant, designed to extract and export 12,000-15,000 b/d of LPG. This plant
is expected to be sited at Port Harcourt near the proposed LNG facility, and
the industries plan to use the same pipeline for collecting gas supplies. Together
the LPG and LNG industries would consume about 1,500 million cf/d of natural
gas, thereby using nearly all of the natural gas currently being flared.[15]

Finally, a comprehensive study for the construction of a petrochemical industry was due for completion in early 1973. A number of foreign companies— ENI, Shell, ICI, Elf, Total, and several Japanese firms—have shown an active interest in becoming partners with NNOC in this venture.[16]

In sum, forward linkages are of large potential importance to the Nigerian economy. The refinery at Alesa-Eleme already makes a fairly substantial contribution to the generation of foreign exchange and also to the employment of local resources. Discussions concerning the construction of a second refinery, a gas liquefaction facility, and liquefied petroleum gas and petrochemical industries have been underway for some time and may soon reach fruition.

Technological Linkages

While technological linkages do not have great impact on the Nigerian economy, there are a few which warrant brief discussion. The petroleum industry has created a limited amount of infrastructure for use by other sectors of the local economy. In the process of opening up well sites, several miles of roads, used as farm-to-market feeder routes, have been constructed in the Nigerian hinterland. The petroleum industry has also stimulated the development of some Nigerian ports, but these new facilities have not significantly benefited the non-oil industry. Finally, power stations, hospitals, schools, and other types of social overhead capital have been constructed by the oil companies for their own use and for the use of their employees. These structures could eventually provide external benefits when the petroleum companies turn them over to other sectors of the Nigerian economy. At present, however, the petroleum industry transmits only very limited benefits to the Nigerian economy via technological linkages.

Final Demand Linkages

Two kinds of payments made by the petroleum industry—wages and salaries, and residual payments (retained economic rent, profits, interest and return of capital)—can lead to final demand linkages. Since 1970, residual payments have been increasing, and in 1970 and 1971 they made up about one-eighth of the total value of output. The firms that supply the petroleum industry also have residual payments. The scope for final demand linkages through residual payments is limited, however, since almost all of the exploring and producing industry and many of the supplying firms are foreign-owned. Consequently, most of the residual earnings are transferred abroad, without benefit to the Nigerian economy.

Wages and salaries also hold only limited potential for final demand linkage effects. In 1970 and 1971 direct wage and salary payments comprised only 1.0 to 1.5 percent of total expenditures. Supplying firms also have wage and salary payments, so they, too, can contribute to possible final demand linkages. The actual significance of these linkages effects depends upon the manner in which the payments are expended. Because portions of expatriate salaries are paid directly overseas, there is only limited remittance of domestic wages and salaries. But expatriates tend to consume relatively large amounts of imported goods, and thus wage and salary payments to expatriates do not greatly benefit the Nigerian economy. The impact of wages and salaries paid to Nigerians also depends upon the pattern of their expenditures. To the extent that Nigerian or expatriate wage-earners in the oil industry demand locally produced food and consumer goods produced by Nigerian import-substitution industries, the petroleum industry contributes some limited gains to the Nigerian economy through final demand linkages.

Fiscal Linkages

Fiscal linkages are perhaps the most difficult of all linkage effects to evaluate, since it is nearly impossible to trace the chain of causation from government revenues to expenditures and related effects. Yet, this problem is less severe for Nigeria than it is for many other countries. As of early 1973 the oil industry was providing 75 percent of total government revenue. To a considerable extent, therefore, government expenditures can be related directly to payments of the petroleum industry.

The present philosophy of the Federal Government is that a high proportion of the revenue from oil, a nonrenewable asset, should be used for the benefit of the country as a whole.[17] In accord with this philosophy, in March 1970 the government announced a new system of allocating oil revenues among the central government and the twelve states. The new decree, retroactive to April 1969, leaves petroleum profits taxes, the source of more than two-thirds of total petroleum revenues, in the hands of the Federal Government, but also provides for a larger redistribution of petroleum royalties to the non-oil producing states.[1]

One of Nigeria's most important priorities is to use oil revenues for agricultural development. The first progress report on Nigeria's 1970-74 development plan suggested that stagnation in the output and export of some agricultural crops was due to marketing board policies. In an effort to correct this situation, the Nigerian government announced in January 1973 that the existing system of marketing boards would be changed. Under the new system, producer prices are set by the central government—not by the eight individual marketing boards—and export duties on marketed produce are abolished, allowing marketing boards to raise the effective price for producers. In addition, the Federal Government has agreed to compensate for any loss of state revenues due to the abolition of the export duties and to compensate the marketing boards for any losses resulting from the central determination of prices. Depending on the relative levels of export and producer prices, these policies could result in agriculture being subsidized from general government revenues.

---

[1]Under the new system the Federal Government will continue to retain all profits tax payments, but will keep only 5 percent of royalties and rentals compared with 20 percent previously. The state of origin will receive 45 percent of royalties and rentals compared with 50 percent previously. The remaining 50 percent will be divided among all twelve states, half distributed equally and the other half distributed on the basis of population. Formerly, the remaining 30 percent was allocated among the four regions on a population basis. "Nigeria—Reallocation of Revenues," *Petroleum Press Service,* April 1970, p. 151.

As is exemplified by its expenditures on agriculture, the government's development policy is shaped by its desire to obtain maximum financial and social benefits from crude oil and natural gas production. Hence, fiscal linkage effects, resulting from the expenditure of rising government revenues, hold great promise for future development. The extent to which this large potential will be realized depends upon the success of government policies in guiding and participating in the future development of the Nigerian economy.

Provision of Skilled Labor

Initially, managers, technicians, and other skilled workers were brought to Nigeria from abroad as international oil companies undertook the search for petroleum. In this way, the petroleum industry contributed to the supply of skilled expatriate labor. In addition, the petroleum industry has augmented the supply of skilled Nigerian labor through the establishment of training schemes, strongly encouraged by the Nigerian government. Under the Immigration Act of 1963, the government imposed tight controls on the number of expatriates that petroleum companies could employ in Nigeria. Moreover, Decree 51 of 1969 stipulated that the companies Nigerianize their operations within a specified time period.[m] Many of the agreements which the government has signed with the petroleum companies require the training and upgrading of Nigerian labor through scholarships, in-house training programs, or on-the-job training. Three of the most recent concessions agreements—with Japan Petroleum, Occidental, and Henry Stephens and Sons—include provisions for financial contributions to create and support a petroleum technical institute. To this end, in mid-1972 the Nigerian government signed an agreement with the Soviet Union for the establishment of an oil-production training center.[n]

In spite of the contributions of the petroleum companies to the supply of expatriate and local skilled labor, the need for additional skilled labor is a serious concern for Nigeria. With the growth in the availability of foreign exchange and government revenues, shortages of skilled labor rather than foreign exchange or investment capital now seem to constitute the major hindrance both to Nigerian economic development and to Nigeria's attempts to Nigerianize this and other industries.

Implications for Policy

Major government policy decisions affecting the petroleum industry in Nigeria include equity participation, financial arrangements, petroleum

---

[m]Decree 51 provided that all companies would have to hire locally at least 75 percent of their manpower, including senior management, within ten years of the beginning of their operations, and thereafter increase the hiring of Nigerians as rapidly as possible.

[n]The Soviet Union's Technoexport will provide the teachers and equipment for the petroleum institute, which will be governed under an autonomous board established by government decree. *Petroleum Intelligence Weekly*, 1 May, 1972.

processing, and membership in OPEC. Three factors influence all of these policy issues. First, there are still large quantities of oil and natural gas in Nigeria which have not yet been produced. Highly conservative estimates of Nigerian petroleum and natural gas reserves indicate that even if no new discoveries were made, Nigeria could maintain 1972 production levels at least through 1990.[o] Second, all concession agreements will terminate beginning in the early 1990s. Hence, the Nigerian government must also determine optimal policies with respect to expired concessions. Finally, as we have already noted, the rapid growth in world petroleum demand is expected to continue, and thus Nigerian policy-makers can anticipate favorable market conditions for the foreseeable future.

The Nigerian government has gradually obtained an increasing share of the growing economic rent associated with petroleum production. Prior to 1967, the amount that the petroleum companies paid the government was to some extent at the discretion of the companies. Although the Federal Government set the provisions under which petroleum taxes would be paid, the petroleum companies themselves determined the value of their output and thus the actual size of the payments. Petroleum Decree 1 of 1967 altered this arrangement by requiring a negotiated posted price upon which tax charges would be calculated. As a result of the increases in the posted price in the following years and other changes in the financial arrangements, in 1971 the government secured more than 50 percent of the total value of petroleum output.

The further extent to which the Nigerian government can extract economic rent associated with petroleum production is circumscribed by the financial arrangements under which the petroleum companies operate in the other countries in which they produce. The multinational petroleum enterprises allocate production to different areas depending on the conditions and costs of production in each area. If the tax squeeze in Nigeria were to become too great, the producing companies would presumably shift production to other areas. The taxation conditions in Nigeria now approximate those of the other major petroleum countries. Hence future tax increases in Nigeria will likely be concerted with those in the other OPEC countries.

Equity participation is an alternative method by which the government can share directly in the rent associated with petroleum production. Following the formation of the Nigerian National Oil Corporation, the government has taken equity participation in the concessions of nearly all producers.[p] Along with transferring rent, participation allows the government to take part in the management and control of the petroleum companies' operations in Nigeria.

---

[o]As of 1 January, 1973, estimated reserves were 15 billion barrels of petroleum and 40 trillion cubic feet of natural gas. *The Oil and Gas Journal,* 25 December, 1972, p. 83.

[p]As of July 1973, Gulf, Mobil, Texaco/Chevron, Mobil/Tenneco/Sun DX and Pan Ocean/Delta Oil had not signed participation agreements with the Nigerian government.

In principle, participation should permit Nigeria to structure operations in a manner which best contributes, directly and indirectly, to economic development. The government has shown no intention of nationalizing the petroleum companies (i.e., taking 100 percent equity), although it has insisted on their increased Nigerianization. This willingness to be a partner will probably continue as long as Nigeria can continue to achieve its objectives—to obtain maximum financial and social benefits from its petroleum resources—through agreements with the petroleum companies.

Forward-linked petroleum-processing industries—refining, liquefied natural gas, liquefied petroleum gas, and petrochemical industries—have great potential importance for the Nigerian economy. These industries can almost surely satisfy domestic demand for processed-petroleum products efficiently and thereby save foreign exchange through import-substitution. Whether Nigeria will become a major exporter of processed-petroleum products will depend on the structure of the processing industry within Nigeria, the development of competitive processing industries in other petroleum-producing countries, and the growth in world demand for processed-petroleum products. Nigeria's prospects appear promising, however, especially regarding LNG and LPG.

Nigeria joined OPEC in July 1971. Because of the implicit most-favored-nation clauses in the company covenants, Nigeria was able, without being a member of OPEC, to obtain treatment from each petroleum company at least equal to the most favorable treatment accorded to any other nation within which that company was operating. There thus was little reason for Nigeria to seek OPEC membership simply to gain bargaining strength. However, if OPEC should ever be faced with the problem of dividing exports of world petroleum into country quotas, by being a member Nigeria may be better able to serve its interests and obtain as large a quota as possible. Of more immediate importance, as a member Nigeria may be better able to influence and assist implementation of the policies which OPEC seeks to promote, including retention of the existing posted-price structure (and hence the generation of large economic rents) and continuation of unified pressure to alter financial arrangements to obtain ever-increasing shares of these rents for producing countries.

Conclusion

The production of petroleum has contributed most importantly to Nigerian economic development by providing revenues and foreign exchange earnings to the government and to a much lesser degree through contributions to the supply of skilled labor, the construction of infrastructure, and the establishment of forward-linked industries. Nigeria thus finds itself in an enviable position among tropical African export economies. Its petroleum is a lucrative export commodity—faced with a growing, income elastic demand and stable or rising prices—from which the Nigerian government has been highly successful in extracting enormous economic rents. But even though the resource base derived from petroleum is substantial, sustained and broadly based development in Nigeria is by no means assured. The important potential contributions of oil to Nigerian development depend now more than ever upon government decisions guiding the use of resources provided by this extensive, nonrenewable asset.

Notes

1. See Scott R. Pearson, *Petroleum and the Nigerian Economy* (Stanford, Calif.: Stanford University Press, 1970).
2. Ibid., p. 31. For a summary discussion of Nigerian economic development, see *Ibid.*, pp. 31-38.
3. Ibid., p. 32.
4. "Riding the Economic Tiger," *African Development,* March 1973, p. N5.
5. "A Dowry for a New Oil Corporation," *Petroleum Press Service,* June 1971, p. 228.
6. "The Next Stage in Nigeria," *Petroleum Press Service,* December 1971, p. 445.
7. "What's Happening in Those Oil Talks?" *African Development,* March 1973, p. N19.
8. "Nigeria Revenues Jump with New Oil Currency Pacts," *Petroleum Intelligence Weekly,* 3 July 1972, p. 7.
9. L. Dudley Stamp, *Africa: A Study in Tropical Development* (New York: Wiley, 1953), p. 53.
10. "Riding the Economic Tiger," loc. cit., p. N5.
11. "Office of Economics World Energy Supply-Demand Analysis . . . ," Hearings before the Committee on Interior and Insular Affairs, United States Senate, 93d Congress, on the issues attendent to current and projected reliance on oil and gas imports, 11 January 1973, p. 630.
12. "Inflation—Bugbear of an Oil Economy," *African Development,* March 1973, p. N37.
13. "Nigeria's Expanding Oil Output," *Petroleum Press Service,* June 1971, p. 216.
14. *Petroleum Press Service,* October 1972, p. 362.
15. M. O. Feyide, Director of Petroleum Resources, "Petroleum Resources of Nigeria," presented to the 13th Annual Conference of the Science Association of Nigeria, Nsukka, 27 March 1972, p. 3.
16. "Nigeria: Bright Future for Oil Industry," *Africa/Middle East Digest,* February 1973, p. 29.
17. "New Deal for Nigeria's Farmers," *West Africa,* 13 April 1973, p. 458.

8

The Copper Economy
of Zaire

Raymond F. Mikesell*

Evolution of the Copper Industry

Copper played an important role in the history of the Belgian Congo beginning with the formation of the Union Minière du Haut Katanga (UMHK) in 1906 to exploit the rich Katanga copper reserves. By the late 1920s copper had become the Congo's most important export. Output reached 139,000 tons in 1930, increasing to 176,000 tons in 1950 and to 302,000 tons, or about 6.7 percent of world production, at the time the Congo became independent in 1960.[a] Following the establishment of the Democratic Republic of the Congo[b] in June 1960, Katanga Province, where the bulk of copper and other minerals are produced, seceded (July 1960-February 1963) thus depriving the central government of its most important source of revenue. Continued internal political strife plus a serious dispute between the government and Union Minière reduced copper output and exports so that the 1960 output level was not surpassed until 1966. Accordingly, real GDP of the Congo remained nearly stationary between 1960 and 1967.

Although Zaire won political independence from Belgium in 1960, economic domination by Belgian firms continued. The conflict over the control of the copper industry has played a major role in the efforts of President Mobutu (who succeeded Prime Minister Tshombe in November 1965) to unify the country and to achieve autonomy over the nation's economy. The achievement of Mobutu's political and economic objectives depended heavily upon obtaining a substantial measure of control over Union Minière which dominated the country's mining and metallurgical industries.[c] Mobutu's objective with respect to the copper industry was essentially to achieve national

*This article reflects a portion of the research of the author financed by a grant from Resources for the Future, Inc., to the University of Oregon.

[a]Tonnage figures are in metric tons.

[b]The name of the country was changed to the Republic of Zaire in 1971.

[c]The political importance of Mobutu's struggle with Union Miniere is illustrated by the company's open support of former Prime Minister Tshombe and of the successive rebellions in Katanga Province.

179

control over the major policies relating to the industry while maintaining the foreign management, technical personnel, and marketing outlets of Union Minière. To this end Mobutu sought to move the headquarters of Union Minière from Brussels to Kinshasa (or to make Kinshasa the headquarters of a new Congolese company organized to operate the properties of Union Minière) and to increase the share of the Congolese government in the ownership of the properties from 18 percent to 50 percent.[d]

An agreement on a joint venture along these lines was actually reached in principle in late 1966, but the agreement collapsed over the issue of the control of the marketing of copper and other matters.[e] The government then formally expropriated the assets of Union Minière in the Congo. In the ensuing struggle the Congolese government was under great pressure to maintain copper production and exports on which it depended for nearly 70 percent of its foreign exchange earnings. The government was also anxious to maintain the international credit standing of the Congo and to avoid being accused of an act of confiscation. In late December 1966, the Congolese government tried to promote an international consortium consisting of Belgian, British, French, and American interests, to acquire shares in a Congolese company that would operate the expropriated properties of Union Minière. When this effort failed, Mobutu made an agreement in February 1967 with the Belgian interests that controlled Union Minière. This agreement took the form of a convention of technical cooperation between the newly organized Congolese corporation, Generale Congolaise des Minerais (Gecomin) and the Société Générale des Minerais (SGM), a subsidiary of Société Générale de Belgique.[f] This convention stated that SGM would provide the managerial recruitment and other technical services for Gecomin, and sell Gecomin's output of copper, cobalt, and other minerals and metals in the world markets. In effect, the agreement provided that the mines would continue to operate under Belgian management much as before nationalization.[g]

---

[d]Prior to the nationalization of Union Minière's properties in the Congo in 1967, the Congolese government was actually the largest equity shareholder (17.9 percent). The principal foreign shareholders of Union Minière were Tanganyika Concessions Ltd. (14.4 percent) which was mainly owned by British interests, the Compagnie Financière du Katanga (8.9 percent), and the Société Générale de Belgique (4.6 percent). The latter company also had shared both directly and indirectly (through its subsidiaries) in Compagnie Financière du Katanga and in Tanganyika Concessions. Voting rights were weighted in favor of the Congo government and the three aforementioned companies. The general public owned 53.9 percent of the shares, but held only 36.1 percent of the voting rights. However, Société Général de Belgique controlled the management of Union Minière.

[e]For a good review of the history of the relationships between Mobutu and Union Minière and the nationalization of the Congolese copper industry, see *Mobutu's Congo*, Fabian Research Series, 266 (London: The Fabian Society, January 1969).

[f]SGM was Union Minière's marketing agent before the nationalization, and is a part of the large Belgian corporate group, Société Générale de Belgique. Union Minière, although deprived of its Congolese properties, has mining and other interests throughout the world, including Canada, Australia, Iran, and Belgium.

[g]See "A Convention of Technical Cooperation between Générale Congolaise des Minerais, Kinshasa, and the Société Générale des Minerais, Brussels, concluded in Kinshasa,

No formal agreement for compensation for the nationalized properties
of Union Minière, valued by Union Minière officials at about $800 million,
was reached at the time of the technical cooperation convention of February
1967. The Congolese government and the foreign shareholders in Union
Minière had a mutual interest in maintaining production out of which earnings for compensation would be generated, and production could not continue without the Belgian management and technical personnel. Settlement
of Union Minière's claims on the Congolese government took the form of
an agreement between Gecomin and SGM on 25 September 1969, an agreement under which SGM was to receive 6 percent of the value of production
for a period of 15 years and 1 percent for another 10 years thereafter, the
agreement running for a period of 25 years. However, the payments are not
based on actual output but on a formula according to which the output
base for the calculation of the annual payments increases by 20,000 tons
each year starting at the 360,000 ton level for 1969. Thus the former owners
have no risk of interruption of compensation payments as a consequence of
output variation, but the amount of the payments varies with the price of
copper on the London Metal Exchange (LME).

Neither the Congolese nor the SGM officials refer to the September 1969
accord as a compensation agreement. (The text has never been published.)
Instead it is referred to in terms of "restitution." The form of the arrangement has provided a politically convenient means of dealing with the sensitive
issue of compensation for the expropriated properties since what is paid to
SGM appears as compensation for services. However, so far as the author has
been able to discover, all of SGM's out-of-pocket costs are covered, including
the salaries of managers, the cost of technical services, etc., out of Gecamines'
revenues.[h] Hence the 6 percent payment appears to be entirely compensation
for the nationalized properties.

February 15, 1967." This text has been published, but the 1969 agreement covering the
compensation arrangements for the expropriation of Union Minière's properties and the
full details relating to the payment for SGM's services to Gecomin have never officially
been made public although most of the terms are well known.

[h]Gecomin's name was changed in May 1970 to Générale Congolaise des Mines
(Gecomines) and again in October 1971 to Générale des Carrières et Mines du Zaire
(Gecamines). In 1970 Gecomines paid 17.8 million zaires (approximately $35.5 million)
to SGM in accordance with the September 1969 convention. The corresponding amount
for 1971 was 14.2 million zaires, reflecting the decline in the price of copper from the
1970 level. It is not possible to project the amounts to be paid to SGM over the 15-year
period without forecasting the price of copper over this period. Moreover, the annual
output of Gecomines on which SGM's payments are based will increase each year as
indicated above. Although an annual payment of $35 to $40 million per year over a
15-year period is scarcely adequate compensation for properties valued at $800 million,
we have no idea of the basis for Union Minière's estimate of the value of its Congolese
properties. Even if we knew Union Minière's net return on its investments in the Congo
prior to nationalization, this would scarcely provide a basis for valuation since, in the
absence of nationalization, taxes would almost inevitably have been increased by the
Congolese government following the pattern of other mineral-producing countries.

The relationship between Gecamines and SGM in the management of the nationalized copper industry is rather unusual. The February 1967 convention of technical cooperation can be interpreted as giving SGM full responsibility for management as well as for marketing the mineral products of Gecamines, or it can be interpreted more narrowly as providing SGM with the more limited responsibility of securing for Gecamines the necessary personnel for the operation of the mines and marketing the products as an agent for Gecamines. In the course of conversation with the general manager of Gecamines, Mr. R. Cayron, it was said that SGM had no managerial responsibility with respect to Gecamines. Broad policy powers are vested in the president of Zaire, who appoints the Administrative Council, but policy and administrative control is centered in the Permanent Executive Committee within the Administrative Council. The Permanent Executive Committee consists of four members, two of whom are Belgian, namely the general manager and deputy general manager of Gecamines, and the other two are Zairian. Mr. Cayron and his deputy were former employees of Union Minière, and their services were made available as a part of the contractual agreement between Gecamines and SGM.[i] Although conflicts of interest are possible between SGM and Gecamines, they have a strong mutual interest in the successful operation of Gecamines.[j]

---

[i]It would appear that SGM personnel not only have full control of the operations of Gecamines but also have a large measure of control over its policies. However, in the course of an interview with Mr. Cayron he went to considerable length to emphasize that his position and that of the entire expatriate staff of Gecamines was that of wholly loyal employees of Gecamines and denied that they were in any sense employees of or beholden to SGM. It is true, of course, that they are paid directly by Gecamines and their contract is with Gecamines. And while there is apparently no formal relationship of Mr. Cayron and his expatriate staff to SGM, it is indeed difficult to believe that at least certain managerial decisions taken by Mr. Cayron are not in some way reviewed in Brussels by the Belgian industrial complex of which SGM is a part. In fact, Cayron emphasized that Gecamines must conduct its business in accordance with sound commercial principles and that he personally had certain responsibilities for carrying out these principles. It seems likely that his special responsibilities arise out of Gecamines' contract with SGM and that Cayron is, in fact, both an agent of SGM and an official of Gecamines. In stating this, however, it is not suggested that Mr. Cayron is not seriously dedicated to the success of Gecamines and its contribution to the Zairian economy.

[j]This author has discussed his interview with officials of Gecamines in a paper entitled *Recent Developments in the Zambian and Zairian Copper Industry,* an External Research Study published by the Bureau of Intelligence and Research, U.S. Department of State, 3 January 1972. SGM and its affiliates have interests in a variety of business firms both in Zaire and abroad covering mining, metallurgy, manufacturing, and marketing. Since the sales of copper by SGM are made under contract at prices related to the LME price, there is probably little latitude for shaving prices to SGM affiliates. However, there are a number of reimbursable expenditures incurred by SGM in the marketing of Gecamines' copper, including refining abroad of blister copper, transportation and other charges which, relating to the sale of copper, provide opportunities to involve SGM affiliates. More important perhaps are the large numbers of equipment and materials suppliers who, controlled by SGM and its affiliates in both Zaire and abroad, may benefit from SGM's special relationship to Gecamines. SGM has an office in Lubumbashi and a large staff in Kinshasa.

International Market for Copper

Most copper produced outside the United States is sold on a contract basis with the price determined by the 3-month forward London Metal Exchange (LME) price. Since the abandonment of the producer price system in Europe (employed during the period 1964-1966) the market has been competitive[k] and the LME price fluctuated widely in 1970 and 1971 from a high of £749 per ton to a low of £394 per ton in response to world demand and supply conditions. The four CIPEC countries[l] accounted for 58 percent of world exports (excluding Communist countries) and 39 percent of world production (excluding Communist countries) in 1969. Other important exporters are Canada, Australia, the Philippines, and South Africa. CIPEC members have been studying and discussing the possibility of exercising control over world prices by means of production or export quotas, buffer stocks, or other devices, but at the time of writing they have not reached an agreement on an approach.[m]

According to the Convention of 15 February 1967, the minerals are delivered by Gecamines at African embarkation ports to SGM, which ensures the further transport, processing, and sale *on behalf* of Gecamines. Consequently, the price due by SGM to Gecamines is the actual selling price of the minerals obtained by SGM less transport, refining, and marketing costs. SGM pays Gecamines 70 percent of the value of the copper exported (less marketing, refining, transport costs) based on the average LME price at the time of export and pays the other 30 percent when collection is made from the buyer.

Foreign Investment in the Copper Industry
and the Investment Climate

The Zaire government is anxious to attract foreign investment in mining but in most cases requires an equity participation in the mining enterprise.

---

[k]The producer price system has been employed in both the United States and Europe as a means of holding down the price of refined copper in order to make it competitive with copper substitutes. While producer copper prices were lower than free market prices, producer copper was rationed and excess demand had to be satisfied by purchases on the open market.

[l]Chile, Peru, Zaire, and Zambia are members of the Intergovernmental Council of Copper Exporting Countries (CIPEC), whose headquarters are in Paris, France.

[m]A recent unpublished study by an international agency concludes that the ability of the CIPEC countries alone to increase their export earnings by cutting back on exports is only marginal in the short run and is clearly not feasible in the longer run. Nevertheless, they might well be able to exercise a stabilizing influence on world market prices through a buffer stock or some other kind of arrangement. Ability to modify short-run fluctuations in copper prices would be enhanced by an international buffer stock arrangement in which all, or nearly all, copper-exporting countries cooperated.

Several copper-mining concessions are held by two foreign groups. One is the Société de Developpement Industriel et Minier du Congo (Sodimico),[n] a company formed in April 1969 with 15 percent Zaire government participation and 85 percent participation by a Japanese firm controlled by the Nippon Mining Company.

The second group, frequently referred to as the American Consortium, created two companies in September 1970, namely, Société Internationale des Mines du Congo (Simico) and Société Congolaise du Tenke-Fungurume (Socotef). The two companies have a common management and identical ownership, but were incorporated separately for the purpose of acquiring exploration rights in several zones. The percentage participation in both companies is as follows: AMOCO (Standard of Indiana) and Charter Consolidated Company, Ltd., each have a 28 percent interest; the Zairian government, a 20 percent interest; Mitsui and Company, a 14 percent interest; Bureau de Récherches Geologiques et Minières (BRGM) of Paris, 7 percent; and Leon Tempelsman and Sons, Inc., together with Robert Anderson, 3 percent. Apparently Charter Consolidated supplies the management while Tempelsman-Anderson were the promoters.

Socotef has a concession of 1,425 square kilometers, including the towns of Tenke and Fungurume, which were formerly a part of Union Minière's holdings and are known to contain deposits of 4.5 percent copper. Socotef will submit an investment proposal after further exploration, including a proposal for a refinery.[o] Simico initially had exploration rights covering several zones totaling 30,692 square kilometers but were required to give up 50 percent of the concession area after 18 months; its several concessions must be reduced to 5,000 square kilometers at the end of 36 months (in late 1973).

Expenditures by the two firms in 1970 are estimated to be in excess of $1.7 million. There is considerable optimism about the quality of the ore in these concessions, and eventually their investment may be as much as $300 million. Sodimiza initiated production in 1972, but at the time of writing Simico and Socotef had not applied for a mining concession. In addition to these companies, Falconbridge Nickel Mines of Canada has a team of geologists working on two concessions in the Katanga area.

The concession agreements are not uniform and are apparently subject to negotiation regarding such matters as taxation and the right of the Zaire government to acquire an additional equity interest. The Sodimiza convention provides that for the first five years of production the company is free of

---

[n]In October 1971 the name of the company was changed to Société de Developpement Industriel et Minier du Zaire (Sodimiza).

[o]Since the completion of this study, Socotef has been renamed Société des Mines de Tenke Fugurume (SMTF). SMTF plans to begin production at an annual rate of 130,000 metric tons toward the end of 1975.

both the export tax and the income tax, with a gradual reduction in tax benefits over the following 15-year period. For a period of five years the Zaire government has a right to increase its initial participation (which it received in return for the concession) from 15 percent to 50 percent. The tax arrangements for Simico-Socotef, on the other hand, provide for a straight 50 percent profits tax instead of the usual 40 percent profits tax and 9 percent tax on concentrates. (The normal export tax rate varies with different types of copper exported.) The Simico-Socotef arrangement reportedly does not require that the foreign companies sell any additional equity to the government beyond the 20 percent of the initial shares in both companies given to it without compensation. A fixed capital amortization schedule (with varying rates applying to different types of capital) is written into the agreement. The Zaire investment code also provides for reduced taxation on reinvested profits.

It is of interest to note in connection with SGM's role in Zaire that SGM sought to prevent the American Consortium from obtaining its concession. After the negotiations with the American Consortium had begun, SGM sought to form a consortium consisting of U.S. Steel, Shell Oil, and other companies for the purpose of acquiring what is now the Socotef concession. It is reported that SGM employed the Belgian government to bring pressure on the Zaire government to grant the concession to the SGM group.

Current and Projected Copper Production

In 1971 Gecamines produced 406,000 metric tons of copper of which about 208,000 tons was electrolytic ingot copper.[1] Output is expected to increase gradually to 460,000 tons by 1974. Gecamines' expansion program involves an investment of over $100 million, half of which is required for expansion of the mines and the remainder for the construction of concentrators, smelters, and refineries. Gecamines expects to obtain external financing for a portion of this investment, including a loan of $16 million from the European Investment Bank negotiated in March 1971 and a $5 million Export-Import Bank loan negotiated in November 1970. Gecamines has plans for a further expansion of productive capacity to 600,000 tons by 1980.[2] However, this will require a substantial increase in electrical capacity in Katanga Province.[P]

Gecamines is also an important producer of other minerals, including cobalt (14,518 tons in 1971) and zinc (195,000 tons of 56 percent zinc concentrates in 1970). The data on the analysis of Gecamines export earnings,

---

[P]In October 1971 the name of Katanga Province was changed to Shaba Province.

domestic employment, and other domestic expenditures discussed below include all the mineral operations of Gecamines and not just copper alone.[q]

In addition to Gecamines' planned expansion of copper production, the Japanese company, Sodimiza, began production in the fall of 1972 at an annual rate of 40,000 tons; production is expected to rise to 80,000 tons by 1975. Sodimiza is initially exporting concentrates for smelting and refining in Japan, but transportation costs are very high. The construction of a refinery in Zaire will depend upon the level of ore output and the availability of power. The American Consortium hopes to be in production in the next five years. (See note o.)

Structure of the Economy

Zaire is a country of about 22 million population with a per capita GDP in 1969 of about $100.[r] Following the achievement of relative political and economic stability in 1967, real GDP rose rapidly during the 1968-70 period at an average rate of about 8 percent. All economic sectors contributed to the expansion, but mineral output plus the rise in world copper prices played a dominant role in the country's recovery from the long period of stagnation following independence.[3] The decline in copper prices during 1971 lowered the rate of growth in real GNP from 11 percent in 1970 to 5 percent in 1971.

The primary sector of the Zaire economy accounted for 21.5 percent of monetized GDP in 1969, almost equally divided between agriculture and mining. The secondary sector accounted for 26.6 percent of monetized GDP, of which 18.2 percent was mineral processing and only 4.6 percent was manufacturing. Thus mining and mineral processing together accounted for 29 percent of monetized GDP and nearly 40 percent of domestic production at factor cost.[4] In 1968 mining accounted for 46 percent of value added in the primary sector and 67 percent of total value added in the secondary sector. Copper, in turn, dominated the mining and mineral-processing sectors, accounting for over 80 percent of value added in the two sectors combined.[5] Other important minerals produced in Zaire include diamonds, cobalt, zinc, cadmium, tin, and manganese. Cobalt, zinc, and cadmium are found in association with copper ores and are produced almost entirely by Gecamines. Diamonds are largely produced by the Société Minière de Bakwanga (MIBA), a firm which is jointly owned by the Zaire government (50 percent) and Belgian and U.S. interests.

---

[q]In 1968 Gecamines produced about 60 percent of the total world output of cobalt; however, the vast bulk of Gecamines' export earnings are derived from copper.

[r]The country's currency, the zaire, has a par value of 1 zaire = 2 U.S. dollars. The relationship between the dollar and the zaire remained unchanged following the general currency realignments of December 1971 and February 1973.

Despite the importance of mining and mineral processing in the economy, these industries provide employment for a very small proportion of the population. In January 1968, of 576,000 persons employed in large public and private enterprises, only 57,000 were employed in mining and mineral processing. About 364,000 were employed in large agricultural enterprises; 51,000 were employed in manufacturing; 15,000 in construction; 60,000 in transport and communications; and 30,000 in commerce, banks, and other services. About 320,000 were employed in government, of which 170,000 were permanent staff employees and 150,000 contractual workers.[6] The vast bulk of the working population is employed on small farms and in small nonagricultural industries.

Economic Impact of the Copper Industry

Information on the economic impact of the copper industry must be obtained mainly from the operations of Gecamines which, prior to 1972, was the only copper producer in Zaire. However, Gecamines also produces cobalt, zinc, silver and other minerals associated with copper ore, and revenues and expenditures of Gecamines reflect all mining and mineral-processing activities. In 1968 copper production constituted about 83 percent of Gecamines' value added and that percentage was probably somewhat higher in 1970 as a consequence of the higher copper prices. Gecamines' annual reports provide no breakdown between foreign and domestic expenditures or between wage and nonwage outlays, but there is available some breakdown of expenditures based on unpublished Gecamines budget estimates for 1968. Using these estimates together with the annual reports for Gecamines, this author constructed a disaggregated statement of revenues and expenditures for 1968 (Table 8-1). On the basis of the estimates in Table 8-1 for 1968, Table 8-2 breaks down Gecamines' expenditures between domestic and foreign outlays for 1968 and 1970; 1970 figures are based on the application of certain ratios from the 1968 data to the figures given in the Gecamines annual report of 1970. It is difficult to separate investment from current expenditures in the financial statements because of the special accounting system employed in mining. During 1970 the value of fixed assets after depreciation rose by about 5.0 million zaires, and expenditure for expanding the capacity of the mines (less depreciation) was 3.4 million zaires.[7]

Payments to the government by Gecamines totaled 95.6 million zaires in 1968, or 51.4 percent of total ordinary government revenue. These payments rose to 132.4 million zaires in 1969, or 49.1 percent of ordinary government revenues, and to 159.5 million zaires in 1970, or 50.6

percent of ordinary government revenue.[s] Payments to the government include a variety of taxes, the most important of which are the export tax, the net profits tax, the turnover tax, import duties, and the payroll tax on foreign employees.

This author estimates that, in 1968, 14.4 million zaires were paid out in domestic wages, excluding that portion (50 percent) of the expatriates' salaries which are permitted to be transferred abroad. The corresponding estimate for domestic wage payments for 1970 was 18.7 million zaires (Table 8-2). Actually, total employment declined slightly between 1968 and 1970 from 23,800 in 1968 to 23,530 in 1970. Salaried employees (personnel de cadre) declined from 2,128 in 1968 to 2,077 in 1970, of which expatriate employees accounted for 1,581 in 1968 and 1,415 in 1970. The rise in domestic wage payments between 1968 and 1970 was based on an estimate of increase in wage rates.

Purchases of domestic materials, equipment, and services employed in production were estimated to be 10.3 million zaires and 12.0 million zaires in 1968 and 1970, respectively. Expenditures for transporting the copper from the mines to African ports are given as 23.0 million zaires for 1968 and 26.3 million zaires for 1970. They constitute payments to the Bas Congo-Katanga (BCK) railroad. Although the principal export route for Gecamines' products is the so-called national route via railroad and river barge to the Zaire port of Matadi, over half of the copper is shipped via three other routes—to Lobito on the coast of Angola, to Dar-es-Salaam on the coast of Tanzania, and to Beira on the coast of Mozambique.[8] Hence, a substantial portion of the transportation expenditures to African ports takes the form of foreign exchange.

Taking domestic wage payments, local materials and services, and domestic transportation together, we have an outside estimate of domestic expenditures by Gecamines (excluding payments to the government) of 48 million zaires and 57 million zaires in 1968 and 1970, respectively, out of total receipts of Gecamines of 199 million and 274 million zaires, respectively (Table 8-2). Foreign exchange expenditures for imports, payments to SGM, expenditures connected with shipments to African ports and with marketing overseas and expatriate salaries transferred or paid abroad totaled 45.4 million zaires in 1968 and 69.2 million zaires in 1970 (Table 8-2). Thus we see that the direct domestic impact of copper mining and related operations is relatively

---

[s]Data on Gecamines' tax payments to the government given in the Gecamines annual reports differ from those available from the Banque du Zaire in unpublished reports. The difference is mainly the inclusion in the latter of taxes on net profits earned during the pervious year, taxes which do not appear in the Gecamines annual reports. The estimates in Table 8-2 reflect the Banque du Zaire information. It is for this reason that in 1970 the total outlays of Gecamines, including tax payments to the government, exceeded by 11.5 million zaires the receipts of Gecamines for the same year. Presumably the net profits tax was paid out of reserves accumulated in the preceding year.

Table 8-1

Gecamines' Revenue and Expenditures, 1968 (Zaire)
(million zaires)

Revenue		199.4
Sales	199.1	
Other revenue	.3	
Payments to government		95.7
Export tax	58.9	
Turnover tax	16.5	
Payroll tax	4.7	
Import duties	4.6	
Profits tax	10.0	
Other taxes	1.0	
Production costs (excluding taxes)		49.4
Salaried workers (personnel de cadre)	13.9	
Unskilled labor	5.2	
Domestic materials, equipment and services	10.3	
Imported goods	20.0	
Export costs		34.8
Domestic transportation	23.0	
Other expenses (foreign)[a]	11.8	
Payment to SGM		8.9
Net asset loss		1.8
Net profits and reserves		8.9

[a]Includes 0.9 million zaires interest on borrowed funds.

Sources: *Gecomines Rapport Annuel, 1969* and unpublished Gecamines budget estimates.

Table 8-2

Estimates of Domestic and Foreign Expenditures of Gecamines, 1968 and
1970 (Zaire)
(million zaires)

	1968		*1970*	
Domestic expenditures		*143.3*		*216.5*
Payments to government	95.6		159.5	
Wages of domestic unskilled workers	5.2		6.9	
Wages of domestic salaried workers	4.6		5.5	
One-half wages of expatriate workers	4.6		6.3	
Domestic material, equipment, and services	10.3		12.0	
Domestic transportation	23.0		26.3	
Foreign expenditures		*45.4*		*69.2*
Imports	20.0		27.3	
Transfer of salaries of expatriates	4.7		6.3	
Payment to SGM	8.9		17.8	
Other, mostly transportation	11.8		17.8	
Total receipts		*199.4*		*274.2*
Foreign	196.4		270.2	
Domestic (estimate)	3.0		4.0	
Residual—reserves, dividends, etc.		*10.7*		*−11.5*

Sources: *Gecomines Rapport Annuel, 1969* and *1970* and Table 8-1.

small. Even Gecamines' domestic expenditures for wages, materials, and transportation have a relatively high import content. The largest share of the wage
payments go to the salaried workers whose level of living enables them to
purchase a variety of manufactured goods, including consumer durables imported from abroad. Many of the materials purchased locally are either imported or have a high import content. Among the products that are produced
in Zaire and used by the mining industry are sulfuric acid, explosives, cement,
and coal (which is not suitable for metallurgical purposes). Thus the major
economic impact of the copper industry arises from the payments to the
government, and the nature of that impact depends upon how the government allocates these revenues.

Copper exports accounted for about 67 percent of Zaire's total mer-
chandise exports in each of the years 1968, 1969, and 1970.[9] Zaire's total
exports in 1970 are estimated at 368 million zaires, of which 247 million
was accounted for by copper. Gecamines' sales[t] of copper and other minerals
totaled 274 million zaires in 1970, but at least 70 million zaires in foreign
exchange expenditures must be deducted to arrive at the net foreign exchange
contribution of Gecamines. Gecamines' sales of minerals declined to 246 million zaires in 1971 as a consequence of the fall in copper prices.

Governmental Budget and Investment
Projects

In 1968 the excess of governmental revenues over current budget expenditures was only 20.5 million zaires and the corresponding figure for
1970 was 65.1 million zaires.[10] About half of total capital expenditures in
recent years has been allocated to public works, much of it for the construction of public buildings. Included in public capital expenditures are the
purchase of military equipment, construction of airports, and a hydroelectric
power project on the Zaire River. Plans are going forward for the construction
of a continuous rail route between southern Katanga and the Atlantic port of
Matadi; the required investment is estimated to be roughly $300 million.[11]
Expenditures for improving transportation—especially highways and ports—
have been relatively small. In the private sector new investment is directed
mainly to housing and equipment for large agricultural and mining enterprises. Little new investment appears to be going forward in manufacturing.[12]
Industrial projects are being planned which would use the large amount of
power to be generated from the hydroelectric power project on the Zaire
River at Inga. These projects include a steel complex, a caustic soda and
polyvinyl chloride factory, a nitrogenous fertilizer plant and an aluminum

---

[t]A small amount was sold for local consumption, but the vast bulk was exported.
Gecamines Rapport Annuel, 1971, p. 8.

smelter—all highly capital intensive projects. These projects would be either fully government owned or joint ventures.[13] Foreign financing, including suppliers' credits, is expected to provide much of the capital for these projects.

Contribution to Labor Skills, Linkage Effects and Social Impact

Like all Central African countries, Zaire is extremely deficient in skilled labor and in workers with sufficient education to occupy supervisory or managerial positions. The government has sought to replace expatriate salaried workers with nationals as rapidly as possible without impairing efficiency, and over the period 1967-71 the number of "personnel de cadre" in Gecamines increased from 251 to 720.[u] No data are given on the turnover of national skilled and supervisory workers in Gecamines, but in other countries with similar export industries this has been an important means by which the skill level of the nation has been raised. Throughout the entire nation the demand for nationals with skills and experience greatly exceeds the supply, and modernization of the country will require a very rapid increase in the supply of trained and educated personnel. In fact, this shortage of skilled manpower may be the greatest constraint on growth. Meanwhile, it would appear desirable to retain as many expatriates as possible in Zaire since their replacement by nationals in one industry simply denies other industries the opportunity of hiring trained nationals.

Since no breakdown exists on either the purchases of the copper industry from local manufactures and agriculture or on the industries using copper as a raw material, little can be said quantitatively about linkage effects. Between 1966 and 1968 the output of metal manufactures declined sharply— by a considerably larger percentage than the decline in value added by manufacturing generally. On the basis of available data, almost no industry that appears to be a likely candidate for being either a supplier to the copper industry or a user of copper products increased its output in real terms between 1966 and 1968.[v] Hence it would appear that linkage effects of the copper industry have been quite small.

The mining and mineral-processing activities of Gecamines are highly mechanized and quite capital intensive. In spite of the large supply of unskilled labor, the company prides itself on adopting the most advanced capital-intensive techniques. The sharp expansion of output in recent years

---

[u]As of 31 December 1971, Gecamines employed 24,588 workers in all categories, of which 1,409 were expatriates. *Gecamines Rapport Annuel, 1971*, p. 30.

[v]One reason suggested for the decrease in manufacturing output in 1967 and 1968 is the liberalization of imports and the inability of inefficient domestic industries to compete with imports. See "Democratic Republic of the Congo," *op. cit.*, p. 35.

has, therefore, been accompanied by a decline in the number of workers, both skilled and unskilled. The reason is that the major objective of the company and of the government is to maximize net foreign exchange revenues from operations and not to expand employment opportunities. The issue of whether metal mining can be made more labor intensive without sacrificing revenue has never really been faced.

Gecamines has continued the activities of its predecessor, Union Minière, in providing housing, health, education, and other social services for its workers and has made a contribution to the communities where the workers live. As is the case with major export industries in other countries, the copper workers constitute an elite group with a relatively high level of living in what is otherwise a very low-income country. There are both advantages and disadvantages of this situation for the development of the country. On one hand, there is the demonstration effect of sanitary communities, improved living conditions, and better social services which communities throughout Zaire will demand from their government. On the other hand, there is the creation of an automobile, durable household goods, jet-flying economy which requires a large amount of infrastructure in the form of roads, gasoline stations, airports, power facilities for running household gadgets, and the like, which contribute to the welfare of only a very small percentage of the total population. Likewise, much of the nation's foreign exchange income goes to support this elite group. From a welfare standpoint, this would appear to be a serious misallocation of capital and of foreign exchange resources.

Notes

1. *Gecamines Rapport Annuel, 1971* (Lubumbashi, Zaire, 1972), p. 12.
2. Ibid., p. 14.
3. Data on the Zaire economy have been largely derived from "Democratic Republic of Congo," *Surveys of African Economies,* Vol. 4 (Washington, D.C.: International Monetary Fund, 1971), Chap. 2.
4. Ibid., p. 18, Table 1.
5. Ibid., p. 24, Table 3, and p. 30, Table 5.
6. Ibid., p. 57, Table 8.
7. *Gecomines Rapport Annuel, 1970* (Kinshasa, 1971), p. 36.
8. "Democratic Republic of Congo," op. cit., p. 47.
9. Data from *International Financial Statistics,* IMF, April 1973, p. 402.
10. "Democratic Republic of the Congo," op. cit., p. 65.
11. Ibid., p. 47.
12. Ibid., p. 41.
13. Ibid., pp. 42-43.

9

Copper and Zambia

James Fry and Charles Harvey

Historical Background

Apart from slave-raiding, some fairly small-scale attempts at more peaceful types of trade and some equally small-scale missionary efforts, Zambia's contact with the rest of the world really begins with mineral exploration. The country that came to be known as Northern Rhodesia was initially a sort of fief of the British South Africa Company (the BSA Co.). The company even had formal responsibility for administration, law, and order until the 1920s, in return for which the British government passed various acts purporting to legalize the rather dubious mining and prospecting concessions obtained from local rulers.[1]

The search for minerals was initially unprofitable, so that the territory was a financial burden on the BSA Co. Although lead and zinc were mined at Broken Hill (now Kabwe) from 1915, large-scale copper production did not begin until the 1930s. The period before 1930 therefore offers a chance to see what the economy was like before the development of the copper-mining industry but after the colonial administration had been established. This is of more than purely historical significance since the copper industry has since become so dominant that it is now extremely difficult to imagine what the economy would be like without it.

There is a good description in Baldwin[2] of the economy in the 1920s. From the point of view of this paper, which is to analyze the impact of copper on the Zambian economy, the most important point is that the railway from Salisbury and Bulawayo had already reached Broken Hill in 1905 and had linked up with the Congolese railway system in 1909.[3] There is some doubt as to whether the railway would have survived financially had copper traffic not come to its rescue, but having survived the 1920s unprofitably it would probably have lingered on. It was not *built* however as a result of copper-mining development in Zambia—it was built as a result of excessive optimism, which took a very long time to be justified. The railway and Broken Hill apart, the only significant "development" before 1930 was the establishing of a small number of white settler farmers along the line-of-rail, an even smaller number at Fort Jameson (now Chipata) in the East, and the colonial administration itself, which, being based on the principle of indirect rule, was skeletal to say the least. In all, a total of 3,623 Europeans were in the country in 1921, mainly Afrikaners in the case of the farmers (who made up one-third of the adult males) and mainly English in the case of the administrators.[a] Only 133 were employed in mining; the other main source of white employment was the railway.

It is possible that if copper mining had *not* developed in Zambia, then other development possibilities, especially agriculture, would not have been so badly neglected. Certainly the large foreign exchange earnings from copper, and the ease of access to relatively well-developed Rhodesian and South African sources of supply, made it only too easy to import. In addition, it is probable that without the copper wealth Southern Rhodesia would not have been so interested in a federation with Northern Rhodesia, the federation proving to be a major instrument for the development of the southern partner at the expense of the northern.

Even when these possibilities are taken into account, and they are only speculations, it is true to say that there would have been virtually no development in Zambia without the copper mines. The economy remains, in the 1970s, overwhelmingly dependent on copper. The key figure is that copper supplies 95 percent of export earnings from visible trade.[b] Since development is still tremendously dependent on imported capital goods and imported skilled labor, it depends on continued earnings from copper. Furthermore, up to two-thirds of government revenue comes directly from copper profits, so that the demand generated by government spending is also dependent on copper. In short, the economy *is* copper to a quite extraordinary degree.

Impact of Copper Mining on the Economy before 1964

The initial impact of copper was small, creating an extreme example of an exporting industry working in an economic enclave. Almost all skilled labor had to be imported at first, and the unskilled African workers worked only on short contracts.[c] This was inevitable given the initial conditions in which the mining companies had to operate. But it was deliberately maintained by the imported white labor force which quickly acquired a vested interest in the status quo. Similarly, the migrant nature of African labor was reinforced by company policy on, for example, wages and housing, and was used as an excuse for not improving working conditions and for not providing training.

Similarly, white settler farmers tried to prevent competition from African

[a]It is almost universal in Southern and Central Africa to use "European" and "white" as synonyms. It can be seriously misleading if it suggests that white people in Zambia came mainly from Europe, as happened in Kenya, for example. Zambia was settled mainly from the south. The figures are taken from the 1921 census of Europeans quoted by Rev. K. Quinn in C. M. Elliott, ed., *Constraints on the Economic Development of Zambia* (Nairobi: Oxford University Press, (1971), p. 62.

[b]Tourism is the only important potential source of invisible earnings, but it has declined. The number of tourists fell from 22,000 in 1965 to under 6,000 in 1968.

[c]Even unskilled labor was imported initially, since local Africans were at first afraid to go underground.

farmers in supplying the new urban work force with food. Settler political power was used to introduce discriminatory marketing policies for maize and beef, and at the same time white trade unions preserved jobs for their members.[d] The example of black engine drivers yielding to white ones as trains crossed the border from the Congo is well known, and it was typical.

While some of this dualism was natural at first, the degree of African advancement and participation could have been quite rapidly improved had the revenues from copper been used for development. But royalties on mining production were paid to the BSA Co. until 1964. The company's right to the royalties was challenged (by the colonial governor) quite soon after large-scale and profitable mining began in the 1930s, and the royalties continued to be disputed after World War II. In 1950 the company agreed to yield one-fifth of its royalty income to the Northern Rhodesian government in return for undisputed enjoyment of the remaining four-fifths until 1986. In 1964, however, a few hours before independence, the company gave up all rights for token compensation.[4]

Another factor limiting the impact of the mining sector before 1964 was federation. As had been the intention, the main economic effect of federation was to allow Southern Rhodesia to use the fiscal yield from copper mining to develop the Southern Rhodesian economy; the scale on which this was done was massive.[5] In addition, because the federation was a common market, Southern Rhodesian industry had free access to the market in Northern Rhodesia— which further hindered the latter's development.

These adverse political factors, brought about by the very success of mining, undoubtedly delayed Zambian development. In spite of them, however, the mining sector did have a growing impact. Firstly, African labor became rapidly less migrant despite the obstacles of wages and housing. By the 1940s the monthly turnover rate fell to 5 percent, and in the 1950s to 2.6 percent. In the late 1920s the average period of African employment on the mines had been only six months or so.[6] Africans began to form trade unions in the 1940s, and even before this were able to organize strikes (in 1935 and 1940), though at the cost of some loss of life.

Secondly, again in spite of discouragements, many African farmers took advantage of the new urban market for food. For example, in 1936-37 African farmers sold 234,000 bags of maize, compared with 321,000 bags from Europeans. African sales grew erratically to 839,000 bags in 1963 and 1.5 million bags in 1968.[e] Another example is the fishing industry that developed in the Luapula valley. The fishing and the transport of fish to the Copperbelt are

---

[d]Efforts were more successful in the case of beef than that of maize; see Baldwin, op. cit., pp. 150-62.

[e]See Richard Hall, *Zambia* (London: Pall Mall, 1965), p. 271 and Elliott, op. cit., p. 277. Sales are erratic not only because of the weather and the relatively low level of technology, but because a substantial proportion of the crop is consumed on the farm. Even subsistence farmers produce a "normal surplus" in most years, which can be sold if there is a market for it.

entirely African, and have brought considerable prosperity to the area.[f]

Thirdly, skills learned and savings acquired on the Copperbelt have provided opportunities for both whites and blacks to start their own businesses. Unfortunately, this impact is not much documented, apart from a few case studies.[7]

Fourthly, although the fiscal impact of copper mining was greatly limited by the payment of royalty to the BSA Co., by the fiscal transfers to Southern Rhodesia already referred to, and by the heavy bias against Africans in government spending, there was of course some impact. Since it was not a government objective to develop the country in general, nor to promote African development in particular, the most important impact of government spending was simply in creating additional domestic expenditure and thus widening the local market beyond that created directly by the mines—although even this effect was limited by a tendency to underspend revenue in the 1930s. The bias against Africans is best illustrated by spending on education. Thus although a growing proportion of current spending was devoted to African education, with a considerable acceleration in the immediate pre-independence years, by independence in 1964 there were still "less than a thousand young men and women with school certificate, less than a hundred who had been to university."[8] This was significantly worse than in other African countries, themselves poorly prepared in educational terms for independence.[9]

Impact of Copper Mining on the Economy since 1964

The real breakthrough occurred at independence. The acquisition of the royalty by the Zambian government was not the only factor adding to tax revenues. In addition, the copper price rose rapidly if erratically, and in 1966, when the producers abandoned their attempt to keep the price down in the interests of long-term stability, the government imposed a third tax on the copper mines (to add to royalty and income tax), raising the marginal tax rate for copper price increases from 52 percent to 74 percent. The combined disincentive effect of the three taxes may have had substantial ill effects on investment in copper mining, but the taxes were very successful in yielding a high revenue for government in the boom conditions between 1966 and the tax reform which accompanied the takeover in 1969.[10]

Two other important factors increased the effectiveness of the newly acquired revenues: the end of federation meant that tax revenue from copper mining no longer went to Southern Rhodesia; and political independence and the ending of federation together gave the government its first opportunity to protect Zambian industry from Rhodesian imports. In 1965, Rhodesia's

---

[f]Fishing in the Luapula Valley was developed as much to supply the Katangan as the Zambian Copperbelt; the former market is now largely closed to Zambians.

Unilateral Declaration of Independence gave enormous added impetus to
the desire to diversify import sources and develop import-substituting industries.
The immediate impact of UDI on Zambian industry was to create a profits boom
(profits sent abroad in 1966 were over 80 percent greater than in 1965). The
longer-term effect was to add greatly to the stimulus to local production and
investment already being provided by the rapid increase in government spending,
and by other government policies. Thus value added in manufacturing rose from
K28mn in 1964 to K73mn in 1967. In particular, of the 67 items of which more
than K200,000 was imported from Rhodesia in 1965, all but five will be produced in Zambia by 1975. Although a considerable amount of import-substitution
took place in the direct supply of inputs into copper mining, it was the general
expansion of government spending (made possible by the acquisition of the
royalties, the ending of federal fiscal transfers, and the rising copper price) which
provided the opportunity for such rapid growth.[g] Although government capital
spending rose by more than five times between 1964 and 1969 (and current and
capital spending combined rose nearly three times), in 1969 the government still
had a large budget surplus and a large balance-of-payments surplus.

At the beginning of 1970 the outlook still appeared favorable. But the
copper price fell from the exceptionally high level of K1252 per metric ton in
March 1970 to K746 by the end of that year and failed to rise much above that
level for three years. In addition, the mining disaster at Mufulira in late 1970
caused a large loss of production, perhaps as much as 250,000 metric tons over
two years, so that foreign exchange reserves fell rapidly. As a result, the government discovered that falling revenue and inexorably rising current expenditure,
made necessary by the earlier capital spending, would leave the second national
development plan with very much less finance than had been hoped, and vastly
less than had been available for the first plan.[11] An analysis of the copper-
price fluctuations and a more thorough examination of copper's relative impact
on other sectors of the economy, on imports, and on employment are undertaken below.

The Takeover[12]

In August 1969 President Kaunda announced a 51 percent takeover of the
copper-mining industry. Payment for the state's shareholding is being made from
the profits on that shareholding—to that extent there is an element of expropriation in the terms of the takeover. But under the rules announced at Mulungushi
in April 1968 the mines (with other foreign companies) had been forced to
retain 50 percent of their post-tax profits in Zambia. Since the takeover, all of
the profits on the residual 49 percent shareholdings have been allowed to be
remitted abroad, and two-thirds or more of the government's share is used to
make compensation payments. As a result, the *cash flow* to private shareholders

[g]See below for a detailed analysis of inputs into the mining sector.

is substantially increased as a result of the takeover; given the probable attitude of non-Zambian shareholders to funds compulsorily held in Zambia, this change is a substantial benefit to them. Another shareholder gain is that a minimum level of compensation payments is guaranteed by the Zambian government, so that if the price of copper falls, or for some other reason the state's dividend falls below K28mn a year, compensation payments will be maintained out of general revenue. Finally, default on any aspect of the agreement would directly endanger Zambia's other international borrowing arrangements, since default made all the compensation bonds repayable in full immediately; in addition, as part of the takeover package, Zambia joined the World Bank-sponsored International Center for the Settlement of Investment Disputes, providing another element of security for the shareholder.

Financially, Zambia gained little if anything from the takeover. There is a small increase in the already high proportion of mining profits accruing to the government, but only so long as profits remain sufficiently high. Otherwise the government could find itself having to use general tax receipts to maintain compensation. The companies retain control of all important decisions at least during the 1970s. As a result of the takeover package—perhaps mainly because of the major tax changes which were included in the deal, but probably also because of the reduction of uncertainty and the general stabilizing of expectations as a result of the takeover itself—major new expansion plans have been announced. Lack of expansion was one of the government's main criticisms of the mining companies before the takeover, so that increased investment was one of the stated objectives of takeover, and even though it was not achieved through "control" via the government's majority shareholding, it was nevertheless achieved.

The takeover thus probably went quite near to the limit of what could have been achieved with the Zambian government's bargaining power as it existed in 1969. Further shifts in the proportion of benefits retained in Zambia may occur as a result of the changes announced by President Kaunda in August 1973— most notably the immediate repayment of the compensation bonds and the ending of the management, sales, and recruiting agreements. No doubt negotiations on the latter issue will follow. And no doubt there will be further Zambian moves on these issues as education, training, and experience accrue over time.

Export Instability

Zambia is an extreme example of an economy dependent on a single export commodity which yields excessively unstable export earnings. Not only is the copper price itself very volatile indeed. In addition mining is a risky business; vital inputs have to come long distances over routes which are both politically and physically vulnerable, and the copper has to face the same hazards on its way to the main markets in industrialized countries. All of these factors have been operative in the period since independence. The impact on the Zambian economy of the fluctuating copper price and the Mufulira disaster have already been mentioned; in addition the mines were forced to cut back production after UDI because of coal shortages, and there must still be copper wire bars lying in the bush along the once infamous Hell Run, the emergency road to Dar-es-Salaam which was used for both oil imports and copper exports during the post-UDI crisis. There was even a brief and very expensive attempt to fly copper out of the country.

The post-independence period also demonstrates the varying effects on the economy as a whole of unstable export earnings. Variations in the price of copper *above* the breakeven point (the point of approximate balance of payments equilibrium however defined) are reflected mainly in the level of foreign exchange reserves, the size of the government's budget surplus, the level of profits remitted abroad, and the level of profits retained by the mining companies. None of these changes has much short-term effect on the rest of the economy. The only effects are on the level of government expenditure and the level of capital spending by the mining companies. Government spending, however, is fairly stable in the very short term, upwards or downwards, and *ought* to be decided, when there are adequate reserves, by the internal capacity of the economy to meet the demands made on it. That capacity is not altered by changes in the price of copper. It is, of course, harder to resist ministerial requests for increased spending when both the balance of payments and the budget are in surplus, but even if these requests are met, there can be a substantial time lag before additional spending takes place.[h] Equally, a fall in the copper price and thus in government tax revenue and foreign exchange reserves (below what they would otherwise have been) may induce a more cautious attitude to spending, especially if such a price fall induces expectations of further falls in the future, but again this only operates after a considerable time lag.

Much the same sort of argument applies to the level of investment spending by the mining companies. Because of the long-time lags between finding commercially mineable deposits and actual production, and the further problems of expanding capacity in transport, refining, skilled labor, etc., investment spending is normally not altered as a result of copper-price fluctuations, unless the price changes so much as to induce a major shift in expectations as to its future level.

More surprisingly, perhaps, fluctuations in export volume may have very

---

[h]In some of the post-independence years the budget was actually underspent in money terms as well as real terms, in spite of considerable inflation; and 1971 was used as a "year of consolidation" to allow the completion of uncompleted projects left over from the first plan (which ran from 1966-70) before the introduction of the second plan in 1972. For comparisons of actual and estimated government spending, see Harvey's paper on inflation, op. cit., Table 1, p. 43.

minor repercussions on the economy. Thus the production cutback in 1966 and
1967, which was caused by fuel shortages, did not result in any fall in employment in mining. The reasons were, firstly, the normal labor hoarding arguments
enhanced by the extreme shortage of skilled labor in Zambia, and secondly, the
political difficulty of dismissing Africans in post-independence Zambia. Both
arguments depend on the mining companies believing in the temporary nature
of such a change in production. For the same reasons the increase in output in
1968 had similarly small repercussions on the economy.

Increases in output, as a result of increases in mining capacity, however,
although adding to aggregate supply, have the effect of tightening various constraints, especially in transport, power supply and skilled labor, and only allow
noninflationary demand increases insofar as the availability of goods and services
has been constrained by shortage of foreign exchange.

As already suggested, a prolonged fall in export earnings, or an extended
period during which earnings are *below* balance of payments equilibrium, ob-
viously causes rapidly mounting economic and political difficulty. This happened
in 1971 and 1972. The previous periods of balance-of-payments surplus had
left the country at end-1970 with large foreign exchange reserves, more than a
year's (visible) imports. But such is the economy's vulnerability that within
18 months the country was faced with a major financial crisis. Furthermore,
several features of the economy limit the potential effectiveness of a devaluation.
Firstly, the small local industrial base means that a devaluation puts up the
prices of a wide range of goods. Secondly, the expatriate labor force, on which
the economy is still very dependent, is mobile internationally and so can expect
to maintain its real income. Thirdly, containing post-devaluation wage demands
by the local labor force would be difficult. There is evidence that wages throughout the economy tend to follow the lead of the African mine-workers. They
are well organized in a powerful union which cannot be counted on to support
government policy. In addition, devaluation increases mining profits and so
weakens the companies' resistance to wage demands.[13] The success of a devaluation is likely, therefore, to depend to a large extent upon whether the miners
could be persuaded to accept a fall in their standard of living or whether devaluation would stimulate an inflationary round of wage increases.

The Direct Impact of Mining on
Other Sectors

Table 9-1 summarizes 1967 data for inputs, outputs, and gross fixed
capital formation of the Zambian mining sector.

A striking characteristic is the low share of imported goods required in
copper mining—a mere 7 percent of gross output in the case of current inputs,
and 30.2 percent of gross fixed capital formation. Mining is also much more

capital-intensive than the rest of the economy. In mining, the gross operating surplus plus indirect taxation amounts to 50.7 percent of gross output.[i] This fact partly explains why the import share of inputs in mining gross output is relatively low. For the other sectors of the Zambian economy (excluding subsistence farmers), the percentage has an average value of only 22.5 percent.

The mining sector is less labor-intensive than the other sectors of the Zambian economy. Wages and salaries make up only 18.6 percent of the gross output of the mining sector, compared with 30.9 percent for the rest of the economy.

The differences in labor-intensity are much more marked when one looks at the number of people employed per million Kwacha of gross output in the copper mining and other sectors. In 1967, an African mining worker was paid an average of K1322 per year. Other African workers got an average of K547. Expatriates on the mines earned an average of K7608 per year; those off the mines received an average of K3557. Thus the copper mines employed 95.5 Africans and 12.9 expatriates per million Kwacha of gross output. The other sectors of the economy employed, on the average 344.5 Africans and 27.8 expatriates.

Later on we shall examine the indirect effects of the copper mines through use of the input-output table. It is appropriate to comment here on the large proportion of current and capital inputs which appear to come from the copper-mining sector itself. Since raw copper, cobalt, lead, and zinc are unlikely to serve as inputs in the production of these same commodities, it is best to assume that the input-output table records the flow of other goods and services (such as sulphuric acid) produced by one mine and sold to others. However, the copper input into mining capital formation is rather harder to explain. Presumably this consists of activities such as shaft-sinking; yet much of this is done by outside contractors, and there is no record of any construction component in mining gross fixed-capital formation. Therefore, we assume that the appearance of mining as an input in capital formation is an error, resulting from the treatment of "capital" inputs such as construction, transport equipment, machinery, and electrical equipment as current inputs credited to the copper-mining sector. Adjustments to correct for the error do not, however, significantly alter our earlier conclusions regarding the relative import-, labor-, and capital-intensities of the copper-mining sector.[j]

---

[i]Gross operating surplus is determined mainly by the price of copper in the short term. In 1967, it was K810 per metric ton—compared with K1090 in 1966 and K886 in 1968. Over this period costs were also rising very rapidly; cost of sales, excluding indirect taxes, rose from K198 to K335 per metric ton between 1964 and 1969. See Bostock and Harvey, op. cit., Table 5.3, p. 117.

[j]We have replaced the K20.2 mn of mining inputs to mining capital formation with inputs from construction, transport, machinery, and electrical equipment, and reduced all

Table 9–1
Zambian Metal Mining Sector, 1967

Domestic and Imported Inputs

Sectoral Source	Domestic	Imported
	(millions Kwacha)	
Agriculture, forestry and fishing	0.3	0.2
Metal mining	13.5	–
Other mining and quarrying	0.9	3.4
Other food	–	0.2
Textiles and wearing apparel	0.1	0.4
Sawmills, joineries, etc.	0.5	0.3
Paper products, printing and publishing	0.3	0.5
Rubber products	–	0.9
Chemicals and petroleum products	2.4	7.5
Bricks and other clay products	–	1.2
Cement, cement products, etc.	0.7	0.1
Foundries and metal products	12.6	5.7
Machinery	3.8	7.0
Electrical equipment	0.8	4.2
Transport equipment	0.7	2.2
Other manufactures	0.2	0.5
Construction	16.3	–
Electricity and water	15.3	1.5

Gross Output

Source	millions Kwacha	% of gross output
Domestic intermediate inputs	98.4	19.9
Imported intermediate inputs	37.9	7.7
Depreciation	15.8	3.2
Wages and salaries	91.9	18.6
Customs duties	0.1	–
Royalties and other indirect taxes	105.1	21.2
Operating surplus	145.8	29.4
Gross output	494.9	100.0
Distribution		
Metal mining	13.5	2.7
Electricity and water	1.4	–
Exports	437.8	88.5
Gross fixed capital formation	20.2	4.2
Stock building	21.8	4.4
Gross output	494.9	100.0

Distribution	15.3	–
Banks and insurance, etc.	5.7	–
Real estate	0.8	–
Railway transport	3.7	–
Road transport	1.3	–
Other transport	0.5	0.5
Posts and telecommunications	1.2	3.4
Business services	3.4	–
Unspecified	3.2	1.5
Total intermediate inputs	98.4	37.9

Gross Fixed Capital Formation

Sectoral source	Domestic	Imported
	(millions Kwacha)	
Metal mining	20.2	–
Sawmills, joineries, etc.	0.1	0.2
Foundries and metal products	0.8	0.2
Machinery	1.6	4.3
Electrical equipment	–	4.1
Transport equipment	0.1	1.4
Distribution	1.1	–
Total gross fixed capital formation	23.9	10.3

Source: *National Accounts and Input-Output Tables* (Lusaka: Government of Zambia, 1967).

Since 1967 certain changes have occurred which would modify our findings based on the 1967 input-output table. More inputs into the mines are now made locally. An explosives factory has been established at Kafironda on the Copperbelt to manufacture blasting materials out of ammonium nitrate produced by Nitrogen Chemicals' plant at Kafue. The mines' coal needs are met increasingly from Maamba in Zambia's southern province, rather than Wankie in Rhodesia. The Kafue Gorge hydroelectric plant will raise the Zambian component in electricity supplies (though it is not clear how much one should treat the present electricity from Kariba as an import, since the Kariba power station belongs 50 percent to Zambia). Furthermore, many small moves toward import-substitution have taken place, such as the manufacture of rubber conveyor belts, mining boots, electric wire, and a whole variety of metal products.

On the end-use side, a notable development has been the inauguration of a copper fabricating industry (Zamefa) producing K4 million of copper wire annually, with hopes of a sizeable export market.

Thus far, our field of vision has been restricted to the direct effects of the copper sector on the rest of the economy. Later we shall use standard input-output techniques to evaluate indirect effects, but we have to leave out one notable indirect effect—that of government tax revenue spent throughout the country. In many ways, this last effect is the most important for the development of Zambia, yet adequate analysis of it will have to wait until it is possible to prepare a dynamic input-output model for the country.

Social Opportunity Costs

The lack of any suitable dynamic model to take account of all the repercussions of the copper mines' activities upon the rest of the economy limits our

---

the current inputs from these four sectors by the same respective amounts. As a result we obtained the following revised values for current and capital inputs into mining:

Revised Current Inputs	
Sector	Revised value of inputs Kmn
Construction (domestic)	1.1
Transport equipment (domestic)	0.1
Machinery (domestic)	0.3
Electrical equipment (domestic)	0.1

Revised Capital Inputs	
Sector	Revised value of inputs Kmn
Metal mining (domestic)	–
Construction (domestic)	15.2
Transport equipment (domestic)	0.7
Machinery (domestic)	5.1
Electrical equipment (domestic)	0.7

ability to give quantitative estimates of the social opportunity costs of the factors involved in copper production. This does not proscribe, however, verbal "estimations" of their magnitudes. Nevertheless, it should remain clear that copper mining has long been, and still is, overwhelmingly the most important sector of the Zambian economy. As we have seen, without copper, Zambia would probably have been a poor, labor-exporting, agriculturally based country, much like Malawi, or, until recently, Botswana. The "with copper" and "without copper" situations are so unalike and the changes involved in moving from one situation to the other are so decidedly nonmarginal that most of the conditions necessary to attempt a true evaluation of social opportunity costs are just not satisfied.

With these strong provisos ever-present, a few points can be made. Little-Mirrlees' techniques have tried, when estimating social opportunity costs, to take into account the marginal productivity of agricultural labor (i.e., the foregone agricultural production) and the imports required to meet the extra demands of a worker once he has gotten a mining or industrial job.[14] A rough attempt by economists in the Ministry of Trade and Industry to use this technique as a basis for shadow pricing of local labor when appraising some industrial projects in Zambia has indicated a shadow price equal to 60 percent of the market price. Nevertheless, this does not give due consideration to various factors which, though unquantifiable, raise the true social opportunity cost of local mine labor. The most important is the demonstration effect of copper wages on wages elsewhere in the economy. This effect helps to explain why the minimum agricultural wage in Zambia is 70 ngwee per day, compared with 25 ngwee per day in Kenya, and why the Zambian Government now finds itself forced to subsidize the country's main agricultural export, tobacco.[k]

Another demonstration effect of the mining labor force on the rest of the economy results from the miners' rather ostentatious luxury expenditure (e.g., on beer, which budget surveys suggest takes up to 25 percent of a typical copper miner's income, or on imported goods) being emulated by other industrial workers. Copper wages influence those in other sectors via both trade unions and political pressures.[15]

On the other hand, the copper mines generate some spill-off of skills, particularly mechanical skills; and savings made by copper miners often provide the capital necessary for the establishment of small businesses on the Copperbelt, and elsewhere. So there are some advantages for the rest of the community from the copper miners' high incomes. But taking everything together, the demonstration effect of copper wages on wages elsewhere probably outweighs such advantages. Hence in strictly social terms, the opportunity cost of a Zambian copper miner may well be as high as his actual wages.

---

[k]One might add that copper also makes it possible to pay such high wages.

The position of expatriate labor is much like that of the local copper miners inasmuch as the demonstration effects of their consumption expenditure must considerably offset the benefits they bring to the community through their training of local workers. For a start, expatriate miners are very highly paid, and their heavily subsidized housing, fringe-benefits (sports, education, and health facilities), free international travel, etc., further increase the real money cost of their employment. They have very favorable conditions for the repatriation of earnings and for the importation of household goods and cars, duty-free. And on top of this, they face the most generous income tax system in Africa. Their high incomes and opulent way of life do not pass unobserved by the Zambian mine workers, and the persistence of the differential between the standards of living of the two groups remains a visible target for Zambian mine workers. In any event the social opportunity cost of expatriate employment is surely at least equal to the salaries paid.

In the case of capital, the social opportunity cost depends upon the extent to which investment in the copper mines is undertaken at the expense of investment in other sectors. And this in turn depends upon the institutional aspects of the control of the remittance of funds out of the country.

Before Mulungushi Economic Reforms of April 1968, all post-tax profits of the mines could be freely remitted out of Zambia. Accordingly, the retention of such funds for investment within Zambia could be considered as being equivalent to raising investment funds from abroad. Since practically all investment in mining is financed either out of profits or by raising funds abroad, the immediate social opportunity cost of capital in mining prior to 1968 might be taken to be zero. After April 1968, the exchange control regulations were amended to prevent the remittance of more than 50 percent of post-tax profits, and a choice was therefore created between investing blocked funds in copper mining or investing them elsewhere. What actually happened was that the blocked funds accumulated as liquid assets in Zambia (incidentally driving the interest rate of Treasury Bills down to just over 1 percent) until they were released as part of the takeover agreements. The period involved (about 18 months) was too short for any substantial changes in mining investment plans to have been made, especially in light of uncertainties about the future form of the tax structure and about the possibility of takeover.[16]

Since the takeover, it has once again become possible to remit freely the privately held share of profits. But the changes introduced by the takeover have induced a large expansion of investment in copper. The mining companies may now write off 100 percent of capital expenditure against tax liabilities in the year in which the expenditure is made, thus producing an investment bias towards copper. The takeover agreements specify that the private sector directors have a veto over any use of profits in non-mining investment. In practice, there have been some non-mining investments since 1969, but they have been small. The position is thus much as it was before the first restrictions were imposed in 1968—finance for mining investment is noncompetitive with other types of investment so that there is a social opportunity cost for mining investment only to the extent that induced investment in coal, electricity, etc., strains the internal resources of the economy.

The case of foreign exchange is especially interesting since Zambia was long in the strange situation of enjoying a balance-of-payments surplus with a currency which was generally accepted as being overvalued. This seemingly inconsistent state of affairs came about as a consequence of the rigid physical constraints that applied to Zambia's transport routes. This constraint led to a considerable inelasticity in the supply of imports to the Zambian market, where an attempt to raise the volume of imports only increased delays at the ports (Dar-es-Salaam, Beira, and Lobito) serving Zambia. While this transport constraint was operative, copper with its high value/weight and value/volume ratios was able to leave the country and more than pay for the incoming imports. Furthermore, in practically every year in the recent past there has been a serious crisis over the importation of some essential, bulky and low value/ weight commodities, e.g., petrol, fertilizer, wheat, maize, coal, and cement. At any given point in time, there are probably as much as K100 million of imports tied up en route to Zambia, a significant amount when compared with Zambia's annual visible import bill of K350 millions.

The other factor leading to balance-of-payments surpluses has been the very high recent price of copper. Because a high copper price removed the immediate need to devalue, the diversification of the economy was substantially hindered. This then is one reason Zambia has been so slow to develop alternative exports, and, for example, food imports are still so substantial. By every criteria except the financial balance of international payments, the Kwacha has been overvalued. Balance-of-payment deficits were only prevented at current exchange rates by substantial intentional (licensing, tariffs) and unintentional (transport) limitations on the inflow of imports. Thus wages are twice as high (or more) as in neighboring countries like Malawi, Zaire, and the East African nations. The point is further demonstrated by the government having to provide a subsidy for tobacco, and the heavy protection needed for local manufactures, even in industries such as clothing with negligible economies of scale.

Impact on Imports and Employment

Earlier we discussed the direct current and capital inputs into the copper mining sector, and then suggested some improvements to be made in those figures. A much better way to understand the relationship between a sector and the rest of the economy is given by the use of standard Leontief input-output techniques, which permit us to quantify both the direct and indirect effects of one sector upon the others. Accordingly, we use a slightly amended version of the 1967 Zambian input-output table, which when taken with other data such as the 1966-68 employment statistics produced by the Central Statistical Office, allows us to calculate the total (direct plus indirect) effect upon imports, Zambian employment and expatriate employment of a unit change in the final demand for any sector.

We start with the amendments. The published Zambian input-output table lists thirty-eight productive sectors. The final demand comes from private consumption, government consumption, exports, gross fixed capital formation, and change in stocks. Primary inputs come in the main from wages and salaries, and gross operating surplus; royalties and indirect taxation, depreciation, subsidies, and customs duties also appear.

The first amendment is to reconstruct the sector called "Agriculture, Forestry, and Fishing." We first went back to the 1967 National Accounts to eliminate the subsistence-farming sector. This was quite straightforward, since all inputs to subsistence farming were attributed to gross operating surplus, and all outputs were considered as going to private consumption. Then we consulted with the Central Statistical Office to break down the remaining figures into two distinct sectors: commercial farming and forestry, and fishing.

Our second amendment is to make private consumption endogenous to the model. This involved estimating the shares of wages and salaries, and profits, which found their way through to private consumption in each sector. Using the employment and earnings data, we were able to estimate the total wage payments to Zambians and expatriates in each sector, and on the basis of the findings of Urban Budget Surveys and information in the National Accounts on the level of personal remittances out of the country, we assumed that Zambians consumed 90 percent of their earnings, while expatriates consumed only 60 percent. Our estimates of the proportions of profits consumed in each sector were based upon reasonable guesswork. In fact, changes in these proportions do not seem to affect our conclusions at all significantly.

Our final amendment was to make use of the changes made above in the inputs to the mining sector.

Using our 40 X 40 input-output table, and standard input-output techniques, we consider for each sector, in turn, the import and employment repercussions of a unit increase in the final demand for that sector's product while all other final demands are unaltered. The results are summarized in Table 9-2.

The copper-mining sector holds a low ranking in each of the columns, A, B, and C. Compared with other sectors, copper generates little demand for imported current inputs, or expatriate or local labor. Indeed the spread effects of copper on the current input side are rather limited.

When one looks at the rankings in this table, one can distinguish five different types of sectors:

1. sectors whose activities are restricted to mere mixing or assembly of imported inputs, with low rankings in columns B and C, but a high ranking

in column A, e.g., other food, or machinery;
2. labor-intensive service industries, with high rankings in columns B and C,
    and with a low ranking in column A, e.g., education;
3. sectors that are intensive in skills with a high ranking in column B and low
    rankings in columns A and C, e.g., banking and insurance or electrical
    machinery;
4. sectors where a relatively high value in rank in one column is "balanced"
    by lower values elsewhere; and
5. two sectors, beverages-tobacco and metal mining, with low ranks in every
    column.

Profits can be broken down further into gross operating surplus, and a large
measure of royalties and indirect taxation. Thus we are left with two possible
reasons for the two unusual sectors in Group 5. Either they are much more
capital-intensive than the others or they are able to secure a large measure of
economic rent, which is then partly taxed away.

Copper-Mining Linkages

In addition to the effects on the Zambian economy of government expenditure of copper revenues, the copper industry has had forward and backward linkages with other sectors.

There are only two possible forward linkages. The first one is very minor,
consisting of the manufacture of copper ornaments, lamps, vases, bowls, and
so on; this is a dubious sort of linkage since the ornaments are made from
specially treated imported copper. The major linkage consists of a K3 million
copper fabrication plant, Zambia Metal Fabricators, which is planned to produce
around 6,000 tons per annum of copper rod and wire, with up to 30 percent intended for export. In the 1972-76 Second National Development Plan, there is
listed a 300,000 ton copper fabrication plant, to export semimanufactures such
as sheet, tubing, wire, and rod. In fact, such a project seems unrealistic as long
as the main export markets remain sheltered behind high protective tariffs.
Nevertheless, a Zambian plant to fabricate copper sheet and tubing for the
Zambian and East African markets is a definite possibility. But the potential
Zambian home and export markets seem to be nowhere near large enough to
justify local manufacture of other copper-using products, such as copper sul-
phate or metal alloys.

With respect to backward linkages the Zambian picture is rather more encouraging. Some important sectors of the Zambian economy depend very
heavily on the copper industry. For instance, the foundries and metal products,
machinery, electricity and water, and other mining and quarrying sectors depend directly and indirectly on the mining sector for a half or more of their
sales. And the sawmills and joineries, chemicals and petroleum products, cement

Table 9-2
Impact on Imports and Employment of Sectoral Demand Changes (Zambia)

Sector whose final demand is raised by one unit	% of wages assumed spent on private consumption[a]	% of profits assumed spent on private consumption	A Imports (in K) generated per Kwacha of final demand [rank]	B Expatriate workers employeed per 1000 K of final demand [rank]	C Zambian workers employeed per 1000 K of final demand [rank]
Commercial farming and forestry	87	50	0.76 [4]	0.034 [23]	1.266 [3]
Metal mining	76	0	0.24 [40]	0.025 [32]	0.204 [36]
Other mining	86	30	0.50 [22]	0.034 [25]	0.783 [10]
Meat processing	80	0	0.84 [2]	0.034 [24]	0.623 [16]
Dairies	76	0	0.65 [8]	0.044 [15]	0.910 [7]
Grain mills	79	10	0.67 [7]	0.035 [22]	0.676 [13]
Bakeries	81	50	0.56 [17]	0.039 [19]	0.536 [17]
Other food	79	10	0.73 [5]	0.017 [40]	0.198 [37]
Breweries and tobacco manufacture	76	0	0.34 [37]	0.019 [39]	0.181 [39]
Textiles and clothing	83	30	0.62 [10]	0.025 [31]	0.435 [19]
Sawmills, joineries	83	20	0.58 [13]	0.038 [21]	0.574 [16]
Paper and printing	72	0	0.93 [1]	0.108 [2]	0.709 [12]
Rubber products	78	0	0.46 [29]	0.031 [28]	0.298 [30]
Chemical and petrol products	77	0	0.64 [9]	0.023 [35]	0.249 [32]
Bricks and clay products	88	30	0.49 [23]	0.028 [30]	1.046 [4]
Cement products	80	0	0.42 [35]	0.032 [26]	0.392 [21]
Foundries and metal products	76	10	0.58 [14]	0.039 [19]	0.309 [29]
Machinery	78	0	0.61 [11]	0.022 [37]	0.207 [34]
Electrical equipment	72	10	0.48 [26]	0.062 [9]	0.364 [26]
Transport equipment	75	10	0.54 [20]	0.024 [33]	0.205 [35]
Other manufactures	73	10	0.58 [12]	0.052 [12]	0.347 [28]

Construction	83	10	0.52	[21]	0.042	[16]	0.756 [11]
Electricity and water	76	0	0.68	[6]	0.022	[36]	0.185 [38]
Distribution	72	50[b]	0.42	[34]	0.054	[10]	0.383 [22]
Banks and insurance	65	0	0.28	[39]	0.086	[5]	0.216 [33]
Real estate	80	0	0.30	[38]	0.024	[34]	0.266 [31]
Railway transport	75	0	0.47	[28]	0.049	[13]	0.380 [24]
Road transport	79	10	0.45	[31]	0.040	[18]	0.455 [18]
Other transport	71	0	0.49	[25]	0.089	[4]	0.415 [20]
Posts and telecommunications	78	0	0.55	[18]	0.032	[27]	0.350 [27]
Government administration	79	0	0.46	[30]	0.066	[8]	0.818 [8]
Education	74	0	0.44	[32]	0.140	[1]	0.966 [6]
Health	76	50	0.48	[27]	0.067	[7]	0.603 [15]
Business services	68	50	0.38	[36]	0.075	[6]	0.374 [25]
Recreational and nonbusiness services	78	0	0.54	[19]	0.107	[3]	1.024 [5]
Hotels and restaurants	82	30	0.42	[33]	0.053	[11]	0.810 [9]
Other personal services	88	50	0.49	[24]	0.045	[14]	3.377 [2]
Unspecified	79	n.a.	0.78	[3]	0.020	[38]	0.179 [40]
Private consumption	n.a.	n.a.	0.57	[15]	0.031	[29]	0.383 [23]
Fishing[c]	90	90	0.56	[16]	0.041	[17]	7.513 [1]

[a]As mentioned above, expatriates were assumed to consume only 60 percent of their earnings, while Zambians consumed 90 percent. Accordingly, in this table, a higher value indicates a larger proportion of earnings paid to Zambians. In particular a sector consuming over 75 percent of its wages can be taken to pay a larger wage bill to Zambians than to expatriates. The reverse holds true when the percentage falls below 75—banks and insurance are an extreme example of this.

[b]We have also carried out this exercise with the assumption that the distribution sector consumed only 30 percent of its profits. This made only a very minor difference to the results, and left almost all rankings unaltered.

[c]On the basis of consultations with people in the Ministry of Lands and Natural Resources we have taken the number of full-time fishermen to be 5,000—implying an annual average level of earnings, net of inputs, of K140.

Sources: Central Statistical Office, Lusaka: *1967 National Accounts and Input-Output Table (amended)*; *Report on Employment and Earnings 1966-68.*

and cement products, banks and insurance, road transport, posts and telecommunications, business services, and "unspecified" sectors, all depend on copper for at least 10 percent of their sales.

The impact of political independence in 1964 and Rhodesia's UDI in 1965 on manufacturing development have already been discussed; much of this expansion has been to supply the mines, and nearly all has been indirectly linked to mining insofar as the whole economy is copper-dependent. UDI also hastened the decision to build the railway to Dar-es-Salaam. Although this is being financed by an exceptionally generous Chinese loan, there are some costs because this loan is unusually closely tied, all local costs having to be financed out of the local receipts from the sales of imported Chinese goods. However, this does at least remove much of the potential inflationary effect of such a large scheme upon such a relatively small economy. There are many other costs associated with this railway, but it is clear from the chain of events that have followed the illegal Rhodesian regime's blockade of Zambia's southern import routes in January 1973 that, on purely strategic grounds, Zambia would have been extremely unwise to have continued to rely on the southern route.

Conclusions

Lack of indigenous political power in Zambia before 1964 meant that nothing was done about dependence on the one international transport route through Rhodesia, about dependence on South Africa and Rhodesia for 60 percent of imports, or about foreign dominance of industrial ownership and of virtually all skill levels except the lowest, and meant that the Kariba Dam on the Rhodesian border was built (with the power station on the southern bank) before the Kafue Dam which is inside the country. Since 1964 new roads have been built North and East, a railway is being built to Dar-es-Salaam, South Africa and Rhodesia now supply only 20 percent of imports, the government owns 51 percent of nearly all major firms and education and training have been enormously expanded, the Kafue Dam is built, and Kariba North is under construction. But the economy remains as dependent on copper as ever. In fact it is in a certain sense more dependent. Zambia has given its people a standard of living—including government-supplied services—which depends on higher earnings from copper than were necessary in the past. The economy is no nearer to being able to export agricultural goods, manufactured goods, or tourist services on any increasing scale. On the contrary, exports other than copper have actually fallen since 1964, and food imports were at a record high level in 1972. Since noncopper exports would have to double in order to pay for a modest 6 percent growth in imports, and assuming that the government cannot rely on a rising copper price and needs its foreign exchange reserves to guard against price falls, it is clear that growth depends in the short term on expanding production of copper.

But increasing copper production will lead to ever-increasing dependence on copper. The question remains therefore whether 70 percent of wildly fluctuating mining profits (87 percent after 1980) can be used to develop a country that has been dependent on copper for so many years in so many ways, that must remain dependent on copper for a decade or two and probably longer, that will always be landlocked, and that cannot at the moment cooperate with at least four out of its seven neighbors.

Clearly, Zambian industry could develop in such a way that, based on import substitution in consumer goods only, it will simply become more dependent on imports. Equally, there could develop a class whose interest was to exploit the majority within Zambia, and encourage the exploitation of the country by external capitalism, but it is at least arguable that this pattern has not yet emerged. In any case, the Russian alternative—the prior development of heavy industry in an economy largely cut off from the capitalist world—is not really viable in Zambia, both because of the absence of the necessary skills, and the small size of the economy.

One can add that although the urban population in general, and certain parts of it in particular, have done better out of the post-independence boom than the rural population, this fact has already produced a political reaction. The price of maize has been raised substantially, thus producing a big shift in the rural-urban terms of trade, and agriculture is receiving high political priority. Zambia is probably unique in having at times spent more in agricultural subsidies than the entire marketed output of agriculture; that may be inefficient, but it is hardly exploitation. (Not all subsidies benefit the rural areas, some being spent on subsidizing imports and some on covering the losses of an inefficient parastatal marketing body.) What is more, there is an almost complete absence of landlordism in Zambia, and a surplus of land in most areas. There is thus the potential, still very far from being realized, of increases in both production and exports, and of exercising some choice in the products to be exported in order to avoid those which are a drag on the market.

Thus while industrialization will no doubt continue, the government would seem to be right in having shifted the avowed emphasis in the Second National Development Plan, since it is in agriculture that the best hopes lie for alternative exports and for extending development to the majority who are also the poorest. Unfortunately, however, quantitative projections for the period of the plan are not completely consistent with the proclaimed emphasis on agriculture. Output of agriculture over the plan period is predicted to grow more slowly than that of the mining sector (5.5 percent annually as against 6.1 percent), and less than half as fast as manufacturing output with its projected growth rate of 14.7 percent.

Notes

1. For a recent discussion of the legality of the BSA Co.'s mineral concessions, see Peter Slinn, "The Legacy of the British South African Company: The

Historical Background," in Mark Bostock and Charles Harvey, eds., *Economic Independence and Zambian Copper* (New York: Praeger Publishers, 1972), especially p. 47.

2. R. E. Baldwin, *Economic Development and Export Growth—A Study of Northern Rhodesia 1920-1960* (Berkeley: University of California Press, 1966), pp. 16 ff.
3. For a chronology of significant events, see Bostock and Harvey, op. cit., p. xviii.
4. See Peter Slinn in Bostock and Harvey, op. cit.
5. For the figures see Arthur Hazelwood, ed., *African Integration and Disintegration* (London: Oxford University Press, 1967), p. 249.
6. See Rev. K. Quinn, "Industrial Relations in Zambia 1935-69" in Elliott, op. cit., pp. 60-61.
7. See, for example, A. Oberschall, "Small Enterprises in Kapwepwe Compound," (Lusaka: Institute for African Studies, 1971). One example given is of a man who saved £500 during 20 years as a miner, started a grocery, and now nets K700 a month.
8. Speech by President Kaunda in 1965, quoted in Trevor Coombe, "The Origins of Secondary Education in Zambia: Policy-Making in the Thirties," *African Social Research,* No. 3, p. 173.
9. "Manpower Report" (Lusaka: Government Printer, 1966), p. 1.
10. For discussion of mining taxation, see Harvey's chapter, "The Fiscal System," in Elliott, op. cit., Harvey's chapter, "Tax Reform in the Mining Industry," and Andrew Gordon's chapter, "The Prospects for New Mine Investment," in Bostock and Harvey, op. cit.
11. For a more extended account of post-independence growth, see Harvey's chapter, "Growth and Structure of the Economy," in Bostock and Harvey, op. cit., and for slightly earlier but more detailed accounts see Harvey's chapter, "Financial Constraints," in Elliott, op. cit., and Harvey, "The Control of Inflation in a Very Open Economy: Zambia 1964-69," *Eastern African Economic Review,* June 1971.
12. This account is derived from Bostock and Harvey, op. cit. For a briefer account see Charles Harvey, "Economic Independence: A View from Zambia," to appear shortly in a conference volume edited by Dharam Ghai. An alternative account can be found in M. J. J. Faber and J. Potter, "Towards Economic Independence: Papers on the Nationalisation of the Zambian Copper Mines" (Cambridge: Department of Applied Economics, 1971). No further references will be given in this section.
13. For relations between the governing party and the mine workers union, see R. H. Bates, *Unions, Parties, and Political Development* (London and New Haven, Conn.: Yale University Press 1971), passim. For a contrary view, see M. Buraway's review in *African Social Research,* No. 13, June 1972. For detailed evidence of the wage-leadership role of the miners in 1966 and 1967, see J. B. Knight, "Wages and Zambia's Economic Development," in Elliott, op. cit., especially Table 4.3, p. 102.
14. I. M. D. Little and J. A. Mirrlees, *Manual of Industrial Project Analysis in Developing Countries, Vol. II* (Paris: Organization for Economic Cooperation and Development, 1968).

15. See J. Knight in C. Elliot, op. cit., and J. Fry, "Prices, Incomes, Employ-
    ment and Labour Productivity" and "Issues in Wage Determination," in
    J. Fry, ed., *The Labour Market in Zambia,* (Lusaka and Manchester:
    Manchester University Press for the Institute of African Studies, forth-
    coming, 1974).
16. For a detailed discussion of influences on investment decisions before and
    after the takeover, see Bostock and Harvey, op. cit., pp. 152-57.

General Notes

1. *Copper mining:*   Zambian copper mining has been organized in two major
   companies since the early 1930s when modern mining began on a large
   scale. The two groups are Anglo-American and RST (Roan Selection Trust,
   previously Rhodesian Selection Trust). In 1969 the Zambian government
   acquired 51 percent of the mines in both groups, although management
   contracts gave control of all important decisions to the existing managements. In 1970 RST was taken over by American Metal Climax. The new
   jointly owned operative groups are called NCCN and RCM.
       Copper production in Zambia is about 700,000 metric tons a year, roughly
   the same as in Chile. The two are the world's largest producers after the
   U.S.A. and the USSR. Most (85 percent) of the copper is fully refined in
   Zambia, and exported in the form of electrolytic wirebars.
2. *Currency:*   Until 1967 the Zambian pound was the same as the pound
   sterling. Zambia did not follow the British devaluation of November 1967,
   so that the Zambian pound remained equal to U.S. $2.80. In January 1968
   the Zambian currency was decimalized on the basis of £1 Zambian =
   2 Kwacha, 1 Kwacha = 100 ngwee. The Kwacha thus equaled U.S. $1.40,
   and retained this value during the period after 1968 covered by this paper.
       We have used pounds for the prewar period, when £1 = U.S. $4.00
   (after 1931), and Kwacha as much as possible for the postwar period. It
   would have been anachronistic to try to use Kwacha throughout.
3. *Weights:*   Copper production and ore reserves were in the past quoted in
   "long tons" (2240 lbs) and "short tons" (2000 lbs). In this chapter we
   have used metric tons (1000 Kgm = 2204 lbs approximately) to which
   the world is gradually moving.

10 The Developmental Impact of Mining Activities in Sierra Leone

Tony Killick*

During the two decades after the end of World War II, mining emerged as the leading sector in Sierra Leone's economy. In the absence of a reliable series of national accounts, this result is best indicated by export statistics. While agricultural exports fluctuated around an essentially horizontal trend line, the value of mineral exports expanded very rapidly. In consequence, the share of minerals rose from 45 percent of total exports in 1950 to 85 percent in 1967.[1] This expansion, largely brought about by foreign-owned companies, enabled Sierra Leone to achieve an increase in the total value of exports at an average rate of over 9 percent per annum in the period from 1959 to 1969.

This important change in the structure of Sierra Leone's economy had the further effect of adding substantially to the volume of wage labor employment[a] and also to the government's ability to finance developmental expenditures, both directly by means of export and excise taxes, and indirectly by permitting larger receipts from taxes on incomes, profits, and imports.[2] Since it appears that domestic food production was expanding slowly, if at all, such growth as occurred in the 1950s and 1960s can be attributed in large part to the expansion of the mining sector.

In the same period a modest amount of import-substituting industrialization also occurred, but the economy remained essentially based upon traditional agriculture, with 35 percent of national income estimated to originate from agricultural activities in 1968-69.[3] Manufacturing remains very small in spite of the postwar expansion; the output of this sector, including handicrafts, is estimated at about 6 percent of GDP. In this, as in other respects, the economy of Sierra Leone is characteristic of many African countries. It is small when measured by the size of its population (2.5 million in 1968), tiny when measured by the size of its GDP (£145 million in 1968-69) and minuscule when measured by the size of its market for manufactures (perhaps £50 million). It is heavily

*This chapter incorporates the substance of the author's article "The Benefits of Foreign Direct Investment and Its Alternatives: An Empirical Exploration," *The Journal of Development Studies* 9 (January 1973), pp. 301-16, and the editor's permission to use this previously published material is gratefully acknowledged. The author wishes to thank R. W. During and Lou Wells for helpful suggestions.

[a]The 1963 census of population showed that of a total labor force of 107,000 in the "modern" sectors of the economy, viz., mining, manufacturing, construction, electricity, gas, and water, some 47,000, or 44 percent, were employed in mining. *Population Census of Sierra Leone,* Vol. 3, *Economic Characteristics* (Freetown: Government of Sierra Leone, 1963).

217

dependent on foreign trade; the mean value of exports and imports of goods and services in 1966-67 to 1968-69 was equivalent to about 27 percent of GDP. It is sparsely populated and estimates of population growth range from 1 percent per annum upwards.

Four economic minerals are produced on a significant scale in Sierra Leone: diamonds, iron ore, bauxite, and rutile.[b] Diamond mining is easily the most important, with exports of £30.94 million accounting for five-sixths of the total value of mineral exports in 1969. All of these minerals are produced wholly for export and, with one minor exception, are shipped in an unprocessed state. During the 1960s the mining of iron ore, bauxite, and rutile was solely undertaken by wholly owned subsidiaries of companies registered in the United Kingdom and the United States. The structure of the diamond industry, however, was more interesting. About two-fifths[c] of diamond production was recovered by a wholly owned subsidiary of a British firm, the Sierra Leone Selection Trust (SLST). The remainder of the output was won by Africans working in small teams and using only the simplest equipment—buckets, spades, bowls, sieves, and, in rare cases, mechanical pumps. This part of the industry will be described in more detail later; for the present, attention will be confined to the activities of the foreign companies.

During 1969, the Sierra Leone government announced its intention of taking a controlling share in foreign mining operations in the country, and it has since partially implemented this decision. It reached an agreement in 1970 with the parent company of SLST, which provided for the reconstitution of the company, with the government holding 51 percent of the shares but with the day-to-day running of the company in the hands of the management of the former SLST.

This study is mainly concerned with the period when the companies were wholly foreign-owned. In a later section an attempt is made to throw some light on the economics of the takeover, and by so doing to enable something to be said about the extent to which the benefits derived by an economy from mining investment are influenced by the nationality of ownership. But the principal purpose of this essay is to examine the developmental benefits derived by the host economy from the activities of foreign-owned companies and, in the case of diamonds, to compare these with the benefits derived from an alternative mode of production.[4] The selection of the mining sector is a significant one, for in choosing between alternative modes of production the decision is especially critical in the case of mineral extraction. In the nature of things, this is a once-and-for-all process, and the problem therefore arises, how to derive

---

[b]In chemical terms, rutile is titanium dioxide and is used for making pigments and titanium metal, and for welding-rod coatings.

[c]It is impossible to be very precise because of the difficulties of estimating the value of diamonds smuggled out of the country.

the maximum benefit for the national economy from the exploitation of this wasting asset.[d]

The following criteria are employed:

1. the directly attributable net addition to value added within the national economy of the host country,[e]
2. linkage effects, of the type recorded in an input-output matrix, and
3. the generation of external economies.[f]

Foreign-Owned Mining Operations

Direct Contributions

We commence with an examination of the direct contribution of the foreign mining companies to various national accounting concepts, as shown in Table 10–1. Two methods are available to compute value-added. The first is to subtract from gross output the value of material inputs utilized for current production. This is done in items 1 through 3 of the table, on the basis of rather approximate estimates of current inputs. Alternatively, we can sum payments for current factor inputs (including depreciation), which are listed in items 4 through 7. If this is done, there is a discrepancy of £0.09 million with the total at item 3 and this is liable to have arisen partly because of rather poor wage and salary statistics. A balancing item has therefore been inserted (item 8) on the assumption that the item 3 figure is the correct one. The small size of the item makes the question of whether the error should be attributed to the estimates of material or factor inputs of no consequence. No attempt is made at this stage to adjust these valuations for the opportunity costs of the factors employed, but this point is taken up later.

The value obtained for gross domestic value-added is £9.63 million (item 3).

[d]Bad agricultural or silvicultural practices on virgin land can result in soil erosion so severe as to make subsequent cultivation difficult or even impossible, and in this event the result is comparable with the once-and-for-all extraction of minerals.

[e]The emphasis here is on the contribution to the *national* economy as distinguished in national accounting from the domestic economy. There may be a major difference between these because of the return flow of profits and other foreign factor rewards. To take the by no means exceptional example of neighboring Liberia, one-fifth of estimated GDP is remitted as property income paid abroad. Cf. Clower, Dalton, Harwitz, and Walters, *Growth Without Development* (Evanston, Ill.: Northwestern Univ. Press, 1966), Table 13, who stress the small stimulation derived by Liberia's economy from foreign-owned primary production.

[f]We may take external economies to refer here to any stimulating effects that are not subsumed as backward or forward linkage effects on the rest of the economy. This is an interpretation similar to Rostow's "lateral effects"; cf. W. W. Rostow, ed., *Economics of Take-off into Self-sustained Growth* (London: Macmillan, 1963), pp. 5-6.

Table 10–1

Output, Inputs and Value-Added of Foreign Mining Companies (Sierra Leone)

		£ millions[a]	
1.	Gross output[b]	13.23	(13.23)
2.	*Less* material inputs		
	(i) Imported	2.36	(2.36)
	(ii) Locally produced	1.24	(1.24)
3.	Gross domestic value-added	9.63	(9.63)
	of which –		
4.	Wage and salary payments[c]		
	(i) To expatriates	0.90	(0.90)[i]
	(ii) To Sierra Leoneans	1.55	(1.55)
4a.	Compensation payments and management fees	–	(1.75)[j]
5.	Direct tax payments[d]	2.65	(2.91)[k]
6.	Depreciation[e]	1.18	(1.18)[l]
7.	Profits to foreign shareholders[f]	3.26	(0.61)[m]
7a.	Profits to Sierra Leonean government	–	(0.64)
8,	Errors and omissions[g]	0.09	(0.09)
9.	Gross national value-added (item 3 minus item 4a minus item 7)[h]	6.37	(7.27)
10.	Net national value-added (item 9 minus item 6)	5.19	(6.09)
11.	Item (10) as % of item (1)	39%	(46%)
12.	Item (10) as % of item (3)	54%	(63%)
13.	Production costs (item 2 plus item 4 plus item 6)	7.23	(7.23)
14.	Production costs as % of gross output	55%	(55%)

Note: Figures in parentheses reflect hypothetical "after nationalization" values. See p. 233.

[a]To minimize distortions created by temporary abnormalities, the values recorded are the means of the years 1963-65. Values are expressed in pounds sterling. In the course of 1964 Sierra Leone introduced a new national currency, the principal unit of which was known as the Leone and exchanged for sterling at the rate Le2.0 = £1.0. During the period from which the data are drawn sterling exchanged against the U.S. dollar at £1.0 = $2.8.

[b]Taken as equivalent to export values.

[c]Including payments in kind.

[d]Including diamond-marketing rules service fees.

[e]As recorded in company returns.

[f]Including undistributed profits but after tax and depreciation.

[g]This is the difference between item 3 (assumed to be correct) and the sum of items 4 to 7. The error is most likely to have resulted from poor wage and salary statistics.

[h]Besides deducting profits from gross domestic value added there would be a case for doing the same with wage and salary payments to expatriates [see item 4 (i)]. This has not been done in the table because these workers are residents of Sierra Leone on the usual national accounting definition (U.N., 1960, p. 7). Very few of them, on the other hand, will stay for more than a few years and meanwhile they will remit substantial proportions of their current incomes to their home countries. It was estimated that some 32 percent of expatriates' current incomes are repatriated and another 22 percent spent on imported goods and services (Killick and During, p. 292). Thus, it could be plausibly argued that of the average payment of £0.9 million to expatriates only about £0.4 million truly contributed to national value-added. This figure, moreover, makes no allowance for the often substantial lump-sum repatriation of accumulated savings at the end of an expatriate's sojourn in Sierra Leone.

[i]It is assumed that the composition of the labor force and their earnings would be un-affected by the nationalization in the medium term.

[j]This has been estimated by assuming the value of compensation to all the companies taken together would bear the same relationship to their 1963-65 average total assets as was actually the case for SLST. The figure is for one year's compensation plus 5.5 percent interest on half the total estimated sum of compensation. An arbitrary £250,000 has been added to cover management fees to the former owners and, for the purpose of estimating the contribution to national product, this sum has been taken as being in the nature of a capital outflow or payment to a foreign-based factor of production.

[k]At 70 percent of profits after depreciation.

[l]It is assumed that factor proportions and techniques (and hence depreciation) would be unchanged in the medium term.

[m]Profits allocated 51 percent to government, 49 percent to former owners.

Sources: Tony Killick and R. W. During, "A Structural Approach to the Balance of Pay-ments of a Low-income Country," *Journal of Development Studies* 4, no. 4 (1969), and previously unpublished data.

This is gross because it includes depreciation, and domestic because it in-cludes the factor rewards of non-nationals. This sum was equivalent to 8.7 per-cent of the mean value of the GDP at factor cost in 1963-64 to 1965-66.[g] If gross domestic value-added is the relevant indicator, it is evident that the mining companies made a significant contribution to income, output, and expenditure in Sierra Leone during this period. But a much better indication is given by figures that have been adjusted for the outflow of profits, for these accrued entirely to the incomes and asset values of foreigners and are excluded from estimates of the national product. We call the adjusted figure, shown in item 9 of Table 10-1 as £6.37 million, gross national value-added; it was equivalent to 5.9 percent of the mean value of GNP in 1963-64 to 1965-66.

Profits were about one-third of domestic value-added and 25 percent of gross output.[h] However, profits are more appropriately set against the capital investment that produces them. If we measure profits against the mean value of fixed assets employed, this calculation results in a rate of return to fixed capital of 24 percent per annum, net of Sierra Leone tax.[i]

Two qualifying points should be made. First, aggregation of the profits of the companies in question conceals large differences in their individual records

------

[g]The national accounts are computed for financial years, which run from July to June. The estimates for these years were the first to be computed in Sierra Leone and are subject to fairly wide margins of error [cf. Central Statistics Office, *National Accounts of Sierra Leone, 1963/64 to 1965/66* (Freetown, Sierra Leone: Government of Sierra Leone, 1967), p. 40]. Revisions of the national accounts would not, however, change the substance of our results.

[h]The profit figures to which we refer are net of Sierra Leone tax but were subject to additional taxation in the U.K., which reduced disposable profits to about 22 percent of gross revenue. We are speaking here of both distributed and undistributed profits.

[i]This calculation is based on company valuations of their fixed assets, and these may not reflect their true economic worth, depending on the methods of depreciation employed.

over these years. In fact, one company was showing net losses, while the profit rates of one of the remaining two were much higher than those of the other. Second, the profit figures in Table 10-1 include undistributed profit. Of the £3.26 million total profits after Sierra Leone tax, £1.28 were reinvested, and did not, therefore, truly represent a "leakage" from the Sierra Leone economy. Nevertheless, it is appropriate to exclude these reinvested profits from national value-added on the grounds that we are here concerned with the effects of past investment and that the reinvestment of profits is contingent on the perception of new investment possibilities that will in due course generate their own return flow to the investors.

Because depreciation expenditures were substantial, there is a significant further gap between the companies' contribution to GNP and their contribution to NNP.[j] Thus the relative size of the mining companies' contribution to the Sierra Leonean economy in the 1963-64 to 1965-66 period depends considerably upon which national accounting magnitude is used. The companies provided 8.7 percent of GDP, 5.9 percent of GNP, and 5.2 percent of NNP in the period studied.

Expansion by the mining companies which increased GDP by 1 percent in a given period would increase the NNP by only 0.6 percent. The difference would be even larger if we were to include foreign transfers of expatriate company employees in our measurement of foreign factor payments.

Industrial Linkages

There are good reasons for expecting weak linkages in this case: the national economy is very small and at an early stage of development; the companies are undertaking primary production and will thus have small requirements for inputs from other sectors of the economy; and since all output is sold abroad, there are no forward linkages. The small size of any backward linkages is demonstrated by the estimate in item 2 (ii) of Table 10-1 that inputs of local materials and nonfactor services averaged £1.24 million per annum, or 9.4 percent of gross output. Information on this aspect was admittedly poor, but even if the estimate is subject to a large margin of error, the nature of our conclusion would be unchanged.

External Economies

Although we make no attempt to carry out a systematic analysis of all the

---

[j]A small adjustment was made to the published GNP estimates to allow for subsequent revisions of the "net factor income from abroad" estimate. All valuations are in current prices and at factor cost.

potential external economies that might raise social benefits relative to private returns, several points can be made.

Employment. Since there is in Sierra Leone a high incidence of unemployment whose reduction is regarded as an economic objective in its own right, the creation of employment may be regarded as a type of external economy, to the extent that the social opportunity cost of labor is less than the going market wage. Productive techniques employed by the mining companies are rather capital-intensive, with fixed assets of £3,560 for every person employed. Total numbers employed by the companies averaged 7,790 over 1963-65. This was equivalent to 0.83 percent of the total labor force in the census year 1963, which can be compared with the companies' contribution to the GDP of 8.7 percent. The relatively small number of jobs created by the companies must have limited their ability to make a favorable impact on the creation of a permanent wage-labor force and on the rates of urbanization and social change.[k] This question of employment creation is discussed more fully below.

Creation of Skills. The two larger companies have their own training schemes for mechanics and other artisan skills, and they send some of their more promising workers for further training overseas. While some of the skills imparted may be fairly specific to mining, there is no doubt that a "wastage" of trained workers into other sectors has occurred, creating an external economy in the strict Marshallian sense. It is true, however, that for higher-level technical personnel the companies remained heavily reliant upon expatriates in this period. It is, moreover, doubtful whether there has been much spill-over of managerial skills from the companies into other sectors. Until recently they relied very largely upon expatriates to fill most supervisory and managerial posts, and only in rare cases would these employees go on to secure employment elsewhere in the local economy. As seen from Table 10-1, item 4, payments to expatriates are estimated to have taken up £900,000 out of an annual total wage bill of £2,450,000, even though expatriates comprised under 3 percent of the numbers employed. It should in fairness be added that there was some change during the 1960s and even without the state takeover Africanization could have been expected increasingly to penetrate into supervisory, higher-technical, and managerial positions. The small external economies created in the past may in this context be a rather poor guide to the future.

Infrastructure. The creation by the companies of infrastructural facilities whose utilization is not exclusive to the mining sector is another form of

---

[k]Saylor, op. cit., pp. 138-42, shows that the company mining iron ore expanded output by about two and a half times between 1945 and 1962 while actually reducing the size of its labor force a little. He attributes this to labor-saving investments stimulated by rapid increases in statutory wage rates.

external economy. In this connection, the diamond company maintains some 60 miles of road which are undoubtedly used for purposes additional to the company's. The company extracting iron ore operates a 50-mile railway to its own port at Pepel, but the use of this is largely confined to the haulage of ore.[l] Both the main companies have built housing and hospitals for their employees, and the latter are also used by local communities. In short, it seems probable that the infrastructure created by the mining companies generates real but not massive external economies. This, however, is a matter that would warrant considerably more investigation.

Taxability.   Tax receipts from foreign investors can be treated as a species of external economy in cases where a shortage of government revenue operates as a development constraint. In Sierra Leone during the years in question a strong case could be made that this condition was fulfilled. During these years the government ran into increasing financial difficulties, stemming partly from an inelastic tax structure, and as a result had recourse to IMF stand-by support and deflationary fiscal policies.[m] It can be calculated from Table 10-1, items 5 and 7, that tax payments were 45 percent of pretax profits. Tax agreements were subsequently revised and substantially larger revenues were expected thereafter.

Foreign Exchange.   The treatment of the foreign exchange earnings of the companies is somewhat similar, for in this period the nonmining sectors of the economy were running large and increasing balance-of-payments deficits, which contributed to a crisis in 1966 and the need to obtain IMF support.[n] In other words, it could be argued that the official rate of exchange did not at this time reflect the true value to the economy of foreign exchange and that the social benefit derived from the net foreign exchange earnings of the companies was in excess of their "market" value. This case is strengthened by the recurring nature of the country's balance-of-payments difficulties and its decision to follow Britain's devaluation of 14.3 percent in November 1967. The companies were making foreign exchange available at the rate of £9.0 million (see footnote n). If we assume a shadow price for foreign exchange corresponding to the new exchange rate established at the end of 1967, the value of this contribution to

---

[l]This railway was originally financed by a British government loan on aid terms, although the direct benefits therefrom accrue almost exclusively to the company. See Saylor, op. cit., p. 139.

[m]From 1963-64 to 1965-66 current government revenue receipts increased at the rate of 2.8 percent per annum while current expenditures rose at the rate of 9.5 percent per annum (Cf. Central Statistical Office, op. cit., 1967, Table 8).

[n]Tony Killick and R. W. During, "A Structural Approach to the Balance of Payments of a Low-Income Country," *Journal of Development Studies* 5, no. 4 (1969), Table 6, show that the nonmining company sectors generated deficits on current and nonmonetary capital accounts as follows (£m): 1963, 9.8; 1964, 7.9; and 1965, 11.0. During this period, the companies were making foreign exchange available at the rate of £9.0 million per annum (p. 280).

the Sierra Leonean economy increases by one-sixth.[o] However, the net benefit on current account was much smaller than the value of exports, and the ability of the companies to provide foreign exchange depended upon a capital-funds importation that may not have continued in the future. Moreover, when certain indirect factors were taken into account, the overall contribution of foreign exchange fell to £5.7 million per annum (at the then existing exchange rate), or only 43 percent of the value of export earnings.

This discussion of this section has shown that a number of factors limited the impact on Sierra Leone's economy of the investments of the foreign mining companies. Among these were low ratios of net national value-added to gross output and gross domestic value-added, slight industrial linkages, high capital intensity, and heavy dependence on expatriate skilled manpower. Some external economies, notably, a diffusion of lower-level technical skills, fairly large tax payments, and substantial net earnings of foreign exchange, were generated. In general, however, the balance of the argument is consistent with the views of those who stress the limited developmental effects of foreign private investment.[p] The next stage of this study is to examine the developmental effects of alternative methods of exploitation in the diamond industry.

An Alternative: The Alluvial Diamond Scheme

An interesting aspect of the Sierra Leonean case is that the diamond industry in this period exhibited a markedly dualistic character. On the one hand, a British company, Sierra Leone Selection Trust (SLST), won diamonds using techniques requiring large inputs of capital and managerial expertise. This company usually accounted for about two-fifths of diamond output. The rest, on the other hand, was won by African diggers using tiny amounts

---

[o]Some justification for using this rather crude proxy for a more carefully estimated shadow exchange rate is provided by the fact that the 1967 devaluation was followed by a substantial improvement in the external payments position. The trade balance moved into surplus in 1968 and 1969 and the country's external reserves went up from £5.7 million at the end of 1967 to £12.6 million two years later. International Monetary Fund, *Balance of Payments Yearbook* Vol. 23 (Washington, D.C., 1971), and *International Financial Statistics* (Washington, D.C., May 1972).

[p]Possibly the best-known expression of this view is by Hans Singer, "Distribution of Gains between Investing and Borrowing Countries" (1950), *American Economic Review Papers & Proceedings* 2, no. 2 (reproduced in his *International Development* (New York: McGraw-Hill, 1964), who argues that conditions today are such as to weight the distribution of gains from international investment heavily in favor of the investor. Berrill is even more skeptical, suggesting that although the bulk of nineteenth-century investment was beneficial to the recipients, there were some important cases in which the effects were actually harmful. India, Egypt, Latin America, Black Africa, and China are mentioned as examples and they practically embrace the whole of the present-day underdeveloped world (see his paper in Rostow, op. cit., pp. 287-89).

of capital and economizing on managerial skills.[q] This subindustry has a four-tier structure. First, about thirty-thousand laborers, who do the digging, are called tributors. Second, people misleadingly called diggers organize the tributors into gangs. Third, dealers buy diamonds from diggers and dispose of them legally to the Government Diamond Office or illegally by smuggling them to Liberia or elsewhere. Fourth, the Government Diamond Office is a marketing organization managed for the government by a subsidiary of the de Beers Group. The whole structure is known as the Alluvial Diamond Scheme (ADS).

All the tributors and diggers are African, most Sierra Leonean but including an admixture of people from other West African nations. Although there is a substantial minority of Sierra Leoneans among the dealers, in value terms an overwhelmingly large part of dealing is undertaken by Lebanese nationals. It would therefore be rather misleading to describe this industry as indigenous for, in common with the rest of the mining sector, the ADS has come to depend upon the assistance of foreign enterprise.

Direct Contributions

Comparisons between the ADS and the mining companies are made much more difficult by there being practically no solid information about the distribution of the earnings of the former. This problem is tackled by making two alternative sets of assumptions, designed to illustrate the most extreme possibilities. The main bone of contention relates to the repatriated profits of the Lebanese dealers, with apparently knowledgeable opinion differing greatly on this point. Our alternative assumptions take repatriated profits to be 2.5 percent of gross domestic value added in the "high-benefit" case and 25 percent in the "low-benefit" case. In the judgment of the author the true proportion is likely to be considerably nearer to 2.5 percent than 25 percent.[5]

Estimates comparable with those in Table 10-1 are set out below (Table 10-2), showing both high- and low-benefit cases. The output figures include a provision for smuggled diamonds. There is no depreciation figure in Table 10-2 and hence no distinction between gross and net value-added. This is because only tiny amounts of fixed capital are employed in the ADS and the figures on imported materials [item 2 (i)] are in this case calculated to include replacement buckets, spades, and other simple pieces of equipment.

The figures tabulated permit a number of direct comparisons between the ADS and the companies. It can rightly be protested that the relevant comparison

---

[q]Cf. H. L. Van der Laan, *Sierra Leone Diamonds* (London: Oxford University Press, 1965) p. 76 and passim, who estimated that SLST required about one-quarter of the labor needed in the alluvial diamond scheme per carat of diamonds produced. The saving on management skills is perhaps not quite as great as is sometimes imagined, for some managerial functions are undertaken by the Government Diamond Office and by the dealers.

Table 10-2

Output, Inputs and Value-Added of Alluvial Diamond Scheme on Alternative Assumptions (Sierra Leone) (£ millions)[a]

	(1) High-benefit case	(2) Low-benefit case
1. Gross output[b]	12.30	12.30
2. *Less* material inputs		
(i) Imported	0.10	0.10
(ii) Locally produced	0.02	0.02
3. Gross domestic value-added	12.18	12.18
of which—		
4. Payments to tributors	4.26	3.04
5. Payments to diggers and other Sierra Leoneans	5.78	4.87
6. Tax payments	0.91	0.61
7. Current consumption and local savings of dealers	0.91	0.61
8. Repatriated profits of dealers	0.30	3.04
9. Gross national value-added (= net national value-added) (item 3 minus item 8)	11.88	9.14
10. Item 9 as % of item 1	97%	74%
11. Item 9 as % of item 3	98%	75%
12. Production costs (item 2 plus item 4 plus item 5)	10.16	8.03
13. Production costs as % of gross output	83%	65%

[a]Values are the means of the years 1963-1965.
[b]Taken as equivalent to officially recorded exports plus an allowance for smuggling.
Sources: Tony Killick and R. W. During, "A Structural Approach to the Balance of Payments of a Low-income Country," *Journal of Development Studies* 4, no. 4 (1969), and previously unpublished data.

is with the diamond-mining concern SLST only, and not with all the companies taken together. Although it is not possible to make this comparison without disclosing confidential information, the general nature of results from comparing ADS and SLST is indicated in the text.

The first comparison is of the proportions of net national value-added to gross output and gross domestic value-added:

	Net national value-added as % of:	
	Gross output	Gross domestic value-added
Companies	39%	54%
ADS (high-benefit)	97%	98%
ADS (low-benefit)	74%	75%

From the point of view of the host country, the objective is to maximize the contribution to national income from the exploitation of a given deposit of diamonds. Even on the most pessimistic assumptions the extraction of a given value of diamonds by the techniques embodied in the ADS makes a contribution to national income clearly superior to that from equal extraction by the technically superior methods of the companies. This important conclusion holds also for a direct comparison with the diamond company, for SLST's figures are only slightly higher than those for all the companies. The relative disadvantage of the companies is derived partly from their proportionately greater use of material inputs, and partly from the greater "leakages" from the national income in the form of depreciation and profit repatriations.

Another interesting aspect of these statistics is revealed by a comparison of the bottom lines of Tables 10–1 and 10–2, which compare costs of production relative to gross output. The production costs of the companies are smaller relative to output than in either ADS case. The same is true on a direct comparison between SLST and ADS. In that "global" sense the companies are clearly the more efficient producers, and yet they clearly make a smaller contribution to Sierra Leonean national income.

A major line of objection should be dealt with at this point. It is sometimes argued that the SLST, because of its technically superior methods, will extract a larger quantity of diamonds from a given diamondiferous area than will the ADS. This, however, is a disputed claim; if it is conceded that areas covered by the ADS are likely to be dug over more than once and that the SLST may exclude as unpayable areas that would be profitable to exploit using ADS methods, it ceases to be self-evident which segment of the industry would achieve the higher extraction rate.[r] Assuming for the sake of the argument that the SLST would be higher, Table 10–3 permits a judgment about the extent to which the SLST rate would have to exceed that of the ADS in order for the former to produce a larger net national value-added from a given diamond deposit. Using the proportions reported above, the following figures show the net national value added that would be derived from an area containing diamonds worth £100 at alternative extraction rates. The companies' contribution to national income even with a 100 percent extraction rate is smaller than all the ADS high-benefit cases and all but one of the low-benefit cases. In only one combination, 100 percent extraction by companies and 50 percent extraction by the ADS (low-benefit case), do the companies contribute more to national income. Since this extreme combination is not at all a plausible approximation of reality, we may take the evidence as demonstrating quite firmly the superior contribution of the ADS to national income from a given diamond deposit. Use of SLST data would change the numerical, but not the substantive, results.

---

[r]This argument is developed more fully in Killick and During, pp.286-87; see also Van der Laan, pp. 79-81. In the absence of firm evidence to the contrary, our treatment of this problem assumes extraction by both techniques to be achieved over an identical time-span.

Table 10–3
Net National Value-Added Derived from an Area Containing Diamonds Worth
£100, at Alternative Extraction Rates (in pounds) (Sierra Leone)

Rate of extraction	(1) Companies		(2) ADS (high-benefit)		(3) ADS (low-benefit)	
100%	39	(36)	97	(84)	74	(62)
95%	37	(34)	92	(80)	70	(59)
85%	33	(31)	82	(71)	63	(53)
75%	29	(27)	73	(63)	56	(47)
65%	25	(23)	63	(53)	48	(40)
50%	20	(18)	49	(42)	37	(31)

Note: Figures in parentheses reflect certain adjustments made by the author. See pp. 231-2.
Source: Author's calculations.

Industrial Linkages

It is obvious from a glance at the estimates of material inputs [Table 10–2, item 2 (ii)] that the ADS possesses virtually no backward linkages with other productive sectors; since all production is directly exported there are no forward linkages either. It is true that the figures for inputs are merely the numerical results of more or less arbitrary assumptions, but everyone connected with the industry agrees that material inputs are very small indeed, so the conclusion is firm even though the statistics are unsure. This test is thus to the advantage of the companies. Small as their linkages were seen to be, they are certainly more powerful than those of the ADS. And what is true of the companies collectively holds also for SLST alone.

External Economies

Employment. The number of tributors employed in the ADS, about 30,000 in recent years, is about four times greater than employment in all the companies, because of the labor-intensive techniques used. Since full employment is itself a policy objective, the greater capacity of the ADS to create jobs is one of its advantages. Thus, to obtain an annual gross output of £1 million the companies employed about 590 workers in this period whereas the ADS employed about 2,400. However, the work involved is not of the kind usually described as wage labor and does not do much either to create a permanent modern labor force or urbanization in its beneficial aspects. (See below for further discussion of the employment aspect.)

Creation of Skills. There is no diffusion of skills comparable with the case of the companies. This is both because the skills called for are fewer and the skills that are needed, e.g., in sifting alluvial deposits or in valuing diamonds, are highly specific. The ADS has probably generated even less diffusion of managerial skills than the companies have. This is similarly due to the small usage and specificity of managerial expertise in the ADS.

Infrastructure. The ADS has not created or caused to be created much social overhead capital. Partly this is because of the lack of bulk of the end-product—the marketing of diamonds does not call for the construction of major roads or railways. Power and piped water are not used; housing is so primitive as to have caused official concern in the past.

Taxability. The ability of the government to tax the ADS is markedly weaker by comparison with the companies. Tax evasion is easy because of the small risks involved in smuggling an easily concealed commodity over frontiers so long and inaccessible as to be virtually uncontrollable.[5] In fact, an attempt in 1967 to raise the export duty payable on ADS diamonds had to be abandoned because it was resulting in disproportionately more smuggling and smaller sales through official channels. In 1963-65 tax revenues attributable to the ADS were a little over 5 percent of mean annual exports, as compared with 20 percent for the mining companies and a higher figure yet for SLST by itself.

Foreign Exchange. During the period reviewed the ADS was a large net earner of foreign exchange.[6] Measuring its direct impact on the balance of payments, net earnings were estimated at between £27 million and £36 million over the three years, and these figures fell to £18 million and £12 million after certain indirect factors were taken into account. A comparison with SLST revealed that in its direct effect on the balance of payments, both on current account and overall, even the ADS low-benefit case yielded higher net foreign-exchange earnings, relative to its exports, than the companies (or SLST taken separately). Taking indirect factors into account raised the relative overall contribution of SLST slightly above the ADS low-benefit figure. Since the true contribution of ADS is likely to lie nearer to the high-benefit limiting case, we may be fairly confident in drawing the conclusion that for every pound's worth of exports, the technically primitive part of the diamond industry brought greater net relief to the balance of payments than the modern mining company. If it is the case, however, that the company achieved a higher extraction rate than the ADS, it remains an open question which would achieve the greater net foreign-exchange earning from a given alluvial deposit.

---

[5]Smuggling is made even simpler by facilities in Liberia that encourage diamond smuggling from Sierra Leone.

Objection could reasonably be taken to the treatment so far of employment creation. It has been suggested above that the ADS has a superior employment effect because of the greater labor-intensity of its operations. However, it is an oversimplification merely to compare labor-intensities, for we have no idea how many of those employed by the companies and by the ADS, respectively, would otherwise have been unemployed (or underemployed). In the face of this objection, we are forced back on the more qualified assertion that unemployment and rural underemployment are commonly regarded as existing on a serious scale in Sierra Leone and that because of its greater labor-intensity the ADS will tend to give rise to a greater net addition to employment from a given level of output than the companies. But imagine, for a moment, that prior to the existence of the mining sector all labor resources were fully employed. In that case the labor-intensity of the ADS would tell against it, for we would then have to debit as a cost to the economy the output foregone as a result of the transfer of labor into mining. Since there is no doubt among those who know the Sierra Leone situation that many of those now engaged in mining were formerly active in other sectors, especially agriculture, could it be that if we debit the opportunity cost of labor against the respective contributions to national income of the companies and ADS, the alleged superiority of the latter would disappear?

This can be tested, but only in a stylized manner. We assume (1) that all Sierra Leoneans engaged in mining were formerly fully employed in farming, and (2) that the output foregone per worker was equivalent to the average value-added per worker in agriculture in 1963, which can be estimated at £50.[7] Note that these assumptions are biased in favor of the companies, by positing no unemployment and by overlooking that the companies are relatively larger employers of workers with modern skills whose opportunity cost is understated by the average productivity of agricultural labor. Yet, on the basis of these assumptions, the opportunity cost of labor can be estimated as £389,500 in the case of the companies and £1,500,000 in the case of the ADS. Subtracting these sums from their respective net national value-added estimates, we obtain the following results:[t]

| | Adjusted net national value added as % of: | |
	Gross output	Gross domestic value added
Companies	36%	52%
ADS (high-benefit)	84%	97%
ADS (low-benefit)	62%	72%

----

[t]In principle, the opportunity cost of all the factors employed should be subtracted but since neither the ADS nor the companies utilize domestic savings generated in other sectors of the Sierra Leone economy and since they can be regarded as equal users of natural resources, only the opportunity cost of labour is significant for our present purpose.

The relative advantage of the ADS is reduced but remains decisive.

The figures above can be used to rework the results of Table 10–3 and the results are set out in that table in brackets. The general nature of the results is unaffected by the adjustment for the opportunity cost of labor; with an extraction rate above 85 percent the companies are superior to the 50 percent extraction low-benefit ADS case, but in all other cases the ADS is superior.

The Impact of Nationalization

The above comparison of the ADS and the foreign company has shown that each has its strong points and weaknesses. The company has larger, even though small, backward linkages with other productive sectors; it contributes more to the diffusion of modern skills; it has created, or caused to be created, more important contributions to the country's infrastructure; and it is much more amenable to taxation. The Alluvial Diamond Scheme, on the other hand, produces a substantially larger contribution to national income from a given gross domestic value-added, and almost certainly from diamond deposits of a given value; it creates more employment; it provides a larger contribution to the balance of payments from a given value of production, although not necessarily from a given deposit.

Considerably more information gathered over a longer period of time would be needed before any final judgment could be formed. Crucial data are lacking on the distribution of the gross income of the ADS and on extraction rates achieved from the two methods, and we cannot confidently generalize from a study of only three years. Nevertheless, the balance of advantage does appear to lie fairly firmly with the ADS. The one really solid advantage of the company was its superior taxability, but against this must be set the greater overall impact of the ADS on the Sierra Leone economy in all other important respects.

To what extent can these results be attributed to the different nationality of ownership of the alternatives and to what extent do they derive from the radically different techniques of production employed? In some ways it is unreal to attempt a sharp distinction between these two factors. Given Sierra Leone's stage of development, the importation of foreign capital and management was at that time practically the only feasible means of creating technologically advanced items. Yet, the question does have some merit, not least because of the recent government takeover of SLST.

The answer is that both techniques and nationality of ownership are important explanatory factors. The contrasting technologies employed, for example, result in big differences arising from the large depreciation costs of the companies as against the negligible value of capital consumption in the

ADS. The same is true of the somewhat different pattern of inputs of the diamond company as against the ADS and of the contrasting employment-creating effects of the two. These factors help to explain the differences in the respective ratios of net national value-added to gross output, and in the linkage effects and externalities generated. The nationality of ownership, on the other hand, affects the outflow of profits and also the extent to which the companies rely upon expatriates for the provision of technical and managerial skills. These also influence the ratios, linkage effects, and externalities.

What, then, are likely to be the effects of the Sierra Leonean government's policy to take a controlling interest in the mining companies? It is possible to provide an approximate answer by taking the historical data already presented in Table 10-1 and adjusting them for the effects of the takeover, on the assumption that the announced terms of the agreement between the government and SLST will be applied to the other companies as well.[u] The results are set out in parentheses in Table 10-1. In interpreting these results it is important to be clear that they refer to a period in which compensation would be paid to the companies, i. e., within eight years of the takeover. It is similarly assumed that in this period factor employments would remain as they were under private control.

Comparison of the entries on lines 11 and 12 of Table 10-1 shows that, in the medium term, government participation would result in only modest improvements in the ratios, which would still remain well below the ADS figures. There would similarly be only a small net gain in current foreign exchange earnings—less than £1 million—against which should be set an almost certainly larger reduction in capital inflows from the former owners, which actually averaged £4 million per annum in 1963-65. Dependence on foreign skills and on capital-intensive techniques is likely to diminish only gradually and is unlikely to be much changed in the medium term.

In the longer term, government participation in mining could bring substantial benefits to Sierra Leone's economy. The payment of compensation would have been completed.[v] The government could have introduced intensified training schemes to reduce dependence on expatriate managerial and technical personnel and could have modified production techniques by substituting labor for capital. Against these potentialities should be weighed the possibility that government control will result in a decline in the efficiency

---

[u]This agreement provided, inter alia, that 51 percent of the shares would be taken over by the government, which would nominate a majority of the board of directors; that SLST would continue to be responsible for day-to-day management (presumably for a management fee, although no sum was stated); that SLST would be compensated by bonds bearing 5½ percent interest and maturing in 16 semiannual installments; and that taxation would be at the rate of 70 percent of profits. See London's overseas newspaper *West Africa* 19, September 1970.

[v]For example, reallocation to profits of the compensation payments and management fees raises net national value added in our hypothetical example to £7.58 million, or 79 percent of gross domestic value added.

of the mines, for the early post-independence experiences of West African
countries point unmistakably to the conclusion that the state makes a poor
industrialist.[w] Whether nationalization will ultimately have a beneficial effect
on the national economy therefore remains to be seen.

Conclusion

What conclusions that have a more general validity may be drawn from
this study? One such is that overgeneralization is only too easy! The factors
determining the distribution of gains from foreign direct investment as between
investor and host economy are numerous and complex. The end result is
likely to be strongly influenced by the techniques of production and other
characteristics of the industry in question, and by the nature of the host
economy. This is not a topic on which broad generalizations are likely to be fruitful. Indeed, while the case studied in this paper is not untypical of quite a
lot of others, it is certainly not typical of all or even most cases.

In a number of respects the foreign mining companies in Sierra Leone are
archetypal of the foreign enclaves about which so much has been written. They
were in the period covered wholly foreign-owned, they engaged in primary
production for export and thus had only slight connections with other productive sectors, and they made substantial post-tax profits. Even so, it has been
possible to demonstrate that they did make positive and significant contributions to the Sierra Leonean economy. Thus, our conclusions do not support
those who argue that receipt of foreign capital in these forms may do positive
harm. We have also shown the possibility, on the other hand, that exploitation
of the country's alluvial diamond deposits by technically simple, labor-intensive
methods might have brought a larger social benefit than was obtained from the
expatriate diamond-mining concern. This serves to emphasize the importance of
considering all available alternatives when determining in which activities
foreign investment should be encouraged or discouraged, although the range of
choice available in other industries and in other countries may often be more
limited than in the case of Sierra Leone diamonds. If an important new diamond
field were discovered in Sierra Leone (an unlikely but not impossible event),
the government would be mistaken to decide that this should be mined by
modern methods, with or without foreign participation, except after very careful
consideration of the rival claims of the ADS.

Implied in this view is a familiar warning against confusing technical with
economic efficiency. There is a quite generally held view in Sierra Leone that
the creation of the ADS was economically harmful to the country and was

---

[w]The author is currently researching the economic policies in Ghana during the
sixties for a study in which it will be shown that acquisition by the state led to drastic
reductions in the efficiency and financial performance of the gold mines that were taken
over in 1961.

justified only on political grounds.[x] Our results do not support that view. There
is a sense in which SLST belonged technically to a different age from the
African diggers and their laborers, working with bucket and spade, and we have
seen that SLST was the lower-cost producer. But it was the ADS, by utilizing
in a greater degree locally available resources, which imparted greater benefits
to the economy.

Various factors isolated here have a direct bearing upon the distribution
of gains from foreign direct investment and may be influenced by state action.
We have been reminded, for example, of the importance of taxation paid
by foreign companies. Governments can influence the distribution of gains by
varying their tax provisions. Efforts directed towards changing the employment
and training policies of foreign concerns and the extent to which firms utilize
domestic as against imported materials can also influence the benefits
accruing to the national economy. Governmental participation is another
method of increasing the developmental value of some foreign-owned industries,
but the net results of this policy are uncertain, and it should thus not be
embarked upon without very careful consideration.

Notes

1. For a discussion of this trend and a general survey of the structure and
   performance of Sierra Leone's economy up to about 1963, see Ralph
   Gerald Saylor, *The Economic System of Sierra Leone* (Durham, N.C.:
   Duke University Press, 1967), passim. The 1969 export data here and
   below are taken from the U. N. *Yearbook of International Trade Statistics,
   1969* (New York, 1970).
2. See Saylor, op. cit., pp. 186, 190.
3. These and other references to national accounting data are derived from
   the U.N., op. cit., pp. 606-14.
4. The interested reader should also see a not dissimilar study of the
   Chilean copper industry by C. W. Reynolds in Mamalakis and Reynolds,
   Essays on the Chilean Economy (Homewood, Ill.: Irwin, 1965).
5. Details of the full range of assumptions made are set out in Killick
   and During, op. cit., pp. 295-97.
6. Cf. Killick and During, op. cit., passim, for details of the results summarized in
   this paragraph.
7. Computed from the national accounts (Central Statistics Office, op. cit.,
   1967) and data on the industrial distribution of the labor force contained
   in the *1963 Population Census of Sierra Leone: Vol. 3, Economic Characteristics* (Freetown: Government of Sierra Leone, 1963).

[x] There was increasing lawlessness in the diamondiferous areas of the country in the
1950s, and the creation of the ADS legalized and, in some degree, regulated what had
previously been illicit digging on a large scale.

11

Comparative Results and Analysis

John Cownie and Scott R. Pearson

Introduction

Our concluding chapter has two broad purposes: to compare information on the relationships between commodity exports and the development process, and to assess the impacts of governmental policies on these relationships.

To provide historical perspective for the comparative analysis, institutions which have influenced past production of the various export commodities are examined, with special emphasis given to factors that help explain similarities and differences in the developmental roles of exports. Particular attention is focused on the nature of ownership of the export activity, on the relationships between export producers and governments of the respective export-producing countries, and on the trends in the local economies as they are interrelated with export production.

Within the limits of available data, the methodological framework specified in Chapter 1 is applied to a comparative analysis of case study results. The components of net social gain are specified, net gain coefficients are calculated, and domestic resource costs are estimated. Results from the various country-commodity cases are compared and analyzed.

In assessing the roles of government policymakers in influencing the growth and the developmental effects of export industries, policy issues are discussed as appropriate to countries and commodities. Particular attention is given to comparisons of the impacts of various policies on net social gain, employment generation, distribution of income, and nationality of ownership.

We conclude by looking briefly at remaining problems in evaluating the prospective future roles of commodity exports in developmental processes. Assessment of available information clearly shows that answers to many questions about the role of exports in development must await further empirical study. By pointing out the most critical areas in which lack of information is the barrier to determining optimal policies toward exports, we hope to identify fruitful lines for continuing investigation.

An implicit point of caution should be stated explicitly. Data and coverage of countries and commodities are insufficient to permit categorical conclusions about the developmental roles of exports. Although suggestive inferences can be drawn from available data, definitive results must await further analysis.

Export Activities in Historical Perspective

This section is organized to provide a country-by-country summary of the historical contributions of export activities.

Ivory Coast

Timber, cocoa, and coffee have each at various times led export growth in the Ivory Coast, and in the post-World War II period the growth of the three together has provided tremendous impetus to the Ivorian economy. Patterns of exploitation have differed considerably. Timber has remained a medium- and large-scale enterprise, characterized by the participation of European-owned firms with capital-intensive methods. In cocoa and coffee production, European-operated plantations co-existed with small-scale African operations until World War II. Following the war, forced labor was no longer available to Europeans, and cocoa and coffee production gradually became almost entirely African activities. Production of each commodity at one time or another encountered transportation bottlenecks, and the need to break such bottlenecks was an important factor in the development of transportation infrastructure.

Between 1947 and 1969, the value of Ivorian exports increased sevenfold; cocoa, coffee, and timber accounted for approximately 80 percent of this rapidly growing total throughout the period. The government has used revenues generated to encourage both industrialization and a diversification of agricultural production. Final demand linkages, especially strong for cocoa and coffee, have made a wide range of activities economically viable, and all three exports have provided labor skills, domestic savings, and foreign exchange, all crucial for Ivorian growth. It is likely that the rapid expansion of cocoa, coffee, and timber exports is reaching an end, although each will continue to be important. But the period of growth they have spearheaded may be a watershed in Ivorian development.

Ghana

Cocoa production began in Ghana in the 1880s, and within three decades Ghana became the world's leading cocoa producer. Production has always been dominated by small-scale African enterprise, and cocoa has had a wide influence on the country's economic development. Cocoa has provided employment, cash income, foreign exchange, government revenue, and domestic savings. These benefits have varied from year to year, however, because cocoa faces erratic and widely divergent international prices, and cocoa has produced only limited linkage effects. Cocoa processing and the production of insecticides and cocoa bags have produced small net gains. Somewhat more significant linkages have occurred in transport, but potentially large final demand linkages have never been fully realized because of the high import content of consumption expenditures. A large proportion of government revenues has been supplied by cocoa, although specific fiscal linkages are difficult to evaluate.

Timber has long been exported from Ghana, with large-scale exploitation beginning after British colonization. Early increases in timber production both followed and encouraged improvements in transportation infrastructure—particularly the spread of rail lines and the improvement of port facilities. The timber industry suffered drastically in the Depression years. Recovery began prior to World War II, however, and continued during the war years, so that by 1945 production had rebounded to the levels of the early 1920s. Prior to 1945, logging was largely carried out by small-scale, local entrepreneurs using highly labor-intensive methods. After 1945, foreign investors established larger-scale, capital-intensive operations. Many of the innovations introduced—feeder roads to eliminate manual haulage, for example—spread to Ghanaian producers. The fixed (private plus public) costs of timber production were increased, but the marginal (private) cost of increasing output was greatly lowered, and total production and log exports each increased more than threefold in the 1950s. After independence, the government emphasized local participation, first by encouraging small- and medium-scale Ghanaian operations and more recently by assuming majority control over the largest multinational companies. Industry output has fluctuated since 1960, with government policy seeking to promote domestic processing and to de-emphasize the export of unprocessed logs. Forward linkages therefore have become increasingly important. Backward linkages and other external effects have not, however, been particularly significant.

Cocoa is likely to remain Ghana's leading export and its most important single commodity in the foreseeable future. The diversification of Ghana's economy should continue to have high priority—one reason being the opportunity to realize increased linkage effects from cocoa—but adequate resources should also be allocated to the encouragement of cocoa plantings and the control of persistent diseases and pests. Ghana has built a good physical infrastructure and has achieved a laudatory level of overall education for its population. Difficult and delicate balances will be required if developmental planning is to take full advantage of the nation's economic potential and in the process reap the potential gains from cocoa and timber exports.

Ethiopia

Coffee has grown in Ethiopia for as many years as reliable records exist. Originally it grew wild, and although some wild trees are still harvested, in our case study it is argued that the majority of Ethiopian coffee is produced from cultivated trees. Exports are moderately important in Ethiopian GDP; in the late 1960s, the export sector accounted for approximately 7 percent of total GDP and about twice that percentage of monetized GDP. Exports are predominantly agricultural, with coffee by far the most important commodity. As a member of the International Coffee Organization, Ethiopia's quota is 2.5 percent of world exports to quota countries. The quota has not constrained exports, however. Recent coffee exports have been below Ethiopia's quota, and government policy has sought to ensure that all coffee of sufficient quality is in fact exported rather than diverted to domestic consumption. Although land-tenure arrangements result in very unequal distribution of the revenues from coffee, coffee provides cash income to large numbers of small-scale farmers, middlemen, and merchants. As a result, while investment linkages have not been particularly strong, final demand linkages have been important in a wide range of consumer goods industries. Diversification of Ethiopia's exports remains a goal of government policy, but coffee is essentially noncompetitive with other potential exports. The absolute importance of coffee exports thus could well remain undiminished as diversification takes place.

Uganda

Cotton was introduced into Uganda by the British about 1900. Cotton provided a means for small-scale African farmers to pay the taxes imposed by the colonial government, so African workers were essentially forced to provide an important raw material for British industry. Early production of cotton was constrained by the interrelationships of ginning capacity, transport, and labor. Ginning capacity was inadequate and poorly distributed, so bulky raw cotton had to be transported, and roads were inadequate or non-existent. The resultant requirements for head transport meant that production was constrained by the availability of labor. Between 1913 and 1938 cotton production increased steadily as ginning capacity and transport infrastructure expanded, and cotton became the dominant export and cash crop in the economy. From 1938 to 1948, cotton acreages declined as the importance of coffee greatly increased. In the mid-1950s the earlier high acreage levels in cotton were again attained, and recent years have seen stabilization at somewhat higher levels.

As acreages expanded in the 1920s and 1930s, farmers earned incomes above amounts required for tax payments. This incentive undoubtedly spurred production further, but taxes on cotton growers continued to outrun services provided to them. Resources transferred from cotton largely remained in Uganda and helped finance modern sector development in a small number of urban centers. Cotton-processing industries understandably played a prominent role, creating important forward linkages.

In the 1950s coffee passed cotton as Uganda's leading export, and the relative importance of cotton as an earner of foreign exchange and a source of government revenue steadily diminished. Cotton retains a broad influence, however, because it continues to be cultivated by three-fourths of adult African male workers in Uganda and it constitutes the chief source of cash income for most of them. The wide distribution of cotton incomes has also led to significant final demand linkage effects. Government policy toward cotton therefore will continue to shape the economic prospects of a majority of Uganda's population.

Nigeria

For more than half a century before the discovery of petroleum in 1956, Nigeria had been a thriving export economy; leading export commodities were ground nuts, cocoa, palm products, rubber, and cotton. Agricultural activities continued to contribute substantial shares of export earnings and of GDP prior to the outbreak of the civil war in 1967. Beginning with the disruption caused by the civil war, however, agriculture has declined in importance, and oil production now dominates the Nigerian export economy.

Following the initial production of oil in 1958, output levels rose only gradually during the 1960s and then were severely disrupted during the war. But after the resolution of the conflict in January 1970, oil production increased rapidly, reaching 2 million barrels per day in 1973. This rapid growth allowed Nigeria to become the world's sixth largest exporter of crude petroleum.

The impact of petroleum production on the Nigerian economy has also increased markedly over time. The Nigerian government has succeeded in securing a continually growing share of the economic rent associated with petroleum production and in influencing more directly the petroleum industry's role in Nigerian development. Through a series of changes in taxation terms, most notably the April 1971 settlement, the government has more than tripled the amount of revenue it receives per barrel of oil produced. In addition, a government oil company—the Nigerian National Oil Corporation—was established in 1971, and it has subsequently taken substantial equity participation in many of the oil companies operating in Nigeria.

Petroleum production has contributed to Nigerian development through the generation of government revenues and foreign exchange, the training of a limited number of Nigerian skilled laborers, the construction of infrastructure, and the establishment of forward-linked industries. Because the petroleum industry is composed mainly of relatively large, foreign-owned and managed firms which use capital-intensive production methods, it has very small backward linkage effects with other sectors. Although forward linkages have not as yet made widespread contributions, several industries planned for the near future, especially natural gas liquefaction, have great potential.

The Nigerian government's current task is to shape its policies both to allow petroleum production to contribute indirectly to economic development through its interrelations with other sectors and, even more importantly, to make the best possible developmental use of the oil industry's massive (and growing) contributions of public investment resources and foreign exchange.

Zaire

Copper has played a critical economic and political role in what is now the Republic of Zaire. Exploitation of copper in the Belgian Congo began in 1906. By the late 1920s copper was the Congo's most important export. At the time of independence (1960) the Congo was producing 6.7 percent of the world supply of copper. Encouraged by European interests, the copper-producing province of Katanga seceded, ushering in a period of political and economic instability which lasted until President Mobutu took control of the government in late 1965. Because of copper's importance in providing income, foreign exchange, and government revenues, it has played a key role in recent efforts to unify the country, to Africanize the economy, and to promote economic growth. The government wished to establish Zairian control of the industry while maintaining the critical technical abilities and marketing outlets of the Belgian operators. Negotiations for a joint-venture arrangement were unsuccessful, and the government finally nationalized the Belgian mining operations in 1967. Under heavy pressure to maintain copper production—which has recently accounted for some 70 percent of foreign-exchange earnings—the government reached an agreement under which operations would be managed by its former owners on behalf of Gecomin, its new Zairian corporate owner (Gecomin was later renamed Gecomines, and then Gecamines).

Copper production has not been closely linked to other sectors of the economy. Employment generation has been small in proportion to output. With the industry taking pride in its adoption of modern capital-intensive techniques, employment has actually declined in recent years even as output has increased. Workers in the industry constitute a well-paid elite—a situation that has both advantages and disadvantages for long-run economic development.

A major goal of the government is to increase copper output and net foreign exchange earnings. To this end it has pressured Gecamines in various ways, including the establishment of joint ventures with Japanese and American interests which Gecamines (even though a nationalized company) apparently regards as competitors. Copper will continue to play a vital role in Zairian economic growth, providing a major share of revenues for operating and development expenditures of the government and an important impetus for the development of interior transportation and other infrastructure.

Zambia

Zambia is an extreme example of an economy critically dependent on a single export commodity. Large scale production of copper began in the 1930s, and Zambia now ranks with Chile as the largest producer in the world after the U.S.A. and the U.S.S.R. Copper has recently provided 95 percent of Zambia's foreign exchange earnings and up to two-thirds of government revenue.

Before independence in 1964, the impact of copper was largely limited to a small enclave. Initially skilled labor was entirely imported out of necessity, but later African workers were deliberately excluded from training and skilled employment. European settler-farmers meanwhile sought to monopolize the cash market for food to feed the mining enclave. Furthermore, federation with Southern Rhodesia worked to the sharp disadvantage of the North. Copper-mining revenues were used to develop Southern Rhodesian industry which then had free access to the North. This situation led to obvious drawbacks for northern industrial development. Despite these factors, some positive benefits spilled over to Africans, but substantial progress began only after independence. New tax arrangements and rising copper prices caused government revenues to rise rapidly in the late 1960s, and these expanded revenues were, of course, no longer shared with the South. As a result of Rhodesia's Unilateral Declaration of Independence in 1965, additional impetus was given to diversification of Zambia's economy, and copper revenues were instrumental in financing the boom in import-substituting industries that extended through 1969. Beginning in 1970, falling copper prices and production losses resulting from the Mufulira mine disaster have cut government revenues sharply, necessitating cutbacks in capital spending in the second plan period. In August 1969, the government assumed a 51 percent interest in the copper-mining industry. While major decisions remain temporarily in the hands of the mining companies, the stabilization of expectations following the takeover produced investment commitments that should substantially expand production capacity.

It is difficult to measure linkage effects of Zambian copper because of the unusual extent to which the entire economy depends on copper in one way or another. Zambian employment in mining itself has increased substantially and will continue to do so as the effects of recent training programs are felt. Increases in mining wages have shown tendencies to spread to other industries, but unless such increases are based on productivity gains, the effect may simply be to drive up prices. The second development plan gives considerable emphasis to remedying agricultural shortages and to effecting successful import-substitution. Nevertheless, the success of all such efforts continues to depend in a major way on revenues generated by copper. While providing Zambia with a relatively high standard of living, returns from copper production have not lessened the copper-dependence of the economy. Unless new reserves of copper are discovered, this dependence could cause severe economic problems in the future.

Sierra Leone

Mining emerged following World War II as the leading export sector in the Sierra Leonean economy. Minerals increased from 45 percent of total exports in 1950 to 85 percent in 1967, with diamonds constituting approximately 80 percent of the mineral total in the late 1960s. The performance of the mining sector contrasted sharply with sluggish growth elsewhere in the economy, but the benefits from mining were limited by the heavy dependence of the sector on foreign investment. Foreign-exchange earned and government payments made by the mining sector financed some developmental activities, and some lower-level skills undoubtedly were diffused into the nonmining economy. Linkage effects were very slight, however, and a large fraction of gross foreign-exchange earnings constituted repatriated profits and payments for imports of capital and skilled labor. Since 1969, the Sierra Leonean government has taken a controlling share in major foreign mining companies. The extent to which this participation will increase net benefits to the domestic economy in the long run is uncertain, because the companies remain tied to capital-intensive, enclave-style operations.

Perhaps the most interesting aspect of the Sierra Leonean case is that diamond production has simultaneously been carried on by a combination of labor-intensive activities known collectively as the Alluvial Diamond Scheme (ADS). In our case study it is argued that under any reasonable assumptions ADS production will contribute a greater net social gain from a given diamond output—net foreign exchange generated will be greater, employment larger, final demand linkages stronger. From the government's point of view the greatest single advantage of the large company is that it is easily taxable, whereas ADS operations lend themselves to smuggling and hence tax evasion. It seems unlikely that governmental control of mining-company interests will change the conclusion that, on balance, ADS operations are economically more efficient.

Developmental Contributions of
Export Activities

In this section we compare the developmental contributions of our selected export activities in specific recent years.[a] The methodology employed is described in Chapter 1, and it is important to make clear the issues raised by this approach. Our comparisons provide static or virtually static pictures of economic structures at particular points or for very short periods in time. They allow us to see fairly clearly what export activities have contributed to economic development within the specified periods. The critical question, however, is the extent to which these static comparisons improve our understanding of exports' roles in the long-run dynamics of the developmental process. There are two kinds of problems to confront in considering this question—problems with the nature of the methodological framework itself, and problems with the adequacy

---

[a]Results presented here are derived from the case studies of Chapters 2-10. Where possible, case study estimates are presented directly. Where necessary to preserve comparability, case study results have been used as the bases for further calculations.

of data available for application of the framework. Before turning to quantitative comparisons, we consider briefly the limitations which these problems pose.

First, our methodology is basically comparative-static. With it, we can compare the contributions of different export activities at particular points in time and also the contributions of the same export activity at different points in time. Hence, we are able to draw highly suggestive inferences concerning how the activity may mesh into the dynamic process of development. We cannot, however, attempt to predict the exact influence of an export activity on the time path of the developmental process, nor can we provide either deterministic or stochastic predictions of future courses of development. As a theoretical matter, this limitation is fundamental. Given the current "state of the art" in dynamic developmental models, however, the limitation does not have great practical significance. Such models themselves are not yet refined to the point where their more detailed predictions can be used in policy analysis.

The second type of limitation is a greater cause for concern. We have argued that our methodology gives a good measure of what an export activity has contributed to an economy during a given period. It is also true that, when rigorously and completely applied, the framework provides highly suggestive and extremely useful indications of what the export's contributions are likely to be over a much longer period. But a "rigorous and complete" application of the framework is often impossible because of the limitations of data currently available, and it is particularly troublesome that these limitations are generally most severe in the areas directly connected with longer-run impacts. One purpose of the remainder of this section, therefore, is to indicate problem areas in which (1) the framework is adequate, but the available data are not, and (2) the development of additional information is feasible and especially important.

Income Generation by Export Activities

In Chapter 1 we defined the net additional income generated by an export activity as the *net social gain* (NSG) from that activity. In the technical appendix to that chapter we demonstrated that NSG can be separated into three components: economic rent evaluated at market prices, an adjustment to reflect more accurate (shadow price) valuations of inputs and outputs, and the social value of all external effects generated by the export activity.

The Contribution of Economic Rent to Net Social Gain. Economic rent is equal to the domestic value of net foreign exchange generated by the export activity (at official exchange rates) *minus* the total value (at market prices) of domestic factors used directly and indirectly in production. In Table 11-1 we

Table 11-1
Contribution to Net Social Gain of Economic Rent from Export Activities

	Ivory Coast	Ivory Coast	Ghana	Ghana	Ethiopia	Uganda	Nigeria	Zaire	Zambia	Sierra Leone	Sierra Leone
	Timber	Cocoa and Coffee	Cocoa	Timber	Coffee	Cotton	Oil	Copper	Copper	Diamonds, large-scale	Diamonds, ADS[a]
	1967	1967	1969-70	1970-71	1969	1969	1971	1968	1967	1963-65	1963-65
(Dollars, in millions)											
Gross output (u_j)	80	158	334	31.9	69	53	1,467	399	1,386	37.0	34.4
less											
Foreign factor costs ($\bar{m}_j$)	29	5	28	14.7	3	6	233	91	149	10.7	.3
Imports of goods and services	13	5	28	11.8	—	6	233	67	106	7.4	.3
Others	16	—	—	2.9	3	—	—	24	43[b]	3.3[b]	—
less											
Residual rent to foreign owners (r_j)	—	—	—	2.2	—	—	205[b]	21	273[b]	9.1[b]	.8[b]
equals											
Net foreign exchange earned ($u_j - \bar{m}_j - r_j$)	51	153	306	15.0	66	48	1,029	287	964	17.2	33.3
Market exchange rate (w_1) (local/$)	250/1	250/1	1.02/1[c]	1.02/1	2.5/1	7.14/1	.3571/1	.50/1	.3571/1	.3571/1	.3571/1

(Local currency, in millions)											
Domestic value of net foreign exchange at market exchange rate $(u_j - m_j - r_j) w_1$	12,750	38,250	312	15.3	165	339	368	143	344	6.1	11.9
less Domestic factor costs at market prices $(\sum_{s=2}^{m} \bar{f}_{sj} w_s)$	9,250	24,250	180	9.3	90	286	57	48	191	3.5	11.0
equals Net social gain deriving from economic rent of the jth export activity (R_j)	3,500	14,000	132	6.0	75	53	311	95	153	2.6	.9
(Dollars, in millions) Net social gain deriving from economic rent of the jth export activity (R_j)	14	56	129	5.9	30	7	871	190	428	7.3	2.5

Note: The symbols for and relationships among these variables are discussed in the technical appendix to Chapter 1.

[a]High benefit case is used in all Sierra Leone ADS calculations.

[b]Residual rent to foreign owners is overstated because "normal" profits are not separated out.

[c]Ghanaian exchange rate is cedis per dollar. Gordon uses pounds per dollar in Chapter 3.

present calculations of economic rent for the case studies presented in this volume. Several conclusions can be drawn from the summary results contained in Table 11-1. Most obvious is the enormous range in the absolute size of the export activities. At one extreme is Nigerian oil, with gross output in 1971 of $1,467 million. Ghanaian timber, with gross output of $32 million in 1970-71, is at the opposite end of the spectrum. In general, mineral activities generated the largest export earnings, with agricultural and silvicultural activities ranging from the lower to the middle end of the scale. (The sole exception to this generalization in the examples studied is the moderate-sized diamond industry in Sierra Leone.)

There is also wide variation in the importance of foreign factor costs and residual rents accruing to foreigners. In activities characterized by foreign ownership (oil, copper, and foreign-owned diamond and timber operations), the value of net foreign exchange earned is reduced to about 45-75 percent of gross output. In domestically operated activities, foreign-exchange leakages are small, and net foreign exchange earned is in each case at least 89 percent of gross output. Conversely, domestic factor costs assume far greater importance in the latter activities. When all deductions have been made from gross output, the amounts of economic rent remain greatly different in absolute size.

Economic rents accrue to host country governments and/or to domestic factors of production. The relative sizes of the public and private shares of these rents may be critical in determining the nature of the export's developmental contribution. Rent centralized in the hands of government is more likely to be used in centrally planned development programs, and to "pull" the development process by direct participation in it. Rent accruing to domestic factors tends to be much more widely distributed, to be channeled into the range of consumption and investment activities pursued by the private sector, and to "push" the development process by increasing the potential viability of numerous enterprises.

In instances involving foreign producers, the only possible contribution of economic rent to NSG is payments made to the local government.[b] The government in these instances maximizes the rent by maximizing the total payments that it is able to extract from the foreign owners who operate the export activity. The objective is to negotiate favorable contractual terms in order to obtain as much of the economic rent as possible while at the same time maintaining sufficient profitability for the foreign owners to ensure that production continues. The government, of course, has a second option—to take equity participation in the activity involved and perhaps to take control of the export operation. Such a strategy aims at increasing the contribution of economic

---

[b]In some instances foreigners face exchange controls that prevent them from repatriating all of their profits and residual rents. For these instances one can make the simplifying assumption that the time stream of remittances is changed but that the present value of this stream remains unchanged because of earnings on investments of funds held in blocked accounts.

rent by transferring residual rents from the previous foreign owners to the new domestic government owners. If a government were pursuing a participation or nationalization policy only for the sake of raising its share of rent, its implicit judgment would be that it could generate residual rents more effectively as an owner than it could by altering financial arrangements to squeeze foreign owners more tightly.

Finally, a methodological observation is in order. Since economic rent is in almost all cases the component of net social gain most accurately and most readily estimated, it is tempting to make comparisons on the basis of this component alone. Yet common sense valuations of the roles of various exports would often show such comparisons to be seriously misleading. The inclusion of social valuations and external effects in our framework enables us, however roughly, to consider relationships which may be at the heart of the developmental process.

The Effect of Shadow Price Adjustments on Net Social Gain.   In many instances, it is desirable to take account of the fact that official exchange rates and market prices do not always reflect real domestic values in the local economy. Therefore, we correct the contribution of net foreign exchange to NSG by multiplying net foreign exchange by the difference between the shadow price of foreign exchange and the official exchange rate. We also adjust the domestic costs to be charged against the export activity by multiplying the net quantity of each domestic factor used by the difference between its market price and its shadow price.

On a priori grounds, we suspect that the shadow price of foreign exchange is usually equal to or higher than the official exchange rate. If foreign exchange is more valuable to the economy than the official exchange rate suggests, the export activity (providing net foreign exchange earned is positive) contributes more to the developmental process than it will be credited with in nominal terms.[c]

Domestic factors of production may be either under- or overpriced at their market rates. Capital is underpriced to large producers if they have access to credit at subsidized or controlled interest rates. The same factor would be overpriced to small-scale producers of agricultural exports if imperfect capital markets force them to pay interest rates inflated well beyond the social opportunity cost of the borrowed funds. Skilled labor is clearly scarce in most developing economies, and its market price in most instances may well be a

---

[c]On the other hand, it is worth considering the case in which net foreign exchange earned is negative, and the activity costs the economy more than it is charged in nominal terms. Instances would be rare if only exports were considered, but our methodology is applicable as well to import-substitutes, which often, at least initially, lose foreign exchange. It is entirely possible that long-run considerations and externalities will make such ventures desirable, but it is important that even short-run foreign-exchange losses be adequately charged.

Table 11-2
Contribution to Net Social Gain of Adjustments in Market Prices and Existing Exchange Rates

	Ivory Coast Timber	Ivory Coast Cocoa and Coffee	Ghana Cocoa	Ghana Timber	Ethiopia Coffee	Uganda Cotton[a]	Nigeria Oil	Zaire Copper	Zambia Copper	Sierra Leone Diamonds, large scale	Sierra Leone Diamonds, ADS[b]
	1967	1967	1969-70	1970-71	1969	1969	1971	1968	1967	1963-65 mean	1963-65 mean
Net foreign exchange earned $(u_j - m_j - r_j)$ ($) times	51	153	306	15.0	66	48	1,029	287	964	17.2	33.3
Correction for existing exchange rate $(v_1 - w_1)$ (loc/$) equals	0	0	0	0	0	0	0	0	0	.0596	.0596
Correction to domestic value of net foreign exchange earned $((u_j - m_j - r_j)(v_1 - w_1))$ (loc) plus	0	0	0	0	0	0	0	0	0	1.0	2.0

Corrections to costs of domestic factors used	0									
$(\sum_{s=2}^{m} \bar{f}_{sj}\,(w_s - v_s))$ (loc)	0	0	1.0	0	63ᶜ	3	0	0	1.2	8.5
Unskilled labor correction	0	0	1.0	0	63ᶜ	3	0	0	1.2	8.5
Skilled labor correction	0	0	0	0		0	0	0	0	0
Domestic capital correction equals	0	0	0	0	0	0	0	0	0	0
Net Social Gain deriving from adjustments to market prices and to existing exchange rate (P_j) (loc)	0	0	1.0	0	63	3	0	0	2.2	10.5

Note: The symbols for and relationships among these variables are discussed in the technical appendix to Chapter 1.

($) – quantity is expressed in millions of dollars.

(loc) – quantity is expressed in millions of local currency.

ᵃHigh assumption case is used in all Uganda cotton calculations.

ᵇHigh benefit case is used in all Sierra Leone ADS calculations.

ᶜCorrections reflect changes in growers' income and in ginning and marketing wages, and are not broken down between skilled and unskilled labor.

roughly accurate measure of its social opportunity cost. Unskilled labor is widely thought to be priced above its social opportunity cost, but in only half of our case studies do the authors support this contention.

If a domestic factor is underpriced, the NSG from the export activity must be adjusted downward, because the full social opportunity cost of the factor—which should be charged against the export activity—is not reflected in the market price that the export producer actually pays. Similarly, while the full nominal cost of an overpriced domestic factor of production is charged against the export activity in computing rent, only the social opportunity cost should be charged against the social desirability of the export activity. By paying a factor an amount greater than its shadow price, the export activity makes the factor a recipient of net social gain from that activity.

Shadow prices are difficult to measure accurately, a point emphasized frequently in the case studies. Table 11-2 shows the results of the rare cases in which authors were able to quantify shadow price adjustments. In many instances adjustment effects may actually be (approximately) zero—market prices and the official rate of exchange can, after all, be correct reflections of scarcity values. But often shadow price adjustments are set equal to zero more or less by default. It is difficult to believe, for example, that existing official exchange rates accurately represented the true value of foreign exchange in every case study but one of this volume. But because available data are generally inadequate to support anything more than educated guessing, case-study analysts are understandably reluctant to make quantitative estimates of shadow prices. Substantial elements of net gain may thereby be concealed, and these elements are potentially among those most crucial to an understanding of the developmental process.

Adjustments reflecting the overpricing of unskilled labor dominate Table 11-2. For Ghanaian timber, Nigerian oil and foreign-produced diamonds in Sierra Leone, the adjustments are small in absolute terms. Still, they represent, respectively, 11, 5, and 34 percent downward adjustments of the corresponding factor costs charged in Table 11-1, and they result in upward adjustments of NSG by amounts equal to 17, 1, and 46 percent, respectively. More remarkable are the adjustments in the analyses of small-scale, local (alluvial diamond scheme) diamond production in Sierra Leone and of cotton in Uganda. In the latter case, shadow price adjustments for all labor cause NSG to more than double. In the former, valuation of unskilled labor at shadow prices lowers domestic factor costs by 77 percent, and increases NSG tenfold. Shadow price adjustments of the existing exchange rate further raise NSG in each of the Sierra Leonean activities.

Two conclusions seem inescapable. First, the results cited must be viewed with extreme caution, because they are dependent on the willingness of case study authors to make very rough quantitative estimates. Second, the making and refinement of such estimates are critical to the measurement of NSG from export activities. Clearly, the size, distributional effects and final demand linkages of shadow-price adjustments to NSG are items for more intensive future study.

Contribution of External Effects to Net Social Gain. The third component of NSG is made up of contributions from external effects—changes in NSG in other sectors of the economy as a result of their economic relationships with the export activity. We have divided external effects into two groups: linkage effects, and the residual of all other external effects. In both groups of external effects, NSG is generated in related activities as a result of the existence of the export activity. Note that the mere fact that related activities exist does not imply that they generate positive net social gains to be credited to the export industry. In particular, large payments to government do not always imply positive fiscal externalities. Such external gains arise only if a government uses export revenues, already credited to NSG in the rent term, to generate opportunities for the creation of additional NSG.

External effects subsume many of the more subtle interactions that make up the export-development relationship. While the present state of analysis does not allow quantification of the external effects component of NSG, qualitative indices of the overall magnitudes of external effects have been estimated, and these indices are presented in Table 11-3. (In compiling Table 11-3, we have to some extent violated our own stricture and taken the existence of linked activities as strong a priori evidence that some NSG is generated.)

1. *Backward Linkages* have been considerable only for Zambian copper and to a lesser extent for Ghanaian cocoa. In Zambia, development of the economy has been built largely upon and around the copper industry. Much of early industrialization was geared to supplying inputs to the industry, and the guaranteed outlet has made the production of such inputs attractive. The long importance of cocoa in the Ghanaian economy has encouraged domestic production of cocoa bags and chemical pesticides, and considerable transport infrastructure was built to facilitate the marketing of cocoa.

2. *Forward Linkages* appear strong for Ethiopian coffee, but this result is strongly influenced by the fact that the author of the case study has defined the export activity narrowly, making coffee an input into packaging, marketing, and transportation sectors. In Ghana, timber and some cocoa are processed domestically, producing moderate forward linkages. More important are the Ugandan cotton-processing industries which have been a significant part of that country's industrial sector.

3. *Technological linkages* have not generally been great, principally because most export activities are highly specialized and do not tend to spin off their methods to other sectors. Moderate technological linkages have resulted where export activities have built transportation infrastructure useful to other sectors, notably the road and rail development in Ghana, the Ivory Coast, and Zambia.

Table 11-3

Contribution to Net Social Gain from External Effects

	Ivory Coast Timber	Ivory Coast Cocoa and Coffee	Ghana Cocoa	Ghana Timber	Ethiopia Coffee	Uganda Cotton	Nigeria Oil	Zaire Copper	Zambia Copper	Sierra Leone Diamonds, large scale	Sierra Leone Diamonds, ADS
	1967	1967	1969-70	1970-71	1969	1969	1971	1968	1967	1963-65 mean	1963-65 mean
Linkage effects of the jth export activity $\left(\sum\limits_{\substack{k=1 \\ k \neq j}}^{q} L_{jk}\right)$											
Backward linkages	I	II	II	I	I	I	I	I	III	I	I[a]
Forward linkages	II	I	II	III	III[a]	III[a]	II	I[a]	II	I	[a]
Technological linkages	I	II	II	II	I	I	I	I	I	I	I[a]
Final demand linkages	II	IV	III	I	III	III	I	I	I	I[a]	II
Fiscal linkages	II	III	II	I	I	II	V	III	IV	III	I
Social valuation of other external effects $\left(\sum\limits_{\substack{k=1 \\ k \neq j}}^{q} T_{jk} \cdot b_k\right)$	II	II	II	II	[a]	I	I	I	III	II	[a]
Impact on net social gain deriving from external effects (E_j)	II	III	II	II	I	II	II	I	III	I	I

Scale: (very weak) I   II   III   IV   V (very strong)

Note: The symbols for and relationships among these variables are discussed in the technical appendix to Chapter 1.

[a] Insignificant.

4. *Final demand linkages* have been strong in countries such as the Ivory Coast and Uganda, in which domestic factor incomes from export activities have been large and these incomes have been channeled into demand for domestically produced goods and services. In such countries as Zambia and Zaire, on the other hand, significant amounts of domestic factor incomes have been used to purchase imports, and potential final demand linkages have not been realized.

5. *Fiscal linkages* have been relatively strong in our case studies. Export revenues typically provide a large proportion of government funds, although it is usually not possible to assign individual government activities to particular sources of revenue. Fiscal linkages have been especially significant for the very large-scale mineral operations in Nigeria, Zambia, and Zaire.

6. *Other external effects,* chiefly the provision of labor skills for other sectors, have been moderately strong in the Ivory Coast, Ghana, Zambia, and Sierra Leone. In Zambia, savings out of domestic factor incomes have financed a significant number of small businesses. The modernization of traditional farmers, including their accumulation and use of farm cash incomes and their adoption of increasingly efficient innovations, is often a highly significant benefit of agricultural export growth.

Comparative Indicators of Income Generation by Export Activities. In Table 11-4 we present a summary of NSG components from Tables 11-1 through 11-3. We are unable to sum the three NSG components for each case because the terms measuring external effects are not comparable to the measurements of the first two components of NSG. As an alternative, we have summed economic rent and the shadow price adjustments, and we have included the indices of overall external effects from Table 11-3. In the remainder of this chapter, we use the sums of the two measurable effects as proxies for NSG figures and the indices as indicators of the relative size of adjustments that we believe would need to be made if external effects could be adequately quantified. It must be remembered that the numerical values of NSG used here are not estimates of true values. Where external effects are thought to be significant, their quantification is critical to a realistic assessment of the NSG derived from an export activity.

With this proviso in mind, we consider Table 11-4. NSG values are economic rent components, modified by shadow price adjustments; these values have previously been examined. We wish now to consider domestic resource cost ratios and net gain coefficients for the selected export activities.

The domestic resource cost of producing a net unit of foreign exchange (DRC) is given by the ratio between total domestic resource costs incurred and total net foreign exchange generated. If the domestic resource cost per unit of foreign exchange is less than the true unit value of net foreign exchange as measured by its shadow price, then the export activity is socially profitable (provided only that net foreign exchange earned is positive). As shown in Table 11-4, all case study exports are highly profitable by this test.

Table 11-4
Net Social Gains, Net Gain Coefficients, and Domestic Resource Cost Ratios

	Ivory Coast Timber	*Ivory Coast* Cocoa and Coffee	*Ghana* Cocoa	*Ghana* Timber	*Ethiopia* Coffee	*Uganda* Cotton	*Nigeria* Oil	*Zaire* Copper	*Zambia* Copper	*Sierra Leone* Diamonds, large scale	*Sierra Leone* Diamonds, ADS[a]
	1967	1967	1969-70	1970-71	1969	1969	1971	1968	1967	1963-65 mean	1963-65 mean
Net social gain from economic rent (R_j) (loc)	3,500	14,000	132	6	75	53	311	95	153	2.6	1.0
Net social gain from adjustment to market prices and to existing exchange rate (P_j) (loc)	0	0	0	1	0	63	3	0	0		
External effects (E_j)[b]	II	III	II	II	I	II	II	I	III	I	I
Net Social Gain $(R_j + P_j)$ (loc)	3,500	14,000	132	7	75	116	314	95	153	4.8	11.5
Net Gain Coefficient $[(R_j + P_j)/u_j \cdot v_1]$	.18	.35	.39	.22	.44	.31	.59	.48	.31	.31	.80
Domestic Resource Cost Ratios $\left(\sum_{s=2}^{m} \bar{f}_{sj} \cdot v_s /(u_j - \bar{m}_j - \bar{r}_j)\right)$	181	158	.588	.553	1.36	4.70	.052	.167	.198	.134	.074
Exchange rate (v_1) (loc/$)	250/1	250/1	1.02/1[c]	1.02/1	2.5/1	7.14/1	.3571/1	.50/1	.3571/1	.4167/1	.4167/1

DRC/v_1	.72	.63	.58	.54	.54	.66	.15	.33	.55	.32	.18
Efficiency factor $(1 - DRC/v_1)^d$	.28	.37	.42	.46	.46	.34	.85	.67	.45	.68	.82
Foreign exchange factor $\left(1 - \dfrac{\overline{m}_j + r_j}{u_j}\right)^d$	.64	.97	.92	.47	.96	.89	.70	.72	.70	.47	.98

Note: The symbols for and relationships among these variables are discussed in the technical appendix to Chapter 1.

(loc) – quantity is expressed in millions of local currency.

(loc/$) – quantity is expressed in units of local currency per dollar.

[a]Scale: (very weak) I II III IV V (very strong)

[b]High benefit case is used in all Sierra Leone ADS calculations.

[c]Ghanaian exchange rate is cedis per dollar. Gordon uses pounds per dollar in Chapter 3.

[d]The net gain coefficient is the product of these two factors. See p. 258.

More interesting for comparative purposes are the ratios of DRC to the respective shadow prices of foreign exchange. These ratios reveal the fractions of the value of net foreign exchange which are absorbed by domestic costs of production. Table 11-4 indicates that Nigerian petroleum and the Sierra Leone ADS scheme are extremely low-cost producers of foreign exchange, with domestic resource costs amounting to only 15 percent and 18 percent, respectively, of the value of net foreign-exchange generated. At the opposite extreme is Ivorian timber, for which domestic costs amount to more than 70 percent of the value of net foreign exchange generated.

If the estimates of Table 11-4 were more refined, they would provide an indication of the comparative advantage of countries in the production of the various commodities.[1] The results of Table 11-4 (as presented) indicate comparative advantages for Zaire over Zambia in copper production and for Ghana over the Ivory Coast in timber. (They also indicate a preference for ADS-type production of Sierra Leonean diamonds.) The present results, however, are subject to all of the qualifications described above concerning shadow prices and externalities; and they provide at best only a static measure of comparative advantage. The potential usefulness of suitably refined results should nonetheless be apparent and should provide a spur to future research.

The net gain coefficient (NGC) measures the fraction of gross output which constitutes NSG—all quantities involved being evaluated in local currency at their true (shadow price) values. The NGC is the product of a foreign exchange factor, the fraction of gross output which does *not* leak out to foreigners, times an efficiency factor, the fraction of net foreign exchange earnings *not* expended on domestic resource costs. The efficiency factor has been discussed above. The foreign exchange factor is critical because an activity efficient in the sense of a low DRC/v_1 ratio (and hence a high efficiency factor) might be so dependent on foreign inputs and ownership that only a small fraction of export earnings is retained in the domestic economy. Conversely, a less efficient activity may compensate by having lower leakages to foreigners. The NGC provides a combined measure of the two characteristics.

As an example, we can compare (from Table 11-4) large-scale diamond production in Sierra Leone with Zambian copper production. Sierra Leonean diamond production is more efficient in the sense that domestic resource costs constitute only 32 percent of the value of net foreign exchange earned, as compared with 55 percent for Zambian copper. But 70 percent of the foreign exchange earned by Zambian copper production was retained domestically, as compared with 47 percent of that earned by large-scale diamond production in Sierra Leone. The result is that the NGC, the fraction of total output constituting a net social gain for the producing country, is roughly the same (.31) in each case. The exact numerical values, of course, must be viewed with extreme caution, but the possibilities they indicate are important.

Even though the results of Table 11-4 are approximate, they suggest some cautious generalizations. The range of NGCs is wide, from .80 for ADS diamonds

in Sierra Leone, to .18 for timber in the Ivory Coast, but net gain coefficients
for mineral commodities do not appear to be greatly different from those for
agricultural commodities. The similar net gain coefficients conceal significant
differences, however. Agricultural commodities have relatively high domestic
resource costs; DRC/v_1 is always at least .54 for agricultural commodities but
in only one case greater than .33 for minerals. Hence the efficiency factor in
NGC is considerably lower for agricultural exports, reflecting their relatively
high domestic resource costs in producing foreign exchange.

Mineral commodities, by contrast, give up much greater fractions of foreign exchange earned to foreign costs and foreign rent receivers than do agricultural commodities. In only one case is the fraction of foreign exchange leaked
less than .28 for a mineral, whereas for agricultural commodities it is never
greater than .11. The foreign-exchange factor in NGC is therefore considerably
higher for agricultural commodities, reflecting the fact that very little of the
foreign exchange they produce accrues to foreigners.

Finally, NGCs for timber in both the Ivory Coast and Ghana were very low.
For the years studied, silvicultural exports combined the high domestic costs
typical of agricultural commodities with the high foreign costs of minerals. Our
case studies indicate that the leakages of foreign exchange associated with timber production are largely factor costs rather than rent payments to foreigners—
the clear implication being that NGCs for timber production can be substantially increased only if associated economic rents are increased also.

Employment Generation by Export Activities

In Table 11-5 we summarize employment figures for the export activities
of the case studies. As expected, the production of agricultural exports uses far
more labor per unit value of output than do mineral extraction activities (Sierra
Leonean diamonds are a conspicuous exception). Dollar output per employee is
approximately equal in Ethiopian coffee production and in combined coffee
and cocoa production in the Ivory Coast (about $140 per employee), and some
two and one-half times greater in Ghanaian cocoa production. At the opposite
extreme, output per employee is on the order of $50,000 in oil production in
Nigeria, and averages $16,800 and $25,800 in copper production in Zaire and
Zambia, respectively. Figures for timber production fall between agriculture and
minerals.

If employment generation is considered as an objective in its own right,
this result may be taken as a plus for agriculture, but agricultural employment
is most often in unskilled jobs or in jobs utilizing very specialized skills which
are largely nontransferable. A relatively small amount of employment in
skilled industrial jobs may have a large long-run impact, as workers who have
acquired such skills later find employment elsewhere in the economy. (A skilled

Table 11–5
Employment Generation and Income Distribution

	Ivory Coast[a] Timber	Ivory Coast[a] Cocoa and Coffee	Ghana[b] Cocoa	Ghana[c] Timber	Ethiopia[a] Coffee	Uganda[a] Cotton	Nigeria[d] Oil	Zaire Copper	Zambia Copper	Sierra Leone Diamonds, large scale	Sierra Leone Diamonds, ADS[e]
	1967	1967	1969-70	1970-71	1969	1969	1971	1968	1967	1963-65 mean	1963-65 mean
Employment	16,636	1,088,000	512,200	11,666	500,000	900,000	3,703	23,800	53,647	7,790	30,000[f]
Local	7,541	972,000	n.a.	n.a.	499,950	n.a.	3,158	22,219	47,263	7,556	n.a.
Expatriate	9,095	116,000	n.a.	n.a.	50	n.a.	545	1,519	6,384	234	n.a.
Output/employee (dollars)	4,800	143	368	3,225	138	59	52,250	16,800	25,800	4,760	1,130
(Dollars, in millions)											
Gross output	80	158	334	32	69	53	1,467	399	1,386	37	34
Production costs	66	102	204	23.8	39	37	393	187	684	20.5	31.0
Accruing to:											
Domestic	37	97	175	9.1	36	31	160	96	535	9.8	30.7
Foreign	29	5	28	14.7	3	6	233	91	149	10.7	.3
Accruing to:											
Labor	15	43	58	4.1	25	24	17	38	257	7.1	30.7
Capital	17	35	91	4.0	10	4	—[g]	18	44[h]	33[h]	—
Intermediate inputs	34	24	55	15.7	4	9	376	131	383	10.1	.3
Rent	14	56	130	8.1	30	16	1,075	211	701	16.5	3.4
Accruing to:											
Government	14	47	143	3.0	6	6	870	190	428	7.4	2.6
Domestic	—	9	-13	2.9	24	10	—	—	—	—	—
Foreign	—	—	—	2.2	—	—	205[i]	21	273[j]	9.1[j]	.8[j]

elite, can, of course, pose its own policy problems, as the Zambian and Zairian cases amply illustrate.) Still, comparison of net gain coefficients shows agricultural commodities to be on a par with minerals as earners of foreign exchange, while employing the usually abundant domestic factor of production—unskilled labor—in relatively large quantities. Case-study authors estimate that over one million workers participate in the production of coffee and/or cocoa in the Ivory Coast, nearly one million in the production of cotton in Uganda, and approximately one-half million (each) in the production of Ethiopian coffee and Ghanaian cocoa. By providing large numbers of such workers with cash income, agricultural activities assist the spread of developmental benefits and the developmental process itself, and promote a more equal distribution of incremental income (NSG) from exports.

It is of course important that arguments for employment generation not be converted into arguments for pure inefficiency. Unless unemployment is an overwhelming problem, there is certainly no advantage in adding workers to an export activity just in order to drive down the ratio of output per worker. There are almost always better and more efficient ways to reduce unemployment.

Employment generation effects could in principle be evaluated for related activities in the same manner as contributions from such activities to NSG. In practice, such indirect employment effects are difficult to estimate, and we have not attempted to do so here. As urban unemployment problems become increasingly severe in many African nations, questions of employment generation will receive closer scrutiny. Export activities and enterprises linked to them will be evaluated carefully in terms of their potentials for creating urban employment and/or economic opportunities in rural areas.

Income Distribution Effects

Assessment of the effects of an export activity on domestic income distribution involves the question of who receives the incremental domestic income

---

Footnotes for Table 11-5.

[a]Output and employment figures are for 1963. Factor payments and rent data are for 1967.
[b]Output and employment figures are for 1960. Factor payments and rent data are for 1969-70.
[c]Output and employment figures are for 1969. Factor payments and rent data are for 1970-71.
[d]Output and employment figures are for 1965. Factor payments and rent data are for 1971.
[e]High benefit case is used in all Sierra Leone ADS calculations.
[f]This entry includes tributors only.
[g]Return to capital is included in the entry listed as foreign rent.
[h]This entry includes depreciation only; it does not include return to capital.
[i]This entry includes interest, return of capital, profits and economic rent.
[j]This entry includes return to capital plus rent.
n.a. = not available

(NSG) which the export activity generates. (It is important to remember that factors of production are not recipients of incremental income when they participate in the export activity, but receive returns only equivalent to those they would earn in alternative employment.) The income distribution issue can be separated into two questions.

First, how are the amounts of NSG which remain in private hands distributed? This question is essentially an accounting problem. If comprehensive and sufficiently detailed information existed on factor payments, the solution would be straightforward once the three components of NSG itself had been completely quantified. In the absence of these estimates we have not attempted a detailed quantitative comparison of distributional effects. Table 11-5 contains evidence that agricultural activities are more likely than mineral or timber industries to leave economic rent as measured by market prices in the hands of domestic factors of production.

Second, how does the portion of NSG which accrues to the government affect income distribution? This question is in principle much harder to answer. Fungibility among budget categories generally prevents imputation to specific revenue sources of the gains from government-financed developmental programs. To the extent possible, however, specific governmental programs need to be identified as being funded either by payments from export activities or by the entire range of governmental revenue, and the distributional effects of the relevant governmental programs have to be assessed. The difficulties are apparent, but they must be confronted if income distribution is to be used seriously as a criterion for comparing export activities.

A carefully measured answer to the first question above is itself of interest. But the usefulness of this measure will be sharply limited and its potential misuses numerous if payments to government form the greater part of NSG. In many cases, the nature and impact of governmental programs will be the final determinants of the distributional effect of export activities.

Summary of Developmental Contributions

In concluding this section, we present a brief country-by-country synopsis of the recent developmental contributions of the exports covered in our case studies. Policy implications are drawn in the following section.

Ivory Coast: Timber, Cocoa, and Coffee, 1967. The three commodities were closely matched in gross earnings. Direct and indirect foreign factor costs, only 3 percent of gross output for cocoa and coffee, constituted 36 percent of gross timber output, and timber therefore accounted for just 25 percent of net foreign exchange earned by the three commodities. Domestic factor costs were equal to about 46 percent of the value of output of timber and 61 percent of cocoa and coffee; market prices were assumed to be a fair estimate of the social opportunity costs of the factors used. Linkage effects were estimated to be moderate for timber and fairly strong for coffee and cocoa. Final demand and fiscal linkages were the strongest in each case. Excluding external effects, coffee and cocoa showed an NGC of .35 as compared to timber's .18—with coffee and cocoa production characterized by much lower foreign exchange leakages and a somewhat lower DRC/v_1 ratio. Cocoa and coffee scored slightly worse than cocoa in Ghana. Employment in cocoa and coffee production was very large and predominantly local; employment in the timber industry was much smaller, and more than one-half expatriate.

Ghana: Cocoa, 1969-70. Gross output of $334 million was the largest for any agricultural commodity in the case studies. Foreign factor costs were only 8 percent of gross output, and domestic factor costs were about 53 percent of total earnings. Linkages were weaker than for Ivorian coffee and cocoa, largely because of the high import content of final demand and fiscal expenditures. With very low direct foreign exchange leakage and a DRC/v_1 ratio of .58, Ghanaian cocoa showed a moderately high NGC of .39. Employment, predominantly Ghanaian, was over one-half million.

Ghana: Timber, 1970-71. Gross output of $32 million was the lowest of all commodities included in our case studies. Substantial foreign factor costs together with some foreign rent reduced net foreign exchange earned to $15 million. Domestic factor costs at market prices were 60 percent of this total, although a shadow price correction for unskilled labor adjusts this figure downward slightly. Linkages were slight, save for forward-linked processing, and employment somewhat higher proportional to output than for timber in the Ivory Coast. Ghanaian timber production showed an NGC of .22—slightly higher than that of Ivorian timber because of a substantially lower DRC/v_1 ratio.

Ethiopia: Coffee, 1969. Gross output was $69 million, and foreign factor costs, $3 million, were minimal. Domestic factor costs were slightly more than 50 percent of gross output, closely comparable to the cocoa-coffee average for the Ivory Coast. Dollar output per employee and the NGC of .44 were also very close to the Ivorian results. Total employment of one-half million, virtually all Ethiopian, again illustrates the generally broadly based nature of agricultural export production considered in this volume. Linkage effects, led by final demand linkages, were moderately strong.

Uganda: Cotton, 1968. Gross output was $53 million, of which about 11 percent was paid abroad to foreign factors. Domestic factor costs were extremely high, constituting 75 percent of gross output at market prices and 59 percent at shadow prices, because of the author's contention that all farm income should be taken as wages to cotton farmers (i.e., there were no scarcity rents to cotton land). The resulting NGC of .31 was the lowest for an agricultural activity. External effects are not reflected here, however, and forward linkages to cotton-processing industries are significant. Furthermore, cotton production was a source of cash income to an extremely large percentage of African workers. Despite the emergence of coffee as Uganda's leading export, cotton remains the predominant cash crop in many regions of the country.

Nigeria: Petroleum, 1971.   Gross output of $1,467 million in 1971 was in absolute size the largest of any export activity studied. It was almost double the level of 1970, partially as a result of rising output and partially because increased realized prices reflected the change in fiscal terms in April 1971. Foreign factor costs declined slightly between 1970 and 1971, and foreign rents rose much less rapidly than output because the Nigerian government succeeded in extracting an increasingly higher share of economic rent. Domestic factor costs, relatively small in any case, also increased only slightly. As a result the NGC for Nigerian petroleum operations rose to .60 in 1971. Fiscal linkages have enormous potential, and important forward-linked processing industries are being planned; other external effects are quite insignificant, and employment is low.

Zaire: Copper, 1967.   Gross output for 1967 was $399 million, approximately 30 percent of the Zambian total. Although relying more heavily than Zambia on foreign inputs, Zaire nevertheless retained a higher percentage of gross foreign exchange earned because factor payments and economic rent accrued to and remitted by foreigners were considerably lower as a percentage of gross earnings. Domestic resource costs were proportionally lower than in Zambia. As a result, the NGC in Zaire, .48, was substantially higher than in Zambia, .31. Linkage effects were weak, and employment was confined to a small, relatively well-paid segment of the labor force. The latter, although not the former, was true also in Zambia.

Zambia: Copper, 1967.   Gross output for 1967 was valued at $1,386 million, second only to Nigerian petroleum among the commodities studied in this volume. Many characteristics have been noted above in comparison with the Zairian case. Linkage effects have been considerably more important in Zambia than in Zaire. A wide range of activities is geared to providing inputs for the mining sector, and workers' skills have spread to other industries. Furthermore, workers' savings have provided capital for small-business investments. Consumption expenditures have been import-oriented, however, and some potential final demand linkages have not been realized.

Sierra Leone: Diamonds, 1963-65.   The Sierra Leonean case provides an opportunity to compare results obtained in producing the same export commodity using two radically different technologies. Annual averages for the years 1963-65 show approximately equal gross outputs from foreign-owned mining production ($37 million) and from alluvial diamond scheme operations ($34 million). But foreign factor costs and rents take more than one-half of the former and virtually none of the latter. Hence, the ADS earned almost twice the net foreign exchange provided by the mining company. If domestic inputs are valued at market prices, the advantage of ADS disappears. If, however, shadow prices reflecting lower social opportunity costs of domestic factors are employed, the ADS shows an NGC of .80 compared to .31 for foreign-owned mining. Accurate estimation of shadow prices, therefore, is critical for a valid comparison of the production methods. Neither method of diamond production has strong external effects, but the ADS has a clear advantage in employment generation.

Exports, Governmental Policies, and Economic Development

Governmental Goals

It is clear that past governmental policies have significantly shaped the roles and contributions of the export activities of our case studies. Early colonial governments often encouraged the exploitation of export commodities but only occasionally with any substantial benefit to the local economies. Later colonial governments were somewhat more enlightened. But maximizing the developmental benefits of exports has become the overriding goal of governmental export policy only in the post-independence period.

Despite the difficulty of generalization, it is useful to attempt to sort out the criteria by which alternative export strategies can be evaluated and to assess the policy instruments available for the attainment of various governmental goals. We have suggested in this study that three criteria—the maximization of incremental domestic income (net social gain), the creation of productive domestic employment opportunities, and the effects of incremental income on the equality of domestic income distribution—are the most important economic standards by which export activities should be judged. However, two important qualifications must be explicitly stated.

The first is that governments clearly have non-economic as well as economic objectives. To take one example, domestic ownership and/or control of export activities may have a national political importance over and above any potential economic benefits; it would be no exaggeration to state that non-economic benefits played important parts in all five of our case studies in which participation or nationalization has occurred. To cite another example, regional or urban-rural developmental balance may be important for a variety of social and political reasons; the policy change affecting the distribution of royalties from

Nigerian oil reflects these kinds of concerns. Clearly there are many other examples of non-economic objectives.

The second qualification is that even if our methodology is accepted as valid for assessing the economic impact of exports, in this study the methodology could not always be applied completely or rigorously. Many critical items theoretically covered by the methodology are not reflected in the numerical estimates we are able to make, and it is legitimate to ask whether the methodology itself might be modified for policy analysis. If, for example, there is no real prospect of quantifying external effects, then it can be plausibly argued that they should be removed from the definition of NSG and accorded the status of a separate indicator—analogous to that of employment generation or income distribution. On theoretical grounds, this change would be undesirable because it would mean a potentially confusing breakup of the NSG term, which is designed to encompass all income effects of an export activity. However, this alteration would have the desirable practical effect of emphasizing that external effects are not included in the NSG, DRC, and NGC numbers that we are able to present.

Under the circumstances it is not surprising that in calculating income benefits from export activities governmental policy makers often select less sophisticated measures than those that we have proposed. Choosing to maximize net foreign exchange earned or total government revenue from exports is generally not the wisest developmental course—either in theory or in practice. But this course has the undeniable advantage of making clear just what is included and what is not, and it eliminates inconvenient apologies for not adequately quantifying external effects, shadow price adjustments, and the like.

We feel strongly that the methodology we have introduced is appropriate, and we are acutely aware of the need for caution in its application and of the duty to urge this caution on others. We further recognize the necessity for government planners to take account, even if only intuitively, of many kinds of developmental relationships which may have to be excluded from an empirical analysis. Given the present realities, we propose four areas in which planners should evaluate governmental policies dealing with export activities:

1.   the incremental effect on local income, evaluated first using market prices and then using best estimates, however uncertain, of shadow prices for foreign exchange and domestic factors;

2.   actual and potential external effects, including especially those linkages which seem important in the dynamic processes of long-run development;

3.   effects on urgent economic, political and social goals, including the need for real and perceived Africanization of important export activities and the desirability of broadly based and relatively egalitarian economic development balanced across regional and urban-rural lines; and

4.   the long-run effects on the growth, modernization, and diversification

of the economy's productive base, goals on which all the criteria of our methodology implicitly converge.

This fourfold division draws a balance between desirable and practical criteria in assessing developmental effects of exports. It also provides a useful framework for the discussion of specific policy instruments.

Governmental Policies

The following discussion is organized around the four areas of governmental concern identified above. Our purpose is not to attempt an exhaustive review of the principal implications for policy in each of the case studies, but rather to indicate some of the possibilities open to governmental policy makers in most tropical African countries.

Increasing Domestic Income. Governments may increase domestic rent accruing from export activities either by increasing net foreign exchange earned, by increasing domestic efficiency in the activities that produce foreign exchange, or by doing both simultaneously.

Increasing Net Foreign Exchange Earned. If external demand is price elastic, gross foreign exchange earnings can be increased by expanding export sales. Even if international demand is price inelastic, as seems to be true for coffee and cocoa, a single country may be able to increase its own export earnings—although total earnings to all exporters fall.

For most agricultural commodities, the expansion of output involves a combination of increasing the farmers' incentives to produce and expanding their opportunities for production. Increasing production incentives generally implies making available a wider range of consumer goods and, more fundamentally, providing higher prices for producers. The setting of producer prices for cocoa in Ghana, to cite a counterexample, seems to have been done mainly with an eye toward immediate fiscal considerations rather than a concern for the medium-term supply response of farmers. Increasing opportunities for production entails the provision of rural extension activities, improved infrastructure (especially transportation facilities), and a wide variety of other activities. In these respects, the governments of the Ivory Coast and Ghana appear to have done relatively more than the governments of Uganda and Ethiopia to promote small-holder growing of cash crops for export.

Increases in output in large-scale mineral and timber operations generally involve major investment decisions by the foreign and/or government owners of the export activity. Major investments have recently occurred or are planned in Nigerian petroleum and in Zambian and Zairian copper, and increases in export output are anticipated in all three of these economies.

Gross foreign exchange earnings from exports may also be increased as a result of price increases for the export commodities. To this end, producing countries may seek to maintain or raise prices by entering into international agreements to restrict commodity supplies. As a member of the Organization of Petroleum Exporting Countries (OPEC), Nigeria has effectively elevated the realized price of its oil exports by increasing per barrel payments to government (though some of the major gains were negotiated prior to Nigeria's joining OPEC). Both Zambia and Zaire are members of the International Council of Copper Exporting Countries (CIPEC), but it is still too soon to assess the effects of this organization. The International Coffee Organization, of which both the Ivory Coast and Ethiopia are members, has probably been effective in reducing coffee price fluctuations, though undoubtedly at the cost of restricting the world market shares of most African producers. In addition, an International Cocoa Agreement has recently been negotiated; its future effectiveness remains uncertain unless the United States becomes a signatory. In brief, with the important exception of OPEC for petroleum, the international commodity agreements and producing-country organizations in which African countries have participated have not yet been notably successful in raising long-run price trends of primary exports.

Net foreign-exchange earnings may also be increased by decreasing leakages to foreign factors or to foreign recipients of economic rent. The first objective is a prime target of efforts to Africanize work forces and managements—an active concern in all of our studies of mineral and silvicultural exports. The second objective, the reduction of rent payments to foreigners, can be achieved in either of two basic ways: taxation or participation. Taxation involves the negotiation or renegotiation of the fiscal terms under which foreign concessionaires are permitted to operate in order to increase host-government revenues from profits taxes, royalties, export taxes, and concession bonuses. Our previous analysis has pointed out the relative degrees of success which the governments studied in this volume have had in extracting economic rent; again oil in Nigeria is a notable case because both the total amounts of rent and the Nigerian government's share have increased as the government has been able to achieve progressively more favorable tax settlements.

Equity participation by the government is an alternative method of transferring rents from foreigners to the government. This option may be attractive when institutional or other constraints prevent governments from taxing all rents away from foreign owners. As we have previously noted, much more than economic rent is usually at stake in decisions to transfer ownership of the exploitation rights to nonrenewable resources. Apart from the full nationalization of the copper industry in Zaire, participation—usually 51 percent equity—has been the rule in our mineral case studies and, most recently, in timber in Ghana. Because the government in each of these instances has assumed ownership within the past six years, it is too early to evaluate the long-run economic profitability of public ownership to the countries concerned.

Increasing Domestic Efficiency. In virtually all export activities included in this study, possibilities exist for increasing the efficiency with which domestic factors are employed. This is particularly clear when efficiency is evaluated using social opportunity costs of all factors. The establishment of correct relative factor prices is much easier to recommend than to implement, however, because exchange rate, financial, and other reforms involve a redistribution of income which generally is resisted by powerful political forces who have a vested interest in retaining the "distortions." To cite just one example, it is widely believed that the downfall of the Busia government in Ghana in early 1972 can be attributed in important part to the large devaluation introduced in late 1971.

Efficiency depends on factor proportions as well as factor prices. The design of appropriate technologies for use in developing countries is a matter of increasing concern. For example, the opportunities for factor substitution are largely unexplored in many large-scale industries; expatriate managers often claim that there is only one "right" method of production, but more labor-intensive, more economically efficient techniques might be introduced in many activities if the proper incentives were provided. Sometimes completely different technologies can be used in mineral or timber production. Comparison of the labor-intensive ADS method of producing diamonds in Sierra Leone with the capital-intensive joint venture between an expatriate firm and the Sierra Leonean government demonstrated that greater gains were obtained by employing the labor-intensive means of production. On the other hand, scattered evidence points to the opposite conclusion in the case of the Ghanaian government's attempt to encourage small-scale, labor-intensive logging firms.

Maximizing External Effects. Our analysis of linkage effects, presented in the previous section, indicates that primary exports in Africa, as elsewhere, generally have very few important backward linkages and that the majority of forward linkages involve little more than first- or second-stage processing of the commodity for export in a weight- and/or bulk-reducing operation. Technological linkages and skill-training effects have also been limited. The main scope for linked development rests with final demand linkages from agricultural exports, and with fiscal linkages from mineral commodities (especially) and from most agricultural crops as well.

Fiscal and final demand linkages are maximized by channeling expenditures into areas where NSG can be realized. Encouraging local production of those goods in which the local economy can be reasonably competitive can promote local industry while also reducing consumption imports. Equally important, governments can, where possible, encourage industries technologically linked to exports—linked not merely by being related, but by being potential sources of NSG. Export revenues should, of course, be used to subsidize related industries only when such industries can in the long run stand on their own developmental merits.

Achieving Political and Social Aspects of Economic Development. "Economic independence" is an important objective of many African nations. While this independence does not imply isolation or self-sufficiency, it does require perceived African hegemony over major economic activities. For most agricultural commodities, independence is a dead issue; foreign-owned plantation agriculture was an early casualty of Africanization. Among our case studies, foreign plantations were important only in the production of coffee and cocoa in the Ivory Coast, and they virtually disappeared in response to changing economic circumstances long before the country became independent. In minerals and timber, however, the issue is exceedingly topical. Economic advantages of government ownership may or may not be great. It can at least be argued that in many circumstances the governments could successfully tax away as much economic rent as they could realize as owners. But the political and psychological advantages of African ownership are plain enough, and these considerations may in themselves produce additional economic benefits in the long run.

Africanization of skilled occupations is a social as well as an economic goal. The training of Africans for the more economically rewarding opportunities of professional and technical employment is a critical objective in its own right, and it is important also in order to remove a social-economic dependence of many African economies on expatriate skills. A well-recognized danger is that an African elite may replace the elite of expatriates. Elite groups of Zambian or Zairian mining workers, for example, pose special problems for these economies, but they also offer certain opportunities—and they most assuredly are preferable to an elite of expatriates. Generally, however, the larger the number of workers drawn into an export activity and the more equally income from the export is distributed, the greater are the likely contributions to development. Some of the most difficult decisions of developmental planning, therefore, will increasingly revolve around the issues of employment generation and income distribution.

Promoting Diversification and Long-Run Development. Diversification of an economy's productive base and of its exports is almost always a concomitant feature of genuine economic development. Virtually every nation studied in this volume is pursuing or would like to pursue some form of diversification. The question of the proper mix of diversified activities can be answered on two levels. For a realistic, contemporary policy maker, the answer lies in a carefully reasoned and coordinated application of the policies and criteria suggested above. For the practical empiricist, however, the trail leads back to the "rigorous and complete" application, over a sufficiently long period of time, of the sort of framework specified in this volume. Adaptations will be required in evaluating domestic industries, and some rather heroic assumptions and projections will need to be made. But the more subtle opportunities and necessities for development can only be identified by specifying and quantifying external effects, by measuring social opportunity costs with some accuracy, and by considering a variety of social objectives, including growth and distribution of income, generation of productive employment opportunities, and a multitude of non-economic goals.

Conclusion

Many of the contributions of exports to African economic development are clear enough, and no particularly elaborate framework is needed to identify them. Other developmental effects are, however, more elusive. We have proposed a methodology to identify and evaluate all significant effects of exports in the development process. Case-study authors have applied the methodology to the extent that available information allowed, and in the process they have provided a valuable set of essays on the roles of principal exports in the development of eight African countries.

The authors of our case studies have also identified the data necessary to undertake a reasonably complete application of our methodology and earmarked several avenues for additional research. The most serious present deficiencies are in estimates of shadow prices and in the measurement of external effects. More accurate assessments of the roles of exports in development will necessarily pay increasing attention to remedying these deficiencies, and to weighing such incommensurates as the income, employment, distributional-equality, and political effects of export activities.

Note

1. For an elaboration of this argument, see Scott R. Pearson and Ronald K. Meyer, "Comparative Advantage Among African Coffee Producers," *American Journal of Agricultural Economics* 56 (May 1974), forthcoming.

Index

About the Authors

Scott R. Pearson is assistant professor at the Food Research Institute, Stanford University. His research interests have concentrated in two areas: the impact of international trade on economic development, particularly in tropical Africa; and the development of petroleum and natural gas in sub-Saharan Africa and in North America. He is the author of *Petroleum and the Nigerian Economy* (Stanford University Press, 1970) and of numerous professional papers. Dr. Pearson serves as an economic consultant to the U.S. Agency for International Development, the International Bank for Reconstruction and Development (World Bank), and the Department of State. He has been a member of the Stanford University faculty since receiving the Ph.D. from Harvard University in 1968.

John Cownie received the Ph.D. from the University of Southern California in 1967 and was a research associate in the Food Research Institute, Stanford University, in 1967/68. He joined the faculty of Federal City College in 1968, where he is associate professor of economics. Dr. Cownie's research interests include the assessment of economic impacts of alternative technologies available to developing countries, and the analysis of ideological trends within American capitalism. He is the author or coauthor of several articles concerning economic development, and is coeditor (with John E. Elliott) of *Competing Philosophies in American Political Economy* (Goodyear Publishing Company, forthcoming).